Local Journalism and Local Media

Local Journalism and Local Media offers a detailed and comprehensive account of recent and significant changes in local news production including the arrival of online editions, local blogs and fanzines and the seemingly unstoppable march of the citizen journalist.

With contributions from academics, local journalists, government press officers, public relations specialists and press regulators, *Local Journalism and Local Media* examines local news media (including newspapers, radio, television and online) in England, Wales, Scotland and Northern Ireland; analyses their economic organisation and ownership; explores the range of papers available from the new '*Metro* style' free papers to the alternative local press; considers local journalists' changing relationship with their sources of news; and offers a number of case studies exploring the wide-ranging contents of the local press.

Contributors consider developments in the education and training of journalists alongside shifts in journalists' working practices against a backcloth of changing patterns of media ownership, industrial relations, freedom of information legislation and developments in new technology which, in combination, make local media increasingly reliant on 'outsider' sources of news emerging from news agencies and press and public relations offices locally and nationally. *Local Journalism and Local Media* concludes that while local newspapers are highly successful businesses, the contribution of critical local journalism to local political communications and a flourishing local democracy is less evident than a decade ago.

Contributors: Stuart Allan, Chris Atton, Ros Bew, Heather Brooke, Peter Cole, Andrew Crisell, Chris Frost, Ivor Gaber, Gregor Gall, Brent Garner, Sara Hadwin, Martin Hamer, Tony Harcup, Shirley Harrison, Greg McLaughlin, Brian McNair, Rod Pilling, Robert Pinker, Karen Ross, Guy Starkey, Richard Tait, James Thomas, Karin Wahl-Jorgensen, Granville Williams.

Bob Franklin is Professor of Journalism Studies at the Cardiff School of Journalism, Media and Cultural Studies. His previous public~~~ ~~ ~~~~
MacTaggart Lectures (2005), *Packaging Politics: Po.*
Democracy (2004) and *Newszak And News Media* (

Local Journalism and Local Media

Making the local news

Edited by Bob Franklin

Routledge
Taylor & Francis Group

LONDON AND NEW YORK

First edition published in 1998
by Routledge
11 New Fetter Lane, London, EC4P 4EE
Under the title of *Making the Local News: Local Journalism in Context*

Simultaneously published in the USA and Canada
by Routledge
29 West 35th Street, New York, NY 10001

This edition published in 2006 by Routledge
2 Park Square, Milton Park, Abingdon, Oxon OX14 4RN

Simultaneously published in the USA and Canada
by Routledge
270 Madison Ave, New York, NY 10016

Routledge is an imprint of the Taylor & Francis Group, an informa business

Typeset in Perpetua and Gill Sans by Bookcraft Ltd, Stroud, Gloucestershire
Printed and bound in Great Britain by Antony Rowe Ltd, Chippenham, Wiltshire

British Library Cataloguing in Publication Data
A catalogue record for this book is available from the British Library

Library of Congress Cataloging in Publication Data
Local journalism and local media : making the local news / edited by Bob Franklin.
  p. cm.
  Includes bibliographical references and index.
  1. Journalism, Regional—Great Britain. I. Franklin, Bob, 1949–
PN5124.R44L63 2006
072—dc22   2006004793

ISBN10: 0-415-37953-9 (hbk)
ISBN10: 0-415-37954-7 (pbk)
ISBN10: 0-203-96920-0 (ebk)

ISBN13: 978-0-415-37953-3 (hbk)
ISBN13: 978-0-415-37954-0 (pbk)
ISBN13: 978-0-203-96920-5 (ebk)

Contents

Illustrations

Tables

Figures

Contributors

Stuart Allan is Professor in the School of Cultural Studies, University of the West of England, Bristol. His books include *News Culture* (2nd edn, 2004) and the edited collections *Reporting War: Journalism in Wartime* (with Barbie Zelizer, 2004) and *Journalism: Critical Issues* (2005). He is currently writing a book, *Online News: Journalism and the Internet*, for Open University Press.

Chris Atton is Reader in Journalism at the School of Creative Industries, Napier University, Edinburgh, Scotland. His books include *Alternative Literature* (1996), *Alternative Media* (2002) and *An Alternative Internet* (2004). He has published numerous papers in this area and has edited special issues on alternative media for *Journalism: Theory, Practice and Criticism* (2003) and *Media, Culture and Society* (2003). In addition to teaching alternative media he specialises in research methods for media and communication at undergraduate and postgraduate levels.

Ros Bew recently joined the Cardiff School of Journalism, Media and Cultural Studies as a tutor in broadcast journalism after 25 years working, mostly for the British Broadcasting Corporation (BBC). At the BBC she produced and reported for radio and television and worked across both local and national networks for news and current affairs. Her specialist interest is business journalism.

Heather Brooke is the author of *Your Right to Know* (2005), a guide to using the Freedom of Information Act. She has written for all the national newspapers and was runner-up for the inaugural Paul Foot award for investigative journalism. Her project 'Justice by postcode' for *The Times* was one of the first examples of computer-assisted reporting in the UK. Before moving to London, Brooke worked as a newspaper reporter in the United States covering crime and politics.

Peter Cole is Professor and head of the Department of Journalism Studies at the University of Sheffield. He previously held a similar position at the University of Central Lancashire. Before joining the academy, Cole worked as a national newspaper journalist. He was a reporter, lobby correspondent, news editor and deputy editor on *The Guardian*. He was founder editor of the *Sunday Correspondent*, editor of the News Review section of *The Sunday Times*, Londoner's Diary editor on the *Evening Standard*, and reporter, diary writer and New York correspondent on the *London Evening News*. He is on the board of the National Council for the Training of Journalists and the Society of Editors. He chairs the Society's training committee, where he has been responsible for reports on training and newsroom diversity. He writes a weekly column on media affairs for the *Independent on Sunday*.

Geoff Court is a freelance researcher and writer who works mainly in the independent production sector of broadcasting, especially television. He is editorial assistant for *Journalism Studies*.

Andrew Crisell is Professor of broadcasting studies at the University of Sunderland and a member of the editorial boards of *The Radio Journal* and *The Journal of Media Business Studies*. He is the author of *Understanding Radio* (2nd edn, 1994) and *An Introductory History of British Broadcasting* (2nd edn, 2002), both of which are published by Routledge, and the editor of *More than a Music Box: Radio Cultures and Communities in a Multi-Media World* (2004). His latest book is *A Study of Modern Television: Thinking Inside the Box* (2006).

Stephen Cushion is a lecturer in the Cardiff School of Journalism, Media and Cultural Studies, Cardiff University. His research is interested in the relationship between young people, citizenship and news media. He has published several journal articles and reports on the political disengagement of citizens.

Bob Franklin is Professor of Journalism Studies in the Cardiff School of Journalism, Media and Cultural Studies, Cardiff University. He is Editor of *Journalism Studies* and co-editor of a new series of books to be published by Sage, entitled *Journalism Studies: Key Texts*. His publications include *Television Policy: The MacTaggart Lectures* (2005), *Key Concepts in Journalism Studies* (with M. Hamer, M. Hanna, M. Kinsey and J. E. Richardson, 2005), *Packaging Politics: Political Communication in Britain's Media Democracy* (2004), *The New Handbook of Children's Rights: Comparative Policy and Practice* (2002), *British Television Policy: A Reader* (2001), *Social Policy, the Media and Misrepresentation* (1999), *Making the Local News: Local Journalism in Context* (edited with David Murphy, 1998), *Newszak and News Media* (1997), *The Handbook of Children's Rights: Comparative Policy and Practice* (1995), *Televising Democracies* (1992), *What News? The Market, Politics and the Local Press* (1991), *Social Work, the Media and Public Relations* (1991), *Public Relations Activities in Local Government* (1988). He is a member of the Board of Directors of the Voice of the Listener and Viewer and a Trustee of the George Viner Trust (for Journalism Trainees from Ethnic Minorities).

Chris Frost is Professor of Journalism at Liverpool John Moores University, where he heads the Department of Journalism. He is author of *Media Ethics and Self Regulation* (2000), *Reporting for Journalists* (2001) and *Designing for Newspapers and Magazines* (2003). He has also written papers for various academic journals, book chapters and much journalism. He is Chair of the National Union of Journalists' Ethics Council, Chair of the Association for Journalism Education and sits on the board of the Institute of Communication Ethics.

Ivor Gaber is Professor (Emeritus) in broadcast journalism at Goldsmiths College, University of London. Previously he held senior editorial positions with BBC TV and Radio, Independent Television News (ITN), Sky News and Channel Four. He now works as a writer, broadcaster and media consultant. His area of expertise is political communications – his most recent books are *Culture Wars: the Media and the British Left* (with James Curran and Julian Petley, 2005) and *Westminster Tales: the 21st Century Crisis in Political Journalism* (with Steve Barnett, 2001). Gaber has been an editorial consultant to ITN for the past three general elections and currently produces and reports for Channel Four TV, the BBC World Service and BBC Radio Four. He also writes regularly for a range of publications including *The Guardian*, the *New Statesman* and the *Times Higher Education Supplement*.

Gregor Gall is Professor of Industrial Relations and Director of the Centre for Research in Employment Studies at the University of Hertfordshire. He was previously Professor of Industrial Relations at the University of Stirling and lives in Edinburgh. His publications include *Union Organizing* (2003), *The Meaning of Militancy? Postal Workers and Industrial Relations* (2003) and *Union Recognition* (2005).

Brent Garner, Deputy Director of the Central Office of Information's (COI) regional arm, the Government News Network (GNN), is a fellow of Trinity and All Saints University College, Leeds, and joint director of a postgraduate degree programme for government communicators run by the COI and Leeds University. He was formerly a journalist for Yorkshire newspapers and teacher with the Open University. He runs the GNN's central division based in Birmingham and lives in Stratford-upon-Avon.

Sara Hadwin lectures in newspaper journalism at the Cardiff School of Journalism, Media and Cultural Studies, Cardiff University. Previously she edited a regional evening newspaper, was publisher and launch editor of two weekly newspapers and was national vice president and treasurer of the Guild (now Society) of Editors of which she remains an enthusiastic member.

Martin G. Hamer (MA, MEd) has been a journalist since 1983. He spent 12 years with the Press Association and currently works for BBC News Interactive. His roles at the Press Association included Sports News Editor and Editorial Development Manager. He also freelanced for several UK national newspapers in the 1980s. Hamer has taught at Liverpool John Moores University and the University of Sheffield, where he successfully launched and led an MA in Web Journalism. He works part-time for the University of Central Lancashire. His recent publications include the co-authored volume *Key Concepts in Journalism Studies* (2005).

Tony Harcup is Senior Lecturer in the Department of Journalism Studies at the University of Sheffield. He has more than 25 years of experience as a news reporter and feature writer in both alternative and mainstream print media within the UK. He is the author of *Journalism: Principles and Practice* (2004); his research on news values, alternative media, and journalistic ethics has been published in both *Journalism Studies* and *Journalism*; and he is currently writing a book exploring ethical dimensions of journalism, to be published in 2007 as *The Ethical Journalist*.

Shirley Harrison's professional career has been in marketing and public relations. She was Director of Public Relations for Sheffield City Council before becoming a lecturer in the School of Business Strategy at Leeds Business School. Since 2001 she has concentrated on community activities both in the criminal justice field – where she serves as a JP, chairs the South Yorkshire Probation Board and is a member of the Courts Board – and in health, where she represents patients on local, regional and national bodies, largely concerned with cancer education and research. She was appointed to the Human Tissue Authority in 2005. She is a member of the Chartered Institute of Public Relations, the Society of Authors and the Magistrates Association.

Greg McLaughlin is Lecturer in Media and Journalism Studies at the University of Ulster at Coleraine. His research interests are in the area of media and conflict and he is author of *The War Correspondent* (2002). He has written a number of articles on the role of the local media in the peace process in Northern Ireland and is currently writing with Stephen Baker on the ideological relationships between media, politics and culture after the Good Friday Agreement.

Brian McNair is Professor of Journalism and Communication at the University of Strathclyde. He is the author of many books on journalism, including *News* and Journalism in the UK (4th edn, 2003), *Journalism and Democracy* (2000) and *The Sociology of Journalism* (1998). He is a regular contributor to the press in Scotland.

Rod Pilling began his working life as a reporter in regional newspaper journalism before entering teaching. He led the development of a Department of Media and Communication at the University of Central England in Birmingham. He is currently Dean of Media, Arts and Society at Southampton Solent University. He is also British Reviews Editor for *Journalism Studies*.

Robert Pinker has served as a member of the UK Press Complaints Commission from 1991 to 2004, as its Privacy Commissioner from 1994 to 2004 and its Acting Chairman from 2002 to 2003. He currently serves as its international consultant. He recently completed a three-year term as international chairman of the Press Council of Bosnia-Hercegovina. He has held professorial appointments in the University of London at Goldsmiths College, Chelsea College and the London School of Economics. He was elected an honorary fellow of Goldsmiths College in 1999, a fellow of the Society of Editors in 2004 and appointed CBE in the New Year's Honours List 2004.

Karen Ross is Professor in Mass Communication at Coventry University (UK). She teaches research methods and audience studies. She has written extensively on the relationship between women, politics and media, and on broader issues of (in)equality in communication and culture. Previous books include: *Women and Media: A Critical Introduction* (with Carolyn Byerly, 2005), *Women and Media* (with Carolyn Byerly, 2004), *Critical Readings: Media and Audiences* (with Virginia Nightingale, 2003), *Mapping the Margins: Identity Politics and Media* (2003), *Women, Politics, Media* (2002), *Women, Politics and Change* (2001), *Black Marks: Minority Ethnic Audiences and Media* (2001) and *Black and White Media* (1996).

Guy Starkey is the author of *Radio in Context* and *Balance and Bias in Journalism: Issues in Broadcasting and the Press*, published by Palgrave Macmillan. He previously produced and presented news, magazine programmes, phone-ins, music sequences and commercials on radio stations in the Middle East, Italy, Gibraltar, Wolverhampton, Wrexham and Liverpool, as well as being a freelance writer for a range of trade and consumer magazines. In 1991 he began teaching radio journalism and production, most recently becoming Principal Lecturer and Undergraduate Programmes Leader for Media at the University of Sunderland. His research interests include journalism, audiences and pan-European broadcasting.

Richard Tait is Professor of Journalism and Director, Centre for Journalism Studies, Cardiff University. He was editor-in-chief of Independent Television

News (ITN) from 1995 to 2002. He was Editor of ITN's *Channel 4 News* from 1987 to 1995, joining from the BBC where he had been Editor of *The Money Programme, Newsnight* and the 1987 *General Election Results Programme.* From 2000 to 2004 he was Vice Chairman of the International Press Institute. He is a Fellow of the Society of Editors, a member of the Board of the International News Safety Institute and a Governor of the BBC.

James Thomas is Lecturer at Cardiff School of Journalism, Media and Cultural Studies and co-director of its Wales Media Forum. His books include *Diana's Mourning, A People's History* (2002) and *Popular Newspapers, the Labour Party and British Politics* (2005). He has published various journal articles and reports on the relationship of Wales with the media.

Karin Wahl-Jorgensen is Senior Lecturer at the Cardiff School of Journalism, Media and Cultural Studies, Cardiff University. She has worked as a journalist in the United States and Denmark. She is the author of *Journalists and the Public* (2006), and *Citizens or Consumers?* (with Sanna Inthorn and Justin Lewis, 2005). Her work on journalism and democracy has appeared in more than 20 different international journals, including *Journalism Studies, Journal of Communication, Public Opinion Quarterly, Critical Studies in Media Communication, Media, Culture and Society, Journalism and Mass Communication Quarterly, Journalism,* and the *International Journal of Public Opinion Research.*

Granville Williams is Reader in Media and Journalism at the University of Huddersfield. He is a National Council member of the Campaign for Press and Broadcasting Freedom and edits its journal, *Free Press.* He is the author of a number of books and reports on media ownership, most recently *Threats on the Landscape* (2002) and *Eastern Empires* (2003) for the European Federation of Journalists. He is currently working on two projects: an update and development of themes first explored in *Britain's Media: How They Are Related* (1994), and an analysis of the role and impact of corporate lobbying on the formation of media policy.

Local journalism and local media: contested perceptions, rocket science and parallel universes

Bob Franklin

The regional newspaper business is booming. The Newspaper Society's website breaks the good news. Regional and local newspapers attract more than £3 billion in advertising revenue, account for almost half (49 per cent) of UK classified advertising and constitute the UK's largest print advertising medium. Readership figures are similarly bullish. Eighty-five per cent of adults (more than 40 million people) alongside 69 per cent of Britain's influential business community read a regional newspaper, while the number of 15–34 year olds reading the regional press (12.2 million) is 10 per cent greater than those accessing the Internet for news (11.6 million) and 27 per cent greater than the number who read a national newspaper (9.6 million). Every minute 3,764 local newspapers are sold in the UK with 67.4 million copies of regional newspapers sold (37.8 million) or distributed free (29.6 million) every week. UK residents spend £690 million each year on regional and local newspapers (Newspaper Society 2005).

Academic appraisals of the local and regional press are markedly less optimistic. Scholarly research typically emphasises the declining number of local papers, their diminishing readerships and circulations (Chapter 1), as well as the consolidation of local newspaper ownership into a handful of regionally based monopolies that sustain profitability by centralising production in large regional centres (Chapter 8) which, in turn, separate journalists from their readers and local community. Newspaper groups further minimise production costs by reducing the number of journalists employed, which increases local papers' editorial reliance on news agencies (Chapter 19) and public relations sources based in local (Chapter 16) and central government as well as other local interest groups (Chapter 18). Newspapers, moreover, face increasing competition from expansive local radio (Chapter 2) and regional television sectors, which also confront financial and editorial difficulties (Chapter 3). Worse, the development of microlocal news services in BBC regional newsrooms threatens to steal local newspapers' most valuable asset – their ability to deliver detailed and very local news reports (Chapter 3). New digital technologies create even more economic and journalistic challenges for the local press by increasing local communities' access to news via the Internet and mobile telephony, as well as enabling a significant and troubling migration of advertising to online sites. The seemingly unstoppable march of 'citizen journalism' threatens further pitfalls, but also creates possibilities, for local and regional newspapers' profitability and editorial contents (Chapters 3, 10 and 18). One local journalist reflected on the prospects for his career and his local paper in the context of the group's move to centralised printing and the closure of the paper's print room, leaving much of the valuable city centre newspaper premises unused. 'Centralisation is the biggest fear now', he argued.

> The printing press has gone, the wages department has gone, other administrative tasks have shifted and the whole computer is now controlled from Leeds ... when you're in a building nearly half of which is standing empty, it doesn't take a rocket scientist to figure out that's not an economic use of a building. You're still going to need journalists here but how many is another matter.
>
> (interview with author May 2005)

These two highly divergent accounts of the current state and future prospects for local journalism and the local newspaper industry recall Zelizer's identification of the 'parallel universes' inhabited by journalists and those who teach journalism, following her return to university after 20 years of working as a journalist. There seemed to be a marked dissonance between the world of journalism practice and the theorising of that practice, with little consensus or common ground to connect them. 'Nothing I read as a postgraduate student', Zelizer (2004: 2) claims, 'reflected the working world I had just left'. Journalists and academics, she suggests, belong to distinctive 'interpretive communities' reflecting different backgrounds, education and experiences of the world. Zelizer's analysis is undoubtedly correct in rooting these differing understandings in the varied social and professional origins of the interpretive subject, but in the context of local newspapers, these universes collide more than might initially be apparent. Most observers, for example, would agree about the facts of declining circulations in the regional press as well as the enviably high profit margins local newspaper groups enjoy. Similarly, there is a growing consensus, as well as shared concerns about the declining numbers of journalists employed in the regional press, the poor salaries they receive, as well as the impact of these and other cost-cutting strategies on editorial quality (Chapters 1, 7 and 8).

In truth, these contested assessments arise because academics, journalists, managers and owners of local newspapers typically identify distinctive ambitions for the local press and interpret its essential functions and purposes quite differently. For managers and owners, local newspapers are judged to be essentially business enterprises; to quote the Newspaper Society's website, they are a '£3 billion advertising medium read by 40 million adults a week' (Newspaper Society 2005). Judged by business criteria, local newspapers are an undoubted success with groups like Johnston enjoying profit rates as high as 35 per cent on turnover. But while many academics and journalists acknowledge the need for newspapers to be profitable to sustain their existence, far more stress the significance of local newspapers as the chroniclers and archivists of local communities and emphasise the democratic significance of the local press. Local newspapers should offer independent and critical commentary on local issues, make local elites accountable, provide a forum for the expression of local views on issues of community concern, as well as 'holding the ring' in debates on significant issues arising within and beyond the community. Measured by this yardstick, local newspapers are increasingly judged to be failing. A recurrent theme in the essays published here is the inherent tension between newspapers as businesses and as an institution of local democracy (Franklin and Murphy 1998)

The existence of such diverse appraisals of the fundamental character and current state of local journalism and local media, signals that discussion and analysis must encourage the widest possible range of voices into the debating chamber to deliver a well-rounded and comprehensive account. Consequently, this collection of essays includes contributions from scholars with research interests in local journalism and local news media, journalism teachers and trainers, as well as journalists working in newspapers, radio, television and online platforms, freelance journalists, local government public relations officers, government press and information officers and regulators: and from across the four nations/ regions of the UK.

The discussion and debate about local journalism and local news media collected here unravels across five sections. The first details the financial and organisational structures of local news media, as well as the impact of recent policy changes, technological developments and shifts in readership/audience numbers for editorial content of local newspapers (Franklin Chapter 1), radio (Crisell and Starkey Chapter 2) and television (Tait Chapter 3) in the UK, with particular studies focused on local journalism and media in Scotland (McNair Chapter 4), Wales (Thomas Chapter 5) and Northern Ireland (McLaughlin Chapter 6).

The second section focuses on the economics of the local press. Peter Cole examines changes in journalism education and training in recent times (Chapter 7), Granville Williams explores the implications of the increasingly monopolistic structures of ownership of the regional press for local democracy (Chapter 8),

Gregor Gall assesses the state of industrial relations in the regional press, with a particular focus on union re-recognition (Chapter 9), Rod Pilling analyses the changing professional roles of local journalists (Chapter 10), while Bob Pinker details the 'permanent evolution' of the Press Complaints Commission and its workings in the local and regional press setting.

Part 3 explores the wide range of distinctive newspaper types which constitute the local press. Tony Harcup considers the alternative local press (Chapter 12), Sara Hadwin reflects on the problems confronting editors who work on daily and weekly newspapers (Chapter 13), Bob Franklin critiques the editorial content of the traditional weekly 'freesheets' as well as the new *Metro* style daily free papers (Chapter 14), while Stuart Allan assesses the impact of the Internet and citizen journalism on the local press and offers a case study of press reporting of the 7 July London bombings (Chapter 15).

Part 4 analyses and explores the role of a number of agencies and actors in constructing the local news agenda, given decreasing numbers of staff journalists and the enhanced reliance on 'external' sources of news. Shirley Harrison examines the work of local government public relations departments in shaping local news agendas (Chapter 16), while Brent Garner details the increasing incursions of central government news agencies into local communications networks (Chapter 17). Ros Bew assesses the increasing role for freelance journalists in the local press (Chapter 18) and Martin Hamer details the impact of local and national press agencies such as the Press Association on local press reporting.

The final section, 'Read All About It!' considers the wide range of editorial contents of the local press. Karin Wahl-Jorgensen examines readers' letters and how they are selected (Chapter 20), Karen Ross critiques journalists' failure to represent equitably the gender and ethnicity of their readership in their use of sources (Chapter 21), Ivor Gaber takes the *Evening Standard* to task for its coverage of the introduction of a congestion charge in London (Chapter 22), Bob Franklin, Geoff Court and Stephen Cushion examine and compare local and regional newspapers' coverage of constituency campaigns across the last five UK general elections (Chapter 23), Chris Frost considers the ethical implications of local journalists' coverage of issues such as deaths and child protection (Chapter 24) and Chris Atton analyses the growth of football fanzines and assesses their editorial contents and claims to be journalism (Chapter 25). Finally, Heather Brooke explores the implications of the recent Freedom of Information Act for local and regional newspapers' coverage and contents.

The common theme running through all the essays is the concern – if not preoccupation – to describe the changes that are evident in the local and regional press. Studies of local journalism and local media conducted during the 1970s described a relatively stable world, in which the journalists, the newspapers and the production processes and technology employed to produce them had not changed markedly across the previous 50 years. 'Local' newspapers earned that name because they were locally owned, locally produced, employed local people as journalists, reported local concerns of consequence and were read by local people. Cox and Morgan's (1974) seminal research exploring journalism and politics in Liverpool, Jackson's (1971) early study of the role of the provincial press in the community and even Murphy's (1974) eloquent critique of local journalists' and newspapers' role in sustaining local power relations, exemplify this tradition and emphasise the continuity and stability which characterised the local press.

In the new millennium, local newspapers are local in name only; the town or city emblazoned on the newspaper's masthead may be one of the few remaining local features of the paper. Ownership of the local press has ceased to be local across the last two decades with the great majority of local papers owned by monopoly newspaper groups with head offices, where editorial policy and key decisions are made, located in remote cities or towns. Local newspapers, moreover, are literally moving out of their local patch, as their original town centre newspaper offices have become increasingly costly to maintain – as well as a valuable and realisable asset – compared to purpose-built offices on the edge of the town centre. A serious consequence here is the loss of routine contact with the local community in which the paper circulates. The production of the paper is also no longer local as group ownership encourages centralised printing and subediting based in large, specially designed production plants located regionally rather than locally. Journalists are also less likely to be 'local' and spend their entire working life on a particular paper since career development in a newspaper group requires ambitious journalists to move around the country to gain experience in different journalistic roles within the group. The emergence of *Metro* papers with their standardised editorial contents and formats across regions, in tandem with reductions in journalism staff, resulting in increased reliance on imported agency copy and the rewriting of press releases issued by government and other nonlocal organisations, means that local newspapers are less likely to report local stories and issues. Finally, the declining sales of hard copy newspapers, combined with the greater availability of online editions of the majority of local newspapers, means that fewer newspapers are read locally. While local residents used to wait patiently and eagerly for newspaper boys and girls to deliver their copies of the *Birmingham Post*, a 'Brummie' diaspora community can read their favourite columnists from an Internet café in Bangkok, Burma or Belgium as easily as they used to in Birmingham.

Undoubtedly the most substantive change, which is acknowledged in many of the discussions in this volume, has been the shift away from the perception of local newspapers as central to the local political life of communities and a vital ingredient in local democracy, to an understanding of local newspapers as businesses in which the achievement of profit and a preoccupation with the bottom line too readily trumps any journalistic ambition. A growing number of academics, journalists and public relations specialists writing in this collection argue that it will not require the knowledge and vision of the rocket scientist to understand how such a shift threatens to diminish both local journalism and local democracy.

References

Cox, H. and Morgan, D. (1974) *City Politics and the Press*, Cambridge: Cambridge University Press.

Franklin, B. and Murphy, D. (1998) *Making the Local News; Local Journalism in Context*, London: Routledge.

Jackson, I. (1971) *The Provincial Press*, Manchester: Manchester University Press.

Murphy, D. (1974) *The Silent Watchdog*, London: Constable.

Newspaper Society (2005) www.newspapersoc.org.uk (accessed 23 December 2005).

Zelizer, B. (2004) *Taking Journalism Seriously: News and the Academy*, London: Sage.

Part 1

Local newspapers and local media

Chapter 1

Attacking the devil?

Local Journalists and local newspapers in the UK

Bob Franklin

2005 was a bad year for the local press. The latest news about industry trends included the long-running story about the declining number of local newspapers, their falling circulations and disappearing readers. Breaking news revealed that there were fewer owners on the ground. Five days before Christmas, the Johnston group purchased Scotsman Publications, reinforcing trends across the previous decade towards monopoly ownership of the local press. Other stories exacerbated the glut of bad news. Trinity Mirror, for example, announced a long-expected package of 300 job cuts, while the Northcliffe group triggered speculation about the future of the entire industry by 'slapping a for sale sign' on the 110 local newspapers in the group (Cozens 2006: 2): the sign was eventually taken down in February 2006 when the newspaper group failed to achieve its anticipated price (*Guardian* 20 February 2006: 7). Add to this the news of demonstrations outside the October meeting of the Society of Editors to protest against journalists' low pay (Silver 2005: 1), as well as concerns about increasing competition from online advertising, Internet-based news services, an expansive local radio sector, the arrival of BBC micro-local news services along with citizen journalists, and it is perhaps unsurprising that at least one media pundit was prompted to pose the question: 'Has there ever been such gloom in the newspaper industry?' (Fletcher 2005a: 1). In a final twist of postmodern irony, Sly Bailey, chief executive of Trinity Mirror, cancelled the group's Christmas party to save money (Cozens 2006: 2). In the national press the mood was little better; at the *Telegraph* the traditional management Christmas card was replaced by a greetings email (Fletcher 2005a: 1).

But this cocktail of long- and short-term trends should not generate such despondency. The local press has survived endless precocious valedictories by pundits previously. In truth, local newspapers are very successful business enterprises (Mintel 2005). Profits are considerable and expansive, while profit margins (measured as a percentage of turnover) are legendarily high and explain the voracious appetite of groups like Johnston Press for buying newspapers. This, in turn, feeds the growing concentration of ownership in the industry (Milmo

2005a: 21, 2005b: 23). Profits have been sustained in the face of the genuine and long-term decline in sales, by buoyant advertising revenues and a cost-cutting management strategy. But this strategy has reduced the number of journalists, kept their wages low and impacted on the newsgathering and reporting practices in ways that diminish the range and quality of editorial in the provincial press (Barter 2005: 4–5; Franklin and Murphy 1997). These editorial changes provide the real cause for gloom. Local newspapers are increasingly a business success but a journalistic failure. This success and failure are intimately connected.

The UK local press enjoys a distinguished history of journalism, which is placed at risk by current managerial strategies. Chris Lloyd's (1999) celebratory history of the *Northern Echo* adopts for its title former editor W. T. Stead's injunction that journalists should spend their energy 'attacking the devil' and championing the causes of their paper's readers. But cuts in journalistic staff and the growing reliance of journalists on external sources of copy from press agencies (see Chapter 18), the town hall (see Chapter 16) or local interest groups, diminish the prospects for critical or investigative journalism; the contemporary local journalist is less likely to be 'attacking' than 'supping with' the devil.

Managing decline: fewer papers and fewer readers

In 2005, there were 1,286 local newspapers circulating in the UK including 27 morning dailies (19 paid and 8 free), 75 evening papers, 21 Sunday papers (12 paid and 9 free), 526 paid weekly titles and 637 free weekly papers[1] (Newspaper Society 2005). Longitudinal comparison with equivalent figures across two decades reveals the extent of the decline of the UK press title base across the 1990s and its subsequent relative stability (Table 1.1).

Table 1.1 Local newspapers: declining number of titles 1985–2005

Newspaper Type	1985	1995	2005
Morning			
• paid	18	17	19
• free	—	—	8
Evening	73	72	75
Weekly paid	749	473	526
Weekly free	843	713	637
Sunday			
• paid	4	9	12
• free	—	—	9
Total	1,687	1,284	1,286

Source: Newspaper Society database 1985, 1995 and 2005.

Broad comparisons between 1985 and 2005 will foster further despair with an aggregate loss of 401 (24 per cent) titles across 20 years. But Table 1.1 reveals that the last ten years have been a period of virtual stasis in the number of newspapers published. More significantly, it illustrates the marked shifts among the different types of newspapers that constitute the local press. The period since 1995 has witnessed the revival of weekly paid papers to their highest level since 1988 (548 titles), the continued decline of weekly free newspapers to their lowest number since 1995 (713), as well as the emergence of free Sunday and the successful free morning *Metro* titles (Newspaper Society). But again, stability is evident when each newspaper type is considered as a percentage of the overall local press numbers. In 1985, for example, free weeklies represented 52.3 per cent of the local newspaper total compared to 49.5 per cent in 2005 with equivalent figures for paid weeklies (41.7 per cent in 1985 and 41 per cent in 2005), paid mornings (1.1 per cent and 1.5 per cent), evening papers (4.3 per cent and 5.8 per cent) and paid Sunday papers (0.2 per cent and 0.9 per cent) displaying a similar constancy for the local press mix.

The data concerning circulations are less equivocal and signal that fewer and fewer people are reading local newspapers. At their peak in 1989, almost 48 million local newspapers (47,870,000) were sold each week, but by 2004 this figure was reduced to 41 million – a decline of 15 per cent. Mintel (2005) suggests a loss of 13 per cent in total volume sales between 2000 and 2004. Free papers have similarly declined from 42 million copies in 1989 to 29 million copies distributed weekly in 2004 – a drop of 28.6 per cent even when the 4.5 million weekly copies of the *Metro*, *Standard Lite* and *MEN Lite* are included (see Chapter 14). There is some comfort in the 4 per cent growth in paid weekly sales (Mintel 2005), reflecting the expansive number of paid weekly titles, but the majority of newspaper sectors are experiencing serious and long-term circulation falls.

In 2004, ABC data recorded an increase in circulation for only 7 of the 75 listed evening papers; a year later, 18 of the 20 best-selling evening titles registered a decline. Some papers are losing readers at an alarming rate with the *Evening Standard* dropping 11.7 per cent in circulation across the January to July period monitored. The *Birmingham Evening Mail* (–9.5 per cent), the *Yorkshire Evening Post* (–8.5 per cent), the *Sheffield Star* (–6.8 per cent) and the *Nottingham Evening Post* (–5.9 per cent) are experiencing a similar and striking downturn in sales. Two evening papers are enjoying circulation growth, but it is modest: 1.8 per cent at the *Belfast Telegraph* and 0.2 per cent at the *Newcastle Chronicle*. Similar downward trends are evident in the morning newspaper market with only the *Western Mail*, the *Ulster News Letter*, the *Daily Post* and the *Paisley Daily Express* resisting decline among the 20 best-selling papers. All English titles experienced a decline in sales in 2005 and, again, some losses are striking, with the *Yorkshire*

Post selling 8.9 per cent fewer papers than in the previous year. Six of the ten largest Sunday papers (by circulation) experienced a decline (−12.8 per cent at the *Sunday Mercury*) and even three of the eight new *Metro* titles registered falling distribution, with three others showing increases of 1 per cent or less (Newspaper Society 2005).

But the dramatic extent of the circulation decline confronting some titles becomes evident only in longer-term comparisons. Table 1.2 compares circulations of key evening and morning titles across the last decade.

Table 1.2 Circulation of selected evening and morning titles 1995–2005

Newspaper Title	Circulation		
	1995	*2000ᵃ*	*2005ᵇ*
Evening			
Wolverhampton Express and Star	212,739	186,042 (−12.6%)	158,130 (−15.0%)
Manchester Evening News	193,063	176,051 (−8.8%)	144,201 (−18.1%)
Liverpool Echo	168,748	155,848 (−7.6%)	130,145 (−16.5%)
Belfast Telegraph	136,714	114,961 (−15.9%)	96,299 (−16.2%)
Birmingham Evening Mail	201,476	136,743 (−32.1%)	93,339 (−31.7%)
Glasgow Evening Times	138,987	106,839 (−23.1%)	92,088 (−13.8%)
Newcastle Evening Chronicle	120,604	107,346 (−11.0%)	91,703 (−14.6%)
Leicester Mercury	118,594	111,652 (−5.9%)	82,232 (−26.3%)
Yorkshire Evening Post	106,794	100,794 (−5.6%)	68,767 (−31.8%)
Sheffield Star	100,971	84,327 (−16.3%)	62,850 (−25.5%)
Morning			
Aberdeen Press and Journal	108,963	101,642 (−6.7%)	86,942 (−14.5%)
Norwich Eastern Daily Press	79,596	76,579 (−3.8%)	68,599 (−10.4%)
The Northern Echo	77,425	66,032 (−14.7%)	55,979 (−15.2%)
Yorkshire Post	79,094	76,424 (−3.4%)	50,541 (−33.9%)
Western Daily Press	62,692	52,373 (−14.8%)	45,115 (−13.9%)
Western Mail	64,602	55,273 (−14.4%)	42,981 (−22.2%)
Western Morning News	52,123	51,596 (−1.0%)	42,325 (−18.0%)
East Anglian Daily Times	49,217	44,755 (−9.1%)	38,538 (−13.9%)
Newcastle Journal	57,677	50,295 (−12.8%)	38,187 (−24.1%)
Ulster Newsletter	33,233	33,435 (+0.6%)	26,270 (−21.4%)
Birmingham Post	28,054	20,922 (−25.4%)	14,256 (−31.9%)

Source: ABC and VFD data from the Newspaper Society website.

Notes
a Figures in brackets represent percentage circulation decline between 1995 and 2000.
b Figures in brackets represent percentage circulation decline between 2000 and 2005.

There are some striking figures here. Since 1995, the *Birmingham Evening Mail* has lost 53.7 per cent of its circulation, the *Sheffield Star* 37.8 per cent, the *Yorkshire Evening Post* 36 per cent and the *Leicester Mercury* 30.7 per cent. The figures for morning titles are less dramatic but also catalogue severe downturns across the period with 49.2 per cent at the *Birmingham Post*, 33.8 per cent at the *Newcastle Journal*, 28 per cent at the *Western Mail* and 27.1 per cent at the *Yorkshire Post*. Significantly, Table 1.2 reveals that for 17 of the 20 titles, the decline in circulation has been greater in the more recent period since 1995, substantiating that the pace of circulation decline is increasing.

Local newspapers mean business!
Advertising, profits and consolidation

Local newspapers remain highly successful and profitable business organisations despite these long-term downturns in circulations and readerships. The explanation of this apparent paradox is the adoption of a business strategy designed to maximise revenue, especially advertising revenue, while minimising production costs. This strategy has delivered high profit margins for the larger newspaper groups and promises continuing business success (see Chapter 8). Mintel's report *Regional Newspapers*, for example, claims that 'future prospects for the UK regional press sector ... remain good' and identifies 'real growth opportunities' which provide 'grounds for confidence in a healthy future for the sector' (Mintel 2005).

Advertising revenues remain bullish despite declining circulations. Local newspapers effectively enjoy a monopoly in local classified advertising, which constitutes more than two-thirds of their overall advertising revenues (Mintel 2005). A senior local journalist claimed,

> the point is, that advertisers in our area advertise in our paper or they don't advertise at all. And that's the point. We've cornered the market in terms of advertising, unless they go on the television or the radio, which clearly isn't feasible for local people. As a result, local papers manage to keep up the advertising revenues and even if they only sell four copies of the paper, it keeps making a lot of money and we keep producing it.
>
> (interview with the author May 2005[2])

In 2004, advertising revenues in the regional press reached £3,132 million, which represented a 20 per cent share of total media advertising revenues, second only to television at 26 per cent but markedly higher than national newspapers (13 per cent), magazines (12 per cent), radio (4 per cent), cinema (1 per cent) and the Internet (4 per cent).[3] Local newspaper advertising revenues grew by a healthy 5.8 per cent in 2004. The local press is the only medium that has been increasing advertising expenditure year on year for more than a decade – from £1,963 million in 1995 to £2,762 million in 2000, and more than £3 billion by 2004 (Newspaper Society). It is not only the high levels of advertising revenue which are significant to the business success of local newspapers; equally important is advertising's contribution to overall revenue which stands at a massive 80 per cent of the overall income of local newspapers compared to approximately 46 per cent for national papers (Mintel 2005).

This sustained income from advertising revenue is the key to the profitability of the local press. In 2003, Trinity Mirror, the largest group by circulation in the UK, returned a profit in its lucrative regional newspaper division of £123.9 million on a turnover of £525 million – a profit margin of 24 per cent (Pondsford 2004: 3). Figures for 2004 reveal that profits at Northcliffe (£102 million), Johnston (£177 million), and other leading groups continue to rise with unusually high profit margins (35 per cent at Johnston), although figures 'between 25 per cent and 30 per cent' are typical 'for many local newspaper companies' (Dear 2006: 8).

These expansive profits reflect the access of provincial newspaper groups to economies of scale – such as printing and subediting local newspapers at central sites within a group's 'territory' – which are available because the ownership of local newspapers is highly concentrated in a handful of regionally based monopolies. The process of consolidation, which has generated this monopoly structure, has been rapid and particularly marked across the last decade (see Chapter 8). Takeovers and mergers remain a constant feature of the industry. By 2005, for example, the *Yorkshire Post* had experienced 'four owners in ten years. In the 240 years before that, it essentially had just one other owner' (Martinson 2005: 18).

In 1996, ownership of one-third of all regional newspaper companies changed hands (Franklin and Murphy 1998: 19). In December 2002, Newsquest acquired the *Glasgow Herald*, the *Glasgow Evening Times* and the *Sunday Herald* for £216 million, following its earlier purchase of the Newscom group in May 2000 for £444 million, adding titles with circulations of 499,550 to its holdings. Johnston Press has superseded Newsquest as the most acquisitive of groups. In March 2002, for example, Johnston purchased Regional Independent Media's (RIM) 53 titles with aggregate circulations of 1,602,522. In the last six months of 2005, Johnston spent more than £500 million buying local papers. The spending spree began in August when Johnston bought Scottish Radio Holdings' 35 titles for £155 million. A month later, the group purchased The Leinster Leader Group for £95 million and the Local Press Group (£65 million), which includes the prestigious *Belfast News Letter*. In December, Johnston bought Scotsman Publications from the Barclay brothers, a group that includes *The Scotsman*, *Scotland on*

Sunday and the *Edinburgh Evening News*. *The Scotsman* exemplifies the trend for profitability despite falling circulation – a return of £7.7 million in 2004 with sales down from 100,000 in 2000 to 65,392 by November 2005 (Milmo 2005b: 23). On the day Johnston bought Scotsman Publications, the group confirmed it was considering a bid for the Northcliffe local titles recently offered on the market and valued between £1.2 and £1.5 billion (Fletcher 2005b: 7).

One consequence of this merger activity has been a marked reduction in the number of companies publishing local newspapers – from 200 in 1992 to 137 by 1998 and 91 by 2005. But while 43 of these publishing companies each own a single newspaper, the 'big ten' groups own 74 per cent of all local newspapers and account for 87 per cent of the weekly circulation (Mintel 2005). The largest 20 groups own 85 per cent of regional titles and control 96 per cent of the weekly circulation (www.newspapersoc.org.uk/factsandfigures.html).

But the virtual monopoly in local advertising which local newspapers enjoy, along with the possibilities for economies of scale which are derived from industry consolidation, explain only part of the story of their business success. The ability of the industry to minimise production costs by employing new printing technologies and keeping labour costs low are equally significant (Dear 2006: 8).

Across the career range, from trainee to senior positions, journalists get paid much less than equivalent professions. In 2003, National Union of Journalists (NUJ) members at Newsquest Bradford went on strike to protest at pay scales of £17,000 for senior journalists at the daily *Telegraph and Argus* and £15,000 for the weekly papers; trainee journalists earn an average £12,000 per annum (Pondsford 2003: 3). In 2005, senior journalists working on weekly newspapers owned by the Guardian Media Group were earning as little as £17,172 per annum which is '£172 more than a McDonald's trainee manager earns from day one' (Barter 2005: 4); half of British journalists earn less than the national average wage of £26,161 (Greenslade 2004: 9). Little wonder that journalists, according to one NUJ official, 'are streaming out of the industry' (Barter 2005: 4) to 'work in bars and pubs in the evenings' because 'they can earn more money serving behind a till than in journalism' (general secretary of the NUJ quoted in Silver (2005: 1)).

Job cuts and non-replacement of staff provide a long-term complement to the low-wage strategy intended to reduce production costs. The chief subeditor at the *Yorkshire Post*, for example, explains the changes at the paper since he began working there in 1977. 'Two features subeditors producing 25 pages a week' had been replaced by seven subs, but they were required 'to produce 180 pages … Bottom lines have become more vivid', he observed. 'It was a different era then' (Martinson 2005: 18). Job cuts continue as part of managerial attempts to maintain profitability despite declining circulation. The October 2005 relaunch of the

Birmingham *Evening Mail*, for example, prompted the loss of 18 jobs that represented approximately 10 per cent of the editorial workforce.

Group unwillingness to replace even the most senior staff is a common problem for editors. 'Companies look at each other's profits, share prices and they squeeze', an editor complained.

> At the moment there is a freeze on recruitment, but the freeze eventually slides into non-replacement and once again it's a ratchet effect. If you don't get a replacement quickly, you don't get it at all. If you slip into the next quarter, they say 'you've got along this far, why can't you continue? You're still bringing a paper out. If I give you eighteen grand for a new reporter, how many more papers is that going to sell? None at all, so why would I want to do that?'

The NUJ argues that the strategy of cost-cutting by low wages, and staff cuts and non-replacement, triggers a 'spiral of decline' in which you 'end up with fewer page changes, fewer editions, less localised coverage and, inevitably, lower sales' (Dear 2006: 8).

'Yesterday's news tomorrow': editorial decline in the local press

Managerial strategies designed to sustain profitability despite circulation decline have a critical impact on the newsgathering and reporting processes of the local press in ways that reduce the range and quality of editorial content. The organisation of newspaper groups into regionally based monopolies, for example, promises economies of scale through the centralised subbing and printing of local newspapers, but each impacts negatively on editorial. The employment of centralised teams of subeditors to work on a number of remote local titles means subeditors have little, if any, local knowledge of the patch in which the paper circulates. The economic efficiency is high but the tie with the local community is ruptured, while 'little matters like quality, accuracy and integrity ... don't show up on the balance sheet'. A group editor claimed that subbing a paper 'up to 60 miles away' is effectively like working in 'another country' (Lockwood 1999: 15).

Centralised printing brings similar disadvantages. Groups invest heavily in new presses which, as a journalist noted, may be based '30 miles up the M62'. The ambition is to guarantee rapid, cost-effective printing and even 'a better quality print job' but one consequence is 'that we've had to move the line forward. Its gone forward two hours, which doesn't sound a lot but we're bringing newspapers in from Leeds now which is fine unless there's a pile up on the M62'. The real cost of 'efficient' printing is a shrinking news day with less time to investigate and report the news. As one subeditor claimed, local newspapers are increasingly reporting 'Yesterday's news tomorrow' (cited in Barter (2005: 4)). Such moves trigger a predictable uncertainty among journalists. At one West Yorkshire paper, a shift to centralised printing resulted in the redundancy of 27 printing colleagues, which left the newspaper offices in a valuable town centre location underused; there were also plans to introduce remote subbing. A journalist noted:

> When you're in a building that's three quarters empty, it doesn't take a rocket scientist to figure out that this is not an economical use of a building. Centralisation is the biggest fear now and it's going to happen. The printing press has gone, the wages department has gone, other administrative tasks have shifted to Leeds. You just wonder how long it will take before we become a wrap around for the *Yorkshire Post*. Centralisation is going to happen, it's just a matter of how much it happens and to what degree ... There will still be a need for journalists but it will be hard to be a local journalist because newspaper groups mean that to build a career you have to keep moving around the country.

Another journalist picked up the latter point that local journalists and newspapers are losing contact with their local communities. 'You have to wonder where it is all going to end', he claimed. 'I worked in Exeter on a cracking paper but it was on an industrial estate by the M5 so no readers actually came to the office and that's something that all papers have got to be concerned about'. Journalists support the maxim that 'location is important'. The move of newspapers' district offices to cheaper sites outside the towns in which they circulate severs links with local communities and readers; in these remote locations journalism becomes a more desk-based job. Worse, the exclusive stories that callers typically bring to town centre offices are lost. Some editors regret the decreasing opportunities to meet readers and local people, which they judge essential to 'a healthy contacts book and a healthy local paper' (Thom 2004: 21).

Job cuts readily translate into short-term cost cuts but they also mean there are fewer journalists to fill the editorial pages of the local paper. Journalists become increasingly reliant on rewriting the press releases issued by local government or the Central Office of Information (Franklin 2004: 98–102), or copy from press agencies like the Press Association (PA) (see Chapter 18) to fill the editorial gaps.

That local newspapers rely on local government press officers for news about local civic and political affairs is well established (Franklin 2004: 106–11; Davis 2002: 24–5) with Harrison suggesting, with a discernible irony, that journalists' dependence on 'the carefully prepared material provided by professional local government PROs' has become 'so extensive' that 'the town hall is becoming the last bastion of good municipal journalism' (Harrison 1998: 168; see Chapter 16).

The election of successive Labour governments since 1997 has witnessed increasingly routine incursions by national, political and governmental communication organisations such as the Government News Network (GNN) and the Central Office of Information into local media networks in order to manage and set the agenda for local discussions of government policy initiatives (Franklin and Richardson 2002). Since 1999, local newspapers have been specifically targeted as receptive vehicles for government news management initiatives (Hammond 2000; Chapter 3), while parties similarly targeted local papers during the 2005 election (see Chapter 23). An increasingly standardised coverage of policy and politics by local newspapers has been an unintended byproduct of these news management ambitions. Journalist Peter Oborne (1999), for example, claims that a single press release with Tony Blair's byline was published verbatim in 100 different local newspapers: the only word changed was the name of the town in which the paper circulated.

It is local newspapers' expansive use of PA copy, however, which provides the most common surrogate for employing journalists in-house. 'Outsourcing' newsgathering is flexible and cost effective; 'by default, PA has become the UK's monopoly reporter' (Aspinall 2005: 2). The PA's output is certainly prolific: half a million words a day on news, sport, foreign and business news and weather (Hamer 2000: 12). The PA supplies camera-ready pages with text and statistical information for most regional newspapers. Costs reflect whether the content required is general and to be shared with other papers, or 'bespoke', that is, uniquely requested by a particular newspaper. Acknowledging this editorial reliance on PA copy, journalist Martin Wainwright declared the PA to be 'the new heart of British journalism' (Wainwright 2005: 25).

Another editorial consequence of the ambitions of newspaper groups to win increased circulations and readerships has been the shift to a new tabloid size and layout since the mid-1990s, complemented by the transition to an increasingly tabloid content. A greater editorial emphasis on entertainment, consumer items and reports, plus a focus on human interest stories is evident in a higher story count, shorter, 'frothier stories' and a changed layout and page design which features splash headlines, more pictures and a greater use of colour (Franklin 2005). A journalist confided,

> The editor wants a human interest story on the front page every day. And what depresses me is the fact that most days the main story comes from the calls, it's a fire, it's a road accident, it's a court case, it's something that's not

politics. News is seldom anything the council is doing … There's a lot of trivialisation. There's a lot of 'get a story quickly', rather than spending a long
time on a different kind of story. Speed is of the essence, trying to do as
much as you can as quickly as you can, quantity rather than quality, which is
terribly sad.

Many local journalists acknowledge that they are no longer engaged in the critical or investigative journalism which earned the local press the title of 'local
watchdog', even if that title was based more on rhetoric than reality (Murphy
1976); those days, they believe, are long gone. Contemporary low-paid journalists working on short-staffed and under-resourced local newspapers are less likely
to be 'attacking' than 'supping with' the devil. The established local newspaper
groups have little ambition to disrupt the local networks of economic and political power into which they are so closely integrated. The editor of one local
newspaper is highly sceptical about the compatibility of newspaper groups'
strategy to secure profitability and the prospects for quality local journalism. His
comments deserve quoting at some length.

> I've worked on different papers, regional and nationals. Sometimes a
> regional paper would have a two-man investigation team that may throw up
> only a single story in two months, but it would be a belter. No regional
> papers are doing that now. Even the paper I used to work on, which is a
> huge selling metropolitan paper; they've just crashed that down and
> reporters are just re-writing press releases … There's also the actual size of
> the newsroom reducing, so you've got fewer reporters plus an emphasis on
> the *number* of stories, not *quality* of stories. So all you've got is people on the
> end of the phone re-writing press releases. They're not actually out there
> connecting with the community … It's like the police. Not enough Bobbies
> on the beat, only Bobbies on the end of the telephone. So fewer reporters
> expected to fill bigger and bigger newspapers with fewer journalists, less
> training and smaller salaries.
>
> So we're not doing the job that regional newspapers used to do. We're not
> going out and challenging people like the police and the local council. All
> we're doing, and I hesitate to say this, but all we're doing is just trying to
> keep circulation up as a horse for advertising. This is ultimately my great
> fear, that eventually we stop being a newspaper and become just a medium
> to carry advertising.

Regrettably this editor's 'great fear' is the Newspaper Society's proud boast.

The Society's website declares itself to be 'the voice of Britain's regional press – a £3 billion advertising medium read by 40 million adults a week' (Newspaper Society 2005). The prospects for local newspapers to provide a forum for local debate, for journalists to inform that debate and provide a stimulus for a healthy local democracy, seem slight. More worrying are the implications for local journalism conducted in this economic and managerial context. The editor concluded with a comment that places the often-discussed and significant notion of press freedom in an interesting, if alarming, context. 'You won't identify me will you?' he asked. 'I could get the sack for saying that'.

Notes

1 These figures are derived from the Newspaper Society website (www.newspapersoc .org.uk) and are based on Audit Bureau of Circulation (ABC) and Verified Free Distribution (VFD) data for the period January to July 2005.
2 A series of interviews conducted with local journalists in the West Yorkshire region in May 2005 formed part of a long-standing study of local journalism during General Elections which dates back to the 1987 election (see Chapter 23). Journalists' views have changed markedly across the period revealing intriguingly shifting perceptions of their roles and activities across two decades. The number of interviewees was modest (15 in 2005), but the journalists were very consistent in some of their views concerning changing editorial standards. It is, also, reasonable to assume that the views they expressed are typical of local journalists beyond West Yorkshire. Unless otherwise stated all interviews quoted in this chapter are from this source.
3 The figure for Internet revenues reveals a significant expansion from the previous year (1 per cent), although the regional press is also a beneficiary here with online recruitment advertising on regional press websites more than doubling in the last two years to £33 million in 2004 (Newspaper Society).

References

Aspinall, C. (2005) 'The news monopoly', *Free Press*, 144, January/February, p. 2.
Barter, M. (2005) 'It's money that matters', *Free Press*, July/August, pp. 4–5.
Cozens, C. (2006) 'A glimpse into the liquid crystal ball', *The Guardian*, 2 January (media supplement), pp. 1–2.
Davis, A. (2002) *Public Relations Democracy*, London: Sage.
Dear, J. (2006) 'Put people before profits', *The Guardian*, 2 January, p. 8.
Fletcher, K. (2005a) 'A bright future for newspapers', *Media Guardian*, pp. 1–2.
Fletcher, K. (2005b) 'Bad news about the Northcliffe sale', *Media Guardian*, 5 December, p. 7.
Franklin, B. (2004) *Packaging Politics: Political Communication in Britain's Media Democracy*, London: Arnold, 2nd edn.
Franklin, B. (2005) 'McJournalism? The local press and the McDonaldization thesis', in Allan, S. (ed.) *Journalism: Critical Essays*, Milton Keynes: Open University Press, pp. 137–51.
Franklin, B. and Murphy, D. (1997) 'The local rag in tatters? The decline of Britain's local

press', in Bromley, M. and O'Malley, T. (eds) *The Journalism Reader*, London: Routledge, pp. 214–29.

Franklin, B. and Murphy, D. (1998) *Making the Local News; Local Journalism in Context*, London: Routledge.

Franklin, B. and Richardson, J. (2002) 'Priming the Parish pump: political marketing and news management in local political communication networks', *The Journal of Political Marketing*, 1 (1), pp. 117–49.

Greenslade, R. (2004) 'The great pay divide', *The Guardian*, 6 December, p. 9.

Hamer, M. (2000) *The Press Association At Work*, Unpublished MA thesis, John Moores University, Liverpool.

Hammond, S. (2000) *Reaching the Regions: Government Communications and the Regional Media*, Unpublished MA thesis, Trinity and All Saints University College, Leeds.

Harrison, S. (1998) 'The local government agenda: news from the town hall', in Franklin, B. and Murphy, D. (eds) *Making The Local News: Local Journalism in Context*, London: Routledge, pp. 157–70.

Lloyd, C. (1999) *Attacking The Devil: 130 Years of the Northern Echo*, Darlington: The Northern Echo.

Lockwood, D. (1999) 'A substandard service', *Press Gazette*, 16 July, p. 15.

Martinson, J. (2005) 'Yorkshire Post survives the wringer', *The Guardian*, 14 June, p. 18.

Milmo, D. (2005a) 'Johnston pays £160m for Irish news group', *The Guardian*, 17 September, p. 21.

Milmo, D. (2005b) 'Barclay brothers sell the Scotsman', *The Guardian*, 20 December, p. 23.

Mintel (2005) *Regional Newspapers*, Mintel: Newspaper Society.

Murphy, D. (1976) *The Silent Watchdog*, London: Constable.

Newspaper Society (2005) www.newspapersoc.org.uk (accessed 23 December 2005).

Oborne, P. (1999) *Alastair Campbell, New Labour and the Rise of the Media Class*, London: Aurum Press.

Pondsford, D. (2003) 'Newsquest staff at Bradford vote for more strikes', *Press Gazette*, 11 July, p. 3.

Pondsford, D. (2004) 'Big rise in profits at Trinity Mirror after job cuts', *Press Gazette*, 5 March, p. 3.

Silver, J. (2005) 'Pressed for cash', *The Guardian G2*, 17 October, p. 1.

Thom, C. (2004) 'Location is everything', *Press Gazette*, 18 June, p. 21.

Wainwright, M. (2005) 'The new heart of British journalism', *The Guardian*, 20 September, p. 25.

Chapter 2

News on local radio

Andrew Crisell and Guy Starkey

Historical background

In one sense, the 1967 launch of the modern system of local radio in Britain can be seen as history repeating itself, for it marked the arrival of a technology for which there was no apparent demand. We commonly assume that most inventions and new technologies are developed in response to a felt need, or at least that their potential is fairly clear from the outset, but this was not altogether true of the birth of radio in the first years of the twentieth century.

As a means of *private* or point-to-point communication between individuals, wireless telephony, the atmospheric transmission of sounds over distances, had obvious enough uses: during a period that partly coincided with the Great War (1914–18) many of these uses were naval and military. But *broadcasting* was seen as a negative side-effect of wireless telephony. What was the value of exchanges between politicians, diplomats and military commanders if they could be heard by anyone who owned a wireless receiver? Even before the war, problems were created in America and elsewhere by 'irrepressible [wireless] amateurs, already numbering thousands, who were anathema to the military; their chatter was said to interfere with military communication. They were even accused of sending fake orders to navy ships, purportedly from admirals' (Barnouw 1977: 17).

There was at first no demand for wireless broadcasting because it was not perceived to be a separate technology with uses of its own; even the thousands of wireless amateurs continued to think of their own communications as point-to-point and their reception of military messages as 'eavesdropping'. Nevertheless, the positive potential of broadcasting was soon foreseen, most clearly by David Sarnoff, an employee of the American Marconi Company. In 1916 he formed

> a plan of development which would make radio a 'household utility' in the
> same sense as the piano or the phonograph. The receiver can be designed in
> the form of a simple 'radio Music Box' and arranged for several different

wavelengths, which would be changeable with the throwing of a single switch or pressing of a single button ... This proposition would be especially interesting to farmers and others living in outlying districts removed from cities. By the purchase of a 'radio Music Box' they could enjoy concerts, lectures, music, recitals etc., which may be going on in the nearest city within their radius.

(quoted in Armes (1988: 107))

Once the uses of this form of wireless telephony were apparent – as a medium of entertainment, information and education – demand for it could be stimulated through those institutional models of broadcasting that are now familiar to us. That which developed in America was commercial, envisaging broadcasting as a means of selling products to the public, or, put another way, of delivering audiences to advertisers. However, broadcasting in Britain was perceived as a universal cultural resource, rather like schools and public libraries. There were social and political reasons for this, but perhaps the most compelling was technological: spectrum scarcity (Crisell 2002: 19). As a small country situated on the fringe of a multilingual Europe, Britain would be able to command only a few broadcasting frequencies. It was therefore logical to place them in the hands of a single organisation that would cater to the needs and interests of everyone who was prepared to pay for a licence to listen to it. This was the 'public service' model that was established in 1922 in the form of the British Broadcasting Company (later British Broadcasting Corporation (BBC)). Though it began on a local scale, wireless broadcasting was soon developed as a national system under the centralising sway of John Reith, and local radio virtually disappeared (Gorham 1952: 78; Harvey and Robins 1994: 41). What persisted were regional variations within what was, in essence, a network service of mixed programming ('something for everyone'), controlled, if not originated, from London (Scannell and Cardiff 1991: 15).

About 40 years would elapse before local broadcasting was revived. The arrival of VHF/FM technology in the 1950s and 1960s improved the quality of wireless (or, as it was now increasingly called, 'radio') reception. But it had an even more important application: because it afforded low-power transmissions, stations that were a reasonable distance apart could share the same frequency. Hence it made room for many more, albeit local, stations on the spectrum. It was yet another instance of a new technology for which there was little demand (Briggs 1995: 638), perhaps because people felt their needs were already being met by the local press and regional television. The first local stations, a BBC monopoly, were not launched until 1967, and even by 1972 only about 40 per cent of the radio audience had bothered to equip themselves for VHF/FM reception (Briggs 1995: 842). The government therefore allowed the BBC and later the Independent Broadcasting Authority (IBA) to give many of their new stations a low-power AM frequency to support the 'prime system of transmission' on the FM waveband (Briggs 1995: 647). But it was not until the end of the 1980s, when the four national BBC networks switched to VHF/FM in the interests of better sound quality, that the bulk of the radio audience followed suit.

Nevertheless, the arrival of new technology and the proliferation of stations reduced the need to provide a generality of programming on any one frequency. And by so doing, it dealt a shrewd blow to the 'public service' concept, which was largely predicated on the scarcity, and hence 'preciousness', of broadcasting. When BBC television was allowed a single rival in the form of commercial TV (there were, of course, many regional companies but they amounted to only one national network), the Television Act of 1954 required ITV also to provide a 'public service' in the form of a range of programming for the audience as a whole; it was not permitted to target just those sections that were of interest to advertisers. And when a system of commercial or 'independent' local radio (ILR) was launched in 1973, the Sound Broadcasting Act would again require the stations to provide the 'balance of programming' that was a cardinal feature of public service (Barnard 1989: 74–5). This failed to recognise not only the abundance of broadcasting in general, but the fact that, in an age of television, most people no longer required a miscellany of output from a medium they treated as a mere background facility. With even newer technologies arriving in the 1980s and 1990s in the form of cable, satellite, digital transmission and the Internet, the claim that broadcasting was 'precious' was no longer tenable. Indeed, the main aim of the Broadcasting Acts of 1990 and 1996 was to acknowledge its new abundance by deregulating it, and there now seem to be almost more stations, networks and channels than there is material to fill them. It has become increasingly necessary to predicate 'public service' on something other than scarcity, and for the BBC, the provision of news at international, national and local levels has been a key part of the answer. Since it is funded from a licence fee and not from advertising, it has a general obligation to offer what 'the market' cannot deliver to any acceptable standard or extent. This naturally includes news and current affairs, which, in a democracy, the Corporation sees itself as having an especial duty to provide.

The 1990 Broadcasting Act largely divested ILR of its public service obligations; it is not even obliged to provide news. '[T]here is no requirement for [independent] local radio to carry local news and insofar as it does so there is nothing to prevent that local news being bought in from the local newspaper' (Radio Authority 1995: 13). But in practice, the stations do carry it, not from some quixotic attachment to the old public service ideal but from hard business sense: since ILR's main diet is popular music, most of which has no local origins or affiliations whatsoever, the only way it can construct itself as being genuinely different from network radio is by providing local news and information.

Organisational issues

Despite the differences between them in funding, structure and regulation, many organisational issues concern both the BBC and the commercial sector. This is so, even if the journalists on the 'public service' side of the divide sometimes envy the relative glamour of the stations on the other, and those in commercial radio occasionally yearn for the comparatively lavish resourcing, job security and salaries of the BBC. Within the latter, there are also more realistic prospects of promotion to national and even World Service newsrooms in radio, and of course, to regional and national television. This persists despite a certain condescension in the national radio networks towards their provincial cousins that even twenty-first-century ethnic and cultural diversity has not altogether dispelled. The similarities between the BBC and local commercial radio stem from the competitive environment in which they operate. The financial bottom line of a company dependent on advertising revenue – whether it be autonomous or part of a group – is related almost entirely to the regular listening figures produced by Radio Joint Audience Research Ltd (RAJAR) (Starkey 2004: 114–18). The BBC is not immune from the RAJAR imperative either, since even though English local radio represents only 6.31 per cent of its expenditure, every part of the whole £4 billion operation has to be accounted for and justified in terms of its value to licence payers (BBC 2004: 135). Such sensitivities are understandably heightened as each decennial Charter renewal approaches.

The paradox at the heart of the local radio newsroom is that audiences also expect international and national news, whereas many local weekly newspapers – which are, by contrast, perceived as complementary to the national press – can provide a wholly local diet. The first ILR regulator, the IBA, would allow only the best-resourced stations to compile their own mix of international, national and local news, requiring the others to broadcast a live three-minute bulletin from Independent Radio News (IRN), followed by their own two-minute local bulletin. The subsequent 'lighter touch' of the Radio Authority (1991–2003), and now Ofcom, has enabled the majority of stations to mix their own bulletins according to what they take to be the priorities of their audiences.

This practice means that, rather than having to wait until after even the lighthearted item at the end of the national bulletin from London, stories of major local importance that would be too parochial to feature in a national bulletin can make the lead locally. However, neither the commercial nor the BBC local newsroom could provide its audience with such comprehensive bulletins were it not for the economies of scale afforded by the underlying national structures of BBC News, IRN and Sky News Radio. In 2005, IRN was servicing more than 270 UK local and regional commercial stations, and Sky much fewer, having supply agreements with only 24 FM or AM stations, almost all in The Wireless Group and Chrysalis Radio. But Sky was also supplying the Digital News Network, to which we shall return shortly.

One of the more recent threats to the autonomy of local newsrooms has been the increasing regionalisation of resources. The BBC's internal organisation is essentially metropolitan in nature, and extensive programme sharing takes place outside peak times. With ever lighter regulation, the original diversity of ownership within ILR was all but destroyed by the formation of voraciously acquisitive groups in the 1990s. GCap Media was created in 2005 through the merger of GWR and Capital, both of them already market leaders, and further consolidation followed as EMAP acquired Scottish Radio Holdings (Martinson 2005). Table 2.1 shows the number of FM licences held by the biggest groups, which often determine programming and editorial policies centrally. What was intended by the Sound Broadcasting Act of 1972 to be a network of locally autonomous commercial stations is becoming increasingly dominated by ever larger conglomerates; as evidenced by the GWR–Capital merger, the regulators are clearly not averse to giants. Further foreign and cross-media ownership seems likely.

Table 2.1 Group ownership of United Kingdom FM stations, 2005

Group	Number of FM licences held
GCap Media (formerly Capital and GWR)	45
EMAP (incorporating Scottish Radio Holdings)	23
The Local Radio Company	20
The Wireless Group	14
UKRD	11

Source: Boon (2005: 39–40).

A debate about whether the regulator should allow news 'hubs' to operate in the commercial sector began under the Radio Authority and continued under Ofcom. The latter conceded that local stations within a region might be allowed to pool resources, provided that each maintained 'a local journalistic presence' in order to ensure a supply of local news for each of them (Ofcom 2004). It is easy to envisage a situation in which this presence is pared to a minimum by the commercial impulse to save on the cost of duplicating the compilation and presentation of bulletins, only part of which may be sourced locally. In 2002, an experimental news hub began servicing GWR stations across the southwest of England – Plymouth Sound, Gemini FM, Orchard FM, South Hams Radio and Lantern FM – at a fraction of the cost of maintaining fully operational newsrooms in each station. Ofcom's subsequent decision to concentrate on 'content' issues, rather than 'operational' issues, raised the spectre of hubs not even being centred on particular regions but serving stations much farther apart.

Technological advances

It is important to stress that the new technologies that allow these developments are not wholly contrary to the interests of either the listener or the local radio journalist. The concept of 'the flying journalist', no longer taken up with such mundane roles as sequencing agency copy and lining up corresponding audio from national feeds but able to move nimbly about a larger editorial area as stories break, is an attractive one. With relative ease, a central, suitably equipped newsdesk can now create bespoke bulletins for each of the different stations within its area and send them out on cue or at a predetermined time.

Provided that the content addresses their priorities and interests adequately, the most alert listeners would care little if, within their area, the same voice is presenting different bulletins on different stations at the same time. Many would simply not know. Furthermore, the practice of prerecording bulletins, even though it contradicts broadcast journalism's image of itself as live, dynamic and up-to-the-minute, is already well-established where companies transmit complementary services on different frequencies in the same area; one such is EMAP, whose Metro Radio on FM and Magic 1152 on AM transmit to overlapping areas centred on Newcastle in northeast England. In the less rigidly regulated sphere of digital radio, the Chrysalis Group has for some time been fooling listeners of Digital Audio Broadcasting (DAB) into believing that its pioneering national rock music and rolling news stations, The Arrow and Digital News Network (DNN) are regional services. It does this by inserting different regional news bulletins and traffic news at predetermined points in the otherwise national programming in each service area. Bespoke branding carefully applied to each regional version positions the service as 'for the northeast', 'for Yorkshire', and so on, and the deception is revealed only in the occasional operator error or computer glitch.

Local radio news and the reporters behind it have already benefited significantly from technological advances. Reporting from remote locations – that is, anywhere away from the newsroom – has been made easier by digital data transmission technology. Since the early 1990s, the increased availability of Integrated Services Digital Network (ISDN) lines and equipment has allowed the sending of both live and recorded sound between distant studios, and between other suitably equipped locations and the studio. Thus, for a fraction of the cost of the permanent studio-quality 'music lines' that radio stations would once hire in order to cover special events or connect remote contribution studios, material that reflects higher production values than those obtainable via the ordinary telephone network can now be easily sourced.

This has considerably reduced the cost of maintaining basic 'satellite' studios – often consisting of little more than a mixer, headphones and a microphone – around an editorial area. An unconventional twenty-first-century manifestation of this has been the arrival of the BBC Community Bus, variously used by Radios Derby, Lancashire, Wales and others, as an interface between the otherwise distant and monolithic organisation that is the BBC and small, often disadvantaged, communities within the local radio areas. In each case, the bus is staffed by a reporter on the lookout for local human interest stories that can be fed back to the studio, thus reinforcing the station's links with those communities. The public is lured aboard by the offer of PC-based access to information technology, including the Internet.

Elsewhere, and in the absence of ISDN provision, the Internet itself has opened up new possibilities for the radio reporter. While editing audio tape on location was always possible, if relatively inconvenient, portable digital recording and editing hardware – including the now ubiquitous laptop – allows even the creation of quite elaborate news packages *in situ*, ready for instant transmission to the newsroom. This can be done using a modem or Wireless Application Protocol (WAP) over the Internet or, far more expensively, via a portable satellite uplink – in each case faithfully preserving the broadcast quality of the original recordings. Stories can thus be turned round much more quickly, and since they no longer need to return to base first, reporters are free to move straight to another assignment.

The BBC's 1990s approach to bimedia journalism, in which its local radio journalists were sometimes expected to produce output for television news, has metamorphosed into trimedia journalism – thanks to the public's growing appetite for new technology. The Corporation's policy of '360 degree exploitation' means that even routine items of local news which television would consider worthy of only a brief inclusion on the regional news pages of the teletext service, are likely to be required for BBCi – the brand name of the various interactive platforms for its output, including Digital Terrestrial Television (DTT) and satellite television. These local items are needed for its web presence. The infinite capacity of the web to process, store and archive text, pictures, video and audio for instant public access enables a local radio report not only to reach new audiences but also to enjoy a longevity far beyond the brief existence otherwise allowed it by the ephemeral medium of radio. One of BBCi's most popular features is its 'Listen Again' section where audio may be heard on demand and free of charge.

The imaginative sorting and branding of such material on the Internet has even allowed the BBC to create new editorial areas for places in England that might consider themselves underserved by its network of just 40 local radio stations (BBC 2005). One such place is Wearside in the northeast of England, sandwiched between the provocatively named Radio Newcastle to the north and Radio Cleveland based in Middlesbrough 30 miles to the south, which is quite distinct in character and allegiance yet hitherto unrecognised by the restricted budget of BBC Nations and Regions. 'BBC Radio Wear' remains an unfulfilled and unfinanced aspiration somewhere down the Corporation's long list of future expansion plans – most of which will fall victim either to other, higher-profile demands on its limited licence income or to the protectionist lobbying of the commercial radio companies (Milmo 2004). On the Internet, though, BBC Wear is a reality, albeit a 'virtual' one, and there are many other examples of local services to which new listeners are directed, simply by entering their postcodes in the appropriate place on the BBCi home page.

In a further example of how Internet technology, combined with increasing editorial sophistication, is empowering audiences to access local radio news of their own choosing, the Internet has created a 'technological' localness in addition to the 'geographical' localness we have previously understood to limit community membership. BBC and some local commercial stations are now streamed live or available as podcasts, not just nationally but internationally. On one level, this simply offers enthusiasts and professionals alike the opportunity to listen to local radio stations that are too distant to be received by traditional means. A more sophisticated and perhaps noteworthy phenomenon, though, is that of increased listening to local radio by those who have moved away from their birthplace but who maintain personal and ethnic ties to it. Thus, Geordies in London can hear Radio Newcastle as easily as Scousers in Scotland may listen to Radio Merseyside, and Brummies may enjoy Radio WM in New York. There are clear similarities between this diasporic listening and the old tradition of sending local newspapers to sons and daughters overseas to help them feel in touch with home and ease the dislocation often felt when living away from those who share their backgrounds, experiences, aspirations and even accents. This trend fulfils the prediction made by McLuhan (2001) back in the 1960s that geographical displacement will be rendered less significant by the growth of the mass media.

Editorial issues

Not all change is positive though, nor is every community as strongly bound by that sense of shared identities and values on which, if it is to find large enough audiences, local journalism depends. In some localities, shared identity is so strong that non-indigenous broadcasting is perceived with a scepticism bordering on resentment; individuals may also feel a sense of belonging simply because their locality seems geographically isolated. The appetite for local news is often at its greatest here. For Merseyside, with a population largely convinced that it has suffered decades of neglect since the decline of its shipbuilding and manufacturing industries, the local television news has traditionally been produced in Manchester, a city whose status as regional capital it passionately disputes. The impact of local radio is such that with a combined share of 30 per cent of all radio listening, BBC Radio Merseyside and EMAP's Radio City together regularly achieve the top two positions in the market (Boon 2005: 23). By contrast, some areas lack the regional identity that binds Liverpudlian audiences together, and their appetite for local news is much smaller. Star 106.6, based in Slough, began broadcasting in 1993 to a collection of commuter towns (including Maidenhead and Windsor) which have little in common other than their economic dependence on, and proximity to, Greater London. It achieves among the lowest ratings, only a 6.2 per cent share in the final quarter of 2004 (RAJAR 2005). As shown in Table 2.2, the very lowest audience shares are almost all in or around London, admittedly the most competitive market in the country, but also where the cosmopolitan nature of communities may render them much less introverted than in the provinces. Among the highest are those stations serving communities that are relatively isolated, such as Radio Borders, Manx Radio and Island FM (Table 2.3).

Table 2.2 United Kingdom FM stations with the lowest audience shares within their own Editorial/Total Survey Areas, fourth quarter 2004

Station name	Audience share (%)
Dream 107.7 FM (Chelmsford)	2.1
LBC 97.3 (London, News/Talk)	2.1
KM-fm for West Kent (Tunbridge Wells & Sevenoaks)	1.9
Time FM 106.8 (Thamesmead)	1.9
XFM 104.9 (London)	1.8
BBC London 94.9	1.7
Jazz FM (London)	1.7
Choice FM (London)	1.5
Time FM 107.5 (Romford, Barking & Dagenham)	1.4
Time FM 107.3 (South East London)	1.3
South City – The Saint (Southampton)	1.2

Source: RAJAR/IPSOS-RSL (RAJAR 2005)

Table 2.3 United Kingdom FM stations with the highest audience shares within their own Editorial/Total Survey Areas, fourth quarter 2004

Station name	Audience share (%)
Radio Borders (Scottish Borders & North Northumberland)	45.8
Manx Radio (Isle of Man)	36.9
Island FM 104.7 (Guernsey)	34.0
102.5 FM Radio Pembrokeshire	33.7
Channel 103 FM (Jersey)	30.5
Moray Firth Radio (Inverness)	26.9
Spire FM (Salisbury)	26.6
CFM Radio (Carlisle & West Cumbria)	25.1
Lincs FM 102.2 (Lincoln)	24.5
BBC Radio Guernsey	24.3
Northsound One (Aberdeen)	21.9
BBC Radio Cumbria	21.8

Source: RAJAR/IPSOS-RSL (RAJAR 2005)

Conclusion

Earlier in this chapter, we suggested that news is integral to BBC local radio because it helps to fulfil the Corporation's public service duty, and to ILR because it affirms the localness of the stations within an output of popular music that mostly lacks any local provenance. We can therefore discuss the future of local radio news and local radio itself in much the same terms, and the key issue for both is the impact of new technologies. Yet we are conscious of the historical lesson that it takes some time for the potential of new technologies to be fully appreciated. The first and obvious assertion we can make is that they threaten localness by allowing economies of scale within the broadcasting industry. But the truth is rather more complex: technology also *facilitates* localness. On the production side, it enables local journalists to generate more stories and, without loss of sound quality, get them on air more quickly. On the reception side, it allows a diasporic localness via the Internet and also enables listeners to access their own virtual stations that can complement the actual ones.

Above all, new technology reminds us of how problematic a concept localness is. Where does it begin and end? In a sense, the object of broadcasting has always been to 'abolish' the sense of locality by spanning distances, and the new technology intensifies this process. A Liverpudlian who lives in Australia can listen to his beloved Radio City as if the station were just down the road; a woman in Sunderland can tune in to the news on BBC Wear, a station that has no objective existence. Localness is no longer geographical – it is a state of mind.

References

Armes, R. (1988) *On Video*, London and New York: Routledge.

Barnard, S. (1989) *On the Radio*, Milton Keynes: Open University Press.

Barnouw, E. (1977) *Tube of Plenty: The Evolution of American Television*, New York: Oxford University Press.

BBC (2004) *Annual Report & Accounts*, London: BBC.

BBC (2005) *Local Radio – Your Guide to English Local Content*, London: BBC, www.bbc.co.uk/england/radindex.shtml?link (accessed 11 February 2005).

Boon, P. (ed.) (2005) *UK Radio Guide & Directory*, Farnham: Goldcrest Broadcasting.

Briggs, A. (1995) *History of Broadcasting in the United Kingdom, Volume V: Competition*, Oxford: Oxford University Press.

Crisell, A. (2002) *An Introductory History of British Broadcasting*, London and New York: Routledge, 2nd edn.

Gorham, M. (1952) *Broadcasting and Television since 1900*, London: Andrew Dakers.

Harvey, S. and Robins, K. (1994) 'Voices and places: the BBC and regional policy', *Political Quarterly*, 65.

Martinson, J. (2005) 'EMAP secures SRH for £391m', *The Guardian*, 22 June, http://media.guardian.co.uk/site/story/0,14173,1511642,00.html (accessed 11 July 2005).

McLuhan, M. (2001) *Understanding Media (Routledge Classics)*, London and New York: Routledge.

Milmo, D. (2004) 'Commercial radio fears community rivals', *The Guardian*, 18 February, http://media.guardian.co.uk/broadcast/story/0,7493,1150485,00.html (accessed 11 February 2005).

Ofcom (2004) *Radio – Preparing for the Future*, London: Ofcom.

Radio Authority (1995) *Media Ownership: The Government's Proposals (CM 2072) – A Response by the Radio Authority*, London: Radio Authority.

RAJAR (2005) *Quarterly Survey*, London: RAJAR, 5 February.

Scannell, P. and Cardiff, D. (1991) *A Social History of Broadcasting: Volume I 1922–1939: Serving the Nation*, Oxford: Basil Blackwell.

Starkey, G. (2004) *Radio in Context*, Basingstoke: Palgrave Macmillan.

Chapter 3

What future for regional television news?

Richard Tait

For more than 40 years, high-quality regional news and current affairs on Independent Television (ITV) and British Broadcasting Corporation (BBC) has been one of the defining characteristics of British public service broadcasting providing the perfect example of the unique British experiment in having two competing and complementary systems – one funded by the licence fee, the other by advertising – both committed to providing high-quality network and regional programming. In 2005, there were 18 BBC regions and subregions and 27 ITV1 equivalents (Ofcom 2005a: 241).

As the most used and trusted source of information about the nations and regions of the United Kingdom, television has always had a vital role in the strength of our democracy; in a postdevolution world, that role has become even more important (Hargreaves and Thomas 2002: 62–76).

But the end of the duopoly, the growth of multichannel television and the new 'light touch' regulation of terrestrial commercial television has resulted in seismic changes. ITV, the dominant regional broadcaster for most of its history, saw its news audiences collapse in less than a decade to be overtaken by a BBC which now, for the first time, proclaims regional broadcasting as one of its central roles. The policy and regulatory argument as the UK nears digital switchover in 2012 is whether commercially funded regional television news will survive at all.

Ironically, while parts of the old system are in danger of disappearing, new digital technology now enables broadcasters to move into local or ultralocal news – and potentially, on a collision course with the local press. In the broadcast newsrooms, the arrival of 'citizen journalism' – viewer-generated content from websites, video cameras and mobile phones – offers huge opportunities for a more interactive and participative regional journalism, but one with complex operational and ethical implications.

Regional news under pressure on ITV

ITV was the dominant player in regional broadcasting from its creation in 1955 till the end of the 1990s. It was set up as a regional network, and the quality and ambition of the licensees' regional programming, particularly news and current affairs, had always been a key determinant in the award and retention of licences.

Clive Jones, the current chief executive of ITV News, who worked in the 1970s on Yorkshire Television's *Calendar*, recalls

> The regional news magazines were quickly established as the flagship output of each of the regional stations ... they were way ahead of the BBC. They were terribly vibrant training grounds. At one stage virtually every programme controller and managing director of ITV had begun in local news.
>
> (interview 2005)

However, the radical changes in the television industry, with the emergence of multichannel television and the new regulatory framework brought in by the 1990 Broadcasting Act, were to have a profound effect on ITV regional journalism. The franchise auction meant that licences were awarded to the highest bidder, once a quality threshold had been met; the companies argued that only by being allowed to merge could they acquire the necessary scale to compete effectively in the multichannel world.

After a decade of takeover battles, by 2004 the Granada–Carlton merger meant there was a single ITV company controlling all the franchises in England and Wales. In Scotland, the Scottish Media Group (SMG) brought together the Scottish Television and Grampian licences in a single company covering all but the border region of the country.

In their bids to win the 1992 licences, many of the companies offered to expand their regional coverage. They had responded to the challenge of devolution by developing enhanced services. On ITV1, as on BBC, there was significantly more coverage of the nations – Scotland, Wales and Northern Ireland – than of the English regions (Ofcom 2005a: 241–5). But as the decade went on, ITV's commitments came to be seen as increasingly unaffordable.

Local news became a lower priority, and the effects of that were compounded by scheduling changes which were little short of catastrophic for the flagship regional programmes in the early evening. Clive Jones described the process: 'as consolidation went on so it [regional journalism] started to lose its sway with the companies. They also then embarked on messing around with teatime, messing around with the news' (interview 2005).

The major change was a consequence of ITV's ill-fated decision in 1997 to kill off its most important news programme, *News at Ten*. The new schedule moved the network news from 17.40 to 18.30, which left the regional news programmes running at 18.00 against the BBC's very successful network news. The loss of the *Home and Away* soap, a mainstay of the ITV teatime schedule, to Channel 5, meant that the 'newshour' from 18.00 had a poor audience inheritance.

The Independent Television Commission's (ITC) own research identified the scale of what it called 'the regional news problem'.

> Viewing of regional news in the English regions and devolved nations has fallen dramatically, from a high of 1.27 hours per month at the turn of 1997 to a current low of 0.47 hours per month ... The pace of decline differs somewhat by region, but the familiar pattern is now for the BBC regional television news programme to have overtaken its ITV equivalent.
>
> (Hargreaves and Thomas 2002: 32)

By 2003, the audience share for ITV's regional news at 18.00 was just 21 per cent – down by a half from 43 per cent in 1994. The BBC's regional news at 18.30, in contrast, had a share of 30 per cent – down by a tenth from 34 per cent in 1994 (Newspaper Society 2005: 39).

In 2002, for the first time in its history, the BBC spent more on its regional output than ITV (Ofcom 2004a: 57–62). In a few short years, the balance of power in regional broadcast journalism was reversed, with apparently no real prospect of ITV ever regaining its preeminence. In March 2005, the BBC was able to claim that its programmes were ahead of ITV's in every part of the United Kingdom apart from Northern Ireland; the total audience for all the BBC's 18.30 regional news bulletins made the slot the most-watched news programme in Britain.

Expansion at the BBC

The BBC's emergence as the dominant regional news broadcaster was not just a consequence of the crisis at ITV. There had been an increased focus on regional news under John Birt and his successive directors of regional broadcasting – Mark Byford, Ron Neil and Mark Thompson. As with BBC network news, there was a new focus on specialist journalism in areas like transport. By 2000, the regional news operations had been integrated into the BBC's network news operation, ending decades of mutual hostility. As Pat Loughrey, the current director of Nations and Regions, recalls 'it had been run as a separated brethren before, with people in one area as contemptuous and as disdainful of the other as you could get' (interview 2005).

The result was a truly integrated operation between 18.00 and 19.00, with satellite newsgathering trucks for fast response, and a more coherent, contemporary approach to set design and graphics. Investment in news continued under Greg Dyke, who took over from Birt in 2000. Pat Loughrey felt Dyke's contribution was to win hearts and minds:

> He felt that unlike almost everyone else who'd ever occupied his seat and thought that nations and regions had to be made like London, Greg passionately felt London needed to be made like the nations and regions, where there was an engagement and a commitment and a lack of exclusive career motivation.
>
> (interview 2005)

The impact of devolution meant that by 2004, the BBC spent three times as much per hour on regional programmes in Scotland than it did in the English regions (Ofcom 2005a: 244). The scale of the investment was all the more effective because television news technology and working practices were changing radically. Lightweight digital cameras encouraged the growth of video journalism. Where once the BBC had struggled to put 80 conventional camera crews in the field each day, it could now rely on up to 400 people trained as video journalists. For Pat Loughrey it transformed newsgathering: 'now between the East region and the Midlands we have more cameras than we had in the whole UK. That's the difference' (interview 2005).

The expansion of television went hand in hand with an ambitious move online – the launch in 1998 of a network of 'Where I Live' websites in the Nations and Regions. By 2003/04, spending in the Nations and Regions at £11.64 million was the second biggest item of BBC online expenditure, after national and international news (Graf 2004: 35).

Light touch regulation

The attitude of the commercial television regulator – from 1992, the ITC, and since 2003, Ofcom, the 'converged' regulator for broadcasting and telecommunications – showed how fast broadcasting was changing. Initially, the ITC, inheritor of a tradition of interventionist regulation, had been concerned about trying to protect regional news. As Steve Perkins, the ITC senior programme officer responsible for news and current affairs, put it, 'The ITC took it [regional news] terribly seriously, possibly to a greater extent than other areas of PSB like current affairs, even possibly than national news in some ways' (interview 2005).

But towards the end of the decade, the emphasis changed. The ITC began to look with a sympathetic eye on ITV's economic problems. As Robin Foster, an ITC executive and then partner, strategy development, Ofcom, explained:

we started doing what I suppose some would call the infamous opportunity cost analysis looking at the real cost to ITV of regional news and other regional programming which I think set part of the agenda for the later work which Ofcom did on that area looking at how affordable the different aspects of PSB obligations were for ITV or likely to be.

(interview 2005)

The research suggested that ITV's traditional role in regional television was under extreme pressure (Kidd and Taylor 2002: 5). The ITC put a figure on what regional programme obligations were costing ITV and came up with an estimate of almost two-thirds of the £210 million opportunity costs for ITV as a whole (Ofcom 2004b: 23). Robin Foster's conclusion was that, 'regional news was probably the most expensive of the PSB obligations facing ITV and one which would presumably come under threat as competition increased' (interview 2005).

The fundamental issue was the cost of producing separate programmes for 15 regions and up to 12 subregions. Ofcom calculated that the average cost per hour of regional programming, including news, was £418,000, compared with an average cost of £86,000 for network programming (Ofcom 2004a: 60–1).

Ofcom's solution to this problem was both to lighten the regulatory obligations of ITV by cutting back the amount of non-news regional programming it had to broadcast, and to adjust ITV's licences to allow it more resources to pay for its regional news services. In February 2005, Ofcom agreed that in England the companies only had to run an hour and a half of non-news regional programming, reducing to just 30 minutes once digital switchover was under way (Dignam 2005: 5). In the nations, public and political opposition resulted in the quotas remaining at four hours, dropping to three hours as switchover begins (Pike 2005: 5).

In June 2005, Ofcom agreed to reduce the annual licence payments ITV was making to the Treasury by the equivalent of £135 million (Revoir 2005: 2). Ofcom believed this would be sufficient to enable ITV to continue to meet its regional news commitments till the end of its new digital licences in 2015. ITV's chief executive, Charles Allen, disagreed, arguing that further financial concessions and/or public intervention would be necessary even to enable regional news to survive to switchover (House of Lords 2005: 2–10).

ITV's last chance?

Until 2004, the growing crisis in audiences and resources was exacerbated by an incoherent and wasteful structure. ITV had always had, in Independent Television News (ITN), a single national and international news supplier. But the regional newsrooms had jealously protected their autonomy. Clive Jones puts it succinctly, 'the only thing that united the ITV regions was their hatred of ITN' (interview 2005).

Stewart Purvis, former chief executive of ITN, remembers endless wrangles over the pictures which the regional newsrooms were meant to supply:

> ITN would 'unreasonably' ask for pictures for the 10 to 6 news which went out before the regional news so often we'd be told 'sorry but the pictures won't be ready for your news, the dispatch rider has lost his way or the taxi has broken down and won't be here in time for you'. Then miraculously the pictures would appear just in time for the 6 o'clock regional news and be available for *News at Ten* and that seemed to me to epitomise the relationship.
>
> (interview 2005)

Even in 1992, when Carlton and Granada, the weekday and weekend London licensees, sensibly put their news operations together to create the London News Network (LNN), they ended up with ITV operating two separate London newsrooms on opposite sides of the river – LNN on the South Bank and ITN at Gray's Inn Road.

However, with consolidation, attitudes began to change. The notorious incident in the 2001 general election, where HTV Wales, an ITV company, sold its exclusive pictures of the 'Prescott punch' to Sky News, ITV's commercial rival, and only then passed the pictures on to ITN, ITV's network news service, brought the dysfunctional nature of the relationship for the first time to the attention of ITV's most senior management. And the search for cost savings, which ITV had promised its shareholders, began to focus on the regional news operations.

In March 2003, with the Granada–Carlton merger in prospect, ITN and ITV jointly approached the ITC with a confidential proposal entitled 'Making ITV News Stronger'. This argued for a new integrated news organisation for ITV, under the aegis of ITN, responsible for network news on ITV1, the ITV News Channel, and all regional news programmes on ITV1 in England and Wales. SMG, Ulster Television and Channel would continue to make their own news programmes for Scotland, Northern Ireland and the Channel Islands (Tait 2003a: 4).

The first sign of change was the closure in 2004 of the LNN newsroom and its integration into the ITN operation. The ITV News Group was created with a senior ITV manager, Clive Jones, as chief executive; an ITN editor, David Mannion, became editor in chief. Another ITN editor, Michael Jermey, joined ITV as editor ITV Regional News. His brief was to bring a new approach:

When I came into this role I saw two overwhelming priorities ... One was to improve the quality of our programmes right across the country, to make better connections with viewers and to do our best either to increase viewing or hold viewing in a world where multi-channel penetration meant that all terrestrial audiences for most slots were falling. And the second was to make ITV Regional News cooperate as one organisation and cooperate with the network news as one organisation.

(interview 2005)

Regarding programme quality, the first issue was the agenda. For Clive Jones, ITV Regional News had lost its way, particularly during the 1990s when the programmes had become hard news vehicles with too much emphasis on crime. He commented that, 'Given that lots of viewers of regional news tend to be older I'm amazed that some people went out at night' (interview 2005).

There was a move away from fires and crime to reflect new trends in journalism such as consumer news, though ITV did not go as far down the road of specialist correspondents as the BBC, partly for financial reasons. Sets and graphics were standardised with flexibility for different regional backgrounds. At the same time, and more controversially, ITV embarked on an ambitious programme, moving its regional newsrooms out of their traditional (and redundant) city centre headquarters in places like Norwich, Southampton and Birmingham.

ITV decided to close and sell these sites, relocating their news operations in much smaller purpose-built facilities in cheaper locations, which could be equipped with the latest digital technology for video journalism and desktop editing. The concept became known as 'business park television'.

In total, ITV estimated its investment in new studios, satellite trucks and digital equipment to be £40–50 million. The changes also meant job losses – primarily among technical staff whose jobs disappeared with new technology. ITV argued that, in the main, the only editorial jobs to go were those who used to make the regional non-news programmes (Tait 2003b: 4).

The new approach got off to a good start. By the end of 2004, Broadcasters' Audience Research Board (BARB) figures showed ITV1's regional share had risen 2 points to 23 per cent, narrowing the gap with the BBC to 6 per cent. On programme quality, an unpublished assessment by Ofcom of ITV and BBC regional news programmes in October 2004 found that both demonstrated high-quality journalism and production values on the big stories. The main differences in the services were that while ITV had a higher overall story count than BBC, the BBC carried more specialist reports and more crafted feature reports.

Local TV and beyond

By 2005, the debate about the future of regional broadcasting had reached a critical point. The government had announced that the process of digital switchover would begin in 2008 and be completed by 2012. At that point the regional network of analogue transmitters would be switched off and with them, ITV argued, went any obligation to provide regional programming unless it was profitable to do so.

The BBC had identified coverage of the nations and regions as a key element in its longer-term strategy. 'Building Public Value', its proposal document for the new BBC Charter from 2007, was explicit in identifying social and community value as one of the five main ways in which it creates public value (BBC 2004: 8).

Ofcom, in its review of Public Service Television, had accepted that ITV would probably wish to withdraw from all regional broadcasting, with the possible exception of regional news, after digital switchover. The BBC might need to play a greater role to compensate (Ofcom 2004b: 63–77). It also thought that its proposed Public Service Publisher, with a budget of £300 million a year, could have a role in sustaining and developing broadcasting in the regions (Ofcom 2004c: 69–80).

However, just at the moment when the future of traditional regional broadcast journalism seemed uncertain, the technology was enabling broadcasters to think ambitiously about a move to local or ultralocal broadcast news using a combination of broadband and some digital television spectrum to target much smaller sections of the audience.

There had been a number of interesting experiments with varying degrees of success – by the autumn of 2005, there were 17 stations with restricted service licences from Ofcom, mostly running city-based local television, such as Channel M in Manchester (Newspaper Society 2005: 30).

The BBC proposed to launch 50–60 local television stations across the country 'to serve an unmet need for local TV news among UK audiences' (BBC 2004: 66). It was planning a pilot in the West Midlands offering a ten-minute bulletin for each of the five areas on a satellite channel, and also making them available on demand via broadband through the 'Where I Live' sites.

The proposal proved controversial – the Newspaper Society, representing the regional press in a submission to government, argued that the proposal should not be allowed to go ahead:

> the regional press has a long heritage of building substantial public value without recourse to public funding. The industry's ability to sustain this role over the long term is at risk from the BBC's planned expansion in local and

regional media. Far from remedying an instance of market failure, this expansion will more likely precipitate one.

(Newspaper Society 2005: 2)

The BBC countered that its proposals did not threaten the local press (Griffee 2005: 14). But Ofcom argued that any decision on local television should be part of the Charter review process and noted that it was undertaking research of its own with DCMS on the future of local television (Ofcom 2005b: 34).

At the same time, the ITV companies were planning their own pilots in Brighton and London, even though they were aware that the economics made it hard to work unless as Clive Jones wondered, perhaps a little ominously for the newspaper industry: 'is there a new stream of revenue advertising from property through to cars to classified?' (interview 2005).

Citizen journalism

The year 2005 was also the year 'citizen journalism' emerged as a major source of material for broadcasters, with particular significance for regional news (see Chapters 10, 15 and 18). Mobile phones with the capacity to shoot and then transmit video plus the wide availability of cheap, high-quality video cameras transformed the rules of the newsgathering game.

The regional and national coverage of the floods at Boscastle and the 7 July 2005 bombings relied heavily on this form of 'citizen journalism'. ITV and the *Daily Mail* paid a reported £65,000 for exclusive amateur video of the arrest of two alleged bombers. ITV's *London Tonight* set up a network of hundreds of viewers who were interested in contributing material and could be text messaged when a story breaks to see if they were in the area. Pat Loughrey built a significant element of citizen journalism into his plans for BBC local television, 'At least a third of the content on the service will be produced by the public and every site will have a producer whose job it is to nurture and facilitate people telling their own stories' (interview 2005).

Conclusion

The growth of citizen journalism is certain to provoke an important debate about its professional implications, just as the growth of blogs has sparked an argument in newspapers. The key issues are verification and mediation – how do regional and local services ensure that the third-party material they offer their viewers is accurate and impartial? How do they avoid being hoaxed or hijacked by lobbies? It also poses questions about broadcasters' responsibilities – how far should they encourage untrained viewers to act in effect as cameramen, particularly in potentially hazardous situations?

Regardless of how those issues were to be resolved, by the summer of 2006 the future of regional television news was as uncertain as at any time in its history. How far it would survive into the digital age would not depend primarily on how skilfully regional television journalists served their audiences but on the success or failure of complex regulatory and political decisions over the next few years aimed at trying to preserve a hugely important part of public service broadcasting. The closure of the ITV News Channel in December 2005 underlined how difficult that task might be as the United Kingdom entered the age of digital television.

References

BBC (2004) *Building Public Value*, London: BBC.

Dignam, C. (2005) 'Detailing Ofcom's vision', *Broadcast*, 8 February, p. 5.

Graf, P. (2004) *Report of the Independent Review of BBC Online*, London: DCMS.

Griffee, A. (2005) 'BBC – we are not an "ultra local" threat to newspapers', *Press Gazette*, 23 September, p. 14.

Hargreaves, I. and Thomas, J. (2002) *New News, Old News*, London: ITC/BSC.

House of Lords (2005) *Minutes of Evidence Taken Before the Select Committee on the BBC Charter Review*, 7 June, London: HMSO.

Kidd, M. and Taylor, B. (2002) *Television in the Nations and Regions*, London: ITC.

Newspaper Society (2005) *Review of the BBC's Charter: Newspaper Society Submission*, London: Newspaper Society.

Ofcom (2004a) *The Communications Market – Television*, London: Ofcom.

Ofcom (2004b) *Review of Public Service Television Broadcasting, Phase 2 – Meeting the Digital Challenge*, London: Ofcom.

Ofcom (2004c) *Review of Public Service Television Broadcasting, Phase 3 – Competition for Quality*, London: Ofcom.

Ofcom (2005a) *The Communications Market – Television*, London: Ofcom.

Ofcom (2005b) *Review of the BBC's Royal Charter: Response to the Green Paper*, London: Ofcom.

Pike, C. (2005) 'NUJ slates Ofcom on ITV public service broadcast cuts', *Press Gazette*, 11 February, p. 5.

Revoir, P. (2005) 'ITV buoyant after fee cut', *Broadcast*, 1 July, p. 2.

Tait, R. (2003a) 'National root to local branches', *Financial Times, Creative Business*, 21 October, p. 4.

Tait, R. (2003b) 'Moments of truth', *Financial Times, Creative Business*, 9 December, p. 4.

Chapter 4

News from a small country
The media in Scotland

Brian McNair

If news is our window on the world, local news is our window on that part of the
world we actually inhabit. In a globalised culture where war-torn, disaster-
strewn images from far-off places of which we know relatively little flow
constantly into our living rooms, local news tells us what's happening in our own
streets and backyards. Parochial by definition, local journalism is part of the
social cement which binds communities together and is widely and rightly viewed
as an essential element in the construction of local identity.

True as a generality, the unique cultural role of local news is even more
important at the level of the 'national' regions of the UK, all of which have
undergone major constitutional reform since the election of New Labour in
1997. Scotland, Wales and Northern Ireland have all seen power devolved
from Westminster to various kinds of constituent assembly, reforms which
have politicised the provision of local news and journalism and at times forced
them to the top of the public agenda. This essay explores recent developments
in the print and broadcast news of one of those nation-regions, Scotland,
against the background of change in the political, economic and technological
environments within which local journalists work. When the first edition of my
book on *News and Journalism in the UK* was published in early 1994 New Labour
and devolution were still a twinkle in Tony Blair's eye. The Scottish and
Grampian commercial television franchises were operated by separate companies, and venerable Scottish newspapers such as *The Herald* were still in Scottish
hands. Online journalism was something indulged in by computer nerds in
California. This essay assesses what has changed since then, and what those
changes have meant for both producers and consumers of local journalism in
Scotland.

Journalism in Scotland: an overview

Scotland has long nurtured a distinct identity (as, of course, have Wales, Ireland
and the people in the English regions), which has shaped its legal and education

systems, politics and media. Scotland was in the forefront of the eighteenth-century intellectual movement known as the Enlightenment and pioneered the development of liberal journalism in the form of periodicals such as the *Edinburgh Review* (Conboy 2004). Ever since, Scotland has supported a public sphere of exceptional richness, given the country's relatively small population. Apart from the UK press and broadcast media to which its population has access (many of which are 'editionised' for the Scottish market with locally produced content), Scotland is supplied with news and journalism by ten newspapers which are to a greater or lesser degree 'national' (in the sense that they are read throughout Scotland, even if they are mainly targeted at one of either Glasgow, Edinburgh, Aberdeen or Dundee), evening papers serving all the major cities, and more than 60 local newspapers, from the *West Highland Free Press* to the *East Kilbride News*. The red-top *Daily Record* leads the field with a circulation of some 471,000, while the broadsheets (including *The Scotsman*, which followed *The Times* and *Independent* by adopting a tabloid format in 2004) record circulations between 60,000 (*Sunday Herald*) and 87,000 (*Aberdeen Press & Journal*).

In broadcast journalism there is the substantial news and current affairs output of British Broadcasting Corporation (BBC) Scotland and its commercial rivals, Scottish TV, Grampian TV and Borders TV, all of which have public service remits under UK legislation. In Scottish radio news, as in the rest of the UK, commercial companies such as Saga and Clyde FM have proliferated in recent years, complementing BBC Radio Scotland's substantial journalistic output with news bulletins, which attract significant audiences even though they form only a minor proportion of schedules mainly dedicated to popular music. A 2002 decision of the Radio Authority requires local radio stations to maintain their own production of news, as opposed to buying material from regional hubs. Stations such as Saga FM thus maintain full-time journalistic staff and other newsgathering resources.

The Scottish media environment: politics and culture

Taking these outlets together, the Scottish public sphere is relatively well-endowed by both UK and international standards. When considering the environmental factors driving its development today, the most important is politics, in particular the advent of devolved government. Devolution means more than merely a change in the way Scotland is run (powers such as the administration of health, education and transport are now devolved from the House of Commons in Westminster to the Scottish Parliament in Edinburgh). It also embodies the assertion of a heightened, and now institutionally acknowledged, Scottish cultural identity, part of but distinct from that of the UK as a whole.

For centuries Scottish national identity has been reflected and articulated not just in the fields of law, education, religion and politics but in a distinctively Scottish journalistic tradition, which since the eighteenth century has been conducted with as much acknowledgement of national identity as that of any independent nation-state. That said, the Scottish print media have not generally been supportive of independence as a political strategy, tending to back one of the unionist parties when called upon to take sides between and during election campaigns. Public support for independence, as measured by the electoral perfor-mance of the Scottish National Party (SNP) over many campaigns, has hovered around 25 per cent, and the percentage of Scottish newspapers extending their editorial support to the SNP has been much less than that. There have been several attempts to establish more pro-nationalist newspapers, most recently the *Scottish Standard*, which was launched in March 2005 just ahead of the general election campaign of that year. Though benefiting from a lot of media publicity (much of which acknowledged the importance, from the point of view of Scottish democ-racy, of an editorial voice for independence), and with a brief to support the SNP, the *Scottish Standard* never managed to sell more than 12,000 copies, and closed after only seven issues. Organised Scottish nationalism remains a movement without a print media voice, as indeed does Scottish conservatism (which despite an unprecedentedly small presence in the Holyrood Parliament retains some 15.8 per cent of the support of those who voted in the 2005 general election).

The expression of Scottishness in Scotland's news media has not extended to anything like editorial enthusiasm for independence. Devolution, on the other hand, *was* supported by most of Scotland's newspapers in the years following Labour's 1997 election victory (the Scotsman titles being the main exception). When the Parliament was established in 1999 it propelled Scotland and its media into a new political era. From the perspective of local journalists a whole new tier of democratically accountable government had come into being, with many significant areas of administrative and financial responsibility shifting from the UK Parliament to Edinburgh. Scottish journalists were presented with both opportunities and additional responsibilities. Here was a whole new sphere of activity from which to extract the precious raw materials of political journalism, and one over which they would have to exercise their fourth-estate task of crit-ical scrutiny. The effectiveness with which they would meet that challenge was acknowledged from the outset to be a measure of Scottish journalism's quality as a democratic resource.

The creation of the Parliament was reflected in the upgrading of political newsgathering facilities in Edinburgh, and expanded resources for political jour-nalism across the range of media. This was accompanied by the expansion of lobbying and political spin (Schlesinger *et al.* 2001). BBC Scotland and Scottish TV launched current affairs programmes such as *Holyrood Live* and *Seven Days*, and newspapers devoted more personnel to coverage of the Parliament's activities than had been applied to local authority politics or the activities of the Scottish secretary of state. BBC's *Newsnight* introduced a Scottish opt-out, produced by BBC Scotland in Glasgow, called *Newsnight Scotland*, which broke away from the UK transmission to give Scottish viewers 15–20 minutes of local news and current affairs four nights a week. 'Newsnicht' Scotland, as it came to be known, was criticised as tokenistic both by senior *Newsnight* figures such as Jeremy Paxman, and by those in Scotland who argued that what was really required in the new political environment was a *Scottish Six*.

This idea was first mooted in the late 1990s, even before the referendum that gave popular approval to devolution. Its proposers viewed it as a daily news magazine produced in Scotland, which would integrate UK national and international coverage. This integrated programme would cover Scottish, UK and world news through a Scottish editorial prism. Nationalists supported the idea as a modest assertion of Scotland's cultural distinctiveness. For those of a unionist persuasion, on the other hand, the *Scottish Six*, by opting out of the BBC's national news at a key moment in the peak schedule, looked like the thin end of a separatist wedge. Despite a 1998 *Herald* poll showing that 69 per cent of Scots supported the idea, the *Scottish Six* never came to pass, largely because BBC managers in London agreed with New Labour ministers (John Birt sought Blair's personal intervention on the matter) that it would fuel Scottish nationalism in potentially dangerous ways. The BBC's 2003 review of its news and current affairs provision in Scotland finally laid the *Scottish Six* concept to rest, trumpeting high levels of audience satisfaction with BBC Scotland's journalism as a whole.

Postdevolution Scottish political journalism

Whole books could be written about the performance of the Scottish media with respect to the Holyrood Parliament. Here I will summarise the experience of the first few years as consistent with that of political journalism in the UK as a whole. Scottish politics and Scottish journalism have been locked in the same relationship of mutual mistrust and 'hyperadversarialism' (Fallows 1996) that has characterised political journalism at Westminster (Lloyd 2004). Whether this amounts to the 'corrosive cynicism' of which journalists are accused by some commentators of the UK media depends on how needful of critical scrutiny one regards Scottish politicians to be. Since the first Parliamentary elections in 1999 Scottish journalists have presented their audiences with numerous exotic tales of scandal, corruption, waste and failure. In many cases the stories have been fully justified by the behaviour of the politicians, as exemplified by the overspend occasioned by the Parliament building (original back-of-an-envelope estimates of £50 million eventually turned into a final bill of £450 million).

Scotland has had its share of sleaze journalism, with everything from cocaine-fuelled prostitution binges to old-fashioned, old Labour clannishness and corruption making headlines. As this essay was being written, former stalwart of Labour in Scotland, Lord Watson of Cathcart, had just been sentenced to one year in prison for attempting to set fire to a hotel curtain following a drunken awards dinner. Earlier that year, the Scottish media indulged in a feeding frenzy around the allegedly inappropriate relationship between senior BBC journalist Kirsty Wark and First Minister Jack McConnell, which extended to him receiving gifts from her in the form of free holidays in Majorca.

The scandal was fuelled, and Wark's position further compromised in the eyes of many, when her documentary production company, Wark Clements, won the contract to produce four films about the building of the Scottish Parliament, at a cost of some £3 million of public money. Evaluated as a documentary, *The Gathering Place*, was, in this viewer's opinion, a welcome counter to the overwhelmingly negative media coverage of the Parliament project which had filled the Scottish media since the project's inception, focusing as it did on the human stories of the main protagonists – Donald Dewar and Enrico Mirales, both dead before the completion of the building; the project managers trying to keep up with what uncertain and fickle politicians thought they wanted; and the tension between dream and reality which every major architectural project involves. Unfortunately, the fact that Wark had also been a member of the committee that selected the Spanish architect reinforced the appearance of small-country cronyism and of an unhealthy closeness between Labour's political elite and key media figures.

Whether or not one blames the politicians for providing the stories which have driven this pattern of coverage, or journalists for their tendency to stress the sensational and the conflictual in political affairs, it is hardly surprising that, against a background of relentlessly negative coverage, by the second Scottish Parliamentary election in 2003 only 49 per cent of the eligible electorate bothered to vote and that successive opinion polls show a general sense of disappointment about the Parliament's impact on the quality of life in Scotland. It remains to be seen if the passing of time will change this perception and what role Scotland's political journalists can play in such a shift (if indeed it is justified by the performance of the politicians).

The economic environment

If a devolved Parliament has boosted local journalism in Scotland by creating a new layer of government for it to watch over, a transformed economic environment has achieved a similar impact on journalists' work. Three trends affecting the local media market have been crucial:

- the consolidation of media capital;
- the rise of the free sheet; and
- the rise of online and other digital media.

Together these have heightened competition and commercial pressures on established companies and outlets.

Scottish media have been affected by trends towards mergers and takeovers arising from the restructuring and consolidation of media capital at the UK and global levels. These trends are far from unique to Scotland, which cannot remain aloof from global trends in the media economy, but they have been more contentious than usual in a context of national, as opposed to merely local, identity (see Chapters 1, 5, 6 and 8). Who owns the Scottish media is more than a pure business matter, but resonates in the political and cultural spheres.

The main ownership changes since 1995 have been:

- 1995 – the sale by Thomson Regional Newspapers of its Scottish titles to the Barclay brothers (*The Scotsman, Scotland on Sunday,* and *Evening News*) and Associated Newspapers (*Press and Journal*);
- 1996 – the takeover of Caledonian Publishing, publishers of *The Herald, Sunday Herald* and *Evening Times,* by the Scottish Media Group (SMG), operator of the biggest Scottish commercial TV franchise;
- 1997 – the takeover by SMG of the northern Scotland commercial TV franchise, Grampian TV;
- January 2003 – the sale by SMG of *The Herald* and *Evening Times* titles to the US-based Gannett, parent company of Newsquest Media Group, for £216 million;
- December 2005 – Johnston Press purchases the Scotsman titles.

The aim of these mergers was in some cases to reduce debt (such as SMG's sale of *The Herald* titles), and in others to consolidate and rationalise in an era of technological convergence and cultural globalisation. Some were politically controversial because they saw the control of Scottish media pass out of Scottish hands, but there were also examples of Scottish media capital expanding overseas and within the UK. The Dundee-based Johnston Press (then the fourth largest UK regional publisher, with control of some 270 papers and 15 per cent of the UK regional market) acquired Score Press in Ireland, and in September 2005 paid £160 million for the Irish Leinster Group (£95 million) and the Local Press Group (£65 million), owners of the *Belfast Telegraph* (*The Guardian* 17 September 2005, p. 21). In December of that year, Johnston bought the Scotsman titles from the Barclays for £170 million. SMG owns Virgin Radio with its lucrative London franchises. Media capital has flowed out of as well as into Scotland in recent years, and will continue to do so.

For journalists it mattered less who owned their newspapers and broadcast media than that the news industry as a whole had been forever changed by increased competitive pressures caused by technological convergence; another cause of concern was the decline of effective trade unionism and related trends such as the casualisation of labour which began with Eddie Shah and the Wapping revolution of the 1980s. In Scotland, as in the UK generally, journalists were less secure in their terms of employment and worse paid on average than they had been ten or twenty years before (Bromley 2005). In July 2002 *The Scotsman* and *Scotland on Sunday* merged key departments, with inevitable job losses. After their takeover by Newsquest, the Herald titles in Glasgow were subject to major cost-cutting economies, with the *Sunday Herald* in particular in a financially precarious state.

On the other hand, media businesses continue to attract major investment. The reclusive Barclay brothers have been praised for investing in the Scotsman titles and transforming them from what one observer calls 'parochial regionals' into 'proud national titles' (Ruddock 2005). According to this source, 'when extra money was needed at *The Scotsman*, such as during the Kosovo war, the Barclays were unquestioningly generous'. However, others criticised the Barclays' stewardship, and that of Andrew Neil, arguing that by adopting a tabloid format for *The Scotsman*, shuffling editors with unseemly regularity and 'alienating the paper from its core Edinburgh readership' they have been a key cause of persistent falling circulation and loss of editorial identity. It remains to be seen if its new, Scottish owners can reverse that trend.

The rise of the free sheet

Another market trend affecting Scottish newspapers has been the rise of the free sheet. The trend began in the 1980s, and by 2005 more free newspapers were being published in the UK than paid-fors. In Scotland, the main free title, the *Metro*, competes for the city commuter market with daily and evening paid-for titles such as the *Daily Record*, *Evening Times* and *Evening News*, forcing more editions and innovative marketing strategies from the established players. In the first half of 2005 the Scottish edition of the *Metro* recorded an average distribution of 118,000, exceeding the sales of all evening titles and broadsheets.

The rise of the free sheets has accompanied the gradual decline of Scottish newspaper circulation, another trend which parallels that of the UK as a whole. Sales of titles such as the once-mighty *Daily Record* have fallen steadily in the face of competition not only from the *Metro* and other free sheets, but from heightened competition from the *Sun* and other UK titles that have localised their content to fit the Scottish market. In 1980 the Audit Bureau of Circulations recorded the *Daily Record* sales at 731,000. In January 2005 the figure was 472,000, down by more than a third. Sales of the *Sunday Post*, once the world's biggest selling newspaper as a proportion of population, fell from 1,000,000 to less than 500,000 over the same period. Comparable declines have affected titles such as the *Evening Times*, *The Herald* and *The Scotsman*. In 2003 News International predicted that *The Sun*'s circulation (then 371,000) would match that of the *Daily Record* (then 475,000) by 2007. As of October 2005 industry observers were estimating that it was closing the gap, helped by price-cutting.

The technological environment

Declining circulations are a feature of the print market everywhere, caused by the proliferation not just of free newspapers but also of new media such as the Internet.

When the first edition of *News and Journalism in the UK* was published, Netscape had not yet been launched, and the World Wide Web was still a tool mainly of academic, governmental and military users. Less than a decade later Oftel reported that Internet access in the UK was available to more than 50 per cent of UK households, and still expanding. Scotland was part of this expansion, though at a slightly slower pace than the UK average (in 2001, Scotland was ninth in the Organisation for Economic Co-operation and Development (OECD) league table of most-connected countries).

Established media companies took some time to respond to the Internet challenge. As late as 1997 online titles could be numbered in the hundreds. Today there are hundreds of thousands, and almost every newspaper and periodical has an online edition. Scotland's news media have been part of this trend, recognising that even if print remains, for the time being, the dominant platform for the delivery of journalism, the future is digital. As yet, however, few established news organisations have been able to make an Internet presence profitable, and the search is on for a viable business model which will allow online journalism to coexist with print.

The Scotsman group, for example, has opted to charge for much of their sites' content, using selected free articles as tasters, then requiring subscribers to pay up for the rest. The Herald titles have more free content, but charge for premium services such as articles from its archive. Some companies are building online gambling and other tried and tested money-spinners into their online packages. No Scottish newspaper company, it is fair to say, has yet found a method of making enough money from the Internet to outweigh the decline of revenue from print sales, although the success of e-businesses such as eBay and Amazon suggest that it may be possible, if the technology can be deployed to do things which consumers want but which print cannot provide. Local newspapers, for example, have always been a key location for local advertising of job vacancies, properties for sale and other niche services which on the face of it seem ideally suited to the interactive, hyperlinking qualities of the Internet. The challenge for local media in Scotland, as everywhere, is to persuade people to pay for these services at a rate which compensates for any corresponding decline in the use of newspapers. Although a solution to this challenge has not yet been found, most media businesses now recognise that the Internet must be made to complement their print operations. As they did with the free newspaper phenomenon in the 1980s and 1990s, established newspaper publishers are seeking to join the Internet revolution rather than beat it.

The globalisation of local journalism

If the Internet is posing a serious commercial challenge to the Scottish press, it is also an opportunity to expand access to local journalism beyond the borders of the locality for which it is primarily intended. Online editions of titles such as the *Evening Times* and *Scotland on Sunday* can be read just as easily in Sydney or Toronto as in Glasgow or Edinburgh. In the past, expatriate Scots and their descendants could, of course, purchase print copies of newspapers from the old country, although with some delay in delivery. Digital printing technologies have made it easier to transmit paper copies of local newspapers overseas cheaply and quickly. Now, however, titles like the *Daily Record* and *Evening Times* are immediately available all over the world to anyone with an online computer. Some 40 per cent of *Scotland on Sunday*'s online users and 20 per cent of BBC *Scotland Online*'s users are overseas. This is a development with intriguing cultural implications, insofar as it breaks down the barriers of time and space which have traditionally separated regions and countries from those places overseas where expatriates have migrated (and indeed within a country such as the UK – Scots working in London now have just as much access to local journalism online as anyone north of the border). Will such access strengthen the distinctive identities of Scots expatriates in Australia and Canada (or of Pakistanis in Glasgow's Pollokshields), and is this likely to be a good thing for the countries where these diasporic communities have settled? Conclusive answers to these questions are unlikely to be forthcoming in the near future, but in a world where cultural identity and multiculturalism are increasingly contentious political issues, they deserve to be asked.

Digitalisation

Another technological trend, the digitalisation of broadcasting, is having major implications for Scottish TV journalism, and commercial broadcasters in particular. As digitalisation proceeds throughout the UK and advertising revenue shrinks, commercial TV companies are coming under growing pressure to reduce or withdraw from their provision of public service programming where it is not profitable. The broadcast regulator Ofcom (2005) has acknowledged this economic reality, while insisting that commercial companies must continue to provide local journalism alongside that of the BBC. Surveys produced by Ofcom and Scottish TV indicate that local broadcast journalism is highly valued by audiences, who also support continuing plurality of provision. BBC Scotland's 2003 review of its own news and current affairs output showed some 80 per cent audience approval. The challenge, then, is to find ways of paying for quality local journalism on commercial TV while preserving the companies' profitability in the digital era.

SMG's plans for its local news include the cancellation of its long-standing afternoon bulletin, and the introduction of a tailored evening bulletin at 22.30. This, should it happen (and as of this writing, many of these issues were still under review by Ofcom and other stakeholders), would be something like a commercial *Scottish Six* integrating Scottish, UK and international news (much of it provided by ITN) within a Glasgow-based production. Reminiscent of Stuart Prebble's early 1990s vision of technology-driven, local news with a strong UK and international content, this programme would utilise the potential of satellite and digital technologies to 'glocalise' TV news and give it a more distinctive footprint. This model of local TV news at peak time would harness the newsgathering resources of ITN in London, while avoiding the political controversy associated with the BBC's *Scottish Six* suggestion.

SMG also plans to provide more niche-targeted services through split digital transmission. Scottish and Grampian will transmit additional opt-outs from a Scotland-wide bulletin. BBC Scotland, too, intends to utilise the new digital technology to tailor and sharpen its provision for more localised audiences than can be serviced by analogue television. Ofcom, meanwhile, has called for a digital news service for the Gaelic-speaking audience, to which both BBC Scotland and SMG have pledged support with programming and resources. In all these ways the likelihood is that digital technology will enhance the provision of local broadcast journalism in Scotland.

Technology and the journalist

There is a downside to technological change, however. In March 2005 BBC Scotland announced a package of job cuts (part of the BBC's UK cutback announced by new Director General Mark Thompson). Of the 176 staff losses announced as BBC Scotland's share of the BBC's overall programme of cuts and economies, 36 were to be in news and current affairs, provoking immediate protests from critics who feared a reduction in the quality of Scotland's local broadcast journalism. Controller Ken MacQuarrie rejected that suggestion, arguing that the cuts represented a painful but essential part of the BBC's refitting for purpose in the digital age. Far from damaging programme quality, he insisted, they would pave the way for BBC Scotland's journalists to benefit from access to a planned £10 million of extra annual investment in the coming years. It would also, he argued, make the BBC in Scotland better prepared to compete for the increase in out-of-London production which the government wants the Corporation to pursue in the future as a condition of Charter renewal. For MacQuarrie, short-term cuts should be seen in the context of a significant long-term expansion.

For local journalists in general, the permanent technological revolution in media has important implications as to how they will work in the future. While training bodies such as the National Council for the Training of Journalists (NCTJ) stick resolutely to a 1950s model based on the supremacy of print, the future needs of the journalism industry will be for individuals competent in multimedia, as comfortable with writing for newspapers as for online titles and broadcast news, and with web design as page layout. The same journalism will increasingly appear on multiple platforms.

Conclusion

As elsewhere in the UK, Scottish local journalism is in a period of change and transformation. New political realities, emerging technologies and the heightened commercial pressures of a globalised media market present challenges as well as opportunities for both print and broadcast media in the coming years. For the press, the key issue is adaptation to a fragmented market of many news providers, including free sheets, online sites and multichannel digital TV news of unprecedented 'localness'. The solution, in all likelihood, will be found in complementarity rather than competition.

In broadcasting, digitalisation presents opportunities for the provision of journalism that is both more global and more local, and for the integration of both within locally-produced packages. Gaelic language news will benefit from digitalisation. While the commitment of both BBC Scotland and SMG to local journalism is not in doubt (not least because regulation requires them to provide it), the commercial sector is clearly more dependent on national and international economic trends, and on the resolution of the emerging funding gap which digitalisation has opened up in the UK.

References

Bromley, M. (2005) *Making Local News: Journalism, Culture and Place*, Unpublished Ph.D. thesis, City University.

Conboy, M. (2004) *Journalism: A Critical History*, London: Sage.

Chapter 5

The regional and local media in Wales

James Thomas

Introduction

Most debates about the media in Wales have revolved around national rather than local issues. These have variously explored broadcasting's relationship to national identity and the Welsh language (Davies 1994), the absence of Welsh national newspapers and the worrying predominance of English media consumption over that produced in Wales (Mackay and Powell 1996; Talfan Davies 1999). This focus encourages a tendency to contrast the 'success' of radio and television in reinforcing national identity with the 'failure' of a 'provincial' press to do so, meaning the latter is often discussed less for what it is, and more for what it is not. That said, in outlining the key features of the Welsh regional and local media, this chapter owes a heavy debt to important recent analyses including the above (Jones 1993; Williams 1997; Barlow et al. 2005; Mackay and Ivey 2004).[1] It begins by exploring the circulation, ownership and content of the regional and local press, before assessing the current and potential impact of broadcasting and summarising the key arguments and areas for possible future focus.

The regional and weekly press

Throughout the twentieth century the Welsh daily morning press has been weak compared to its London-produced competitors, with 85 per cent of the daily morning papers bought in Wales produced in England in 2003 (Thomas et al. 2004a). In Welsh press, free weekly newspapers on the surface appear dominant in circulation, with a weekly circulation of 767,865 in 2005. Among paid newspapers the weekly local press is strongest in circulation (weekly circulation: 427,844). The less impressive daily circulation of both the Welsh-produced evening (171,458) and particularly the morning papers (81,106) has often provoked discussions about its weakness. But in an overall week, the daily press account for the majority of regional and local sales, with evening papers selling just over 1 million (37 per cent) and morning dailies selling

486,636 (18 per cent) (Newspaper Society 2005). Meanwhile, the circulation strength of free newspapers (29 per cent of all weekly circulation) has to be set against the fact that these papers tend to be skimmed compared to the paid dailies and weeklies.

The Welsh daily press is regional rather than national. The *Western Mail*'s circulation is concentrated in the South and has only a very limited penetration in North Wales, where the other morning paper, the *Daily Post*, is concentrated. While not national, these morning papers have too broad a reach to serve a distinct local community. Despite its South Wales base, the *Western Mail* defines itself as 'the national newspaper of Wales'. The *Daily Post* has a more identifiable North Wales identity, visible most notably when it is articulating the region's interests against the alleged domination of the South. But until 2003 it was simply a Welsh edition of the *Liverpool Daily Post*, where it was produced, before it was split into two separately produced editions with a commitment to more Welsh content. These morning papers are joined by a series of evening papers serving a more geographically identifiable and narrower regional community in and around Cardiff (*South Wales Echo*), Newport (*South Wales Argus*), Swansea (*Evening Post*) and Wrexham (*Evening Leader*). Within their readership constituencies are a range of weekly newspapers serving more local communities.

Yet while the Welsh press is regional and local, its ownership is certainly not, with a concentration of ownership among large media corporations 'whose major commercial interests existed outside of Wales' (Barlow *et al.* 2005: 46; see Chapters 1, 4, 6 and 8). By far the most dominant is Trinity Mirror, whose position as the largest UK regional publisher is echoed in Wales, where it owns 27 papers, including the *Western Mail*, *Daily Post* and *South Wales Echo*, accounting for 42 per cent of total circulation (Barlow *et al.* 2005: 45–6, 49).

Table 5.1 Circulation of regional morning and evening daily press in Wales

	1979	1997	2005
South Wales Echo	120,000	74,246	57,852
Evening Post	69,000	67,185	56,487
Western Mail	94,000	61,541	43,247
Daily Post	50,000	52,000	40,835
South Wales Argus	53,000	30,597	30,295
Evening Leader	35,000	31,864	26,331
Total circulation	421,000	317,433	255,047

Sources: Osmond 1983; Williams 2000; ABC January–June 2005

The circulation for daily regional newspapers is plummeting (Table 5.1), and is down by nearly 40 per cent since 1979. Most dramatically, the *Western Mail* has lost nearly a third of its audience since 1997, but this has not led to falling revenue due to lack of advertising competitors and the increased advertising that establishment of the Welsh Assembly has brought. Avoiding losing advertisers rather than readers has been its key priority in recent years (Williams 2003), although in 2004 the *Western Mail* joined the other dailies by shifting from broadsheet to tabloid format. A similar advertising monopoly in the North is enjoyed by its Trinity sister, the *Daily Post*, which has lost a fifth of its readership since 1997, as has the *South Wales Echo*, although the latter remains Wales' biggest selling daily newspaper. The *South Wales Argus* is the only Welsh daily newspaper to have stabilised its readership, no small feat in a declining market with Wales echoing wider UK and international trends. In 2003, only 50 per cent of people in Wales were regular newspaper readers, with a concentration among older age groups (Thomas *et al.* 2004b).

This circulation decline of the daily press has to be set against the greater stability of local weekly newspapers. Between 2002 and 2005, for example, there was only a 2.5 per cent fall in circulation of Audit Bureau of Circulations (ABC)-listed Welsh weekly newspapers, with nine showing slight increases and 16 showing declines. These papers also have a greater balance of younger and older readers. This is partly because most people continue to define their lives around their locality, with working, shopping, schooling and leisure all taking place within a limited radius of around 14 miles (Newspaper Society 2005). Local identity and interest in local news is stronger than regional identities that tend to be served by Welsh dailies. Research shows that interest in media reflecting people's local city/town/village to be very high in Wales, at nearly 80 per cent, with interest in a wider 'region' around 20 points lower (Ofcom, 2004: 43). Local media are also, according to the Newspaper Society (2005) and other sources, highly trusted (although some qualitative evidence discussed in the following contradicts this) and are seen as better at understanding local concerns and lifestyles. Their ability to attract advertising revenue is boosted by their role as a key source for obtaining information and services, job-searching and purchasing products. And, in contrast to the proliferation of competing news services at the UK level, the local media have few competitors.

Little qualitative research exists on the consumption of Wales' local press. But one analysis suggests that it tended to be read on a 'pick and flick' basis – in less depth than daily newspapers, with often little strong reason given for reading. There was an interesting gendering of discussions and consumption, with women reading up on the 'local gossip' in the kitchen while men occupied themselves with weightier news, dismissive of a 'toilet read' that they bought 'out of habit' or for their wives (Mackay and Ivey 2004: 52–3).

Most analyses of Welsh press content focus on politics. They have documented its changing attitude to devolution from opposition in the 1970s to later support (Osmond 1983; Williams 2000). Others have suggested depoliticisation of content (Cushion and Morgan 2003) under the impact of processes of popularisation and tabloidisation (Williams 2003). Another finding reports more restrained coverage of asylum seekers than in the tabloids, but a focus that remains on official issues like cost and numbers (Speers 2001). An analysis of front pages across 400 local weekly and regional daily newspapers' editions illustrates very clearly the key reporting theme of crime and social disorder, much of it alarmist and alarming (Table 5.2).

Table 5.2 Front pages of the regional and local press (May/June 2004)

Front-page headline	Weekly (%)	Daily (%)
Crime	34	40
Accident/human interest	25	13
Politics	10	12
Area development	10	4
Social issues	8	7
Health	4	4
Entertainment and celebrity	3	4
Industrial relations	1	1
Employment	1	2
Sport	1	3

Examples included: 'Teenage gangs "out of control"' (*Newport Argus* 19 May 2004), 'The city of fear' (*South Wales Echo* 5 May 2004), and 'Are you afraid to go out in our city' (*Evening Post* 10 June 2004). The 'imagined local community' portrayed on these front pages was a place to be feared, characterised by social breakdown, teenage criminals and drugs. This corresponds with popular fear of crime and antisocial behaviour. According to MORI (2004), 44 per cent of people believed crime in their local area had gone up over the last year, 37 per cent thought it had stayed the same and only 8 per cent said it had gone down. It is debatable to what extent this much-documented divorce between perceptions of crime increasing and the reality of falling crime rates is down to media coverage. But local crime reporting may have more immediate impact than the more geographically generalised discussion in the national media – or at least the two are likely to reinforce each other. One detailed ethnographic study of Welsh households certainly suggested a link with perceptions and behaviour, with local newspaper reports of crime, violence and drug-related incidents invoked as a rationale for 'not going out' to places 'to avoid' or as proof of a community's 'changed' nature (Mackay and Ivey 2004: 58).

Another strong emphasis, particularly in the weekly press, was on human interest stories. These usually detailed tales of accidental tragedy and misery, along with the odd tale of good fortune in the face of adversity. One view is that the focus on the personal makes debates about abstract social and political issues immediate and intelligible for a wider audience (Sparks and Tulloch 2000). But the majority of these stories echoed a pattern in which 'the personal is not only the starting point but also the substance and the end point' (Sparks and Tulloch 2000: 252). For example, one story entitled 'Fears for his life' (*Rhondda Leader* 20 May 2004) focussed on grandparents scared for their only surviving grandson serving with British troops in Iraq, after the earlier death of their other grandson in a tragic accident. The only link of the personal with the political was latent, in the subject of the story, but its actual focus was firmly on the personal tragedy already suffered and the fear of more. These stories complement crime coverage in depicting the external environment as one where 'danger and despair lurk at every turn' (Langer 1998: 149), and chance and luck determine life experiences rather than political and economic structures. It risks substituting 'any expressed desire to change the world with a fatalistic vision which holds that, however miserable or unrewarding one's life or circumstances might be, people should be satisfied and not complain, because "things could get worse"' (Langer 1998: 153).

The weekly press in particular also paid significant attention to both negative and positive local development issues, usually around new shopping centres, housing and leisure facilities and on social issues such as transport and health. In the period studied 10 per cent of stories in the weekly press and 12 per cent in daily newspapers were devoted to politics. While this is superficially quite encouraging, the sample time frame included the 2004 local and town and community council elections in Wales. When one would expect an intense scrutiny of local democracy, the overwhelming front-page attention still lay with other 'softer' issues. This reinforces the argument that while knowledge of UK and international issues is much easier to obtain, there is a comparative local news hole that contributes both to lack of knowledge of local councils and wider disengagement with the political process (Hargreaves and Thomas 2002: 21, 62–6; Kevill 2002). A linked argument is that the coverage of local councils that does take place is largely negative, reinforcing their poor reputation and public cynicism. A 2002 MORI survey of UK media coverage of local government found that only 6 per cent was positive, compared with 48 per cent negative and 35 per cent neutral, with the report suggesting that repairing local government's image problem was 'like rebuilding the reputation of the US army after Vietnam' (Page 2002).

More detailed analysis (Thomas *et al.* 2004a, 2004b) suggests a distinction between the dailies and weeklies. Daily press coverage of both the 2003 Welsh Assembly elections and the 2004 local elections lacked overall prominence but was quite extensive, largely nonpartisan and concentrated on constituency profiles and the general campaign process. Coverage of the local elections in the weeklies struggled to gain much prominence even on the inside pages, with the most space and prominence reserved for reporting the results, which accounted for two-thirds of election front pages. This proved better at telling its citizens who won than in informing them about the key issues that should have decided this. Little attempt was made at either small- or big-picture analysis that examined Party records, policies and issues, or explained the responsibilities of local councils. Instead, a rather more basic, reactive approach included short biographies, pictures and lists of all candidates, general stories and details about how and where to vote.

More widely, the weekly press has shown little engagement with devolution. Former British Broadcasting Corporation (BBC) Wales head Talfan Davies (1999: 18) has argued that the legitimacy of Wales' new institutions is 'dependent on embedding them into the daily narrative of people's lives through the regular reporting of constituency-based activities ... and of the local impact of Assembly decisions'. Assembly members certainly rate their local press as the most important media to be courted (Cushion and Morgan 2003) and it often provides columns for local politicians. But it lacks the resources, political will and commercial incentive to provide a more sustained scrutiny of the local impact of political decisions taken in Cardiff and Westminster.

Welsh-language local papers: the papurau bro

One unique feature of the local press in Wales is the development of the papurau bro, Welsh-language community newspapers. Between 1973 and 2001, 68 papurau bro were established, with three-quarters of those founded in the ten years after 1973 (Barlow *et al.* 2005: 40). Growth tailed off after this time but more than 80 per cent of them remain in existence despite being totally dependent on volunteers. Individual circulations are often small, but the penetration of papurau bro in local Welsh-speaking homes can be very high and in the mid-1990s their readership was estimated at 280,000 (Huws 1995). Their content includes stories of significance to the Welsh-language community, news about local residents and institutions including sports clubs and societies, columns for children and younger readers, space for readers' reminiscences and, like their English-language counterparts, reader reports of news from local areas. Unlike them, however, no space is devoted to court appearances and scandal.

These papers, produced monthly, grew principally out of an increased concern during the 1970s to safeguard the existence of Welsh-language communities threatened by immigration and economic and demographic change, while also satisfying the demand for 'local, local news'. What is also interesting is their total dependence on a large body of volunteers, with on average 39 maintaining each paper, with 1,000 people across Wales who regularly write or contribute news for them. As Huws (1995: 89) notes, 'one cannot overemphasise the significance of these figures, since they demonstrate the importance of papurau bro as a means of creating social activity', and promoting active citizenship and democratic community media. That said, these papers have been criticised for a backward-looking conservative ethos that has made them more reminiscent of 'a sort of Welsh-language copy of the "Parish News"' (Huws 1995: 91). They have been accused of nostalgic or unappealing content for most Welsh speakers and a concentration on people rather than on the economic and social threats to the communities that they serve. While no readership age breakdowns are available, it is likely, given their links with the chapels and other traditional Welsh cultural communities, that their consumption is overwhelmingly skewed towards older groups, as is true of Welsh television. A number of papurau bro have sought, in the words of one editor, to shift a 'fairly traditional' appeal to one that is also geared to 'young Welsh speakers' (BBC 2002). There is a potential audience here, with the slight increase in Welsh speakers in the 2001 census concentrated among younger groups. But this increase, largely in areas where only 10–20 per cent speak Welsh, has to be set against the further decline in areas where more than 80 per cent speak Welsh as a first language (Thomas and Lewis 2006). It therefore remains uncertain how well the papurau bro can adapt to these linguistic and demographic changes, as well as to the more general problem of attracting younger readers.

Regional and local radio and television

The structure of the press in Wales is characterised by the strength of the local and the weakness of the national, but in broadcasting the reverse is the case. Whereas England has local BBC radio stations, in Wales the national nature of BBC Radio Wales and Radio Cymru means there are no public service local stations. The onus to provide them rests solely with 14 Independent Local Radio (ILR) stations along with one regional ILR service. These commercial stations tend to be a largely 'forgotten medium' (Barlow 2003: 83) in discussions about the media in Wales. While the dominance of the local in the press is often identified as a barrier to strong national identity, the weakness of the local in broadcasting is much less noted. The most detailed work (Barlow et al. 2005; Bromley 2001; Mackay and Powell 1996) paints a depressing picture of ownership and decision makers located outside the locality, concerned with profit rather than any public service commitment. Programming formats are homogenised, with music preferred over speech; a restricted range of popular music, aimed at the key audience of those aged 20–50 and 'the 29-year-old woman' in particular, dominates. Networking of ILR schedules at certain times of the day reduces costs and benefits advertisers but further reduces a commitment to locality. Indeed, the population reach of these 'local' stations varies considerably from 65,000 to 887,000, with little reflection of recognisable local communities. Equally, some ILR stations have proved increasingly unwilling to offer programming in Welsh to reflect the linguistic make-up of their communities.

In terms of news provision, the reality is that local news is not adequately covered, with the bulk of local items usually being outweighed by UK- or Wales-wide subjects. The local news that exists tends to echo those crime and human-interest stories favoured by local papers, while local government reporting and politics receives minimal focus. For example, Wales' regional ILR and largest commercial broadcaster, Real Radio, largely ignored the 2003 Welsh Assembly elections, devoting just a minute of air-time to it until the eve of the poll, with most coverage focussing on quirky stories. Liberalisation of regulation has ensured that commitment to locality has not been, in practice, the chief factor in awarding or renewing radio licences. The experience of the Bridgend ILR licence, awarded in 1999 is typical. The application was won by a local group, Bridge FM, despite the fact that its commitment to local news was lower than the other two rival bidders and, unlike them, it promised no Welsh-language content in a target area where 29 per cent speak Welsh (Bromley 2001 131–34). Within 18 months, its localness had been further diluted, in both content and personnel, when it was taken over by UK radio publisher, Tindle Radio, which had a small 'stalking-horse' share from the start (Barlow *et al.* 2005: 113).

The result is that local radio in Wales echoes a wider UK pattern (Crisell 2002) in which a commitment to locality and public interest is reduced to the commercial success of broadcasters in attracting listeners and advertising revenue. The potential of local radio to empower citizens and democratise media is marginalised. The only alternative emphasising this, access radio, exists more in theory than in practice, with only one such station in Wales, GTFM, based in Treforest, a joint venture between the local community and the University of Glamorgan.

While public service broadcasting is weaker in Wales than England for local news, surveys suggest, paradoxically, that television is the most important source of local news for nearly 60 per cent of people – considerably higher than the UK average – with local newspapers half that (Table 5.3). Radio was also less valued than elsewhere, perhaps reflecting its weak provision in that area.

Table 5.3 Which source for local news do you most rely on?

	Wales (%)	*UK (%)*
Television	58	45
Local newspapers	30	39
Radio	7	12
National newspapers	4	4
Internet	1	1

Source: adapted from survey for Hargreaves and Thomas (2002)

The surprising predominance of television as a source of 'information about your area/region' is also replicated in other studies, which find that reliance on television in Wales is higher than anywhere else in the UK except Northern Ireland (Ofcom 2004: 36). This is somewhat worrying given the obvious limitations of national television in covering local news, but it does play 'some' role. An internal BBC review (2003) revealed that local government coverage accounted for a surprising ten per cent of stories of the most popular Welsh news bulletin, *BBC Wales Today*. This accounted for 45 per cent of all political coverage, making it, surprisingly, the single most important political category compared with 33 per cent on the National Assembly and 22 per cent about Westminster. During the 2004 local elections, *BBC Wales Today* carried a daily average of two minutes of coverage that outlined the key social and political issues facing viewers in half a dozen constituencies. While television cannot provide much consistent reporting on individual localities, the limited amount of local political coverage in weekly papers makes it one key way that citizens can scrutinise the behaviour of their local leaders. Indeed, there is potential for the BBC's proposed new local television news services to fill the gap in the supply of serious local news that currently exists and which is rendered more acute in Wales than in England by the absence of a local BBC radio system.

Conclusions

The media system in Wales is characterised by an interesting paradox between the structure of the press on the one hand, and television and radio on the other. Broadcasting in Wales has a national structure in which a regional and local focus is limited. By contrast, the press in Wales has an overwhelmingly local and regional structure in which 'the national' is almost completely absent. For daily regional newspapers, the picture is one of sharply declining circulation, although this is combined with greater stability for the more local weekly press and a reliance on advertising revenue that keeps the regional and local press profitable.

Large media corporations whose main interests lie outside Wales own the local press and their content appears to be dominated by 'softer' crime and human-interest issues. However, far more detailed content analysis is required in this area and also on the current position and content of Welsh-language local papers and local radio. That which exists for the latter suggests the process of commercialisation to be even more visible than for the press, with the dominance of large companies providing mainstream, centrally dictated popular music while speech, locality, diversity and public service are marginalised. In this regard Wales' position is clearly very similar to England. But the shortcomings of the regional media are also accentuated, as in Scotland, by the fact that BBC Wales' radio and television services are structured around the nation rather than localities. Yet there is clearly the potential – and seemingly the demand – for more local television and radio channels that would enhance knowledge of local public affairs and improve the diversity of local media and democratic participation. This would provide a welcome shift in the balance between public service and commercial local media that currently rests decisively with the latter in Wales.

Notes

1   My thanks also go to John Jewell and Stephen Cushion for their collaboration on earlier research that partly informs this chapter and to David Thomas for help and discussions around the papurau bro.

References

Barlow, David (2003) 'Who controls local radio?', Planet, 158, pp. 79–84.

Barlow, David; Mitchell, Philip and O'Malley, Tom (2005) The Media in Wales: Voices of a Small Nation, Cardiff: University of Wales Press.

BBC (2002) 'Welsh language papers win Euro funds', http://news.bbc.co.uk/1/hi/wales/2416475.stm (last accessed August 2005).

BBC (2003) 'Review of nations and regions' coverage of local government', Internal report.

Bromley, Michael (2001) 'Reporting changing democracy: commercial radio and news in the UK of regions and nations', in Bromley, M. (ed.) No News is Bad News, Harlow: Longman, pp. 127–36.

Crisell, Andrew (2002) 'Radio', in Briggs, A. and Cobley, P. (eds) Media: An Introduction, Harlow: Longman, pp. 121–34.

Cushion, Stephen and Morgan, David (2003) 'If it bleeds it leads: reporting the assembly news', Planet, 158, pp. 49–55.

Davies, John (1994) Broadcasting and the BBC in Wales, Cardiff: University of Wales Press.

Hargreaves, Ian and Thomas, James (2002) New News, Old News, London: ITC/BSC.

Huws, Gwilym (1995) 'The success of the local: Wales', Mercator Media Forum, pp. 84–93.

Jones, Aled (1993) Press, Politics and Society: A History of Journalism in Wales, Cardiff: University of Wales Press.

Kevill, Sian (2002) *Beyond the Soundbite: BBC Research into Public Disillusion with Politics*, London: BBC.

Langer, John (1998) *Tabloid Television: Popular Journalism and the 'Other News'*, London: Routledge.

Mackay, Hugh and Ivey, Darren (2004) *Modern Media in the Home; An Ethnographic Study*, Luton: John Libbey.

Mackay, Hugh and Powell, Anthony (1996) 'Wales and its media: production, consumption and regulation', *Contemporary Wales*, 9, pp. 8–39.

MORI (2004) 'Perceptions of teenage anti-social behaviour', www.mori.com/localgov/statistics.php (last accessed August 2005).

Newspaper Society (2005) www.newspapersoc.org.uk/ (last accessed August 2005).

Ofcom (2004) *Reshaping Television for the UK's Nations, Regions and Localities*, London: Ofcom.

Osmond, John (1983) 'The referendum and the English-language press', in Foulkes, D.; Jones, B. and Wilford, R. (eds) *The Welsh Veto: The Welsh Act, 1978 and the Referendum*, Cardiff: University of Wales Press.

Page, Ben (2002) 'Let's not put up with it any more', www.mori.com/ (last accessed July 2005).

Sparks, Colin and Tulloch, John (eds) (2000) *Tabloid Tales: Global Debates over Media Standards*, Lanham: Rowman and Littlefield.

Speers, Tammy (2001) *Welcome or Over Reaction? Refugees and Asylum Seekers in the Welsh Media*, Cardiff: Wales Media Forum.

Talfan Davies, Geraint (1999) *Not by Bread Alone: Information, Media and the National Assembly*, Cardiff: Wales Media Forum.

Thomas, James and Lewis, Justin (2006) 'Coming out of a mid-life crisis? The past, present and future audiences for Welsh language broadcasting', *Cyfrwng: Media Wales Journal: Cyfnodolyn Cyfryngau Cymru*, 2, pp. 7–40.

Thomas, James; Jewell, John and Cushion, Stephen (2004a) 'The media and the 2003 Welsh assembly elections', *Representation*, 40 (4), pp. 280–7.

Thomas, James; Jewell, John and Cushion, Stephen (2004b) *Media Coverage of the 2004 Welsh Local Government Elections*, www.electoralcommission.gov.uk/ (last accessed August 2005).

Williams, Kevin (1997) *Shadows and Substance: the Development of a Media Policy for Wales*, Llandysul: Gomer.

Williams, Kevin (2000) 'No dreads only some doubts: the press and the referendum', in Balsom, D. and Jones, B. (eds) *The Road to the National Assembly*, Cardiff: University of Wales Press, pp. 96–119.

Williams, K. (2003) 'What's happening at the *Western Mail*', *Planet*, 157, pp. 32–6.

Chapter 6

Profits, politics and paramilitaries

The local news media in Northern Ireland

Greg McLaughlin

An audit of the local media in Northern Ireland presents a picture of seemingly rude health and vigorous media pluralism. The region has seen the launch of new radio stations and newspaper titles, and the adoption of new media technologies. Local media businesses have expanded into Britain and the Republic of Ireland, while there has also been inward investment from media companies in Britain, Ireland and continental Europe. However, there are questions whether these developments represent expansion in real terms or the beginnings of a long overdue reformation. With four TV stations, seven radio stations, five daily newspapers and 73 weeklies, the region has a range and choice of local media out of proportion to its population of just over 1.5 million. To an extent, this is a legacy of the conflict, with readerships and audiences having fragmented along sectarian lines, creating safe, local monopolies for many media outlets. Today, however, market demand is fragmenting along other, more familiar lines in the UK context – age, gender and consumer lifestyle, for example. Internet and digital TV usage in the region is well in line with the UK average, drawing readers and audiences away from the traditional media and prompting major advertisers to review their spending accordingly.

Of course, the transition from conflict to peace also presents profound political challenges to the media in Northern Ireland. Having played a crucial and controversial role in reporting a 40-year war, they must now adapt to mediating a difficult period of conflict resolution. And, despite the dramatic reduction in civil unrest and paramilitary violence, local journalism in the region is still a risky trade. It is important, then, to put the analysis that follows in political as well as economic perspective.

Profits

This section begins with a general look at the local media in the region and then assesses their long-term sustainability in light of current market trends.

Print media

The bigger newsagents and supermarkets in Northern Ireland offer a choice of 23 daily newspapers published locally, and in Britain and the Republic of Ireland. This is a survey of those published locally; unless otherwise stated, all circulation figures are sourced to the Audit Bureau of Circulations (ABC) (January–July, 2005). The region has five daily newspapers (Monday–Saturday), all of them published in Belfast: the *Belfast Telegraph*, the *News Letter*, the *Irish News*, the *Daily Ireland* and the Irish-language newspaper, *Lá* (pronounced 'law').

The *Belfast Telegraph* is owned by the Dublin-based Independent News & Media Group. It publishes a number of editions per day and has an average daily circulation of 94,000 copies. Moderately unionist in editorial policy, it reaches a cross-community readership by virtue of its advertising and consumer content. The *News Letter*, traditionally the voice of official Ulster Unionism, has experienced a dramatic collapse in political influence and circulation in the past 60 years, falling from more than 100,000 copies, post-Second World War, to 29,000 today. The paper has changed ownership twice since 1996 and is now owned by the Scottish media group, Johnston Press plc. The *Irish News* has a daily circulation of more than 48,000 copies (see Chapters 1, 4, 5 and 8 for discussions of local press ownership). Privately owned by the Fitzpatrick family, its editorial line is broadly supportive of the policies of the moderate, nationalist Social and Democratic Labour Party (SDLP). The *Daily Ireland* is a new venture, launched in February 2005 by the Andersontown News Group (ANG). With a circulation of just over 10,000, it publishes a single, all-Ireland edition per day and follows a broadly republican editorial line, supportive of the policies of Sinn Féin. ANG also publishes *Lá*, and estimates its circulation at 3,500. However, these local dailies must compete with the *Sun* (78,000) and the Ulster edition of the *Mirror* (57,000), the circulations of which outstrip all but the *Belfast Telegraph*. Newspaper readers in the region also enjoy a wide selection of Sunday papers. There are three locally produced titles – the *Sunday Life* (84,082), the *Sunday World* (66,963) and the Derry-based *Sunday Journal* (5,824). The market leader, however, is the *News of the World* with 88,500 copies, while the Ulster edition of *The Sunday Times* sells 29,000 (News International estimates).

In addition to the Belfast dailies, Northern Ireland has a total of 73 weeklies, serving an adult population of just under a million. This is because for every unionist newspaper in a large town, there is a corresponding nationalist title; it is unusual to find a local weekly that serves a mixed readership. In effect, therefore, these newspapers have not needed to compete with each other – they have survived on restricted readerships and advertising markets. It is rare to have new titles enter the market and when they do they find it hard to challenge the local monopoly. In the mainly nationalist city of Derry, the launch of the *Derry News* in 2001 challenged the position of the *Derry Journal*, one of Ireland's oldest newspapers. In spite of the new title's low circulation (6,346), the *Journal* (23,000) engaged it in a surreal newspaper war. For example, the *Journal* traditionally published on Tuesdays and Fridays but when the *Derry News* started a new Monday edition, the *Journal* followed suit with two new titles on Mondays, the *Derry on Monday* (2,339) and *Foyle News* (2,692), using for both an identical tabloid format and look to that of its new rival. And when the *Derry News* published a Sunday paper, the *Derry News on Sunday*, in September 2003, the *Journal* followed suit in 2004 with the *Sunday Journal* (5,824). Critics argued that the standard of journalism in both papers suffered as a result, with pages of photographs, sport and advertising but a minimum of news. The war went beyond mere competition in a tight market and it seemed that the *Journal* was bent on the total extinction of its smaller and weaker local rival, which was eventually forced to close its Sunday paper.

As well as the weekly newspapers, there is a small number of monthly magazines but only *Fortnight* qualifies as current affairs journalism. However, a determined reader will find a range of newspapers and newssheets from the political fringes. Some of them are published by loyalist and republican paramilitary groups and are regarded as little more than propaganda. They are irregular in publication and random in distribution but, to a certain extent, they offer an insight into grass-roots republicanism and loyalism that is not possible to find in the mainstream press (McLaughlin and Baker 2004; Baker 2005).

Online journalism

Online journalism in Northern Ireland tends to be satirical or amateur in nature. The *Portadown News* appeared online in 2000 as a satirical commentary on major news stories in the peace process, but closed in 2005; other sites, such as *PureDerry* and *RandomShite*, publish in the same vein. The weblog, *Slugger O'Toole*, features commentary and discussion on politics and current affairs and sometimes feeds the news agenda with breaking stories of its own. *The Blanket*, an online magazine run by republican activists and ex-prisoners, provides a dissident perspective on the Good Friday Agreement and the peace process, and local and international current affairs.

Broadcast media

As with other regions of the UK, Northern Ireland is served by its own local broadcast media. The British Broadcasting Corporation (BBC) provides an extensive news and current affairs service on television (BBC Northern Ireland (NI)) and radio (Radio Ulster and in Derry, Radio Foyle). In the independent sector, Ulster Television (UTV) mirrors the BBC's news and current affairs provision but it has also established a large audience in the Republic of Ireland for its light entertainment programming. UTV enjoys a 2 per cent lead over BBC NI in average audience share (BARB, January–December, 2004) but falls far behind in the production of original programming. Apart from these two major players, there are two community-based television companies in operation. Northern Visions Television (NvTv) serves the Belfast area and is part of a media access project funded by the Northern Ireland Film and Television Commission (NIFTC). Channel 9, a rather more commercial enterprise, is based in Derry and relies heavily on local advertising revenue. About 48 per cent of television viewers in Northern Ireland can receive up to four Irish television channels terrestrially or by cable/satellite: RTE1, RTE2, TV3 and the Irish language station, TG4; cable and satellite viewers can also receive regional UK television channels. However, viewing figures in Northern Ireland for these Irish and UK stations are low.

The independent radio sector is rather more extensive, with five stations in existence (e.g., Downtown and City Beat) and franchises won for another two to be launched in 2006 and 2007. The new stations include U105, which will broadcast to the greater Belfast area. It is owned by UTV, whose commercial franchise allows it to expand its media interests beyond Northern Ireland. UTV already owns 17.8 per cent of commercial radio licences in the Republic of Ireland, making it the largest single player in the Irish market, and also has one of the biggest commercial radio portfolios in the UK, including 16 independent radio stations and stakes in five of the UK's 14 digital radio bundles. In June 2005, the company bought The Wireless Group (TWG) and rebranded it UTV Radio.[1]

Underlying market trends

The evidence might suggest, then, that Northern Ireland is one of the most richly served areas of the UK in terms of print and broadcast journalism. However, less obvious but significant underlying trends undermine the optimistic picture. The media market in Northern Ireland is fragmenting, with people turning to new information sources made available by digital technology. A survey by the Northern Ireland Statistical Research Agency (NISRA) showed that in 2004, 61 per cent of the adult population owned PCs, 53 per cent had Internet access, and 50 per cent had digital television.[2] This has had a negative impact on the traditional media, particularly for the daily newspapers. In the 14-year period 1990–2004, the *Belfast Telegraph* experienced a dramatic 29 per cent drop in sales, while the *News Letter* saw a decrease of 17 per cent; the *Irish News*, on the other hand, enjoyed an increase of 15 per cent. From 2001–4, *Irish News* sales dipped by 4 per cent from its high of 50,000 copies per day in 2000. The *Belfast Telegraph* and the *News Letter* suffered a further decline of 15 per cent and 13 per cent respectively on their figures in 2000. In a review of its advertising spend in the local media, the Northern Ireland Office (NIO) has set these falling sales figures against relatively high advertising rates on the basis of 'cost per 1,000' readers. As shown in Table 6.1, the local dailies compare rather unfavourably with the competitive rates offered by the Ulster edition of the *Daily Mirror*.

Table 6.1 Advertising costs/1,000 in local daily newspapers in Northern Ireland, 2004

Title	Readers	Rate card cost (£)	Cost per 1,000 (£)
Belfast Telegraph	294,742	546.00	1.85
News Letter	74,431	263.70	3.45
Irish News	186,302	289.50	1.55
Daily Mirror	257,824	360.00	1.40

Source: 'A review of government advertising in Northern Ireland', Office of the First Minister and Deputy First Minister, Stormont, Belfast, 2005

In view of these statistics, the government questions 'whether it represents value for money for a significant premium to be charged over normal display rate card costs … and why it should pay a premium for this'.[3] The review went out for consultation in 2005, issuing a clear warning to the local dailies to drop their advertising rates or have them capped. Paddy Meehan, head of advertising at the *Irish News*, concedes that a spending review is a worry for all the daily newspapers but it could be a blessing in disguise for the *Irish News*. He anticipates that a government cap on advertising spend would likely be set against the lowest available rate, the *Mirror*'s £1.40 per 1,000 readers. In that case, the *Irish News* would not suffer as heavily as the *News Letter*, whose rate is two and a half times higher. His paper has long argued that its rates represent better value for money for other major public advertisers such as the four Non-Departmental Public Bodies (NDPBs) set up under the Good Friday Agreement.[4] The NDPBs spent £4.4 million on media advertising in 2003/04; yet, as of 2005, they advertised in only one daily newspaper, the *Belfast Telegraph*, in spite of its evident decline in circulation and readership, and its higher advertising rate.[5] Some of the daily newspapers have responded to prevailing market pressures with high-profile revamps in design and content. The *Irish News* moved to compact tabloid format in 2005 after a brief experiment with the Berliner format now used by *The Guardian*. Its associated company, Interpress, invested in a new hi-spec printing plant at Duncrue, Belfast, using the Man Rowland press to reproduce brighter, cleaner page design and allow for full colour capacity. Although the *Irish News* continues its commitment to comprehensive political content, it also uses other 'tabloid' strategies to broaden its appeal to the affluent youth market,[6] including a human interest oriented page three, daily entertainment and lifestyle supplements, more extensive sports coverage and popular holiday offers. In response to the chronic decline in sales of its traditional evening broadsheet, the *Belfast Telegraph* launched a morning edition in compact tabloid format with improved page design and full colour capacity. It is too early yet to assess whether these marketing strategies will reverse the downward trend in sales and readership, especially for the *Telegraph* and the *News Letter*. General trends suggest that the fragmentation of the media market in Northern Ireland will continue, leaving the traditional newspapers to face a long-term retreat into a niche market.

The local media market has seen significant changes in ownership and control in recent years. In 2004, the European venture capitalist firm, 3i, bought the *News Letter* and the Derry Journal group from Mirror Regional Newspapers for £46.3 million. It set up Local Press Ltd to run its new acquisitions and promised commitment to local journalism, including the start-up of a new title, the *Daily View*. An experiment in nonpolitical, youth-orientated journalism, the *View* promised to cover 'real issues of the 21st Century, not the 17th Century' and published its first edition on 4 April 2005. After only 25 issues, it closed on 6 May. The decision to close the new title so quickly indicated 3i's ruthless instincts for its profit margins and anticipated the eventual sale of Local Press to Johnston Press, just months later, for £65 million.[7] Another related development with local implications was EMAP's purchase of Scottish Radio Holdings (SRH) for £391 million in 2005. The SRH portfolio included the Northern Ireland-based Downtown Radio and the Morton newspaper group, though EMAP immediately sold off the Morton group to Johnston Press.[8] The sale marked the latest in a series of significant acquisitions by Johnston Press in a six-year period, giving it 15 per cent share of the regional newspaper market in the UK. With its purchase in 2005 of the Leinster Leader group, it now commands about 23 per cent of the regional newspaper market on the island of Ireland.[9]

Politics

Northern Ireland has experienced a conflict of nearly 40 years so it is hardly surprising that its newspapers should reflect political and sectarian divisions in terms of readership and content. Recent research puts the *Belfast Telegraph* readership at about 67 per cent unionist, 28 per cent nationalist, probably thanks to its classified and commercial content. The readerships for the other dailies are much more exclusive, although the *News Letter*, with its hard-line unionist outlook, has a 12 per cent Catholic readership (9,000), compared with a

Protestant readership of 5.9 per cent (11,097) for the *Irish News*.[10] Until recently, all the dailies have tried to maintain a degree of political pluralism in their editorial content by hiring columnists 'from across the divide' and encouraging public dialogue and debate in their letters pages. On the eve of the referendum on the Good Friday Agreement, in May 1998, the *Irish News* and the *News Letter* featured a joint, front-page editorial recommending to their readers a resounding 'Yes' vote. However, while the *Irish News* has remained staunchly supportive of the Agreement, the *News Letter* has hardened its editorial outlook in the context of unionist disillusionment with the peace process. The *Belfast Telegraph* boasts an increasingly 'upmarket' readership and is politically conservative in editorial outlook, but it features a weekly column by the radical, socialist journalist, Eamonn McCann, who presents a nonsectarian, class-based analysis of local and international politics that is difficult to find in any other mainstream newspaper in Ireland or the UK. Although the *Daily Ireland*'s political coverage has been critical of the Irish Republican Army (IRA) and of Sinn Féin's response to a number of controversies involving the IRA, it has been the object of disdain among the political and media establishment, north and south of the border. It has been labelled 'hardline' and 'fascist', and Irish Justice Minister, Michael McDowell, has described it as 'a Provo rag'. The political reaction to the *Daily Ireland* is symptomatic of liberal anxiety about the rise of republicanism as a credible electoral force throughout the island of Ireland.

In political terms, the problem with the press in Northern Ireland is not that newspapers reflect or even underpin political ideologies or sectarian divisions. As with all other aspects of social and cultural practice, this is an inevitable outcome of decades of bitter conflict, which may take generations to overcome. Besides, these newspapers at least report politics with greater depth and insight than the press in London or Dublin, and Northern Ireland would be poorer without them. The real problem is that there is no credible political alternative, for example, a progressive newspaper that appeals across the sectarian divide and campaigns on social and economic issues. But there does not seem to be much hunger for such a paper in Northern Ireland. Circulation figures seem to suggest that readers who do not want to deal with politics Northern Ireland style, turn to the *Sun* and the *Mirror*, whose editorial policy is to stay clear of routine local politics.

The two main broadcasters in Northern Ireland, BBC NI and UTV, promote their public service commitment to impartial news but this has always been difficult to achieve or defend in such a deeply divided society. David Butler (1995) shows how the BBC has attempted, without success, to construct a sense of national identity in a society where identity is bitterly and sometimes violently contested. The ideological default has been a 'balanced sectarianism', whereby prejudice is contained rather than interrogated. There is rarely resolution, just a weary, paternalistic attempt by broadcasters to occupy 'the middle ground'. This finds its clearest expression on BBC Radio Ulster's daily Talk Back programme, presented by David Dunseith. The programme is a reliable monitor of the political temperature in Northern Ireland at any given moment. It mixes serious political discussion with some light-hearted diversion, inviting listeners to express their views on air by phone-in, text, email or the very popular 24-hour recorded message service dubbed the Rant Line. It is common to tune in and hear Dunseith engage in tetchy exchanges with listeners about his perceived bias against loyalists or republicans, Protestants or Catholics. However, McLaughlin and Baker (2005) have found a clearly identifiable aspiration on the part of the production team to find common, uncontroversial ground, to domesticate the conflict by conceptualising the audience as one big dysfunctional family. The current producer, Seamus Boyd, took a deliberate decision in 2000/01 to move the programme away from an exclusively political agenda and test a cross section of public opinion on problems such as chewing gum on the streets of Belfast or the state of public toilets in Northern Ireland. The content and direction of these items sometimes take a surreal and humorous turn but there is a danger they might dilute one of the very few broadcasting spaces left in which politics and the problem of sectarianism in Northern Ireland can be discussed openly and honestly.

Local television news and current affairs programming no longer anchors the peak-time, mid-evening schedules as it once did (McLaughlin 2000). After 19.00, news bulletins are decidedly brief and current affairs programmes are consigned to late evening slots after 22.30. This minimalist approach was only too evident in their coverage of the 2005 Westminster election campaign. BBC NI and UTV managed to schedule special eve-of-election debates at the same time. The BBC's format was bland and predictable, featuring a panel of candidates for the leading political parties, and focusing on a narrow agenda of constitutional issues. UTV opened its programme live from Derry at 22.00, took a commercial break five minutes later, broke again for ITV's news at 22.30, only to resume at 23.00 for another 20 minutes. That may add up to a respectable 45 minutes but the frequent breaks made for a very stilted and lifeless debate. To be fair, TV coverage of the results was somewhat better but it was blunted by the agonisingly slow counts in almost all of the counting centres around the north.[11]

Paramilitaries

Given the central and sometimes difficult role of the local media in reporting the conflict in Northern Ireland, it is perhaps surprising that only one journalist has been killed, although others have been threatened and intimidated by paramilitary groups, many of which are still active despite the peace process. In 2001, the

Loyalist Volunteer Force (LVF) murdered *Sunday World* journalist, Martin O'Hagan, because of his investigation into their drug trade. The newspaper continued with his work despite regular threats to its reporters. In September 2005, the situation escalated when the *Sunday World* exposed the luxurious lifestyles of leading figures in the Ulster Defence Association (UDA), implying that it was funded by income from drugs and racketeering. In response, the UDA enforced a boycott of the paper in Loyalist areas of Belfast. They threatened distributors and newsagents, including Sainsbury's, warning them not to stock the paper. Newsagents that resisted the boycott received death threats or had their premises burned. Yet, in a surreal twist, the same paramilitaries were observed buying up copies of the *Sunday World* from newsagents on the nationalist Falls Road so they would not miss an issue of their favourite Sunday paper. The boycott had some immediate impact – the newspaper lost 7,000 in sales in the first week of the campaign. However, the editor Jim McDowell and his staff expressed dismay with the lack of support from their employers, Independent News & Media, and from the British government. They wondered what the reaction would be if such a campaign was launched against a newspaper in Liverpool or Manchester (McDonald 2005). Compared with Iraq or Colombia, Northern Ireland is relatively safe for local journalists, but their uneasy relationship with paramilitary groups underlines the risks that some of them still face. However, the refusal of the *Sunday World* to buckle under paramilitary violence and intimidation has had the support of all local media organisations. It seems a fitting tribute to the memory of Martin O'Hagan and what he tried to do as a journalist.

Concluding remarks

In a political sense, Northern Ireland does not have a normal media market compared to other regions of the UK. Journalists in Manchester or Glasgow do not die for the story, and newsagents in Cardiff or Cornwall do not get burned down for stocking the wrong newspaper. However, it possibly shares other problems relating to general market pressures: declining newspaper circulations and readerships, pressures on advertising revenues, shifting patterns of ownership and control in the interest of business rather than journalism and the marginalisation of local TV news and current affairs from the peak-time evening schedules. The market analyst might point to more positive developments: competition-driven innovation in print technology and page design, improvements in newspaper content and local as well as inward investment in new media businesses. Yet, if the news media scale down political news and soften editorial lines to appeal to larger, and younger, cross-community readerships and audiences, then that cannot be good news for a part of the UK that, after a 40-year conflict, is struggling to build consent for pluralist, democratic structures.

Acknowledgement

Many thanks to my colleague, Colm Murphy, for his invaluable comments and suggestions on earlier drafts of this chapter.

Notes

1 UTV website: www.utvplc.com
2 See 'A review of government advertising in Northern Ireland', OFMDFM, Stormont, Belfast, 2005; www.ofmdfmni.gov.uk/ofmdfm_ad_review.pdf
3 Ibid.
4 The four NDPBs are: Invest Northern Ireland (InvestNI), the Northern Ireland Tourist Board (NITB), the General Consumer Council for Northern Ireland (GCCNI), and the Health and Safety Executive Northern Ireland (HSENI).
5 Paddy Meehan, *Irish News*; interview with the author, 24 October 2005.
6 The youth market is crucial to all the local dailies. Just over 32 per cent of *Irish News* readers are aged between 15 and 34, while the *Belfast Telegraph* and *News Letter* fall some way behind, with 26 per cent and 24 per cent respectively. However, the Ulster edition of the *Daily Mirror* outcompetes its local rivals with 36 per cent of its readers in the age group; www.ofmdfmni.gov.uk/ofmdfm_ad_review.pdf
7 See 3i website: www.3i.com.
8 *Media Guardian Online*, 21 June 2005; http://media.guardian.co.uk
9 The *Village* (Dublin), 23 September 2005.
10 See: www.ofmdfmni.gov.uk/ofmdfm_ad_review.pdf
11 See also Wilson and Fawcett (2004) for an excellent survey of local media coverage of the 2003 NI Assembly elections.

References

Baker, S. (2005) 'The alternative press in Northern Ireland and the political process', *Journalism Studies*, 6 (3), pp. 375–86.

Butler, D. (1995) *The Trouble with Reporting Northern Ireland*, Aldershot: Avebury.

McDonald, H. (2005) 'A boycott that means murder, arson and terror', *The Observer*, 18 September.

McLaughlin, G. (2000) 'The politics and economics of news and current affairs: the case of Northern Ireland, 1985–99', in Weiten, J., Murdock, G. and Dahlgren, P. (eds) *Television Across Europe*, London: Sage, pp. 221–35.

McLaughlin, G. and Baker, S. (2004) 'Alternative media, the "War on Terror" and Northern Ireland', in Nohrstedt, S. and Ottosen, R. (eds) *U.S. and the Others: Global Media Images on "The War on Terror"*, Göteborg: Nordicom, pp. 191–201.

McLaughlin, G. and Baker, S. (2005) ' "Ordinary people", politics and the media in Northern Ireland', paper to conference on *Truth, Power and Ethics in the Media*, Dublin City University, 17 June.

Wilson, R. and Fawcett, L. (2004) 'The media election: coverage of the 2003 NI assembly poll', Democratic Dialogue report, Belfast.

Part 2

The economics of
the local press

Chapter 7

Educating and training local journalists

Peter Cole

Far more people want to be journalists than will be journalists, or could be journalists, or should be journalists. Despite plenty of evidence to the contrary, journalism is still seen as glamorous, exciting and rewarding, which of course it is for some journalists in some jobs. Those aspiring to a career in the media talk of the variety and unpredictability. Some want to write, some to change the world. Some want to meet famous people, by which they mean celebrities; some want to perform, which usually means having their face on television. Some believe journalism is fashionable; some consider it a form of political activity. Some consider it a way of joining a social elite. Some want to be paid for doing what they love best, and would do anyway: watching football or listening to music. Some simply find it deeply satisfying to find things out, preferably things others would prefer not to be found out, and tell other people about them. These are the potential real journalists.

That, it has to be said, is a purist view. There are many other kinds of journalists, and they include those who have achieved, or are on the way to achieving, one of the aspirations just listed. The wannabe journalists, naturally enough, have role models, beacons of hope. At that precious, untarnished moment, when everything lies ahead, they dream of crouching in a Baghdad street while the shots are ringing out, talking breathlessly into a microphone. They dream of being abused by Alex Ferguson at a Manchester United press conference. In their moments of reverie they are interviewing Jude Law or Catherine Zeta-Jones, wandering through the flooded wasteland of New Orleans, taking the prime minister apart with their incisive questions, covering suicide bombings in London or exposing financial corruption in high places. It's good to dream and for some, dreams become reality.

Even on student newspapers, where many future professionals start their journalism careers, the new agenda is evident. Kim Fletcher, former editor of the *Independent on Sunday* and editorial director of the *Daily Telegraph*, in his book *The Journalist's Handbook*, writes:

Jan Webster, a former editor of Sheffield University's *Steel Press*, explained how things had changed. 'Our paper used to boast a fantastic news team. Now many of those joining the paper think journalism is about swanning around talking to celebs. Many of them don't want to make a phone call and are scared to talk to student union officers'.

(Fletcher 2005: 8)

But still the reporter on a local newspaper or in a regional radio or television newsroom is more likely to be interviewing a local councillor about the new bypass proposals, which will probably be shelved just like the last five plans. He or she may be finding out from a dear old couple how they managed to survive 60 years of marriage, or listening to an irate retailer moaning about how increased car parking charges are going to damage business. They may be 'gutting' the Ofsted report on the 'failed' local school or writing about the campaign to raise money to send a child to America for an operation to cure a rare bone disease. They may be recording a radio item about the dangers to health of a mobile telephone mast or a television item about the increase in binge drinking. Local journalism is about local issues and local politics and local people. The October 2005 relaunch of the *Birmingham Mail* in a series of localised editions underlines the acceptance throughout the regional press that local is what sells.

Journalistic careers start in many different ways, and many of them start local. To say that there is a career structure in journalism would be an exaggeration. Yes, there are structures there, but when a former test match cricketer or international footballer can become a sports writer, a weather girl a news reader, a former politician a columnist and the son or daughter or nephew or niece of a national newspaper editor a national newspaper journalist, then there is as much serendipity, or luck, as structure.

Famous journalists tend to romanticise their beginnings, playing down their drive and tenacity and exaggerating the casualness with which they 'found' themselves in journalism. Marr (2004: xvi) is typical. 'I didn't decide to become a journalist. I stumbled into journalism', he writes in his memoir. 'I'd done the requisite English degree, played politics, drawn cartoons and learned how to smoke sixty cigarettes a day without being sick. I'd started a PhD, washed dishes and been turned down for a job in a second hand bookshop'. He was turned down for a British Broadcasting Corporation (BBC) traineeship as well, of course, and found himself as a trainee at *The Scotsman*. In other words, he started in regional journalism, albeit on a Scottish national paper.

The media world has changed. Training used to be by apprenticeship. The school-leaver would be taken on by the local paper, often after O levels, as they then were, and would learn on the job, attached to an experienced reporter or news desk executive. They would take exams, in newswriting, law, public administration and shorthand, and progress from 'junior' to 'senior' with a little more money and a desire to move on. They would cover the courts, the council and local life, and learn the importance of accuracy, of knowing and interesting the audience, of maintaining contacts who would tell them things. And they would learn the crucial importance of trust. Unlike their here-today-far-away-tomorrow counterparts on the national press, they would know that if they upset a member of the local community by getting it wrong, or sometimes by getting it right, he or she would be on the phone to the editor or at the front desk the next day complaining and saying 'I'll never talk to that reporter again'. It was a tough grounding, and while it could hardly be described as glamorous it instilled the basic skills and realities of reporting life. National newspapers recruited the best from the local and regional newspapers – so did the broadcasters – and were well served, to a point.

There is still a residue of local editors who believe apprenticeship was and is the only way. My first editor, during a period of work experience on a Surrey weekly at the end of my second year at university, strongly advised me to abandon my degree and join his reporting staff as a trainee. He was genuinely baffled when I declined, admittedly after toying seriously with taking up his generous offer. And when I moved from national journalism into teaching journalism in higher education, the first local editor I met poured scorn on graduates and said the only people he wanted to recruit were 'boys on bikes from local estates'.

We are in a transitional phase – have been for too long – where journalism education or training (the use of those two words represents a debate that rages on, and to which we will return) remains caught between the old craft apprenticeship and the new graduate economy. The central features of this debate can be headlined thus:

- Is journalism a profession?
- Is journalism a graduate occupation?
- Who decides the nature, duration, content and assessment of journalism education/training?
- Who pays for it?
- Who sets and monitors standards?
- Is journalism pricing itself out of talent?
- Is too much structure the enemy of good journalism?

But first, what makes a good journalist? Hundreds have sought to answer that question, and still more the related question 'What is good journalism?' We'll duck the latter, on the basis that it is not the subject matter of this chapter. The former is.

Max Hastings, distinguished war correspondent, editor (*Daily Telegraph*, *Evening Standard*), now columnist (*The Guardian*, *Daily Mail*) once offered the following advice:

> As a young reporter you need to be curious, hungry and original. At an interview you'll have to convince a jaded and exhausted executive or editor that you've got something different to offer. You've got to believe journalism is the most important thing in the world – of course we know that it isn't – but you've got to feel passionate about what you're doing in a way few other jobs call for. And of course make trouble.
>
> (Hastings 1997)

The most famous definition of what it takes came from Nick Tomalin, a *Sunday Times* journalist tragically killed in his prime.

> The only qualities essential for real success in journalism are ratlike cunning, a plausible manner, and a little literary ability ... The ratlike cunning is needed to ferret out and publish things people don't want to be published (which is – and always will be – the best definition of News). The plausible manner is useful for surviving while this is going on, helpful with the entertaining presentation of it, and even more useful in later life when the successful journalist may have to become a successful executive on his newspaper. The literary ability is of obvious use.
>
> (Tomalin 1975: 77)

Tomalin goes on to say:

> We are obsessed with professionalism, and convinced there is not only a mystery to our craft, but a whole spectrum of laboriously learned techniques. We demand an apprenticeship, examination results, and years of drudgery before we allow entrants a proper chance to show their talents, and yet all the really successful (and really good) journalists have somehow or other managed to escape such a cumbrous ordeal.
>
> (Tomalin 1975: 77)

Note the use of both profession and craft (a confusion that endures – necessarily, I think). Also, note the romance of the first quote (and we must hold on to the romance) and the dilettante anti-education observation of the second (which has no place in our qualifications-obsessed present era).

For a more prosaic and more local journalism-oriented definition, the Holdthefrontpage website offers the following list of required characteristics:

- an interest in current affairs at all levels;
- a lively interest in people, places and events;
- an ability to write in a style that is easy to understand;
- good spelling, grammar and punctuation;
- an appreciation of the part a local newspaper plays in the community;
- a willingness to accept irregular hours;
- an ability to work under pressure to meet deadlines; and
- determination and persistence.

Graduates

While school-leavers still enter journalism, particularly regional and local journalism, and others do short courses in journalism at colleges and commercial training providers, the dominant trend in recent years is for journalists to be graduates. That is hardly surprising given the increase in participation in higher education and government policy to drive it up to 50 per cent of school-leavers.

This trend towards 'graduateness' was pointed out in a study of British journalists by Delano and Henningham (1995). They found that 70 per cent of all journalists went to university or college, six times as many as 40 years earlier. The figure will be greater now. Journalism degrees and diplomas were held by about 10 per cent of those working in journalism; again this figure will be higher now.

The News Breed stated:

> Despite there being no formal barriers to entry into journalism or career progress, the near preponderance of graduates suggests that a higher education qualification has become a de facto requisite. Present-day journalists (and employers) may say that they do not regard any educational or vocational qualifications as essential but the evidence suggests that within the span of a single working generation journalism has come to offer fewer opportunities to anyone with a limited or unconventional education. Its practitioners seem to be drawn from narrowing socio-economic strata and, notwithstanding the increasing enrolment of women, to be predominantly white, male, and, although largely non-practising, Christian.
>
> (Delano and Henningham 1995)

More recently the survey *Journalists at Work* claimed that 97 per cent of journalists had a first or higher degree (Journalism Training Forum 2002: 23–4).

The proportion of women entering journalism has certainly changed since that was written. I have noticed that there is a higher proportion of women each year in the courses offered at Sheffield. In the undergraduate course in 2005, at the time of writing, it is about 70 per cent.

One of the scandals of the regional and local press is its failure to recruit from the ethnic minorities. The Society of Editors produced a report, 'Diversity in the newsroom' (2004), which examined the employment of ethnic minority journalists on newspapers serving areas of high ethnic minority populations, such as Leicester, Leeds, Birmingham, west London and Manchester. Only the *Birmingham Evening Mail* (7 out of 96 editorial staff), Stoke *Sentinel* (5 out of 92), and the *Manchester Evening News* (6 out of 112) appeared to be making real efforts to recruit. Papers like the *Burnley Express* and *Oldham Chronicle* each employed one ethnic minority journalist.

My first full-time job in journalism was as a reporter on the late *London Evening News*, where I was the second graduate they had ever hired. Now the large majority of entrants into journalism, print and broadcast, are graduates. That does not necessarily mean journalism graduates; it means people with degrees. Most graduate journalists do not have journalism degrees, although many have postgraduate journalism degrees. There is a debate among employers as to whether they prefer a traditional degree such as English, history or politics, or a degree in journalism. Many say they prefer the education of a traditional degree plus the emphasis on skills and training provided by a postgraduate diploma or masters.

There remain some employers who are suspicious of degrees, to which the short response is: if approaching half of young people have degrees, do you really want to exclude the brightest half of the population (not always the case, of course, but generally so) from your recruitment? The one area where most employers would agree is that they do not want recruits with media studies degrees, so frequently and unfairly derided by the media themselves.

What really concerns employers is what they call 'pre-entry training'. And this is where the real change has come about. While for years the media industries accepted responsibility for training, through the apprenticeships or indentures described earlier, and through providing time and payment for day or block release at a local college, now a majority expect their recruits to come half-honed, with certificated pre-entry training in journalism skills and knowledge, from shorthand and media law to reporting and writing techniques. It saves them a lot of money.

So the cost of training journalists has to a large extent passed from the employers to the taxpayer and the students themselves, or their parents. Students build up debt (from autumn 2006 and the arrival of top-up fees even more debt) in effect to buy an entry ticket to the world of journalism to which they aspire in such great numbers. Those doing the postgraduate courses preferred by so many employers build up even greater debt, up to an additional £10,000.

Despite this, many employers are often critical of higher education journalism courses, criticising teaching and course content. This is justified in some cases and not in others (we will come to the accreditation of courses later). Just as the media are interested in sales and audiences, so is higher education interested in recruiting students, particularly the less prestigious institutions which find it hard to recruit funded numbers.

Journalism, or the idea of doing it, is so very popular among young people that a number of universities and colleges are quite shamelessly setting up courses and recruiting to them with little thought for what is required from such vocational education and without appropriately qualified staff to teach the students.

The universities' central admissions service (UCAS) lists nearly 700 courses covering journalism at 67 institutions. Around 5,000 places are on offer. And this excludes the hundreds of other courses in media studies or their derivatives. The country is awash with opportunities to study journalism, and many of the graduates will be disappointed when they seek a reporting job. The average local newspaper editor is unlikely to look with enthusiasm on an applicant parading a BA in Human Resource Management and Journalism.

Professional bodies

The 1949 Royal Commission on the Press identified the need for coordinated training of journalists, and led to the setting up in 1952 of the National Council for the Training of Journalists (NCTJ). Through the years of indentures (apprenticeships) it was supported by the industry; every trainee became familiar with Oxdown, the mythical town in which all events written about by trainees doing their NCTJ exams occurred. Only in 2005 was the obliteration of Oxdown signalled, to cries of joy and nostalgic sorrow in equal number.

The NCTJ became the custodian of training standards. Its constituent bodies were the Guild of Editors (representing editors from the regional and local press), the Newspaper Society, representing the publishers, the National Union of Journalists (NUJ) and later the Institute of Journalists, a small alternative to the NUJ. The NCTJ licensed short courses, and most trainees took part in day release or block release, the classroom aspect of their apprenticeships. The syllabus, heavily influenced by employers, focussed simply and basically on the tools of the trade: traditional newswriting to tell it straight, media law to keep out of trouble, public administration to understand what was going on at the council meeting, and shorthand to get the quotes down accurately and verbatim, particularly in court. There were two stages to these exams, and when the second set was passed the trainee became a senior, a qualified journalist. That was it, and apart from the occasional law refresher most journalists passed the next 40 years or so untroubled by further training.

The college short courses prepared trainees for their NCTJ exams, nothing else. Out of these came full-time courses – Preston Polytechnic was an early provider and brought us the editor of *The Independent*, Simon Kelner. Still, the only exams were those set by the NCTJ. Local broadcast journalism also recruited off these courses, or from local papers.

The national press and broadcasting existed outside this training structure. Mostly they recruited the already trained, and 'NCTJd', from the regional press. Until the end of the 1960s there was a diktat from the NUJ, mostly unchallenged by the national press, that all recruits had to have 'served' three years in the provinces before joining a national. There were a few ways round this restriction, usually graduates becoming leader writers on quality broadsheets.

Higher education entered the scene in the late 1970s and 1980s with the introduction of postgraduate diploma courses at institutions like Cardiff, City and Central Lancashire Universities. They offered intensive practical courses with work experience, and they were based on the traditional NCTJ syllabus. Universities were expanding, and these courses offered graduateness to the media. Local papers were not initially enthusiastic – graduates from traditional universities, even if they had added shorthand and newswriting to their repertoires, were not 'boys on bikes'. And they were 22 years old, not 16 or 18.

The dinosaurs despaired, but when many of the bright and focussed graduates proved they could do journalism rather well and had acquired the traditional skills, the postgraduate diploma courses became popular recruiting grounds. The nationals began to find they could recruit a different kind of reporter from the regions. The courses played their part by insisting that their students take the NCTJ exams as well as the university exams, something the NCTJ required before recognising (accrediting) higher education courses. The mould had broken, although the school-leaver entrants and short courses remained.

Broadcasting produced its own professional body, the Broadcast Journalism Training Council (BJTC), which did not set its own exams but did accredit postgraduate courses, which were being set up alongside their print counterparts. The BJTC sought to influence curriculum and made various demands for proper newsroom equipment and work experience.

At the same time as this development of postgraduate courses, industry training schemes, and in some cases colleges, were emerging. The BBC had a prestigious and highly sought-after graduate training scheme and so did Independent Television News (ITN). In the regions Thomson regional newspapers did too, and took on many who later became successful national newspaper journalists. Journalism was becoming a graduate occupation.

Perhaps inevitably, with numbers going to university soaring, undergraduate journalism courses followed in the early 1990s, and have grown in number ever since. Editors who had just about come round to postgraduate courses found a new target in the BA courses. How could you spend three years learning to be a journalist when we used to do it in a few months? The editors wanted only the professional skills; universities insisted that a degree represented more than that: it required reading and reflection and academic study. The tension persists.

Alongside, or perhaps as a consequence of, all this, the NCTJ went through a difficult period. Universities have autonomy. They develop their own syllabuses and are responsible for their own assessment. While it is common for professional bodies in medicine, engineering, architecture and other subjects to be prescriptive about course content, it is unusual for these bodies to set their own exams in addition to the university's, as the NCTJ does. The employers and editors were challenging the NCTJ curriculum and questioning how relevant it was to modern editorial imperatives and trends. Less court and council reporting was being provided in local papers and much court reporting was being subcontracted to agencies. Reporting staffs were smaller, with most interviewing done on the telephone. And editors were demanding more human interest, more consumer-focussed stories and less institutional coverage. Was the NCTJ reflecting this? Was Oxdown news the news they were covering?

The NCTJ is now going through a radical reappraisal of all its activities, looking at syllabuses, accreditation of courses, quality control and standards of examinations. Its board is now more reflective of its various clients and high-profile directors from the national as well as regional press and education providers now sit on the board. Government-imposed standards for vocational qualifications are being adopted. In short, the NCTJ is becoming a much more professional organisation, more in tune with industry, government and educational requirements.

There are National Vocational Qualifications (NVQs) in journalism, but despite government money and considerable promotion, take-up has been minimal on newspapers. The major publishers use the NCTJ postentry qualification.

The BJTC is in a period of self-examination. It is hard to exaggerate the impact of the Hutton report into the Kelly/Gilligan affair, and this is having a direct impact on the training of broadcast journalists. The Neil report explored this in depth; an embryonic BBC training school is developing; new ways of monitoring standards of accuracy and impartiality are being introduced. The BBC is even discussing the case for shorthand for broadcast reporters, which is, at the time of writing of this chapter, not a requirement.

And finally ... pay

Nobody gets rich in the local and regional media, except the owners. The pay situation has worsened over the years and shows little sign of improving. It is worst in the newspaper sector, where a starting salary for a graduate will usually be around £12,000 and is sometimes less (see Chapter 1). While nurses, teachers and policemen will start on salaries several thousand above that, and average graduate starting salaries are nearer £20,000, young journalists are increasingly asked to make sacrifices in living standards that are indefensible. Meanwhile, the huge corporations that own most of the regional and local press are seeking, and achieving, profits running over 30 per cent of their turnover. Cost-cutting is not restricted to economic downturns; it is a constant fact of life. Reporting staffs are cut, to the detriment of local journalism, and many weekly papers are produced by newsrooms consisting mostly of trainees.

Since more and more of these are graduates, bringing with them large and increasing personal debt from their higher education, it is not surprising that increasing numbers move out of journalism into related careers like public relations. Some decide against journalism while still doing their journalism degrees. The employers remark only on the number of applications they receive, although some editors notice the number is declining. The universities and colleges though see no decline in applications for journalism and related courses.

Starting salaries in broadcast journalism and magazines tend to be £2,000 or £3,000 better. There are exceptions to this dismal picture, with graduate training schemes offered by employers such as Reuters and the *Financial Times* paying more realistic sums. But places are few, and applications huge in number.

References

Delano, A. and Henningham, J. (1995) *The News Breed. British Journalists in the 1990s*, London: London Institute.

Fletcher, Kim (2005) *The Journalist's Handbook*, London: Macmillan.

Hastings, Max (1997) 'My Big Break', *Media Guardian*, 24 March, p. 5.

Journalism Training Forum (2002) *Journalists at Work*, London: Publishing NTO, Skillset.

Marr, A. (2004) *My Trade*, London: Macmillan.

Tomalin, N. (1975) *Nicholas Tomalin Reporting*, London: Andre Deutsch.

Chapter 8

Profits before product?

Ownership and economics of the local press

Granville Williams

> Broadly speaking, three factors distinguish newspapers from one another: ambitions, resources and values. Ownership is probably the greatest influence on all three.
>
> (Downie and Kaiser 2003: 76)

The striking common feature of patterns of ownership of the local and regional press across Europe is the horizontal integration of local newspaper titles by media groups to create regional monopolies in newspaper markets (European Federation of Journalists 2002). In the UK this pattern of consolidation and concentration has accelerated in the past decade (see Chapters 1, 4, 5 and 6). The Newspaper Society (NS), the trade association which promotes the regional press in the UK, states 'over £6.8 billion has been spent on regional press acquisitions since October 1995. The top 20 publishers now account for 85 per cent of all local newspaper titles in the UK and 96 per cent of the total weekly audited circulation' (Newspaper Society 2005a). The companies involved in this rapid consolidation of ownership, and its impact on the working practices and quality of journalism in local newspapers, form part of the content of this chapter, but the broader context of government policy concerning the regulation of newspaper ownership provides the first focus for analysis.

Media ownership and democracy: local concerns

Any systematic account of the relationship between media and democracy would be inadequate if it did not include the key role of newspapers in the local democratic process as investigators for, and informers of, the public. In 1997, the *Yorkshire Post*, for example, after a six-month investigation, broke the story of extensive corruption within Doncaster Council and a £60 million planning scandal which became known as 'Donnygate' (Rose 2002). Ideally papers should convey information about local government and local communities, and enable people to make informed choices on issues affecting their immediate environment. However, economic pressures that are the result of structural mechanisms in the industry threaten that role.

The idea that narrow ownership of the local and regional press is a threat to pluralism and diversity is not new. The Royal Commission on the Press, in its 1962 report, concluded that control of the press was a matter of public concern and that the increasing concentration of newspaper ownership in a few hands could stifle the expression of opinion and argument and distort the presentation of news. As a result, the 1965 Monopolies and Mergers Act (subsequently replaced by the 1973 Fair Trading Act) required that transfers which raised public interest issues, or where the average daily paid-for circulation was 500,000 or more, be referred to the Competition Commission. But analysis of the 20 Competition Commission reports since 1990 reveals only four adverse findings delivered. One of those dealt specifically with the suitability of David Sullivan, owner of the *Sport* and *Sunday Sport*, acquiring the *Bristol Evening Post* (HMSO, Cm 1083, May 1990). In another case involving the acquisition of seven newspapers in the Nottingham area owned by T. Bailey Forman Ltd, by the Daily Mail and General Trust, the Conservative Trade Minister, Tim Eggar, overruled the adverse report and allowed the sale to go ahead (HMSO, Hm 2693, October 1994). A 1999 report did find specifically against one aspect of a merger because of 'the increased concentration of ownership that would result from the transfer to Trinity of Mirror Group's Northern Ireland titles' and for the merger to go ahead Trinity would have to dispose of its Northern Ireland publications, including the Belfast *News Letter* and *Derry Journal* (Competition Commission 1999). The fourth adverse report, on the proposed takeover of Trinity Mirror titles by Johnston Press, is considered later in the chapter.

As the government developed policies for what became the 2003 Communications Act, the NS lobbied strongly for a new system with less regulatory interference in local and regional newspaper transfers and mergers. In the Act, however, a specific 'public interest' clause, relating to newspaper and other media mergers, caused the NS concern and it insisted that 'the vast majority of regional and local newspaper mergers will not be subjected to public interest interventions, and references and decisions that block transfers and mergers or impose interventionist controls' (Newspaper Society 2004: 1–2). The outcome seems to have been successful for the NS, as a reading of the Department of Trade and Industry (DTI) guidance document on media mergers reveals (DTI 2004). The inescapable conclusion is that the oft-stated policy intention to protect diversity and plurality in the local press has been a spectacular failure.

Changes in local press ownership

The precipitate sale of regional newspaper holdings by media groups in the mid-1990s went against a prevalent business idea that the ownership of different sections of the media would create synergies through cross-promotion and the use of the expensive commodity of news on different platforms, thus cutting costs by reducing staffing levels. What happened was the reverse of this, as media organisations with extensive cross-media interests sold off their regional press assets. In July 1995 the Thomson Corporation sold all of its English titles to Trinity International Holdings for £327.5 million. The Scottish titles were sold in two parts: the Aberdeen papers to Northcliffe and the Edinburgh titles to the Barclay brothers. Reed merged with the Dutch group to form Reed Elsevier, and announced the sale of Reed Regional Newspapers (four evening papers, 90 weeklies and the largest publisher of free newspapers). A management buy-out was financed by the New York investment institution, Kohlberg Kravis Roberts (KKR), which had a reputation for ruthless cost-cutting. Newsquest was the name of the new company.

EMAP followed the examples of Thomson and Reed when it withdrew from the regional newspaper market in June 1996 and sold its four evenings, 30 paid weeklies and 31 frees to Johnston Press for £210 million. Pearson's Westminster Press went to Newsquest in September 1996 for £305 million. In March 1998 Lord Hollick's United News and Media sold the bulk of United Provincial Media to Regional Independent Media (RIM) for £360 million, having sold United Southern and UPN Wales earlier. Johnston Press purchased Portsmouth and Sunderland Newspapers in June 1999 for £266 million. Also in June 1999, after KKR decided to realise its investment in Newsquest, the US media group Gannett beat off other contenders with a bid of £904 million. Gannett has a controversial history in the US in the way that it developed its media group of 74 daily newspapers, including *USA Today*, 21 television stations and extensive cable interests (McCord 1996). It was able to acquire Newsquest without any reference to the Competition Commission because it did not own any other UK newspapers. KKR made a return of 66 per cent on its investment over three and a half years in Newsquest. Gannett in turn expanded its newspaper empire in the UK, notably with the acquisition of three titles, the *Glasgow Herald*, *Glasgow Evening Times* and *Sunday Herald* from Scottish Media Group for £216 million, after the Competition Commission cleared the takeover. In 2005, Johnston Press continued its expansion with the acquisition of Scottish Radio Holdings' newspaper division Score Press for £155 million in June, two Irish newspaper groups for £160 million in September, and Scotsman Publications, whose titles include *The Scotsman* and *Scotland on Sunday*, from the Barclay brothers in December. In January 2006 the top four groups had 65 per cent of local and regional newspapers in terms of circulation: Trinity Mirror 21.5 per cent, Johnston Press 15.25 per cent, Newsquest close behind at 15.2 per cent, and Northcliffe 13 per cent.

What was striking about these changes in ownership, as Colin Bourne, a National Union of Journalists (NUJ) official, pointed out, was that 'most of those buying up everything for sale are interested mainly, if not wholly, in newspapers', whereas the sellers were selling up because they 'were never able to produce the rate of returns realisable in the electronic media' (Bourne 1996). Northcliffe Newspapers, a division of the DMGT, owners of the *Daily Mail*, *Mail on Sunday*, the *Evening Standard* and *Metro*, with extensive local radio interests, was the exception in this process of specialisation – it did not sell its regional newspapers. Instead, its chairman, Sir David English, attempted to exploit the commercial opportunities of cross-media ownership at a local and regional level (Williams 1998). In a surprise move the DGMT did announce the sale of its regional newspaper group in December 2005, but in February 2006 cancelled the sale because the three bids it had received did not reflect what the company considered to be the long-term value of the business.

There are two sharply diverging views about the current economic health, ownership and future prospects of the local and regional media in the UK. One is relentlessly promoted by the NS and the owners of the large regional media groups. Johnston Press, in its 2004 *Annual Report and Accounts*, is explicit about future strategy:

> We believe it will be possible for us to participate in the anticipated further consolidation of the local publishing industry. Economists and competition experts are increasingly recognising that, in terms of advertising revenues, newspapers compete with a variety of media and that, as far as plurality of editorial voice is concerned, that can be achieved just as well, indeed, sometimes far better, under a small number of owners than it can under diverse, fragmented and under-resourced ownership conditions.
>
> (Johnston Press 2005: 12)

The NS also sees regional press concentration as a positive development: 'Consolidation has left the industry in the hands of regional press "specialists" who have reinvested heavily in their core newspaper businesses' (Newspaper Society 2005a). Another crucial source of the financial health of this media sector is the level of advertising expenditure, and here again the NS emphasised its achievements, with the regional press being the second largest advertising medium with revenue of £3,165 million (20.4 per cent) after television (26 per cent) (Newspaper Society 2005b).

A good insight into the issues posed by regional consolidation is available through an analysis of the relatively insignificant agreement by Johnston Press to acquire eight free weekly titles owned by the Trinity Mirror group in the areas around Derby, Northampton and Peterborough in July 2001. Department of

Trade Secretary, Melanie Johnson, announced that she was referring the matter to the Competition Commission because the transfers would give rise to a significant increase in concentration of ownership of local newspapers. The report by the Competition Commission was unexpectedly robust and advised against the transfer of the titles (Competition Commission 2002).

Johnston Press, now the fourth largest publisher of regional and local papers with 241 titles, grew rapidly in the 1990s, doubling in size with the acquisition of EMAP's regional newspaper business in July 1996. This growth continued with the acquisition of Portsmouth and Sunderland Newspapers in 1999, and RIM in March 2002, just as the Competition Commission report was being prepared. From its origins as a modest local newspaper company in Scotland, it began to win praise from City analysts for

> buying wisely and integrating better … It boosted margins on Portsmouth and Sunderland, its first major acquisition back in 1999 from 19 to 26 per cent in the first year. It took only a little longer to get margins at the regional titles it bought from EMAP up from 15 to 21 per cent. Both of these businesses are now producing margins of 30 per cent.
>
> (Connor 2002)

On the other hand, in 2001, Trinity Mirror, formed by the merger of Trinity plc and Mirror Group plc in 1999, had a lacklustre financial performance: on a turnover of £1,131 million and an operating profit of £37 million it produced a margin of 3 per cent (Competition Commission 2002: 3). Trinity Mirror wanted to sell its eight titles to Johnston for £16.1 million because of their weak financial performance. Trinity Mirror's Midland Weekly Media Division wanted to focus on its titles in Birmingham and Coventry and the eight titles were peripheral to its operations.

As a transaction it fitted well into the way regional paper groups did business. It would tidy up some gaps in the near-monopoly sway which Johnston had in the area, 'create synergies through the publication of a number of overlapping and contiguous titles', and allow increased revenue through a number of cost reductions by integrating editorial, advertising, printing, distribution and other administrative functions within Johnston's divisional structures (Competition Commission 2002: 62–3). But the Competition Commission report identified other concerns, particularly focusing on four titles, which would have given Johnston 'a virtually complete monopoly position in local newspapers' in the Peterborough and Northampton geographical areas and argued that the transfer of the titles would operate against the public interest.

The Commission report recommended that the Secretary of State should not consent to the transfer of the four titles. The report also identified its concern about 'cluster publishing' and the 'implications for local concentration if consolidation in the ownership of regional and local newspapers were to continue'. Local monopolies, it suggested, 'are likely to give rise to a "live and let live" attitude on the part of publishers which would attenuate competition in local markets up and down the country'. The report suggested that the Office of Fair Trading 'should give early attention to whether an industry-wide inquiry into these issues should be initiated' (Competition Commission 2002: 37–8). Such an inquiry has not happened, and it is unlikely it ever will. This is all a long way from the provincial world of Northampton in 1945, and the local newspaper office in Market Square, which Jeremy Seabrook invokes: 'The paper was delivered to almost every household that could afford it; and it served less as a disseminator of news than as a vehicle for gossip ... The local newspaper was a contemporary equivalent of the stocks: shame and disgrace remained constant; only the technology was different'. Now, he argues, 'Contemporary communications systems, global cultural convergence, information conglomerates and transnational providers of entertainment have made deep inroads into worlds that remained for centuries bounded, enclosed and self-reliant' (Seabrook 2005: 233, 241).

Driving the businesses forward

Company reports give us part of the story about how the larger regional newspaper groups operate. All seek to organise their publications in regional geographical clusters to achieve economies of scale by maximising the use of printing, advertising, management, finance and personnel resources. Newsquest, for example, had 17 such clusters at the end of 2004; Johnston Press prints the vast majority of their titles at 13 regional centres, and Trinity Mirror has 12 print sites. Investment in new regional printing plants offering additional colour capacity, which is attractive to advertisers, is also standard: Newsquest in Oxford has opened a new facility; Northcliffe Newspapers in Derby, Stoke and Plymouth; Johnston Press opened a £60 million facility in Sheffield with plans for a £45 million one in Portsmouth; Trinity Mirror in Newcastle, and a £45 million joint investment with Guardian Media Group in Oldham to print the *Daily Mirror* and Trinity Mirror's North West titles. As Johnston Press point out, 'the operation of a relatively small number of larger scale printing centres provides the basis for tight cost control and excellent operational efficiency' (Johnston Press 2005: 9).

But there are sharp differences between the financial performances of different groups which, in turn, puts shareholder and other pressures on the underperformers. Out ahead is Johnston Press (2005) which, in its 2004 *Annual Report and Accounts*, announced an operating profit margin of 34 per cent, the highest in the industry. One City commentator identified its chief executive, Tim Bowdler, as the man who 'has transformed Johnston into a lean, mean machine – slashing costs and closing titles threatening to bring down the company's mouthwatering operating margin' and cited another factor: 'By concentrating on a limited number of regions, but with a near monopoly sway in many of them, Johnston can offer advertisers the chance to hit a fragmented audience with one shot, and charge higher rates for the privilege' (Wachman 2005).

In February 2003 Sly Bailey, formerly chief executive of the Time Warner-owned IPC Media, took over as chief executive of Trinity Mirror. Her job was to 'fundamentally transform the performance of Trinity Mirror by running the Group more effectively and efficiently' and this was to be achieved through a performance-based strategy, 'Stabilise Revitalise Grow' (Trinity Mirror 2005: 10). Scattered throughout the *Annual Report and Accounts 2004* are phrases like 'cost savings targets', 'reducing overall operating costs', 'tight cost management' and driving circulation revenue growth through increases based on the 'little and often' cover price policy. In 2004 Trinity Mirror delivered £23 million in cost cuts, £3 million more than promised, and the target for 2005 was set at £35 million (Davey 2005). In 2004 the result was that the regional newspaper division increased its profit margin by 3.9 per cent to 27.6 per cent. Trinity Mirror chairman, Sir Victor Blank, praised Sly Bailey and her management team, for 'setting itself performance standards that are at the very least equal to those of its rivals' (Trinity Mirror 2005: 9).

Northcliffe's operating profit margins for 2004 were just under 20 per cent, but in June 2005 two long-serving editors on the *Bristol Evening Post* and the *Bath Chronicle* were sacked because they were opposed to major cost-cutting plans. A *Press Gazette* report quoted one Northcliffe employee: 'The pressure is on from the City shareholders who ask why Northcliffe hasn't the same 30 per cent margins of the likes of Johnston and 28 per cent of Trinity. The answer is those kinds of margins are probably unsustainable if you are going to retain editorial quality' (Slattery 2005). Northcliffe introduced its £25 million cuts package with a title redolent of Stakhanovism, 'Aim Higher'.

'A money-making industry'

We can now address a second, and very different, perspective on the state of the UK local and regional press, and one which has disturbing parallels with developments in the American local press. In the 1960s most American papers were privately owned by local proprietors in the towns where they were published. As two US journalists point out, this was not always good for journalism because proprietors might stifle 'aggressive coverage of local institutions', but 'the best proprietors rose above parochial interests and encouraged tough-minded, independent reporting in their papers'. That is no longer the case.

> Today chains own 80 per cent of America's newspapers (and) most of the corporations that own newspapers are focused on profits, not journalism.

Editors who once spent their days working with reporters and editors on stories now spend more of their time in meetings with the paper's business-side executives, plotting marketing strategies or cost-cutting campaigns.

(Downie and Kaiser 2003: 68)

Complaints about the decline in the quality of the regional press are not new, but what is interesting now is that commentators from different sections of the ·UK media share a common view of the negative impact of the race for profits on the editorial quality of the local press. *Media Week* covers the media but with more of an emphasis on advertising and marketing. Its editor, Tim Burrowes, penned a critical editorial after the publication of the Audit Bureau of Circulations (ABC) figures for July–December 2004 were published, revealing an overall sharp decline in regional newspaper circulation. He listed targets for cost-cutting, such as journalists:

They were wasting a lot of time meeting contacts, visiting police stations, covering council meetings, attending courts, that sort of thing. Yet if they did everything on the phone – perhaps followed up a few more press releases and pursued a few less off-diary pieces, everything could be done with fewer staff … The results were fantastic for the publishers – more profitable titles. But over time, circulation seemed to slip. The public didn't seem to feel there was as much useful local information as before and they turned away.

(Burrowes 2005)

One local newspaper journalist in West Yorkshire identified the biggest threat to the independence of the local press as

the systematic gutting of newsrooms and an increasing use of journalists as copywriters. The lack of staff to go out and find stories leads to newsrooms where no one ever leaves the office. To fill a paper there is an over-reliance on press releases (predominantly from the local council, which often go in to the paper completely unchallenged), on contributed copy and on 'safe' community stories.

(interview, 3 August 2005)

The four big regional newspaper groups all issued profit warnings based on a drop in advertising revenue in the summer of 2005. As in the USA, the response of the newspaper groups is not to recognise that there will be ebbs and flows in advertising expenditure which will impact on profits, but to cut costs in an attempt to shore up profit margins. It is a response which speeds the cycle of decline. At the Johnston Press paper, the *Yorkshire Post*, letters were sent out to editorial staff over the age of 55 asking if they wanted to take early retirement. The automatic replacement of staff is supplanted by a culture of cuts, and 'business plans' have to be submitted to prove that a post is essential before it can be replaced. 'Saying "last year we had four reporters and even by replacing the one that's just left will only leave us with three" doesn't cut any ice' (interview, 3 August 2005).

As staff levels are pared back, others see an opportunity to cross into what was once the distinct and protected area of editorial content, capitalising on the pressures facing papers being run as tightly as possible with fewer, and often younger, less expensive staff. 'Well, it's a dog-eat-dog world out there, and the problems of the journalist can represent potential opportunities for good PROs', was how one PR person saw the situation (Nicholas 2005; see Chapter 16 for the influence of local government public relations officers in setting the local news agenda). A PR service, Free Features Ltd, provides an online database of copy that can be downloaded by any editor in the country, free of charge, provided they include information from a commercial sponsor. Janet Kelly, the managing director of Free Features sees the service 'as a natural extension of "advertorial", copy written and designed by the newspaper to promote a product, but paid for by the advertiser ... But where a newspaper will typically headline an advertorial with the words "This is an advertisement", Free Features content is presented as an article'. Almost 400 regional newspapers have signed up (Katbamna 2005).

The Press Association (PA) also fills part of the vacuum left by empty journalists' desks (see Chapter 19). 'It is PA which has the contracts with most publishers and broadcasters ... it is the PA that provides much, if not most of any news organisation's basic material' (Aspinall 2005). Striking confirmation of this is provided by the case of journalists at Newsquest's *Glasgow Herald* who contacted their sister paper, the Bradford *Telegraph & Argus*, when news broke that the men suspected of carrying out the first wave of London bombings in July 2005 came from Leeds, to ask whether they would share copy on the story. The reply was they took copy from PA to save money (*The Observer* 2005).

The two different narratives about the success or failure of the local press are also highlighted when we look at the working experience of journalists. The Newspaper Society Annual Review 2004–5 points out that there are now 13,000 journalists working on local and regional newspapers – up from 8,000 in 1996. The NUJ on the other hand is involved in a protracted struggle to end low pay and sees the situation rather differently. Miles Barter, an NUJ official, points out that journalists are streaming out of the industry because 'as well as low pay journalists on local papers complain constantly of over-work, long hours, bullying bosses and stress' (Barter 2005).

It doesn't have to be this way, of course. There are examples of papers – the *Barnsley Chronicle*, the Wolverhampton *Express and Star* – which invest in news and editorial standards, but if the pressure is to boost the profit margins, then inevitably local newspapers will be diminished in circulation, quality and importance.

References

Aspinall, C. (2005) 'The news monopoly', *Free Press*, 144, January/February, pp. 2–3.

Barter, M. (2005) 'It's money that matters', *Free Press*, 147, July/August, pp. 4–5.

Bourne, C. (1996) 'Reshaping regional newspapers', *Free Press*, 94, September/October, p. 4.

Burrowes, T. (2005) 'Never mind the quality, just feel the profit margin' *Media Week*, 8 March, p. 5.

Competition Commission (1999) *Trinity plc/Mirror Group plc and Regional Independent Media: A Report on the Proposed Merger Situations*, www.competition-commission.org.uk/rep_pub/reports/1999/431trinity.htm#full

Competition Commission (2002) *Johnston Press plc and Trinity Mirror plc: A Report on the Proposed Merger*, www.competition-commission.org.uk/rep_pub/reports/2002/463johnston.htm#full.

Connor, H. (2002) 'Throg street "wise buyer"', *The Observer*, 17 March, p. 8.

Davey, J. (2005) Tempus 'Faith in Sly helps to patch up problems at Trinity', *The Times*, 1 July, p. 65.

Downie, L. and Kaiser, R. G. (2003) *The News About the News*, New York: Vintage.

DTI (2004) *Enterprise Act 2002: Public Interest Intervention in Media Mergers,* London: DTI.

European Federation of Journalists (EFJ) (2002) *European Media Ownership: Threats on the Landscape*, Brussels: EFJ.

Johnston Press (2005) *Annual Report and Accounts, 2004*, Edinburgh: Johnston Press plc.

Katbamna, M. (2005) 'This article is not an advertisement – or is it?', *The Independent Media Weekly*, 4 April, p. 21.

McCord, R. (1996) *The Chain Gang*, Columbia: University of Missouri Press.

Newspaper Society (2004) 'Public interest intervention in media mergers', www.newspapersoc.org.uk/documents/publications/pr2004/memorandum.html (accessed 7 July 2005).

Newspaper Society (2005a) 'Ownership changes, mergers and acquisitions', www.newspapersoc.org.uk/default.asp?cid=351 (accessed 10 July 2005).

Newspaper Society (2005b) 'UK Media Advertising Expenditure 2004', www.newspapersoc.org.uk/documents/Factsandfigures/UK.adspend–2004.pdf (accessed 16 July 2005).

Nicholas, K. (2005) 'PROs can capitalize on journalists' woes', *PR Week*, 15 April, p. 20.

Rose, R. (2002) 'Bad apples back in the barrel', *Red Pepper*, May.

Seabrook, J. (2005) 'The end of the provinces', *Granta*, 90, London: Granta.

Slattery, J. (2005) 'The first casualties in the Northcliffe firing line', *Press Gazette*, 1 July, p. 11.

The Observer (2005) Media Diary 'Down the wire', *The Observer*, 4 July, p. 9.

Trinity Mirror (2005) *Annual Report and Accounts 2004*, London: Trinity Mirror plc.

Wachman, S. (2005) Throg Street 'Johnston is a great read', *The Observer*, 12 June, p. 8.

Williams, G. (1998) 'Local visions: cable television: the new local medium', in Franklin, B. and Murphy, D. (eds) *Making the Local News*, London: Routledge, pp. 51–62.

Chapter 9

Industrial relations and local journalism

Gregor Gall

Introduction

Journalists' collective workplace organisation in the provincial newspaper industry, embodied in the National Union of Journalists (NUJ), experienced large-scale and deep-seated retrenchment following an employers' offensive by aggressive, well-resourced and unitarist-minded newspaper groups in the 1990s. The vehicle for this employer offensive and retrenchment was union derecognition, that is, the unilateral removal by employers of agreements they formerly held with the NUJ covering rights of recognition, representation and collective bargaining. Derecognition had, by the late 1990s, left the overwhelming majority of journalists in provincial newspapers without any institutionalised means of joint regulation of the employment relationship (e.g., the style and content of employer behaviour and policy) or of the wage-effort bargain (e.g., collective bargaining over pay and conditions) and with very few rights of union representation (e.g., over individual grievances and health and safety). Alongside derecognition, employers also introduced personal contracts, under which individual journalists were nominally free to negotiate their own terms and conditions of employment. Despite union opposition, employer unilateralism over the determination of pay and conditions prevailed. This, not surprisingly, detrimentally impacted journalists' wages and working conditions as a result not only of the generalised condition of a capitalist market economy with its competitive and accumulative pressures, but also because a number of specificities of the market in the provincial newspaper environment led companies to try to reduce labour costs.

However, by mid-2005, the rout and retreat experienced by the NUJ had been reversed quite dramatically. Starting in early 2000, and under the shadow of the provisions for statutory union recognition of the Employment Relations Act 1999 (ERA), the NUJ began to win back a substantial number of recognition agreements with a number of employers who had previously derecognised it. This chapter, based on extensive interviews with an array of NUJ personnel between 1997 and 2004 and supplemented by secondary sources such as the weekly *Press Gazette* and the NUJ's monthly *The Journalist*, begins by examining the process by which the NUJ created and mobilised forces that proved capable of re-imposing upon the provincial newspaper employers the institutions of the joint regulation of the employment relationship. It then proceeds to consider whether the NUJ has also proved capable of re-imposing the processes and outcomes of the joint regulation of the employment relationship upon the provincial newspaper employers.

Historical background

Widespread collective bargaining at chapel (workplace branch) level in provincial newspapers dates from the late 1960s and early 1970s. Its development was relatively rapid in this period of overall trade union strength and high level of industrial combativeness, and culminated in the ability to sustain a protracted and relatively successful strike constituting part of the so-called 'Winter of Discontent' revolt of the low paid in 1978–9 (Gall 1992). The motivation behind, and the processes, nature and extent of, derecognition, and the provincial newspapers' offensive against the NUJ have been previously and extensively studied elsewhere (e.g., Gall 1993, 2000; Noon 1993, 1994; Smith and Morton 1990) so as to be not worth reiterating here. Nevertheless, it is important to briefly restate that following the removal of the constraints upon the managerial prerogative represented by the National Graphical Association (NGA) and Society of Graphical and Allied Trades (SOGAT) print unions in the pre-press and press areas of production, the employers sought to prevent the NUJ taking up this mantle under the regime of 'direct entry' (or single key-stroking) by engaging in strategies of disorganisation and derecognition.

Moreover, the inability of the NUJ to resist this offensive was accentuated by the general retreat of trade unionism in Britain during the period. Without suggesting interemployer coordination across the economy or that employers took their cues from Conservative administrations, a generalised offensive against organised labour by capital and the state took place between 1979 and 1997. The demoralisation and disorganisation resulting from the union movement's incapability to resist this offensive meant that when the NUJ experienced its 'derecognition offensive' in the 1990s, the collective resources that were able to help sustain workers in previous industrial battles no longer existed to the same degree, and thus were not potentially available to journalists. Consequently, journalists had to rely far more on their own meagre resources and do so in a less supportive environment. The decimation of the organisational strength of the NGA and SOGAT print unions contributed significantly to this.

The regaining of recognition

Regaining union recognition has been critical to the project of renewal for the NUJ because it provides a measure of legitimacy, stability and effectiveness for union organisation as well as facilities for workplace union personnel (e.g., time off for trade union duties, access to internal company communication systems). With recognition, the NUJ is freer to organise and less of an 'outlaw' or 'bandit'. Moreover, it affords the NUJ the ability to move from merely representing members on an individual basis to that of representation and negotiation on a collective basis. And on the basis of the retention of members, an elementary level of union organisation and the maintenance of a level of collective consciousness and the prospect of, and then arrival of, employment legislation to enforce union recognition, the NUJ has been able to gain recognition from resistant employers.

The extent of the re-emergence of the NUJ as a potential force within the provincial newspaper industry can be assessed by virtue of its recapturing union recognition agreements. Since 1999, 16 agreements have been gained through winning ballots (and no ballots have been lost) while 36 agreements were obtained through membership audits or management intelligence confirming the NUJ's claimed density. Most (active) campaigns to regain recognition took between 6 and 24 months. Of the 52 agreements, only three were set in train via the holding of a ballot or signed prior to 6 June 2000 when the statutory union recognition provisions of the ERA came into effect. This gives some indication of the extent and the depth of the antipathy of the provincial newspaper employers to regranting recognition compared with employers in other sectors who were, in the words of the Confederation of British Industry (CBI), taking the advice of 'sensible human resources directors … to consider negotiating recognition agreements while time is on their side and before the law imposes a statutory procedure' (*Financial Times* 9 February 1999). In total, recognition has been regained for nearly 3,000 journalists in a period of five years after a decade of derecognition. Of these new recognition agreements, 64 per cent were with the five largest provincial newspaper groups (Johnston, Newsquest, Northcliffe, Regional Independent Media and Trinity Mirror).

Employer response and resistance

While all but two of the recognition agreements were voluntarily gained, this should not be taken to suggest that employers were willing to do so. Indeed, the mildest form of employer opposition to granting recognition was simply to state that until the legal position changed, and because the newspaper companies were not acting unlawfully, the status quo would be maintained. Once the legal position had changed, this mild form of opposition then comprised tardiness in meeting the NUJ to discuss recognition with regard to the requisite membership or journalist support thresholds, methods for ascertaining these and the complexion of possible recognition agreements. The tardiness represented a strategy of obfuscation. The stronger forms of opposition comprised the standard tactics of anti-unionism such as anti-union literature and captive meetings with anti-union presentations about the 'union threat' to pay, jobs and profits and the 'evil' of unions vis-à-vis being parasitic and undemocratic, as well as the establishment of non-union forms of employee voice and representation such as company councils (Gall 2004a; Gall and McKay 2001).

At Trinity Mirror (Cardiff) in 1999, the employer signed a single union 'sweetheart' (partnership and 'no-strike') recognition agreement with the Amalgamated Electrical and Engineering Union (AEEU) for the workforce, even though the AEEU had no members amongst journalists. After four years of campaigning, the employer relented and recognised the NUJ. Trinity Mirror (Newcastle) attempted to establish a staff forum with the help of Advisory, Conciliation and Arbitration Service (ACAS) but after ACAS pulled out under protest from the NUJ, the forum was stillborn. Newsquest similarly established staff forums as methods of giving expression to employee voice and gave higher than expected pay increases in response to NUJ activities. But alongside this, it employed more sinister tactics such as unfairly making shop stewards redundant at its Bolton, Belfast, Bristol, Cambridge, Hull and Sheffield centres. Northcliffe has used similar tactics at its Aberdeen, Gloucester and Stoke centres to avoid NUJ recognition.

The process of regaining recognition

The process by which the statutory recognition provisions were created involved a series of compromises between employers, trade unions, the Labour Party and the government. The effect of this was to considerably lessen the utility of the provisions to the unions. Consequently, it is worth examining why the NUJ was able to so extensively regain recognition, for this is significant in its own right and relates to the NUJ's ability to mobilise its membership resources after recognition.

In general terms, the NUJ has benefited from the statutory mechanism's positive influence (the 'shadow' and 'demonstration' effects) on employers following its limited but tactical use by trade unions which helped create a bandwagon effect (Gall 2004b). Nonetheless, the NUJ was operating in one of the most hostile sectors for trade unionism, and therefore, it can be deduced that the actions of the NUJ itself have a direct bearing on its success in regaining recognition. The union was able to maintain its membership and support base throughout the years of derecognition of around 3,000 members prior to June 2000 (which then rose to 5,800 by 2003), as well as augment these in the run-up to the arrival of the statutory mechanism. This was accomplished by adapting well to operating as (i) an illegitimate agent with bargaining or representational rights through the provision of individual membership services (advice, legal representation, training); (ii) being a constant, dogged and high-profile critic of the employers where providing voice was valued and issues of efficacy of voice were not paramount; and (iii) campaigning for statutory union recognition through the Press for Union Rights lobby group which the NUJ helped found with other media unions in 1990 (see Press for Union Rights 1990).

The Father of the Chapel (FoC) at the Yorkshire *Evening Post* explained the situation at his workplace:

> Management of what was then United Provincial Newspapers expected membership to dwindle and the union to disappear. They were wrong ... It's been a hard slog. There were times when we felt out in the wilderness but the members always stayed solid.
>
> *(Press Gazette* 11 May 2001)

His counterpart at Birmingham *Post and Mail* observed of his workplace:

> The union refused to go away. With a team of activists willing to work on the chapel committee we refused to go away. And we started winning little victories ... [like] consultation rights on the health and safety committee [and in 1999] we even negotiated an overall pay increase – despite being derecognised.
>
> *(Journalist* January 2001)

The contexts of these activities – of individual membership representation, dogged critic and campaigner for statutory union recognition – were those of a determined core of long-standing and experienced lay activists, the widespread existence of workplace grievances amongst the provincial newspaper journalists, and the continuing strong presence of the notion of the profession of journalism, with the NUJ acting as a vociferous campaigner for journalism as the 'sword of truth and justice' and dispenser of the press cards.

This strategy was outlined and operationalised in an NUJ (1995) pamphlet subtitled 'What to do when management refuses to listen'. Consequently, the NUJ did not suggest to its members that they should merely hang on for some distant 'better days' but that members could and should struggle in the immediate period to defend their rights and that this struggle was an essential part of rebuilding confidence and union organisation to generate the capacity to regain union recognition in the future. One particular aspect of the NUJ strategy was to target Newsquest's centres for recognition first (where it had the strongest union organisation in centres like Bolton, Bradford and Oxford) in order to create a forward momentum with which to pressurise other employers.

However, the salience of this enforced way of organising is that, while an achievement in itself and consonant with the trade union consciousness of the journalists then, it did not necessarily lay out the strongest foundations for the post-recognition period. Through using a counterfactual method, it can be speculated that more acute collective mobilisations like strikes or occupations to achieve re-recognition may have provided a more tested and robust form of collectivism with which to subsequently face the employers. Here the issue of the developed state of journalists' collective consciousness is less important than their ability to impose significant costs and sanctions on their employer through mobilisations at the point of production. This is not to bemoan the activities of the NUJ as they were, but rather to understand the implications of the processes it engaged in.

After derecognition but before bargaining

In spite of variations in the intensity of employer opposition outlined above, all employers showed lethargy in the two phases prior to the commencement of collective bargaining. First, considerable time elapsed between the NUJ winning a recognition ballot or securing majority membership through a membership audit and the date on which a union recognition was agreed and signed. While some delay may be considered reasonable where the content of a recognition agreement is jointly decided upon, employers went further than this, often deploying the service of lawyers, by deliberately not expediting the process. Commonly, six months elapsed and the NUJ had to involve its general secretary to command meetings with employers in order to bring matters to a positive conclusion for the union. Second, considerable time elapsed between the signing of union recognition agreements and the first bargaining to produce a 'house' agreement, an agreement between the chapel and the employer over pay rises, pay rates and other terms and conditions of work and employment. This period of delay comprised between 6 and 12 months. Employers refused to enter into negotiations shortly after the commencement of recognition as might have been expected because they stated that negotiations could not begin until the date of the annual review of pay had been reached, that is the date of the annual review under the years of derecognition. For example, the *Press Gazette* (11 May 2001) commented: 'The NUJ chapel at the *Oxford Mail* and its sister titles regained recognition last June but the company had been slow in negotiating a house agreement'.

In both instances, the power relations and dynamics of the bargaining relationship dictate that the initiative lies with the employer because the employer is a 'primary organisation' and the union a 'secondary organisation' (Offe and Wisenthal 1980). By flatly stating their position, the employers forced the NUJ into a position of accepting their will or mobilising its resources in order to seek movement. In short, the employers challenged the NUJ's willingness and ability to change their tardiness and obfuscation. Other than remonstrate, the NUJ did not seek to overcome the employers' will here.

The outcomes of collective bargaining

The most obvious, and relatively easier, outcome of the post-recognition period to examine is that of the pay and condition bargaining settlements. Over and above the dry 'pounds and pence' details of the 'wage-effort bargain', this helps inform an assessment of employer and union behaviour and the resources both can bring to bear on the bargaining relationship in the post-recognition period in order to determine its outcomes. It is first important to recognise the basis on which the bargaining took place. For some 10–15 years (the period between derecognition and re-recognition), the employers, save for the influence of the labour market, determined whether there was any uplift in pay and conditions. Indeed, the expanding supply of journalistic labour that exceeded demand in this period allowed the employers even greater discretion here. Therefore, the first bargaining took place after the stagnation of wages and conditions in real terms and relative to other comparable professional groups, meaning that the base line on which the NUJ operated was an impoverished one.

The first rounds of bargaining (2001–04) provide little evidence that the NUJ chapels, judging by their claims, have been successful in achieving their demands in the first rounds of bargaining after regaining recognition despite nine chapels taking 110 days of strike action between them. Nearly all employers' first offers (of between 2.5 per cent and 3.0 per cent) were not substantially different from their final offers and the actual settlements. And the level of the settlements resulted primarily from the influence of the slackness in the journalistic labour market and the willingness of employers to pay what they thought was the going rate. However, the underlying picture is a good deal more complicated than this although it does not negate what has just been said. At the outset, it is worth noting that the initial claims represented 'wish lists' of what it would take to begin making up for the losses incurred during derecognition. In practice, these were political statements of intent for several years ahead and for the consumption of members and employers, rather than an actual bargaining agenda for a particular year. Overall, it appears the chapels were able to obtain very minor concessions on across-the-board annual pay rises, even where striking was used.

Little movement by employers on issues concerned with other working conditions and remuneration outside basic pay can be detected. For example, chapels have had little success in preventing redundancies from taking place, gaining significant improvements in severance terms or ameliorating the conditions of increased workloads on the remaining staff.

However, far greater success was recorded in raising the pay of junior staff through raising minimum rates or pay bands. For example, at the *Spalding Guardian* in 2002, the pay of graduate trainees was raised from £9,500 to £11,000 (16 per cent increase) while that of newly qualified seniors was raised from £12,000 to £14,000 (17 per cent). At the London *News Shopper* series in 2000, the minimum rate was increased from £10,500 to £12,000 (14 per cent) while in 2002, the pay of trainees after one year was increased from £13,200 to £15,200 (15 per cent). At Bradford in 2002, the minimum starting rate was increased by £1,500 (14 per cent) while rises for specific groups were: weekly reporters (3.2 per cent), evening reporters (2.9 per cent) and senior weekly reporters (7.1 per cent). This compares broadly similarly with the Greater Manchester Weekly News series whose chapel had not been derecognised and which, in 2002, gained an increase in the starting rate for trainees from £10,486 to £13,060 (24 per cent). Consequently, the NUJ chapels were not able to secure significant increases for senior staff and tackle the wider extent of low pay in the sector. The recognition of this has led the NUJ nationally, in the case of Newsquest group, to submit a claim aimed to achieve a minimum of £20,000 by 2005 for seniors.

This relatively small degree of success for the NUJ needs to be couched in the specific context of the provincial newspaper sector and the dynamics of its industrial relations. First, the degree of employer intransigence was considerable with many employers seemingly determined to try to maintain *de facto* derecognition. Agreeing to recognition was a tactical manoeuvre, not a strategic change of heart. For example, the FoC at the Yorkshire *Evening Post* stated

> [We] ... fought long and hard to win back recognition, but this is just a start. Now we have to begin the fight to retain some of the benefits we lost during the days of derecognition. ... The company has made it clear that it is not interested in partnership or cooperation. It has agreed to recognition because it had to. We believe it will now pursue every possible obstruction to further progress.
>
> (*Journalist* June 2001)

While the NUJ's Irish secretary commented on the case of the *Belfast Telegraph*'s pay freeze, 'It's hugely ironic but not surprising that having just agreed to negotiate with the union again after 15 years, the company should turn around and pull down the shutters on this year's pay talks' (*Irish News* 25 June 2002), and the NUJ reported:

> At the Bristol Evening Post, the company is encouraging people to opt out of the bargaining unit and are not holding meaningful negotiations. In companies owned by both Johnston Press and Newsquest they have announced, and in at least one case paid, the annual pay award prior to negotiations beginning.
>
> (NUJ 2003: 5)

Although mindful of the unit labour cost implications of bargaining, an additional dimension to this was that after reluctantly conceding recognition, employers had determined against further loss of face by being, as they saw it, 'turned over again' by the NUJ. This mentality was particularly strong in 2003 after the Bradford strike of 2002 where employers dug in against the first major union mobilisation in the sector.

Second, it is apparent that while the results of strikes were limited for those chapels taking strike action, the strikes had a positive, if small, demonstration effect on other employers. Consequently, many employers were rather keener than might have otherwise been the case to make some minor concessions in the face of rejection of first offers or strike ballots and strike threats. Third, the relative success of the first chapel's strike action in 2002 considerably raised the expectations of what chapels could achieve through steadfastness in the 2003 bargaining round. Fourth, outside the annual bargaining rounds, the NUJ has recorded little success in preventing considerable numbers of redundancies and ending policies of not filling vacant posts. While severance terms have been improved, the NUJ has not been able to exert any significant influence on controlling the resulting increased workloads for remaining staff. Fifth, the settlements achieved by re-recognised chapels compare favourably with those made by non-derecognised chapels, although continuing recognition should not be viewed as a *sine qua non* of union strength, given the recent decline in the union wage premium (the positive gap in pay between unionised and non-unionised workers). Thus, the pay gains from collective bargaining amongst those chapels that maintained recognition should not be viewed as particularly significant and, therefore, neither should those from re-recognised chapels. Lastly, and with the degree of relative immiseration of journalists' wages and conditions experienced in the years of derecognition, considerable ground needs to be made up just to compensate for this. For example, in this period the Yorkshire *Post/ Evening Post* journalists in Leeds suffered a significant diminution of their sick pay scheme in 1996 while journalists at the Preston and Blackpool centres had their holiday entitlement reduced in 1996.

Conclusion

In terms of exploring the social relations of production within the provincial newspaper industry in Britain, it is clear that an extensive and ongoing contestation has occurred between the collective organ of the journalists and the employers. Having experienced a widespread and deep-seated employers' derecognition offensive, the NUJ was able to maintain a significant level of membership and in some of these cases also coherent and tangible workplace organisation. Consequently, this offensive was not successful in destroying the NUJ's presence in the industry. While employers did not provide alternative means of 'employee voice' following derecognition, they did take advantage of the weakened position of journalists to erode the relative worth of their terms and conditions of employment. It was from this basis of having the organisational and ideological capacity to articulate journalists' grievances that the NUJ has been able to revitalise itself in the provincial newspaper industry by taking advantage of the influence of the new employment legislation, which it played a large part in bringing about. But the re-emergence of union recognition as a major means of regulating the relationship between the NUJ and the newspaper employers suggests that the predominant employer strategy of derecognition has now been superseded by the predominant strategy of marginalisation, whether of outright 'surface' bargaining or 'hard-nosed' bargaining. Indeed, the case of the provincial newspaper journalists provides a salutary lesson in demonstrating that *de jure* recognition should not be made synonymous with *de facto* recognition. For employers with a deep-seated and historical antipathy towards trade unionism such as newspaper employers (Gall 2000, 2001), merely conceding recognition has been a demonstration of tactical deftness in engaging in a more long and drawn-out war. Indeed, some in the NUJ were far-sighted enough to recognise this early on. The NUJ's Northern Organiser told the 1998 NUJ annual conference: 'Recognition is not the panacea. When we get it we will still have to fight for higher wages and better conditions. On its own it will achieve nothing' (*Journalist* April 1998).

Although the NUJ can rightly praise itself for getting this far, it nonetheless faces a far more difficult challenge in creating the resources and mobilisation necessary to fully transform the potential of union recognition into the actuality of union recognition, that is, improvements in terms and conditions through collective bargaining, whether by mutual consent with employers or through coercion. This concerns the pay of all journalists, and means revisiting and attempting to solve the quandaries that the NUJ faced prior to the onset of derecognition in the 1980s. These centre on how to construct, mobilise and aggregate effective union leverage over the employers within the confines of a regime of decentralised collective bargaining, restrictions on immunities for lawful industrial action and a labour market where supply exceeds demand.

References

Gall, G. (1992) 'The NUJ: a union in crisis', *Capital and Class*, 48, 7–15.

Gall, G. (1993) 'The Employers' offensive in the provincial newspaper industry', *British Journal of Industrial Relations*, 31 (4), 615–24.

Gall, G. (2000) 'Employment relations and the labour process in the newspaper industry: is there the potential for the return of the NUJ?', *New Technology, Work and Employment*, 15 (2), 94–107.

Gall, G. (2001) 'Industrial relations under new ownership; the case of the provincial newspaper industry', *Personnel Review*, 30 (1), 22–41.

Gall, G. (2004a) 'British employer resistance to union recognition', *Human Resource Management Journal*, 14 (2), 39–57.

Gall, G. (2004b) 'Trade union recognition in Britain, 1995–2002: turning a corner?', *Industrial Relations Journal*, 35 (3), 249–70.

Gall, G. and McKay, S. (2001) 'Facing "Fairness at Work": union perception of employer opposition and response to union recognition', *Industrial Relations Journal*, 32 (2), 94–114.

Noon, M. (1993) 'Control, technology and the management offensive in newspapers', *New Technology, Work and Employment*, 8 (2), 102–10.

Noon, M. (1994) 'From apathy to alacrity; managers and new technology in provincial newspapers', *Journal of Management Studies*, 31 (3), 19–32.

NUJ (1995) *A Voice at Work: What to do When Management Refuses to Listen*, London: NUJ.

NUJ (2003) *Review of the Employment Relations Act 1999: The NUJ Response*, London: NUJ.

Offe, C. and Wisenthal (1980) 'Two logics of collective action', in Offe, C. (ed.), *Disorganised Capitalism: comtemporary transformation of work and politics*, Cambridge: Polity Press, pp. 170–220.

Press for Union Rights (1990) *The Union Campaign to Restore the Balance of Rights in the Workplace*, London: PUR.

Smith, P. and Morton, G. (1990) 'A change of heart: union exclusion in the provincial newspaper industry', *Work, Employment and Society*, 4 (1), 105–24.

Chapter 10

Local journalists and the local press: waking up to change?

Rod Pilling

A wake-up call

It is unlikely that the British newspaper editors who gathered for their conference in late 2005 would have needed the exhortation of the opening speech to 'Wake up to a New World'. Shifting circulation and advertising patterns and the rapid growth of Internet traffic would have already alerted them to the scale of the change facing them. They probably did not need 'futurologist' Professor Richard Scase, author of *Britain 2010: the Changing Business Landscape*, to ring any alarm bells.

If they did need a wake-up call, they received one shortly afterwards. An announcement from the Daily Mail group sent seismic shocks through British regional journalism. This group, one of the oldest and most successful, a genuine press dynasty, had decided to jettison its regional newspaper operation, Northcliffe Newspapers.

The decision to sell what was regarded as a prized asset raised all sorts of questions about the future of local papers. Why were such long-term players getting out? Why were they selling the most profitable part of what was still largely a family-owned business? (This part alone had made a profit of £102 million on sales of £520 million in the last year, more profit than the national newspaper division and far more than any other part of the Daily Mail General Trust (DMGT).) It had more than 100 titles, a weekly combined circulation of more than 9 million, and a company lineage of more than 80 years that traced directly back to the founder of the popular newspaper revolution of the 1890s, the first Lord Northcliffe. Regional newspapers had been widely regarded a core part of a press dynasty, although DMGT had signalled its intentions to diversify and re-invent itself.

Alarmist rumours circulated that the current chairman, Viscount Rothermere, or his board had lost faith in the future of local papers. They were getting out whilst they could achieve a high price; a figure of around £1.5 billion was thought likely. Such rumours did not dampen interest from potential buyers; on both sides of the Atlantic, press groups eyed the potential prize.

Tim Bowdler, one of the potential buyers, the chief executive of the rapidly growing local press group Johnston Press, which achieves operating profit of more than 30 per cent, expressed great surprise at the decision: 'I didn't expect this. Local newspapers have tremendous brand strength and connections with their communities. We are better equipped than anybody to manage that challenge' (Rushe and Kleinman 2005: B5).

Former editor and media commentator Roy Greenslade said:

> The sad truth is that Rothermere's managers appear to believe the future for regional newspapers is perilous. They want to offload their 105 titles before potential buyers realise that revenues are about to fall off a cliff.
>
> Yet that projection may be flawed, indicating that DMGT has failed to embrace the Internet as enthusiastically and intelligently as its rivals … rivals such as Johnston Press and Trinity Mirror have set out by different routes – the former by organic development, the latter by acquisition – to create a synergy between papers and websites'.
>
> (Greenslade 2005: 8–9)

Greenslade acknowledges that many aspects of the changes facing traditional newspapers are unclear but feels clear-sighted analysis makes one message clear:

> It may seem ironic but the key to long-term circulation success for newspapers lies in viewing the printed paper as the 'core brand' on which to build a host of digital 'products.' Though we journalists may blanch at those terms and possibly recoil from the concept, we have to appreciate that our future is tied to wooing an audience that is gradually turning its back on our inky output. And we have to do it fast.
>
> (Greenslade 2005: 8)

Steve Eggington of Worldwide Media summarised the position facing print newspapers in the early twenty-first century succinctly: 'If newspapers stick to ink they will sink' (Sargeson and Astill 2005).

This chapter examines the changes that local newspaper journalists are making – or planning – in response to what they perceive as seismic changes in their industry. Few of them expect the landscape to remain the same. Many expect wholesale change.

My study of local newsrooms in the late 1990s found a number of changes. Newsrooms were getting smaller, with fewer journalists covering fewer stories.

Most of the journalists, particularly on weeklies, were trainees and were poorly paid (see Chapters 1 and 8). Both journalists and the Guild of Editors feared a 'sweatshop culture' was emerging. Journalists were being more selective about news and sources of news reporting that had been staples a generation earlier; courts and councils were now sparsely covered. Journalists were relying more on press releases from organisations with an interest in and the capacity for promoting themselves. Many now worked on free newspapers with a high proportion of advertising (Pilling 1998: 183–95).

Yet there was an enduring faith among journalists in traditional local journalism and there were some conspicuous examples of success. Journalists were prepared to put in extraordinary commitment in pursuit of their traditional values when covering the local news. There was also evidence that their coverage was less deferential than it had been and that a wider range of voices were finding their way into the local papers than had done a generation earlier. There was evidence too that the attitude to their audience had changed. Under competition from other attractions for readers' attention, journalists sought more to interest the readers than to tell them what they ought to be interested in (Pilling 1998: 183–95).

New technology – especially the computer-based automation of text handling – was an engine for change in production and was altering some traditional practices and threatening some long-standing roles. Some high-profile figures were advocating further efficiencies. Computer-automated page layout had prompted a call for the 'death of the sub' from one senior figure with an eye on costs. Copy, he argued, could be entered straight into templates by reporters. Similarly, digital text could be recycled around a group's publications at virtually nil cost. The Guild of Editors pointed out that there was now a very marketable database at the heart of most newsrooms. They were calling for reporters to become multiskilled, camera-carrying 'content gatherers' for these multimedia databases. Lest anyone get carried away by technological optimism, commentators warned that these changes would ignore readers' tastes at their peril. Tastes for the local, for allegiance and community needed to be heeded, as did the readers' ability to spot fake localism in recycled generalised content (Pilling 1998: 183–95).

A new prototype for the newspaper business and a new 'mindset' for local journalists

After that study, technological change gathered pace and Internet distribution became more powerful and much more widespread. A more radical strategy for the future of local papers was emerging – one that exploited the distribution potential of the Internet and involved changing the 'mindset' of local journalists. American media commentator Ken Auletta argued that the central quest of newspaper businesses in an age of digital convergence was not to perfect its print output but to search for synergy – to make profitable connections between the printed newspaper and other forms of media. He identified in the late 1990s what he believed to be the model for the newspaper company of the future – the *Chicago Tribune*. He proclaimed:

> *Tribune* has become a prototype for the cutting-edge newspaper company of the future ... its newsrooms are multimedia models with robotic cameras, digital audio and video equipment and a central command desk shared by editors from its TV stations, its 24-hour local cable news channel, its radio stations and its internet publications.
>
> (Auletta (2005) quoted in Lloyd (2005: W10))

Through this approach, the *Tribune* was successful both in gaining market share and cutting costs. A somewhat sceptical Auletta identified a shift in journalistic culture: '*Tribune*'s journalism is called content. And its editors and executives alike blather endlessly about synergy, brand, brand extension, content, branded content, information provider, partnering' (Auletta (2005) quoted in Lloyd (2005: W10).) Their 'blathering' clearly paid off; in 2000, two years after Auletta first published this view in an essay in *The New Yorker*, the *Tribune* acquired Times Mirror Group, publisher of the *Los Angeles Times*.

A similar cultural leap is being made by journalists on the *Manchester Evening News* (*MEN*) in England. They are familiar with the new culture identified by Auletta. They work in an organisation that has embraced such an approach and now go for training to the Newsplex multimedia and convergence centre at the University of South Carolina. They also train on their paper's city television station, Channel M. *MEN* editor Paul Horrocks explains that this training is to help them produce a multimedia portfolio: 'The purpose is to change the mindset of print journalists and teach them how to tell a story in a multi-media fashion, making the best of the Internet, television and video as well as print' (Astill 2005).

The *MEN* has similarities to the *Tribune*: it publishes three paid-for print editions, a free edition, a website and a television station. Video cameras and audio recorders are routinely used by reporters (or 'content-providers') and their video and audio clips are loaded onto the newspaper's website to enhance content. If a story is followed up for television, then elements of the televised story can also be added to the website. Readers are encouraged to comment on what they have found and these comments are then published. Editor Horrocks said: 'Print is still at the heart of the business but we need to understand how best to attract an audience, whatever the media portfolio, and then sell that audience to advertisers' (Astill 2005).

The rise of citizen journalists

The multimedia prototype described by Ken Auletta in the USA and managed by Paul Horrocks and others in England concentrates on producers exploiting the linkages between different media to maximise audiences. Other producers were introducing innovations to exploit a different potential of the new technology – the potential of the audience to be authors of 'content' as 'citizen journalists' (see Chapters 3 and 18).

There is a long tradition in local newspapers in Britain of volunteer contributors – typically from societies, sports associations and residents in the more remote 'patches' of the circulation area – but Korean journalist Oh Yeon Ho attracted international attention in 2002 when he took this idea a significant stage further by exploiting the potential of the Internet. He set up *OhmyNews*, an online newspaper that actually based its content on 'citizen reporters', whose contributions were edited by a handful of professional staff (Mahmud 2005: 1).

By 2005 *OhmyNews* was estimated to have 39,000 freelance contributors who originated 80 per cent of its content. Its full-time staff had grown to 55 and they produced the other 20 per cent. Ho also exploited the potential of the new technology to generate both audience feedback to content and cash flow at the same time. *OhmyNews* has a novel 'tip-jar' system which enables readers to pay authors a 'tip' when they approve of an article merely by clicking on their computer screen. One citizen journalist's article reaped tips of 30,000 dollars from readers. Ho's imaginative use of technology achieved two remarkable things: the mobilisation of thousands of newsgatherers to enrich content and a simple, instant interactive link between audience and content.

Not surprisingly, the rise of 'citizen journalists' at *OhmyNews* has inspired similar ventures elsewhere, including *iTalkNews* in San Francisco. Founder Elizabeth Lee said: '*OhmyNews* has provided a successful model that many citizen journalist sites are using as inspiration. But this is something that has been about to happen for a long time. When *OhmyNews* showed a way, people were ready to go' (Mahmud 2005: 1).

No comparable site has emerged in the UK, possibly because its well-developed local media already capture the potential of citizen journalism. British Broadcasting Corporation (BBC) radio journalist Matt Foster told the *Guardian*'s media section in August 2005:

> We do have a very strong and diverse media in this country and extremely developed local journalism. It's hard to see, then, what an equivalent of *OhmyNews* could offer that we can't get elsewhere. Plus the major media providers in Britain have been good at co-opting the idea of citizen journalism.
>
> (quoted in Mahmud (2005: 2); see Chapters 3, 15 and 18)

However, Ho's two central achievements: the mobilising of citizen journalists and his interactive link with the audience are widely admired and are seen as a model to emulate. An appeal for citizen journalists to join a new photographic agency based in Glasgow, called *Scoopt*, which would exploit the value of such amateur images of news stories, resulted in 1,200 amateur mobile phone photographers becoming members within a week.

Founder Kyle MacRae said: 'The media are profiting from these pictures and I would like to see the photographers profiting as well ... If you are walking around with a camera phone and something happens, you can get a great photo' (Ponsford 2005b: 9).

British local editors were enthusiastic about embracing new production methods. *Barnsley Chronicle* editor Robert Cockroft told fellow editors at their annual gathering that their publications – the local paper – should be 'the local content king'. They had to be very imaginative about how they conveyed news. His own organisation was investigating streaming video, but the key to their preeminence would be their ability to get closer to their readers than any rival organisations. The *Chronicle*'s biggest success story of the year was a special supplement called 'Dandy Dogs'. Cockroft said: 'The readers know you are getting close to them when you don't just visit their school and workplace, but their kennels too' (Astill 2005).

Nick Turner, deputy editor of the Carlisle *News and Star*, urged local papers to develop blogging in their patch. He said that locally based blogs or web-logs attached to papers could bring benefits. Papers should aim to 'head up the local blogging community'. His own paper had advertised for volunteer bloggers and had quickly established a local network which ranged from housewives to Members of Parliament.

> It gives you virtual district correspondents who have an emotional take on their patch. They are always available for case studies and will take part in any feature you suggest. They provide alternative voices from parts of the community not generally heard from in newspapers and they generate traffic to the newspaper's website.
>
> (Sargeson and Astill 2005)

The changing audience

If these journalists were concentrating on the supply side of their business, a formidable figure had focussed his attention on the demand side – the changing audience. Rupert Murdoch, in an address to American editors, urged journalists to appreciate a revolution among the audience: 'What is happening is, in short, a revolution in the way young people are accessing news'. Murdoch, who had been widely regarded as an Internet sceptic in the 1990s, said younger people were not choosing to get their news from the newspaper but from electronic platforms (Ponsford 2005a: 2).

'They don't want to rely on the morning paper for their up-to-date information', he said and he indicated a change in the way they want their news voiced: 'They don't want to rely on a God-like figure from above to tell them what's important'. He told an audience that included 'embedded readers': 'The data may show that young people aren't reading newspapers as much as their predecessors, but it doesn't show that they don't want news. In fact, they want a lot of news, just faster news of a different kind and delivered in a different way' (Ponsford 2005a: 2).

Murdoch advised editors to observe their teenage children closely:

> They want news on demand, continuously updated. They want a point of view about not just what happened but why it happened. They want news that speaks to them personally, that affects their lives. And we in this room – newspaper editors and journalists – are uniquely positioned to deliver that news. We have the experience, the brands, the resources, and the know-how to get it done.
>
> (Ponsford 2005a: 2)

He urged journalists to exploit their unique content: 'We have unique content to differentiate ourselves in a world where news is becoming increasingly commoditised. And most importantly we have a great new partner to help us reach this new consumer: the Internet' (Ponsford 2005a: 2).

However, print journalists needed to rethink their websites. They needed to move well beyond the current bland re-versioning of print stories: 'Instead it will need to offer compelling and relevant content: deep, deep local news; relevant national and international news; commentary and debate; gossip and humour' (Ponsford 2005a: 2).

News should be continuously updated. There should be space 'for conversation'. Bloggers would add a further dimension. 'What is required is a complete transformation of the way we think about our product', he said (Ponsford 2005a: 2).

He feared that too many editors and journalists were out of touch with their potential readers. In America trust has declined in both directions: fewer readers trust journalists, fewer journalists trust the public to make good decisions.

> This is a polite way of saying that reporters and editors think their readers are stupid. In any business, such an attitude toward one's customers would

not be healthy. But in the newspaper business, where we rely on people to come back to us each day, it will be disastrous if not addressed.

(Ponsford 2005a: 2)

Murdoch feared print journalists may be unable to make the necessary changes but if they could, then success online could actually improve printed newspapers. It was a 'monumental, once-in-a-generation opportunity' but, if seized, could lead to great reward. 'Success in the online world will, I think, beget greater success in the printed medium' (Ponsford 2005a: 2).

The new managing editor of one of the Northcliffe group's papers, the *Brentwood Gazette*, was determined to make changes and seize that opportunity. The attention of Matthew Holder, an experienced BBC online journalist as well as former print journalist, was firmly on his potential readers. Like Murdoch, he believed that future developments must be reader-driven:

Future websites will be dynamic and very much a two-way operation. We can get feedback, ideas and opinions from the readers, as well as pictures they may volunteer, which we can then feed into the newspaper. It allows the audience a greater say in the news agenda and enables us to tailor the product to what they want.

(Lagan 2005b: 9)

Newspaper websites had begun purely as a different delivery method for news that had already been gathered for print but now they would be much more dynamic: 'Reader interplay is the future for regional news reporting' (Lagan 2005b: 9).

Back to basics

However, not all high-profile editors were placing their faith in Internet exploitation. The pressures facing local newspapers in urban areas of Britain in 2005 were well illustrated by the challenge faced by the incoming editor of the *Birmingham Mail*, Steve Dyson. His response illustrates a faith in traditional local newspaper values to meet a changing world (Lagan 2005a: 11).

Circulation in Birmingham and the surrounding circulation area had declined remorselessly for 30 years. The *Mail* still enjoyed a potential readership of more than one million people in its circulation area but its sales had fallen from a peak of more than 300,000 in the 1970s to less than 100,000 in 2005 and were still falling.

Successive regimes had trimmed costs and cut journalists. Incoming editor Steve Dyson felt that this had resulted in a move away from localised content and a retreat into generalised content rather than localised news; he wanted to reverse this trend. He admired the way the local rival, Wolverhampton-based *Express & Star*, had retained its close local coverage, its large editorial staff and its circulation of more than 150,000.

Dyson's relaunch was hailed by the trade paper, *Press Gazette*, as a retro move, a return to tradition: 'Brummies go back to basics for £1million relaunch of evening tabloid'. Dyson was doubling the number of local editions, increasing local reporting staff and promising ultralocal coverage including listing all local court adjudications and planning applications. In addition, he was going to be an old-style, hands-on editor, who focussed his time on editing the paper: 'I have taken on this position on the condition that I am the editor. Management do not touch me for meetings until any given afternoon. It needs that focus and direction'. *Press Gazette* commented: 'Some of the key changes could be seen as a return to traditional values: an editor in charge of editing, grassroots reporting, strong campaigning and investing in editorial' (Lagan 2005a: 11).

If some of Dyson's planned changes seem old-fashioned, some were not, but were responses to changes that he saw in potential readers. The paper would have more colour and a more magazine-style appeal to women; its news coverage would be more positive and its news and features would be more emotive. Dyson said: 'We have to challenge ourselves to delve into the human side of it and pull more emotional strings' (Lagan 2005a: 11).

Yet Dyson's major proposed changes clearly appealed to a traditional mindset in journalists. One commentator applauding the moves in the letter pages of *Press Gazette* commented sardonically: 'Local news [in local papers] - that's novel' (Tait 2005: 19).

Conclusion

Both the scale and pace of changes facing local newspapers have increased. The pressures for change centre on two related factors: rapid developments in media technology and shifts in the media habits of the potential audience. First, the emergence and spread of new Internet-based media that can distribute news and advertising without printing and distributing a single copy is seen both as a threat and an opportunity by local journalists. Many local journalists are intent on embracing the ability of new technology to give their stories wider audience through the development of websites. They are increasingly becoming 'content producers' for a range of media. Their executives – now often managers rather than editors – focus on synergy 'across platforms'– including the Internet, local television and even 'podcasting' (the downloading of audio to iPods).

These changes focus on the supply side of the local news business – new sources of 'product' and new means of distribution. But they are partly driven by the second powerful factor, changes on the demand side – shifts in the behaviour of readers. The potential local news audience, especially its younger members, is turning away from print for its information and advertisements. This causes concern but at the same time, the new technology does create opportunity for much greater audience involvement and feedback. Editors can measure responses to individual stories – hits on their websites – to give themselves a surer feel of which stories are attracting interest. They are deliberately developing discussion forums and communities of bloggers on their websites to stimulate debate about local issues. Looked at more broadly, this concentration on involvement of audience is a shift in the balance of the relationship between local newspaper journalists and the readers. Internet optimists welcome the potential democracy; newspaper commentators warn that news can no longer be delivered from on high.

Amongst all this change, one high-profile editor, Steve Dyson, was returning to traditional local values – increasing local coverage and investing in local journalists to halt long-term decline in circulation. In addition, he was returning the paid-for evening paper to hands-on editing. For Dyson, adapting to change involved resisting the trend toward recycled, generalised content and going back to what he saw as the local paper's traditional values which focus on the ultralocal. In advocating this 'back to basics' approach, he was not alone. He could point to examples around the country where cultivating localism has served local paper businesses well. There were, paradoxically, examples of newspaper businesses developing by concentrating on local print news. They were less noticed than the evangelists of multimedia but they were quietly consolidating along traditional lines.

This chapter began with a futurologist's wake-up call to British regional journalists. Professor Scase had a two-edged message. First, he argued that newspapers in Britain had been complacent and risked losing their dominant position. This study suggests that far from being complacent, many local journalists, and at least one high-profile newspaper group, were very concerned and had begun to innovate energetically.

Second and more comfortingly, Professor Scase told his audience that in this rapidly changing world there was still a place for localism: 'Local issues become more important in the globalised world, making local newspapers more important' (Scase 2005). All of his audience will have been fervently hoping that he was right about this – that they could continue to cultivate and satisfy an appetite for the local news and that Viscount Rothermere had made an error in threatening to jettison local newspapers from his portfolio.

References

Astill, P. (2005) 'Local content and multi-media approach the way forward, say editors', *HoldtheFrontPage*, October.

Auletta, K. (2005) *Backstory: Inside the Business of News*, London: Penguin.

Greenslade, R. (2005) 'So what will we be wrapping our fish and chips in?', *Daily Telegraph*, 6 December, pp. B8–9.

Lagan, S. (2005a) 'Brummies go back to basics for £1million relaunch of evening tabloid', *Press Gazette*, 7 October, p. 11.

Lagan, S. (2005b) 'Reader interplay is the future for regional news reporting', *Press Gazette*, 11 November, p. 9.

Lloyd, J. (2005) 'The demise of print mirrors the decline of journalism, as companies transform into cost-cutting "content-providers"', *Financial Times*, 20 August.

Mahmud, S. (2005) 'Analysis: the rise of "citizen journalism"', *BBC Monitoring Media Services*, September.

Pilling, R. (1998) 'The changing role of the local journalist: from faithful chronicler of the parish pump to multi-skilled compiler of an electronic database', in Franklin, B. and Murphy, D. *Making the Local News: Local Journalism in Context*, London: Routledge, pp. 183–96.

Ponsford, D. (2005a) 'Journalists are out of touch with readers, says Murdoch', *Press Gazette*, 22 April.

Ponsford, D. (2005b) '"Citizen Journalism" agency signs up 1,200 snappers', *Press Gazette*, 12 August.

Rushe, D. and Kleinman, M. (2005) 'Flogging the local papers', *Sunday Times*, 4 December, Section 3, p. 5.

Sargeson, N. and Astill, P. (2005) 'Blogs bring benefits to local newspapers', *HoldtheFrontPage*, October.

Scase, R. (2005) 'Wake up to a New World', speech delivered to the Society of Editors, 17 October.

Tait, J. (2005) 'Local news – now there's a novel idea!', *Press Gazette*, 4 November, p. 19.

Chapter 11

Regulating the local press

Robert Pinker

Introduction

In this chapter I will start with a brief review of the role of the Press Complaints Commission (PCC) in its administration of the industry's Code of Practice, and how it seeks to reconcile the rights of freedom of expression and privacy with the claims of public interest. Thereafter, I will focus on describing how the Commission has progressed over the past decade in helping to create a new climate of voluntary Code compliance and how the Code of Practice has been kept up to date in response to new challenges and the impact of new legislation. Where appropriate, I will draw on examples of complaints against regional and local newspapers for illustrative purposes.

The PCC, its constitution and remit

The PCC was established in 1991 as a successor to the old Press Council. The Commission currently consists of 17 members. Ten of them, including the chairman, are lay or public members and seven are working editors. All appointments to the Commission and the Code Committee are subject to ratification by an independent Appointments Commission, which has a majority of lay members. The PCC itself is funded by a Press Standards Board of Finance – or Pressbof – which is an independent body responsible for collecting registration fees from across the entire industry. This arrangement ensures that, in the conduct of its business, the PCC is as constitutionally independent from the industry that funds its activities as it is from government.

The British system of press self-regulation is based on a clear-cut but complementary division of responsibilities between the industry and the PCC. The Code of Practice belongs to the industry, which is responsible for upholding its requirements and keeping it up to date. The Commission is responsible for administering and enforcing the Code. The PCC does not impose fines on publications that breach the Code. In all cases where an adjudication is made, it relies exclusively on moral censure. When a complaint is upheld, the offending news-paper or magazine is required to publish the Commission's critical adjudication in full and with due prominence. No publication has, so far, refused to do so – even in those cases where the editors in question remain convinced that they have not breached the Code.

Freedom of expression, privacy and the public interest

The Code of Practice sets out the principles and guidelines that the Commission applies in its handling of complaints and that editors and journalists are required to uphold.

Press self-regulation serves two main purposes. It protects press freedoms and it protects citizens from abuses of those freedoms by the press. Freedom of expression and privacy are both fundamental human rights but they can seldom, if ever, be treated as absolute rights because they so frequently come into conflict with each other. In seeking to reconcile these conflicts, regulatory bodies must also give due consideration to the claims of public interest.

The fact that such conflicts of principle occur so frequently explains why some form of press regulation is necessary. The dilemma that all democratic societies face is not one of choosing between regulation and no regulation at all but of choosing between two different kinds of regulation – the statutory or the self-regulatory options.

How these frequently competing claims are taken into account in the Code and reconciled in the process of adjudication is best illustrated by reference to complaints about privacy intrusion.

Two examples of complaints against local newspapers illustrate how the Commission balances the right to individual privacy against the right to freedom of expression and considerations of public interest. In 2001, a Mrs Noble complained that the *Jersey Evening Post* had published a letter from a government official which disclosed details of her rental payments in breach of Clause 3 (Privacy). The complaint was upheld on the grounds that the letter contained personal and private information of no public interest. The adjudication also served as a reminder that editors are responsible for all of their editorial content, including readers' letters (PCC Report No. 56/57, 2001–2).

In 2002, Ms Tomlinson, a convicted drug smuggler, complained under Clause 3 (Privacy) that the *Peterborough Evening Telegraph* had published photographs of the inside of her house. Normally such photographs would constitute a breach of the Code, but in this case they had been taken and supplied by the police. The Commission rejected the complaint on the grounds that there was a public interest in illustrating how the proceeds of the complainant's crimes had been spent (PCC Report No. 60/61, 2002–3).

There are two kinds of complaints, other than those involving privacy issues, against which editors can advance a public interest defence. The Code recognises that there may be occasions when payments by newspapers to witnesses in criminal trials and to criminals can be justified on grounds of public interest.

Trends in the pattern of complaints

The Code of Practice consists of 16 clauses and a statement defining public interest. Each clause lays down guidelines for editors on aspects of journalistic practice which might give rise to complaints about unethical conduct. The clauses can be conveniently grouped together under four main headings. The first of these – accuracy in reporting and opportunity to reply – has always accounted for the majority of the complaints received, investigated and ruled upon. In 1997, it accounted for 70 per cent of all rulings made. Since then, the figure has averaged around 60 per cent.

Some typical examples of complaints from local people about their local newspapers include a woman who complained under Clause 1 (Accuracy) that the *South Wales Evening Post* had wrongly reported that her estranged husband had been involved in a fight with her new boyfriend. She did not have a boyfriend and the incident had involved a neighbour. The newspaper published a correction six weeks after the original story appeared. The complaint was upheld on the grounds that inaccuracies must be corrected promptly and that the correction ought to have included an apology (PCC Report No. 58/59, 2002). Another woman complained under Clause 1 and Clause 5 (Grief and Shock) that the *News & Star* had insensitively reported that her husband – a local GP – had died on the morning before the details had been confirmed. The complaints were rejected on the grounds that the newspaper was entitled to report the death of a local figure, that it had done so with sensitivity, and also taken care to distinguish between comment, conjecture and fact (PCC Report No. 55, 2001).

The second group of clauses cover privacy and other related issues including harassment and taking photographs in private places, intrusions into grief and shock, the privacy of children, children who are victims or witnesses in cases involving sex offences, children who are witnesses to or victims of crime, intrusions into the lives of hospital patients and protecting the innocent relatives or friends of persons convicted or accused of crimes. Complaints about privacy-related issues accounted for 21 per cent of rulings made in 1997. Since then, the figure has averaged around 24 per cent.

In 2002, the Commission upheld a complaint from the father of a 12-year-old victim of crime. This was the Commission's first adjudication under the new subclause of what was then Clause 10 and is now Clause 9. The subclause states that 'particular regard should be paid to the potentially vulnerable position of children who are witnesses to, or victims of crime'. In this case, the *Eastbourne Argus* had identified the complainant's daughter – who had been the victim of an attempted kidnap – in an interview with another victim. Sufficient regard to the vulnerability of the girl had not been paid by the newspaper, and the complaint was upheld (PCC Report No. 58/59, 2002).

In the same year, the Commission upheld a complaint under what is now Clause 4 (Harassment) from a Mr Tunbridge who complained that the *Dorking Advertiser* had published a photograph of him without his consent. He was, at the time, taking afternoon tea with a companion in a quiet tearoom. The complaint was upheld on the grounds that Mr Tunbridge was in a place where he had a reasonable expectation of privacy and that such places could include both public and private property (PCC Report No. 58/59, 2002).

Discrimination is the third most frequent cause of complaints. In 1997, complaints about discrimination accounted for just over 6 per cent of all rulings made. In 2000, this figure rose to just over 10 per cent, largely as a result of press reporting on immigration and asylum issues. Thereafter, in the wake of the attack on the New York World Trade Center and other subsequent acts of terrorism, the proportion of complaints about discrimination rose to nearly 20 per cent in 2003. They currently account for 16 per cent of all rulings made but this figure has been rising again since the recent London bombings.

It should be noted that Clause 13 is designed to protect 'individuals' from prejudiced remarks in articles about them. It does, however, attract a very large number of complaints from people who simply wish to register their disapproval of a news item that does not personally affect them or that consists of general remarks about 'groups' or 'categories' of people. When allowance is made for these kinds of multiple complaints about the same article, the number of discrete issues complained about under Clause 13 falls from nearly 20 per cent to just 6 per cent of the total in 2003. Only 24 of these complaints had to be investigated in 2003.

Since 1995, only four discrimination complaints against local newspapers have been taken all the way to adjudication and only one of these was upheld. In 1997, a Mr Bishko complained that the *Evening Standard* had made discriminatory references to his religion in an article about him. The Commission upheld his complaint on the grounds that, in the particular context of the story, the description of the complainant's religion could be construed as pejorative (PCC Report No. 40, 1997).

The fourth group of Clauses covers issues related to newsgathering which include the use of listening devices and resort to subterfuge or misrepresentation, financial journalism, the protection of confidential sources of information, witness payments in criminal trials and payment to criminals. In 1997, all of the complaints on which rulings were made under these clauses accounted for just under 3 per cent of the total. They currently account for a little over 6 per cent. The greater part of this increase is explained by a small but possibly significant rise in the number of complaints about the use of listening devices and resort to subterfuge.

In 2003, the Commission upheld a complaint under what was then Clause 17 (Payment to Criminals) from a Mr McInnes against *The Daily Record*. The newspaper had paid a criminal for information in the genuine belief that it would reveal material of public interest. Although it subsequently revealed nothing of public interest, the newspaper went ahead and published it. The Commission found that the clause on payment to criminals provided insufficient guidance to editors on how to proceed in such matters. It, therefore, upheld the complaint as a technical breach of the Code but did not censure the newspaper (PCC Report No. 62/63, 2003).

The evolution of the PCC

The growth of voluntary Code compliance

The growth of voluntary Code compliance on the part of editors is a better measure of effective press self-regulation than the frequency with which Press Councils have to uphold complaints and impose sanctions. Over the years, the Commission has developed two complementary procedures for the resolution of complaints. Some are resolved by means of informal conciliation and others go all the way to a formal adjudication. Cases that go all the way to adjudication do so either because there are *prima facie* grounds for believing that the breach is potentially so serious that an informal apology, published letter or voluntary correction would not be a sufficient remedy or because the editors concerned are convinced that they have not breached the Code and that a formal adjudication will vindicate them.

When the Commission started work in 1991, its relations with many editors were highly confrontational. Every complaint was the subject of prolonged negotiation and dispute. With the passage of time, they have become much more willing to make voluntary corrections and apologies for breaches of the Code. This change in editorial attitudes provides a crucially important measure of the extent to which the Commission and the industry have created a new climate of conciliation and voluntary compliance in the resolution of complaints.

In 2004, the Commission concluded investigations into 333 cases under Clause 1 (Accuracy) and Clause 2 (Opportunity to Reply) that raised possible breaches of the Code. Out of this number, the editors offered appropriate remedial action to resolve the complaint in all but six cases. This means that in 98 per cent of these cases the newspapers offered appropriate remedies that were, in effect, also opportunities to reply. Almost 60 per cent of these cases were eventually settled by agreement with the complainants and resolved to their satisfaction.

In the same year, the Commission investigated 218 complaints made under the nine clauses relating to privacy. Just over half of these cases were found to involve a possible breach of the Code. In all but two of them, the Commission's staff negotiated proportionate and appropriate offers from the newspapers to resolve the matter.

The average time taken to deal with all complainants received has now fallen to 17 days. The average for cases in which a ruling was required is currently 37 days. For cases that require full investigation, it is currently 60 days. These figures compare very favourably with those of other regulatory bodies.

What sort of outcomes do complainants want from a complaints authority? Few, if any, successful complainants go on to seek further redress in the courts of law – if only because they know that the legal option can be ruinously expensive and take months or years before it is concluded. What complainants want is a prompt apology, a correction or an opportunity to reply. Conciliation and voluntary compliance on the part of editors make it much easier to provide complainants with a service that is not only free and fair but swift in its conduct of business.

Very few editors knowingly and wilfully breach the Code. Nearly 60 per cent of all complaints received are about inaccuracy and most of these are the result of carelessness or a failure to distinguish between comment, conjecture and fact. This, in large part, explains why editors respond so promptly and offer a correction when errors of this kind are drawn to their attention.

Nevertheless, in cases of complaint where editors are convinced that they have not breached the Code, they will always put up a vigorous defence of their position and invest much time and effort in doing so. They would not respond in this way if they did not care about having to publish a critical adjudication against themselves. All the evidence suggests that they care very much. Similarly, editors are prepared to offer prompt corrections and apologies when shown to be necessary because they take the Code seriously and are firmly committed to upholding its provisions.

The success of the Commission and the industry in creating a new climate of conciliation and conflict resolution has seldom been accorded the recognition that it merits. When relevant measures of effectiveness are applied across the whole range of the Commission's work, the true scale of that success becomes evident. Freedom of expression has been protected and the press has learned to exercise that freedom more responsibly. Most importantly, serious breaches of the Code occur far less frequently than they did 10 years ago and when people do complain, they receive a service that is readily accessible, cost-free, efficient and prompt in delivering a resolution or making an adjudication.

Regional and local newspapers have established a very creditable track record in their willingness to resolve complaints whenever possible by means of informal conciliation. The following examples illustrate the kinds of complaint that can be resolved in this way.

A Mrs Bradley complained under Clause 3 (Privacy) that the publication in the *Chester Chronicle* of her daughter's telephone number in a readers' letters column without her consent had intruded into her privacy. The editor wrote personally to the complainant asking her to pass on his apologies for any distress that had been caused to her daughter. He also gave an assurance that the number would not appear again (PCC Report No. 58/59, 2002).

A Mrs Akhtar complained under Clause 1 (Accuracy) that the *Birmingham Evening Mail* had wrongly claimed – on two occasions – that she had pleaded guilty to a charge of racial harassment. In fact, she had strongly denied the charge and the case was formally dismissed. In order to remedy the situation, the newspaper published a wording proposed by the complainant along with her photograph (PCC Report No. 60/61, 2002–3).

Responding to change and updating the Code

Over the past decade, the Code of Practice has been kept under continuous review and updated as required by the Code Committee. Some revisions were made in response to deficiencies exposed in the process of investigating and adjudicating complaints. Other were made either in response to new legislation or in order to obviate the need for further legislation. In this necessarily brief review, I will focus on those changes which I think have had the most significant and lasting influence on the evolution of the Code's remit and requirements.

The Commission started the new decade with the publication of a Complainants' Charter in which it set out a list of service targets against which it would measure its future performance. The targets included improving speed of response in dealing with enquiries and complaints, improving accessibility for all who needed to complain and appointing an internal Charter Officer to investigate complaints about poor quality of service.

The first comprehensive review of the Code took place in 1997, shortly after the death of Diana, Princess of Wales. This review coincided with the introduction of new legislation designed to incorporate the provisions of the EU Data Protection Directorate and the European Convention on Human Rights into UK law.

Under the provisions of the revised Code, the clause on harassment was rewritten in order to ban obtaining information or pictures by means of persistent pursuit. Other significant changes were made at the same time. Digital manipulations of photographs with intent to mislead were banned. The definitions of privacy and private places were clarified and broadened. The protection of children's privacy rights was extended beyond the age of 16 to cover the whole period while they were still at school. Payments to children, their parents or guardians for any information relating to their own welfare or that of any other children was prohibited unless they could be shown to be in the child's interests. Editors were required to provide a justification for any information they published about the private life of a child other than the fame, notoriety or position of his or her parents or guardians. In the past, the Code required editors to show due sensitivity when information was being sought from people experiencing grief and shock. This requirement was extended to include the wording of any news item or story that was subsequently published. As might be expected, the majority of complaints about intrusions into grief and shock are made about reports on inquests published in local newspapers. Very few of these complaints are upheld.

The decision to incorporate the provisions of the European Convention and other EU Directives into UK law made it all the more necessary to develop closer working relationships with government. The requirements of the Convention were incorporated under the provisions of the Human Rights Act in 1998. At the time when this legislation came before Parliament, the Commission and the industry were greatly concerned about its potentially damaging impact on the right to freedom of expression and the possibility that it might be used in the courts to introduce a law of privacy by the 'back door'. The government listened to these concerns and agreed to amend the legislation by introducing a new Clause 12, which provided an important safeguard by emphasising the right to freedom of expression. The clause also highlighted the significance of 'any relevant privacy code' which clearly included the Commission's Code of Practice.

The Data Protection Act incorporated the provisions of the EU Data Protection Directive into UK law in 1998. In its original form, the Act would have classified as private information large amounts of data that were not intrinsically private in nature. As such, the Act would have posed a substantial threat to press freedom. After some months of negotiation with ministers and civil servants, the government agreed to an amendment which reconciled the rights and obligations of newspapers and magazines to report on matters of public interest with the privacy rights of individual citizens.

The amendment allowed editors to advance a public interest defence when faced with an action by the Data Protection Commissioner on the grounds that what they had published complied with a Code of Practice 'designated' by Parliament for the purposes of the Act. This was the first time that the Commission's Code had been 'designated' in this way. A new subclause was added to the public interest statement in the following year which recognised that there was 'a public interest in freedom of expression itself'. This subclause was added in order to make the Code consistent with the requirements of the Human Rights Act 1998 which, like the Data Protection Act, was also derived from the provisions of the European Convention on Human Rights.

The Commission was also successful in negotiating a similar change in the provisions of the Financial Services and Markets Act 2000 during its passage through Parliament. In effect, the government agreed to exclude financial journalists from the provisions of the Act if they were subject to the requirements of the Code of Practice. The Commission subsequently published a Best Practice Note of Guidance on financial journalism after consultations with the industry. In this respect, it is worth noting that the Code's requirements on financial journalism have remained unchanged since 1991. The only serious breach occurred in 1999 when the Commission launched its own investigation into a share-tipping scandal at the *Daily Mirror*. The breach was drawn to the attention of the publisher and the newspaper had to publish a lengthy critical adjudication with due prominence (PCC Report No. 50, 2000).

The Commission's success in negotiating such important amendments to the provisions of these three statutes during their passage through Parliament marked a turning point in the history of its relations with government. Taken together, they demonstrated the growth of government confidence in the effectiveness of the voluntary Code of Practice and of the Commission in its administration of the Code.

In 2002, the Commission raised a complaint of its own volition against a number of national newspapers that had made offers of payment to witnesses in the trial of a school teacher for indecency. Following its investigation, the Commission ruled – on grounds of public interest – that the payments had not breached the Code. Nevertheless, the Lord Chancellor announced shortly after this adjudication that he intended to introduce legislation to ban witness payments by law because such payments might prejudice the course of justice. The Commission and the industry claimed that there was no evidence to suggest that new legislation was necessary and that the Lord Chancellor's intentions could be more effectively realised by clarifying the requirements of the Code on this matter. After extensive discussions between the Commission, the Code Committee and members of his Department, the Lord Chancellor agreed not to legislate. The clause on payment to witnesses was radically revised and strengthened in a matter of weeks.

Permanent evolution

Sir Christopher Meyer took up his appointment as the Commission's new chairman shortly after the launch of a major inquiry into privacy and media intrusion by the Culture, Media and Sport Select Committee of the House of Commons.

The Select Committee started its inquiry in December 2002. The Commission completed and submitted its 250-page response in February 2003. The challenge facing the Commission was to demonstrate that over the previous decade it had succeeded in raising standards of journalistic practice, that the Code of Practice was being upheld by the industry and that the great majority of complaints which raised a possible breach of the Code were being resolved through mediation and voluntary compliance on the part of the editors.

When the Select Committee reported later in the year, it made a number of proposals for enhancing the effectiveness of the Commission's work, but its overall conclusions were that 'standards of press behaviour, the Code and the performance of the Press Complaints Commission have improved over the last decade'. The Select Committee went on to acknowledge that 'the PCC [has] the confidence of the industry', that there was a great deal of praise for the staff of the Commission from complainants, and that PCC jurisprudence on privacy was 'more developed than that of any other regulator'. It also noted that 'the vast bulk of the valid complaints presented' to the Commission were resolved without having to resort to formal adjudication and that these resolutions were achieved 'with great speed' (House of Commons – Culture, Media and Sport Committee 2003: 3, 10, 21).

Since then, the momentum of change in response to the Select Committee's report has been sustained by both the Commission and the Code Committee. In his first major speech made shortly after his appointment, Sir Christopher Meyer outlined the components of a forward-looking policy of 'permanent evolution' directed towards raising still further the quality of the Commission's services to the general public and its authority and national profile as a regulatory body.

Over the past two years, significant progress has already been made in implementing this new programme of 'permanent evolution'. First, in order to reinforce the Commission's manifest independence as a regulatory body, the majority of lay members over press members was raised to a ratio of 10:7 and their appointments were made open to public competition. Second, the Commission's handling of complaints has been made subject to the scrutiny of an external Charter Compliance Panel and an independent Charter Commissioner. The Panel scrutinises all aspects of the Commission's handling of complaints, reviews as many complaints files as it deems necessary and publishes an annual report with advice on how customer service might be improved. The Charter

Commissioner provides dissatisfied complainants with an opportunity to have the Commission's handling of their complaint reviewed by an independent assessor.

Third, new procedures have been introduced in order to keep the Code of Practice up to date and effective as an evolving document. The Code Committee agreed to undertake an annual 'audit' of its provisions and to publish a handbook designed to assist editors in their interpretation of the Code. *The Editors' Codebook*, written by Ian Beales, the Code Committee's Secretary, was published in 2005 (Beales 2005).

In 2004, the Code Committee completed and published another major revision of the Code's provisions. It extended the remit of the Code to include online versions of publications and the requirements of its Privacy Clause to include digital communications. A new clause regulating the use of clandestine devices was added. The clauses on harassment, intrusion into grief and shock, the protection of children and access to hospitals were clarified and made stricter. The clause on payment to criminals was also revised in order to ban the publication of material obtained by such payments in cases where a public interest could not be demonstrated.

The fourth set of initiatives in the 'permanent evolution' agenda have focused on raising the Commission's profile and public awareness of its work. The new Code of Practice now requires editors to include a headline reference to the PCC when publishing critical adjudications. The Commission has also launched an ongoing programme of Open Day meetings throughout the United Kingdom to which members of the public, including local politicians, editors and journalists are invited. Audiences submit questions on any subject related to press ethics and the work of the Commission and people with specific problems or concerns can seek advice on a one-to-one confidential basis. So far, successful Open Day meetings have been held in Edinburgh, Cardiff and Belfast and others are being planned.

Conclusion

In order to succeed, an independent Press Council must win and retain the trust of the industry it regulates and the general public it serves. It must also be able to convince both government and the judiciary that self-regulation is more effective in dealing with complaints about unethical press conduct than statutory regulation or seeking redress in the courts of law.

How does a newly established Council set about achieving these objectives? First, and most obviously, it strives continually to improve the quality of the service it provides. It makes itself easily accessible to complainants, editors and other interested parties. It handles complaints and makes adjudications with efficiency, speed and fairness. It must always be manifestly even-handed in its dual tasks of protecting press freedoms and protecting the public from abuses of those freedoms by the press.

Second, a successful Press Council stays alert and responsive to changes in public opinion and to the pattern and character of the complaints it receives. It must be equally responsive to changes in the law that have implications for the practice of self-regulation. Responsiveness means that the Code of Practice must be kept under continuous review and updated as required. It must be especially prompt and pertinent in its response to complaints that have exposed weaknesses and oversights in the wording and provisions of the Code. It must be just as watchful for new government initiatives and legislation that might have adverse implications for freedom of expression.

From its inception, the Commission has worked unremittingly towards achieving these objectives. The growth of voluntary Code compliance is not a topic that makes headline news. Nevertheless, it is one of the best measures of successful press self-regulation and it could not have happened without the support of the industry across the whole range of the national and local press. Celebrity adjudications are far more likely to be reported than the fact that well over 90 per cent of all complaints are made by so-called ordinary people and almost all of them are resolved by voluntary conciliation.

References

Beales, I. (2005) *The Editors' Codebook*, Newspaper Publishers Association *et al.*

House of Commons – Culture, Media and Sport Committee (2003) *Privacy and Media Intrusion, Fifth Report of Session 2002–2003, Vol. 1 Report*, House of Commons, HC 458–1.

Part 3

Local newspapers:
exploring the range

Chapter 12

The alternative local press

Tony Harcup

The first issue of *Leeds Other Paper* I ever saw was number 20, back in September 1975. It was typical of the alternative local press of the period: 18 A4 pages produced on electric typewriters and Letraset with a few post-hippy graphics thrown in, printed on a second-hand offset litho machine, collated and folded by hand, and distributed personally to those newsagents who could be persuaded to stock it. If the style was rough and ready, the content was a revelation to anyone sceptical about a commercial press that called itself a watchdog while acting like a lapdog. Take the front page, which juxtaposed two stories: the destruction of local working-class communities in the path of motorway construction, and the disruption of a cricket test match by protesters who dug up part of the wicket. The fact that a park had been bulldozed to make way for the self-styled 'motor-way city of the seventies', and that the park had included a cricket pitch, prompted the headline '£10 million damage to Holbeck wicket ... Headingley also hit (damage £5)'. The stories were covered in two detailed double-page spreads inside that certainly took an alternative approach to the laws of defama-tion and contempt of court. Room was also found for a critique of the 'hysteri-cal' way mainstream media covered the story of the campaigners against an alleged miscarriage of justice who had damaged the Headingley pitch.

Inside there were also articles about a children's play-scheme, staff cuts at the city's swimming pools, a woman's battle with her local Social Security office, a police raid on a nightclub, the censorship of library books on political or moral grounds (complete with a leaked copy of the 'restricted list') and several community campaigns against commercial developments. Accompanying the alternative news were features such as book reviews, a legal advice column, read-ers' letters, a recipe for brewing your own beer and rudimentary listings. From the radical message of its front page to the free listing of campaigns, clinics and co-ops, *Leeds Other Paper* (*LOP* to its friends) served a readership that was alienated from mainstream media. And its readership need not remain passive, as a state-ment on page two invited a more active stance:

> We publish *Leeds Other Paper* because we hope people will find it useful and interesting and because we enjoy doing it. We are not aligned to any particular political party but try to support groups and individuals struggling to take control over their own lives – whether it's in the factory, the housing estate, or the home ... If you like the paper and want to make it better or help us get it out to more people, we'd be pleased to hear from you ... We have weekly meetings every Monday evening, and new people are always welcome.
>
> (*Leeds Other Paper* 1975)

I went along, wrote a few stories and soon found myself taking part in open editorial meetings that were often unwieldy and occasionally fractious but always a fascinating learning experience. Every article, every sentence, every word would be passed around, discussed, and approved, rejected or rewritten there and then. Having a roomful of people read your copy and say 'this is boring', 'I think you're wrong and here's why', or occasionally 'that's interesting', was the sort of journalistic training that money could not buy.

Who benefits and who loses?

This experience was far from unique. From the late 1960s through the 1970s and into the 1980s, alternative local newspapers sprang up throughout the UK, drawing from and reporting on the community politics and/or social movements that emerged during this period. Some of the best-known titles included: *Aberdeen People's Press*, *Alarm* (Swansea), *Angell* (South London), *Birmingham Free Press*, *Bradford Banner*, *Brighton Voice*, *Bristol Voice*, *Bury Metro News*, *Bush News* (Shepherd's Bush, London), *Calder Valley Press*, *Cardiff People's Press*, *Chapeltown News* (Leeds), *City Issues* (Sheffield), *City Wise* (Nottingham), *Coventry News*, *Durham Street Press*, *East End News* (London), *Exeter Flying Post*, *Gateshead Street Press*, *Glasgow News*, *Grass Eye* (Manchester), *Hackney People's Press* (London), *Huddersfield Hammer*, *Hull News*, *Islington Gutter Press* (London), *Lancaster Free Press*, *Leeds Other Paper*, *Leigh People's Paper*, *Liverpool Free Press*, *Manchester Free Press*, *Manchester Women's Paper*, *Mole Express* (Manchester), *New Manchester Review*, *Northern Star* (Leeds), *Nottingham Voice*, the *Other Paper* (Burton-on-Trent), *Pak-O-Lies* (Liverpool), *Peninsula Voice* (Cornwall), the *Post* (Hull), *Rochdale Alternative Paper* (*RAP*), *Sheep Worrying*, *Sheffield Free Press*, *Spen Valley Spark*, *Street Press* (Birmingham), *Styng* (Barnsley), *Tameside Eye*, *Tuebrook Bugle* (Liverpool), *York Free Press* and *West Highland Free Press*.

'The most successful ones were somehow the most local', explained Dave Bartlett of *RAP* (quoted in Dickinson (1997: 101)). Even the Royal Commission on the Press (1977: 40) noticed something was afoot:

A multiplicity of alternative publications suggests dissatisfaction with an insufficiently diverse established press, and an unwillingness or inability on the part of major publications to provide space for the opinions of small minorities. On this view, the alternative press provides at least some of the diversity lacking among stable and respectable publications.

Some lasted barely a handful of issues, others survived more than a decade; sales ranged from a few hundred to several thousand. The majority were monthly, run either by informal collectives or workers' co-operatives. A study for the Minority Press Group found that such papers emphasise:

> the question of who benefits and who loses from any particular decision, whether a hospital closure or a housing scandal, and show what the effects and sufferings are to people in the area. They also provide local oppositional forces with an otherwise unavailable platform for their views.
>
> (Aubrey *et al.* 1980: 16)

Such papers utilised as 'primary sources' people who, according to Franklin and Murphy (1991: 126), tended to be 'marginalised by the usual process of news production'. Instead of doing the police and fire calls, or regurgitating the opinions of the local Establishment, the alternative local press reported the views and actions of people living on housing estates, of those involved in community groups, of rank-and-file trade union activists, the unemployed, and those active within the women's and gay movements and the black communities. They were seen as parish magazines of the dispossessed (Harcup 1994: 3).

It would be wrong to talk of the alternative local press as a homogeneous category as, with open editorial policies and a shifting population of contributors, an alternative paper could change its style and direction within weeks, even within the same issue. But most shared an ethos that one of the occasional alternative press conferences described as:

> Local, anti-racist, anti-sexist, politically on the left, overtly rather than covertly political, not produced for profit, editorially free of the influence of advertisers, run on broadly collective principles ... Most alternative newspapers are small, their existence precarious. With one or two notable exceptions their circulations are in the hundreds rather than the thousands. But this tells us nothing about their influence nor their value. As virtually all the mass media are in the political centre or on the right, the voice of the local alternative newspaper is an important counterweight. Small need not mean insignificant.
>
> (National Conference of Alternative Papers 1984: 1)

The same conference also discussed how to cover industrial issues and get away from the predictable 'one closure, two marches' in every issue. A sympathetic industrial reporter from a commercial evening newspaper advised alternative journalists to 'capitalise on trade union suspicion of the straight press and spell out the links between job losses and their knock-on effect ... Fill in the gaps the straight press leaves, and redress the imbalance by setting a broader context' (National Conference of Alternative Papers 1984: 2). One suggestion was to compare how employers tended to benefit while employees suffered during closures and redundancies, a familiar story in those Thatcherite days. Particularly adept at keeping tabs on local business chiefs and the powers-that-be was *RAP*, which developed a detailed microfiche and card index enabling it to investigate those running the town in which its readers lived and worked. A decision was taken by the *RAP* collective to personalise stories as far as possible. They explained why:

> It is precisely that aspect which explains much of the appeal of the straight press. But the 'alternative' nature of our use of this technique lies in the fact that its targets come from a different social class to those typically attacked by the other press. This gives the paper its bite and provides figures that readers can recognise, while seeing them in a new perspective. An average issue of *RAP* will contain over 50 representatives of the local bourgeoisie. The basic recipe is then topped up with features or special investigations. We have covered in depth, and from the alternative angle, a wide range of local institutions: the Rotary Club – membership, connections, activities; the Magistrates Bench – names, ages, political affiliations and the names of the secret committee which chooses them; the local churches ... the death industry; estate agents; bookmakers; the health service etc.
>
> (Aubrey *et al.* 1980: 71–3)

Investigative journalism from the grassroots

Although a few papers such as *Liverpool Free Press* (Whitaker 1981) and *Manchester Free Press* (Dickinson 1997: 98) had been established by journalists working on a local rag who felt the need for an alternative outlet, most were like *RAP* or *LOP*: produced by people with no formal journalistic training or background. Despite – or because of – this position outside the norms of journalistic practice, such papers were capable of genuine revelation. As Hanna (2005: 15) notes: '[T]he grassroots nature of their experiences and contacts, their specialized pool of knowledge and unconventional "take" on the world mean those involved in alternative media sometimes uncover scandals or raise broad issues subsequently pursued by mainstream media'. One example was *LOP*'s investigation into the use of carcinogenic chemicals at a local dye-works. Whereas mainstream media tended to notice health and safety stories only when there was a disaster, or at least a body, *LOP* exposed potential health risks before even the workers or their trade unions were aware of them. This was made possible by the fact that the reporter had previously studied textile chemistry, enabling him to make sense of technical documentation that had been released only in the United States. The story later became the basis of a television documentary produced by Channel Four, with the help of *LOP*.

Other examples of investigative journalism in *LOP* included exposing the government's civil defence bunkers at the height of the Cold War; being the first to publish details from the then secret 'Protect and Survive' instructions on surviving nuclear attack; exposing mortgage lenders who discriminated against inner-city areas; the mysterious death of nurse Helen Smith; land deals involving Freemasons; allegations of brutality in mental hospitals; fascist groups' claims to be working with black Muslims; the secret training in the UK of military personnel from the Chilean dictatorship; the right-wing 'blacklisting' agency the Economic League; conflicts of interest within the government-appointed Leeds Development Corporation; the antics of a 'radical right' Tory administration at Bradford Council; and the contamination of hundreds of houses in the Armley area of Leeds with asbestos. Not a bad record for a perpetually cash-strapped newspaper whose journalists learned their trade as they went along.

A short-lived forerunner called the *Other Paper* (1969) had declared in its first issue: 'We are an alternative news service, a socialist news service. But we aren't quite strong enough to have any other name as yet'. Yet its successor became one of the great survivors of the alternative local press. *LOP* hit the streets in January 1974 – during the State of Emergency imposed during Prime Minister Edward Heath's ill-fated battle with the miners – produced by a group of mostly ex-students who were active in community and anarchist/libertarian politics, making use of the cheap and relatively easy to run offset litho printing presses that became available in the late 1960s (Aubrey *et al.* 1980: 6). The £150 required to buy the first press had been raised by jumble sales, benefit events and a levy of sixpence a week paid by people keen to see an alternative to the conservative local and regional press. *LOP* went on to be published 820 times, first monthly, then fortnightly and later weekly, before closing down exactly 20 years later (Harcup 1994). Initially staffed by people signing on the dole or giving up spare time, from 1978 *LOP* was run as a formal workers' co-operative with (low) paid staff funded by income from sales, advertising, commercial printing, typesetting, and (briefly) creative use of the government's Job Creation Scheme. Unpaid labour and people dropping in off the streets offering to help continued to play a vital role throughout most of the paper's life.

There was no editor and, until near the end, *LOP*'s editorial meetings were open to staff, contributors and readers alike. This 'prefigurative' method of organisation (Atton 2002: 18, 154), involving 'horizontal communication' among producers and audience (Atton 1999: 73), was reflected in the paper's content. This was articulated in an internal discussion paper entitled 'Views on the news': '[P]olitically, a good story for me is one that reinforces the ability of the mass of people to do things for themselves and decreases their reliance on others (especially in work and in the community)' (Leeds Alternative Publications 1980s undated: 1). *LOP*'s news agenda was constructed in opposition to what the paper's workers saw as mainstream journalism's shallowness. Whereas traditional reporters too often seemed content to get a 'line' or an 'angle', *LOP* contributors were encouraged to cover issues in both depth and breadth:

> We are committed to doing justice to the subjects we cover. This means well-researched, in-depth articles often and *LOP* stories are longer on average than those in the commercial press ... We should be conscious of the need to slow down our readers – to reverse the in-one-ear-out-the-other process – and create lasting impressions.
>
> (Leeds Alternative Publications 1980s undated: 2–3)

Sometimes this in-depth approach could result in thousands of predictable words about yet another damp house, accompanied by a blurred photograph of a miserable tenant pointing to an indiscernible dark patch in the corner of a dark room. At other times it meant worthy pieces about faraway international events with tangential local connections. It could certainly be a grim read on occasions. As one reader commented in a questionnaire: 'My mum finds it so depressing she barely looks at it'. But at other times *LOP* could produce uplifting copy about people involved in struggle, from the revolt of low-paid public sector workers in 1978–9 (the 'Winter of Discontent') and the miners' strike against pit closures in 1984–5, to the establishment of refuges for battered women and council tenants turning the tables on a council chief by dumping uncollected rubbish on his desk.

The contrasting approaches to sources and stories adopted by mainstream and alternative media, even when ostensibly covering the same event, are illustrated by comparing how the inner-city riots of 1981 were reported by the commercial *Yorkshire Evening Post* (*YEP*) and by *LOP* (Harcup 2003). In the *YEP* the riots were reported as a straightforward 'law and order' story, with prominence given to the explanations of elite sources such as senior police officers, politicians, and magistrates, using words such as 'mobs', 'mayhem', 'hooliganism' and 'copycat', along with a familiar claim that outside agitators had stage-managed the violence (Harcup 2003: 363–4). But for *LOP* it was more complicated than lawless youths on the rampage, and the paper framed events within a context of poverty, unemployment, dead-end jobs, low pay, alienation, racist attacks and aggressive policing. The elite sources and official explanations that featured so prominently in the *YEP* were almost entirely absent from *LOP*, which instead quoted at length from anonymous witnesses on the streets and even from conversations overheard in the 'kangaroo courts' that dealt with those arrested (Harcup 2003: 364–6). Although perhaps neither paper told the whole story, it could be argued that the material in *LOP* provided an important counterbalance to the hegemonic viewpoint of mainstream media.

'There is no alternative'

However, a combination of counter-hegemonic journalism and the development of a comprehensive 'what's on' listings guide only rarely edged sales of *LOP* above the 2,500 mark. One street survey carried out by the paper's volunteers found that 70 per cent of those questioned in Leeds city centre had not heard of *LOP* even though it was on sale in most newsagents in the area at the time. In 1991 the paper's name was changed to *Northern Star*; a move prompted primarily by the (ultimately futile) hope of boosting sales in the rest of West Yorkshire by dropping the Leeds tag, but which also located the paper within a long tradition of what has been referred to as 'insurgent journalism' (Curran and Seaton 2003: 16). *Northern Star* had been the name of a Chartist newspaper published in Leeds in the 1830s (Cole and Postgate 1961: 283) that had itself taken the name from a paper published by the Belfast Society of the United Irishmen at the end of the nineteenth century (Baker 2005: 377). The *Northern Star* of the 1830s declared its intention to 'disseminate, steadily and consistently, the light of truth' into what was otherwise 'a darksome and gloomy hemisphere' (*Northern Star* 1838); and that was pretty much how it felt in Thatcher's Britain too.

But, just as the first *Northern Star* did not survive beyond the Irish rebellion of 1798, and the Chartist *Northern Star* could not outlive the period of working-class agitation for the People's Charter in the mid-nineteenth century, so the tide eventually went out on the late-twentieth-century version of the paper. The waves of community, social and workplace activism on which *LOP* had depended for its subject matter, its readership and its supply of volunteers, eventually ebbed. In its quest for survival, *Northern Star* joined the rest of the press in chasing a younger readership and gradually became more of a 'what's on' guide featuring cultural and 'lifestyle' features and fewer hard news stories. It still had more substantial content than many publications produced with many times the resources but it was not enough to guarantee survival. Dwindling sales and mounting debts, combined with increasing staff turnover and burnout, a declining number of contributors, chronic undercapitalisation, a zero budget for promotion and a loosening of the bond between producers and readers resulted in the paper publishing its final issue on 20 January 1994.

LOP/Northern Star had fallen victim to political and economic forces that had already killed off most other radical publications; perhaps the only surprise was that it had been able to survive so long in the social wasteland ruled by Maggie ('there is no such thing as society') and Tina ('there is no alternative'). Across the Pennines in Rochdale, *RAP* had run out of steam more than a decade earlier, despite selling 7,500 copies a month. As *RAP*'s David Bartlett recalled: 'There were no sixties people left, and the seventies lot were different' (quoted in Hobbs (1993: 20)). In Bury, Sue Ashby explained the atmosphere around the time the *Metro News* ceased publication in 1983:

> We were exhausted. We saw papers around us folding and we thought 'must keep going, must keep going', but I think there was a tide of apathy coming in which made it difficult ... We went into a time when the sense of community disappeared. It went with Thatcherism.
>
> (quoted in Dickinson (1997: 163))

While they lasted, such papers had challenged the hegemony of the local Establishment and mainstream media by demonstrating that there was more than one way of viewing the world. The alternative local press critiqued media practice in practice, contesting accepted notions of common sense and of who should be allowed to speak. The production of alternative media was 'propaganda of the deed, highlighting the faults of the established press' (Whitaker 1981: 101). But by the mid-1990s the UK alternative local press, as created by 'sixties people', was no more.

A quirkiness of viewpoint

Many of those involved in the alternative press went on to work as journalists in a range of media (Harcup 1998: 114; Dickinson 1997: 6, 208). They took with them their contacts books and what one referred to as 'a quirkiness of viewpoint' (quoted in Harcup (2005: 366)). The ideas of alternative media have influenced the mainstream in other ways too. 'We made the local newspapers in the town sit up and take notice of us', recalled a veteran of the alternative local press. 'They also became more inclusive in their own editorial content'. Another observed: 'Mainstream media are always stealing the styles, content and contributors of alternative media. It's a bit like an underground music scene, things filter through' (quoted in Harcup (2005: 367)).

However, many of such journalists' former readers may now receive little local information. One survey found that a third of *LOP*'s regular readers never read, watched or listened to any other local media; only a fifth regularly bought any other local paper; and half had no contact with other local media beyond picking up the occasional copy of the *Yorkshire Evening Post* or watching *Look North* on BBC TV's regional output. As one former *LOP* journalist commented at the time of the paper's demise: 'It was only a grotty little thing produced on a few sheets of recycled paper that 2,000 people would buy, but that doesn't measure up to the impact it had over the years. It had a profound effect on Leeds in its small way' (quoted in Harcup (1994: 30)). The dispossessed, in Leeds as elsewhere in the UK, had lost their parish magazine; and if I had a pound for every time someone has since expressed regret that *LOP* is no longer published, I would be able to finance a whole string of alternative papers.

Active citizenship

The period discussed in this chapter was not a 'golden age'. All claims of golden ages are suspect in any event, and this one certainly didn't feel like a golden age when the press broke down, when suppliers refused to deliver paper because of unpaid bills, or when pasted-up copy had to be flattened beneath a television set with someone standing on top (as happened with the first issue of *LOP*). More crucially, if the 1970s and 1980s are seen as a golden age, the implication is that it is over. Although the genre of the alternative local newspaper – produced co-operatively, combining news, investigations and listings, published regularly and sold in newsagents – now seems to have been a passing phase, this does not have to be the end of the story. Dissatisfaction with mainstream media persists. In the view of one journalist who has worked in both alternative and mainstream media:

> Mainstream journalism is probably a bit more diverse than in years gone by, but it could still do with more diversity. The quality of some journalism – content in the red top tabloids and the standard of writing and news selections in many local papers – makes you want to cry or just screw up the papers.
>
> (quoted in Harcup (2005: 368))

The functioning of a healthy public sphere – a space in which informed citizens can engage with one another in reasoned debate and critical reflection – depends on a diversity of groups and views having access to media. Yet studies suggest that the less powerful groups in society continue to face structural obstacles in gaining access to mainstream media (Manning 2001: 137, 226–7). It is precisely such groups, under-represented in the mainstream, that have been given voice in alternative media. In this sense, alternative media can offer counter-hegemonic alternatives to mainstream media and, in the process, support active citizenship and help nurture a healthier public sphere than would exist in the absence of such alternatives.

Future waves of alternative local journalism may be located online rather than in print. Many cities, towns and even villages in the UK already have community noticeboards or forums on the web, and numerous opinionated individuals are producing weblogs; none of which is necessarily journalism, but it does indicate some of the potential of the technology. The network of Indymedia websites now includes separate local and regional sites for parts of the UK and, although to date they have tended to be dominated by repetitious reports of demonstrations, who is to say how they may develop? It is to be hoped that we may see these and other sites featuring more investigative and revelatory journalism – on a local, national and international scale – than has been the case to date. It may be relatively early days for online technology, but twenty-first-century alternative media are part of a longer radical tradition, as one of the founders of the Brighton-based *SchNEWS* (2004: 298–9) newsletter notes:

> When you initially get involved in something, you think you're the first person that's ever done this, but it's generally not true ... *SchNEWS* is just following on from the radical media from the past couple of hundred years. We're part of that tradition, just as struggle is part of it.

The struggle continues.

References

Atton, C. (1999) 'A reassessment of the alternative press', *Media, Culture and Society*, 21, pp. 51–76.

Atton, C. (2002) *Alternative Media*, London: Sage.

Aubrey, C.; Landry, C. and Morley, D. (1980) *Here Is the Other News*, London: Minority Press Group.

Baker, S. (2005) 'The alternative press in Northern Ireland and the political process', *Journalism Studies*, 6 (3), pp. 375–86.

Cole, G. D. H. and Postgate, R. (1961) *The British Common People: 1746–1946*, London: Methuen.

Curran, J. and Seaton, J. (2003) *Power without Responsibility: The Press, Broadcasting, and New Media in Britain*, London: Routledge.

Dickinson, R. (1997) *Imprinting the Sticks: The Alternative Press Beyond London*, Aldershot: Arena.

Franklin, B. and Murphy, D. (1991) *What News? The Market, Politics and the Local Press*, London: Routledge.

Hanna, M. (2005) 'Alternative media', in Franklin, B.; Hamer, M.; Hanna, M.; Kinsey, M. and Richardson, J. E. (eds) *Key Concepts in Journalism Studies*, London: Sage, pp. 14–15.

Harcup, T. (1994) *A Northern Star: Leeds Other Paper and the Alternative Press 1974–1994*, London and Pontefract: Campaign for Press and Broadcasting Freedom.

Harcup, T. (1998) 'There is no alternative: the demise of the alternative local newspaper', in Franklin, B. and Murphy, D. (eds) *Making the Local News: Local Journalism in Context*, London: Routledge.

Harcup, T. (2003) 'The unspoken – said: the journalism of alternative media', *Journalism: Theory, Practice and Criticism*, 4 (3), pp. 356–76.

Harcup, T. (2005) '"I'm doing this to change the world": journalism in alternative and mainstream media', *Journalism Studies*, 6 (3), pp. 361–74.

Hobbs, A. (1993) 'Alternative voices', *GMB Direct*, 10, September/October, pp. 20–1.

Leeds Alternative Publications (1980s, undated) 'Views on the news', internal discussion paper.

Leeds Other Paper (1975) 20, September 1975.

Manning, P. (2001) *News and News Sources: A Critical Introduction*, London: Sage.

National Conference of Alternative Papers (1984) Leeds, Spring 1984. Editorial and Workshop Reports.

Northern Star (1838) 'The anniversary', *Northern Star and Leeds General Advertiser* 2 (53), 17 November, p. 4.

Royal Commission on the Press (1977) *Periodicals and the Alternative Press*, London: HMSO.

SchNEWS (2004) *SchNEWS At Ten*, Brighton: SchNEWS.

The Other Paper (1969) 'Editorial', *The Other Paper*, 1, 10 October, p. 2.

Whitaker, Brian (1981) *News Ltd: Why You Can't Read All About It*, London: Minority Press Group.

Chapter 13

Real readers, real news
The work of a local newspaper editor

Sara Hadwin

An anthrax scare, a fuel blockade and a burnt-out circuit board on the press are the stuff of this editor's nightmares. All three, on separate occasions thankfully, threatened to stop my paper reaching its readers, thereby creating some of the most frantic days of my life as editor. Even libel threats and being questioned by police on possible contempt charges failed to create such emotional turmoil. Resolving those challenges could wait until after deadline. These examples underline the first responsibility of an editor: to get the paper out. On a good day an editor does that and much more. On the most taxing days, that and nothing else matters. Readers are an editor's paramount concern. Their relationship with the newspaper, through the person of the editor, is up close and personal, particularly on a local title. It is also profound, complex and often lifelong but, on any given day, failing to get their newspaper to them is the biggest failing of all.

The editor: at work

To avoid such calamities an editor gets her[1] hands dirty – literally and figuratively. Even the aloof find themselves embroiled in production. Newspapers emerge from a manufacturing process conducted to deadlines but with the added dimension of being different every edition. Constant change generates judgment calls and it is never long before a decision is required from the ultimate arbiter: the editor.

For most regional editors, being hands-on is the only way. Whatever their senior management responsibilities, most remain intimately connected with the content and design of every edition. One or more news conferences a day with department heads establish the priority given to each story – the treatment and prominence each receives. Story ideas are introduced, legal queries raised, gaps spotted, accompanying pictures perused. As stories break, more impromptu gatherings take place to adjust priorities. Nearly all editors would expect to sanction a change of page one lead; some would want to know about page lead changes too.

An editor remains a working journalist involved in the day-to-day production of the entire newspaper. That an editor delegates many jobs to the editorial staff does not mean that, if necessary, she should not write a wedding report or sub the television programmes. An editor keeps a constant check on the mechanics of newsgathering and presentation to ensure trained and responsible people are getting the news, that the system for handling, checking and correcting it is working properly and that those executives who are taking major decisions in her name are doing so responsibly, imaginatively and with due regard to the values of the paper.

An editor may focus on certain aspects of her role, depending on personal preference and/or the availability of trusted deputies. An editor should surround herself with reporting talent – assemble and nurture that talent, and harness it to clearly defined objectives. But there is no place to hide. An editor is morally and legally responsible for everything that appears in the paper. If there is doubt about the legality, accuracy or good taste of any article, the editor is obliged not to publish it. This applies equally to letter writers and outside contributors. An editor has to be journalist, writer, manager, legal expert, negotiator, visionary, mentor, publisher and entrepreneur.

The editor: policymaking and the community

Most regional editors write the newspaper's daily leader column. Columnists may express personal views in bylined opinion pieces but the ultimate responsibility for those views appearing in the paper is the editor's, even if she does not share them. The policymaking role of the editor extends further into what the paper stands for, what role it plays in the community, what campaigns it runs, what values it upholds and what attitudes it seeks to discourage. Iconic regional newspaper editor Harold Evans, famous for revealing the Thalidomide scandal, told UK editors:

> It is the editor who has to define the news values. Judgments have to be made on what is important. Ultimately I think they have to be moral judgments; this story is more relevant than that to the health, wellbeing and fulfilment of people's lives. There is a limit to what focus groups and readers can tell you about news and opinion. It is this: they don't know what they don't know. No focus group could have expressed an interest in mad cow disease before it broke out.
>
> (Evans 1996)

An editor has obligations to her staff and employers but most of all she has special obligations at all times to readers: it is in their name she claims independence. Although she is part of a management team, she is not a creature of management; although she is part of the editorial department she is not its delegate (nor of any trade union within it). An editor must resist pressures from whatever source which could restrict her editorial independence and dictate the content of the paper. At the heart of 'policymaking' is service to the community. There is no better way of serving it than publishing the facts about a multitude of activities, identifying and catering to a multitude of interests, and allowing as many people as possible to have their say.

Framing policy is a complicated business. A newspaper must sell, at the right place and at the right time. There is nothing ignoble about this: it must pay its way or disappear. Readers must get their money's worth or they will stop buying the paper. It follows that a paper, to a large extent, must give its readers what they want. That is the major constraint on any editor – not the wicked proprietor nor the unscrupulous advertiser, the twin devils of popular mythology. This involves identifying readers' interests, knowing how they earn their living and how they spend their leisure. It means giving them a constant flow of information which holds their attention. But in addition to giving them what they want, part of our job involves giving them what they need. It is what the Committee of Concerned Journalists describes as the challenge to make the 'significant interesting and relevant' (Kovach and Rosenstiel 2003: 148). Though of necessity a regional newspaper must concentrate on local affairs, it can also project national and international issues by relating them to readers' experience. It is too easy to assume that a factory worker in Barrow has no interest in an international problem: what is required is the journalistic skill to show its significance to his general wellbeing.

Trivialities, half-truths, gossip and celebrity photographs might well be widely read but, in order to take real decisions, readers must be in possession of real information. It might require real thinking power to evaluate it, but in a democracy it is important that citizens should have access to it. (They might ignore it and stick to the cartoons, but that does not excuse us from providing it.) It is incumbent upon all journalists to think about their role in society. The purpose of a provincial paper is not only to present and project the news objectively and imaginatively, but to empower its readers to express themselves more effectively, canalising their aspirations, making more articulate their demands, helping them to improve their community.

A newspaper should reflect the community it serves – warts and all – but it must be prepared to confront unpalatable truths. It would be pretentious to think a local newspaper can change the course of world affairs but locally it can help to get things done. Williams (2005: 18), of the *Western Morning News*, retiring after 30 years as a regional newspaper editor, told *Press Gazette* his role had been about 'making a difference'.

The editor: calling to account

A local newspaper has a positive role to play – at the very least it can right things that have been allowed to happen by default. Those called to account will rarely be pleased. They will occasionally have a genuine grievance and at all times deserve a fair hearing but more often than not they simply object to the newspaper putting into the public domain something they would rather keep to themselves. There are others who feel a newspaper is being disloyal to the community by exposing its failings. They would prefer to resolve issues behind closed doors or, worse, persist in ignoring them. So editors are the focus of considerable abuse. Those who feel the heat of the newspaper's criticism and those neglected in its columns tend to be convinced the editor is prejudiced against them. One of my newspapers was once accused, for example, of being biased against Brownies.

When the *Torquay Herald Express* took its council to task, the muscular coverage provoked a typically hostile and personal attack on the editor. In reply, editor Brendan Hanrahan told the council and his readers:

> I haven't 'got it in' for anybody. I live in the centre of The Bay, listen to what people say in the streets, shops, offices, bars and stands of Torquay United in the belief and hope that it will help me shape and lead a paper that is an important part of their life. It is my responsibility to run a good, professional and independent newspaper and business and to advance the prosperity of the communities we champion to the best of our ability. That means reporting the facts, good or bad, no matter how hard that is at times and even if it involves taking people into the zone of uncomfortable debate. That also means, occasionally, passionate but sincere opinion columns from me that seek to express the anger and frustration of our readers on topics of huge public interest – without fear or favour to anyone.
>
> (Hanrahan 2005)

His remarks encapsulate much of a local newspaper editor's role. Editors are close to their communities. They pick up on readers' concerns because they make a point of building contacts from all walks of life. They also ensure their door is open to all those with news to tell.

But some criticism of editors and their newspapers can be justified on a broader front as well as over specific inaccuracies. Newspapers inevitably highlight the extreme, the exceptional, the dramatic. Readers' perceptions can be warped if individual headline-grabbing incidents are rarely put into context. Fear of crime is one notable example. Perversely, where serious crime is rife it merits less attention. An armed raid in south-east London is hardly worth a mention; in Barrow it would be the front page lead because of its rarity. Editors need to ensure stories are followed through so readers are aware of the bigger picture. When reporting crime that means letting readers know when culprits are ultimately caught and dealt with by the courts, creating awareness of a whole range of crime prevention activity and analysing effectively trends and patterns of offences.

Another danger is that journalists, in adrenaline-driven pursuit of the big story, may produce startling front pages that appear to be revelling in the latest calamity. For a journalist there is an inevitable element of excitement about disaster and an editor has to take great care about the style of the ensuing coverage. The reputation of the newspaper relies on getting it right, not just factually but in tone and presentation too. Being so much closer to it on a regional newspaper actually makes that task easier. Mass job losses or gruesome attacks happen to real people – to people who are probably readers themselves. A local newspaper also witnesses the consequences of any major event and its editor can influence what impact the newspaper has on the outcome. It can report responses but it can also be a catalyst or act in its own right.

The editor: making a difference

A regional newspaper is in a commanding position to expose wrongdoing, underlying failings or impending crises but, having highlighted a problem, it can also seek ways to become part of the solution. So for a local newspaper, a splash on a fatal crash is just the first of a series of reports. An interview with the grieving family may raise safety concerns. A good contact of the health reporter may draw attention to worrying local statistics. Such incidents have spurred newspapers to a wide range of successful campaigns – for reduced speed limits, for pedestrian crossings, to create safe routes to school, for changes in sentencing for dangerous drivers. An effective regional newspaper supports its readers. It does not abandon them in their hour of need but rather looks for ways to galvanise the community response.

Nottingham Evening Post editor Graham Glen, speaking at a Society of Editors conference, asked fellow members:

> Do we simply report events or do we get involved? I think we must do both. Of course, the first requirement is to achieve excellence in reporting. No community activity can be a substitute for that. But with your journalism in good shape, you can add community involvement to the mix ... with this result: You can make a worthwhile contribution. You can demonstrate you are part of the community, not apart from it. You can be the local champion. It starts with an attitude of being positive ... which must go right through the newsroom. One of the dumbest clichés I know is that bad news

sells newspapers. Big bad news sells newspapers – planes crashing on the M1, Fred West. But a diet of dreary small-time bad news turns off readers. We don't ignore it. But we have a positive attitude. A preliminary Evening Post newslist contained the item ... *Vandals trash garden.* The facts? A favourite schoolteacher had died after an illness. In her memory, her inner city primary pupils had created a small garden. Vandals had wrecked it. We got hold of a local garden centre and suggested they donate a few items. We contacted some local conservation volunteers. All co-operated. It cost us little... other than imagination. The result was a positive 'fix it' story. We don't just report crime – we participate in preventing it.

(Glen 1998)

The above expresses an editor's philosophy about the newspaper's role which he shares with staff and readers. It also demonstrates the unique position of a newspaper within a community. An editor who genuinely identifies a constructive way forward and who is motivated by readers' collective interest can harness an amazing reaction. It is hugely satisfying for an editor to know she has struck a chord, said what the readers wanted to be said, prompted them to take action. So while it is true that regional newspapers thrive in communities where local identity is strong they can in turn bolster those communities and the sense of cohesion within them.

Involvement is a dirty word for some editors who fear being seen to be compromised. Being aloof certainly makes life simpler but means the editor, and thereby the newspaper, misses out on readers' experiences and concerns. Glen went on to argue the case for involvement, for instance as a champion of literacy during Nottingham's Year of Reading. 'I'm not important but I bring to the party the *Nottingham Evening Post* and more than a quarter of a million readers a day,' he said (Glen 1998).

An editor must ensure the newspaper is fair to everyone. She must make it obvious she cannot be nobbled and is in no one's pocket. So it behoves the editor to explain the nature – and limits – of her involvement which can be uncomfortable. Glen confronted concerns of being compromised head-on. He argued:

I take the view that a newspaper can be involved and committed provided everyone clearly understands the rules. The *Evening Post* takes partners for projects not partners for life. Severn Trent sponsors our Unsung Heroes campaign. But we'll turn them over if they pollute a canal. And they know that. Similarly with the local authority and hospitals.

(Glen 1998)

An editor's instinct has to be that it is nearly always healthiest to bring a problem out into the open, confront it and deal with it. *The Guardian* editor Alan Rusbridger, addressing the question of whether newspapers are passive observers or active agents of change, rejected a division between the two. He argued that the act of reporting inevitably makes a difference. Newspapers, particularly local titles, make a connection with the readers and the communities they serve, he said. And in making that connection they change the readers and the nature of politics in the community. But a newspaper can only empower readers and communities if it has the credibility to earn their trust. Rusbridger (1998) told UK editors: 'The people with influence are the ones who are trusted. And trust is earned through accuracy and sound journalism.'

Readers are the ultimate arbiters of whether newspapers are earning that trust. Locally, they soon know if a gap emerges between a newspaper's version of events and what is happening in their real lives. Readers may accept a degree of dramatic language but they know if a story is far from the truth. A national can be 'here today, gone tomorrow' in any one community; the local paper cannot and that is predominantly for the good. An editor is exposed to a daily reality check. A local newspaper editor can expect to have to answer for errors and excesses, and in the main to real readers with genuine concerns, not just to spin-doctors (although they are in the mix locally too).

Editors: readers matter most

For their part, readers should be encouraged to participate and to express their opinions, their fears and their hopes in the columns of their newspaper. The local newspaper should provide the individual with a platform – often his only platform. An editor's case for access to information is based on the people's right to know. If her journalists are not working with objectivity and honesty and not giving all manner of people and organisations the chance to have their voices heard, she has no moral justification for many of the claims she makes in the name of press freedom. Yet objectivity in news reporting does not imply impotency in comment. It is an important part of the editor's job to see that this objectivity is maintained in news reporting – and also that the voice of the paper is heard loud and clear through its comment.

Expressed broadly, the role of an editor is to produce a newspaper which serves the community in which it circulates and is bought willingly because it has the long-term interests of its readers at heart, satisfies their curiosity, enriches their lives, expands their horizons and helps an informed enlightened public opinion to emerge.

Editors: who's the boss?

Regional editors are generally not subject to direct proprietorial intervention in editorial decision making. Most regional newspaper companies broadly live up to their commitment to editorial independence. But management makes its presence felt, primarily by controlling the purse strings. There was a time when margins were where editors scrawled corrections in blue pencil. There was a time when editors (and many proprietors) saw themselves as above the financial fray. But there too a regional newspaper editor is now obliged to get her hands dirty. Most evening newspapers are owned by corporations prepared to see circulations and coverage diminish as long as profit margins continue to rise to previously unimagined heights.

Looking back a generation, the role of editor has certainly changed. Long-standing editors such as Bill Deedes and Harold Evans have both bemoaned the decline in the status of editors within most of these corporations. Harold Evans told UK editors: 'The short-term cost cutters have killed more newspapers than they have ever saved.' He added: 'Wise editors and management will keep and embellish their newsgathering operations – so no-one can steal their clothes – and above all they will cherish their editors' (Evans 1996).

A classic editor is beholden to readers and to a newspaper title, not ultimately to her employer. She would not consider herself to have a 'boss' (in the usual sense of a superior) to impress or cultivate. Yet someone has always had the power of hire-and-fire over an editor. What has changed is the seniority and nature of those wielding that power.

Some editors are now appointed by managers with no journalistic experience and little appreciation of the newspaper's wider role and contribution to society. It is no wonder the independence of thought and action central to editing a robust newspaper is being challenged. The autonomous editor is under threat. Few managing directors have the vision and confidence to appoint the editor the newspaper really needs: someone who makes a point of challenging authority of all kinds and will refuse to allow the newspaper to be craven to anyone, even its proprietor.

Companies have adopted the 'if you can't measure, you can't manage' mantra. One of its great weaknesses is the tendency to understate or even ignore that which is difficult to quantify. Given all the intangible benefits of a newspaper and the challenge of assessing quality, rather than quantity, it is no wonder such an approach has been particularly damaging to effective journalism. In any real-world economic equation there has to be an 'x' factor. In newspaper terms someone has to place a value on the dynamism and creativity of a title, its relationship with the community, its very soul.

Managements, and their consultants, will use lowest common denominator benchmarking in an attempt to create a formula which can be applied in semi-automatic fashion to produce newspapers with minimal managerial input or application of judgment. But newspapers do not produce themselves on auto-pilot; their production is not a process which can be set in motion and left to replicate itself. A newspaper 'is' a business but it is so much 'more' than that – and it is the 'so much more' that no one is measuring and that is in danger of disappearing.

Editors know a newspaper must pay its way but for journalists the profit is a means to an end, not the end itself. If there have to be cuts, an editor knows how to make them in ways which will disappoint readers least but it is always with a heavy heart. And now she also faces the question still unanswered by regional newspaper companies: How high do those margins have to go?

An editor knows there is never enough time or talent to do everything that needs doing but that doesn't make it reasonable or sensible to run newsrooms on reduced numbers and poor pay while pushing margins higher. The danger is that the editor runs out of ingenuity, adopts the formula and narrows the scope of the newspaper's operations. If editors who resist such changes are then eased out, newspapers end up being run by those who do not even recognise what has been lost.

An editor has to live with disappointment which means most are born optimists. The newspaper is always less than it could be but the struggle goes on. Every edition is an opportunity to right the wrongs, within the newspaper building as well as in the outside world. Powerful editors are good for newspapers. An editor is the custodian of the newspaper and has to put the newspaper and its readers first. The editor is the personification of the newspaper, particularly in the community. The editor's decisions and judgments make the newspaper what it is.

Editors need all possible encouragement to move beyond increasing profit margins into raising the sights of their journalists and their titles. Otherwise they are hastening the day when those margins collapse and meanwhile selling themselves, their readers and their communities short. Editors may well be taken to task for a lack of modesty as individuals but they should never be persuaded to be modest in their aims for their newspapers.

Notes

1 An editor is referred to as 'her' not only because of my gender but also to highlight the fact that fewer than 10 per cent of UK regional daily newspapers are edited by women.

References

Evans, H. (1996) 'Evans: an editor on how to edit', *Guild of Editors Conference*, newspaper.

Glen, G. (1998) 'Serving the community', *Guild of Editors Conference*, www.societyofeditors.co.uk

Hanrahan, B. (2005) *Editor's 'Grow up' Message to Councillors*, www.holdthefrontpage.co.uk/news/2005/08aug/050802han.shtml

Kovach, B. and Rosenstiel, T. (2003) *The Elements of Journalism*, London: Atlantic Books.

Rusbridger, A. (1998) 'Journalists or agents of social change', *Guild of Editors Conference*, www.societyofeditors.co.uk

Williams, B. (2005) 'Don't mention profits in front of the Colonel', *Press Gazette*, 30 September, p. 18.

Chapter 14

A right free for all!

Competition, soundbite journalism and developments in the local free press

Bob Franklin

At first glance, free newspapers seem to demonstrate a double paradox. First, they are distributed free of charge, but remain a lucrative and expansive sector within the local press. Second, they are 'newspapers' but they report little if any 'news'. Both seeming contradictions are resolved by reference to a third, but highly significant, characteristic of free newspapers; they derive their income uniquely from advertising revenues. Consequently, there is no requirement to sell these newspapers to generate income nor, since the papers are given away, is it necessary to report news to attract readers (Franklin 1998: 125). This distinctive economic logic means that the free newspaper's capacity to deliver news is inherently compromised by the ambition for advertising revenues and profit: an ambition which has flourished with the recent and expansive corporate ownership of the local press. As Preston (2003) notes, these newspapers have 'more to do with business than journalism'.

Developments in new digital technology, moreover, in tandem with this reliance on advertising and the perennial desire to reduce the costs of newsgathering and reporting, have encouraged changes in the editorial style and content of free newspapers. Some observers believe that these developments are fundamental and are redefining the essential nature of journalism. Tim Jotischky, the editor of Associated Press' *Metro*, for example, claims,

> We are reinventing what it means to be a news reporter. What we are doing is soundbite journalism. We are giving people very compact news stories. Our reporters are Internet literate and do a lot of casting around websites. Sometimes a reporter finds a great story and we turn it into a news story.
>
> (cited in Morgan (2001: 14))

More sceptical journalistic voices offer critical assessments denouncing free newspapers as 'dumbed down publications', produced by 'people who can't write for people who won't read' (Preston 2003).

The first phase of what hyperbolic advocates termed 'the free newspaper revolution' occurred during the 1980s. The number of titles expanded at a considerable pace, but in the 1990s, this growth experienced a reversal. Free newspapers remain a significant element within the local press, however, because of the large number of titles which are published, the substantial distribution figures they achieve, the considerable advertising revenues they command and, perhaps most significantly, because of their impact on the already dwindling fortunes of the traditional paid-for weekly local papers (Bourke 2003: 16). Since the turn of the new millennium, the emergence of a new style of 'daily' free newspaper exemplified by the *Metro* and the *Standard Lite*, has reasserted free newspapers' claims to significance within the local press. Competition for readers, advertisers and market position is unprecedentedly fierce, of course, but is not confined to rival free papers in an age of 'ambient news' (Hargreaves 2003: 3). Internet websites, mobile telephones, as well as local television and radio, each deliver news and intensify the competitive market in which free newspapers must operate and attempt to seduce the news-indifferent members of what marketing specialists delight in describing as the 'iPod generation' (Marriner 2005a: 5).

This chapter examines more closely the distinctive economic logic of free newspaper production, considers the development of the 'weekly' free newspaper industry across the 1980s and 1990s and concludes by exploring the recent emergence of the 'Metro style' 'daily' papers as well as considering their implications for the local press.

'More to do with business than journalism'

Free newspapers reverse the traditional assumptions of newspaper economics which suggest that high-quality news coverage, which reports a wide range of issues but with a local news agenda, is the vital ingredient necessary to entice readers to buy a local newspaper. When a newspaper can illustrate a sufficient circulation among local readers, local businesses will advertise in the paper. In this way, the local paper generates income from copy sales and advertising revenues via the sale of two commodities: news to readers and space to advertisers.

But the economic imperatives informing free newspaper production require a reconsideration of these assumptions. Free newspapers redefine the identity of the 'buyers' and the 'sellers' as well as the nature of the 'product' for sale in the free newspaper marketplace. The 'buyers' are no longer 'readers' trying to purchase a 'product' identified as 'local news'. The 'buyers' (readers) are themselves transformed into a 'product' which is offered for sale to advertisers who, in their turn, become the new 'buyers'. In the context of this revised rationale, the quality of free newspapers' editorial has become largely irrelevant to the papers' success. Free distribution guarantees delivery to a closely defined target readership regardless of the paper's editorial merit or even the homeowners' wishes; love it or hate it, the local free paper is pushed through letter boxes every week by a small army of school children, pensioners and other casual workers. But editorial quality is not wholly irrelevant since advertisers must be convinced that these newspapers are read rather than thrown away. Editorial must accomplish a difficult balancing act which requires it to be sufficiently engaging to attract readers' attention, without being so interesting that it diverts them from the advertisements.

All newspapers are reliant to a greater or lesser degree on advertising, but free newspapers' total dependence on advertising revenues is unique and has a number of consequences for their economic organisation, staffing structures, newsgathering and reporting routines and the subsequent character of their editorial.

First, the balance between advertising and editorial typically favours the former overwhelmingly. Only the front page and two or three other pages feature news; the remainder are devoted to advertising copy. The *Cardiff Post*, for example, has an average pagination of 68 pages with 90 per cent devoted to advertising, while the *Croydon Borough Post* with 154 pages typically devotes an average of 88 per cent wholly to advertising (VFD January–June 2005). Second, the reliance on advertising revenues makes free newspapers potentially more vulnerable to advertising interests where they conflict with editorial priorities. All local newspapers must be sensitive to powerful local advertisers' interests, of course, but such concerns are 'more deeply entrenched' in the free newspaper 'commercial model' (Berry 2005: 58). Advertorial is rampant and has grown markedly across the last two decades; for local journalists it is a curse (Franklin *et al.* 2005: 11–12). Certain sections in the papers, moreover, whether motoring, travel, or business, may be dropped, not because of insufficient reader interest, but because these topics fail to attract advertising. Third, it follows that because they report so little news, free newspapers need considerably fewer journalists than paid papers, providing them with a significant cost advantage over their paid sister papers. Journalists, moreover, are less significant to the paper's revenue base than the telephone sales staff; the latter directly generate income. Fourth, the link between journalists and readers is ruptured since free newspapers do not have to win a readership by publishing relevant, high-quality local stories. They are wholly unaccountable and simply distributed to targeted audiences in compliance with advertisers' requirements. Readers' dissatisfaction with the paper has no impact on the number of copies distributed. Finally, free papers are increasingly editorially reliant on non-journalistic sources of news such as the press and public relations departments in nearby local authorities, local businesses and central government, as well as national and local press agencies (see Chapters 1,

16, 17 and 19); alternatively they try to cut the cost of newsgathering by employing freelances (Chapter 18). The resulting copy delivered to journalists by public relations specialists is typically uncritical and, too frequently, speaks to sectional or local elite rather than community interests. Journalists and PR staff pursue distinctive agendas: the PRO's task is to persuade, the journalist's ambition is to inform (Franklin 2004: 106–11).

The developing free newspaper industry, 1975–2000

The first free newspapers were launched in the mid-1970s and for two decades enjoyed a rapid expansion in terms of the number of published titles, the aggregate distribution they achieved and the advertising revenues they attracted. Free newspapers titles grew from 325 in 1980 to 494 the following year – a rate of 52 per cent in a single year. By 1986, free newspapers achieved what was to prove a publication peak of 882 titles. Distribution figures grew at similarly impressive rates from 15 million copies in 1981 to a peak of 42 million copies by 1989 (Franklin 1998: 128). The free newspaper business was booming.

Growth in advertising revenues was similarly bullish. In 1970 free papers earned a meagre £2 million in advertising income, which represented a modest 1.4 per cent share of the total regional/local newspaper advertising market. By 1980, these figures had reached £84 million (13.1 per cent) and by 1985 £263 million (26.2 per cent), a doubling of market share in five years. This growth in revenues continued throughout the 1990s although figures dipped to £578 million in 1990 reflecting the impact of a continuing recession on the advertising industry.

The rapid growth of free papers in the UK during the 1970s and 1980s is readily explained by three factors. First, the poor and uncompetitive state of the existing local paid weekly newspapers, which had been suffering declining circulations for a decade, offered free newspapers a market niche they readily exploited. Local papers' attempts to pre-empt competition from 'invaders' by establishing their own free papers merely, albeit unwittingly, added to the rapid expansion of the free press sector. Second, the lower production costs of these free newspapers, which published little news and employed fewer journalists, allowed them to undercut by two-thirds the advertising rates offered by paid weekly papers. They effectively undermined the local advertising monopolies enjoyed by the traditional press and readily won favour with local advertisers. Third, the absence of trade unions facilitated the introduction of new print technology, which reinforced the relative cost advantages of free newspapers. There would be no highly paid and skilled printers, fewer journalists, no unions, lower wages and more 'flexible' working arrangements on free newspapers. As one editor claimed:

> The free newspaper revolution forced paid-for regionals to challenge the unions, bringing in the new technology which had been available for years. It also radically lowered their cost base. These newcomers had the advantage of lower costs at several points compared to the larger papers. They had less expensive or less extensive overheads: they needed fewer journalists; and they could get the printing done on contract, that is they did not have to invest in the major cost of printers or a press. As the cost of placing adverts with the larger papers rose, so the free sheets were able to pull in the new or small and the regular advertisers who were beguiled by the low costs.
>
> (Hayes 1996: 195–6)

Free newspaper titles and distributions dipped across the 1990s. Distributions peaked at 42 million in 1989 but reduced to 28 million by 1996, a fall of 33 per cent. Across the subsequent decade, distribution has stabilised, with 29.6 million newspapers distributed each week in 2005 (www.newspapersociety.org.uk, accessed 1 November 2005) with free weeklies such as the *Manchester Metro News* continuing to achieve a high distribution of 309,462 each issue. But the number of published titles also reduced from the 1986 peak of 882 to 630 in 1996, a reduction of more than 28 per cent. By late 2005, the figure was almost identical with 637 titles published weekly although the composition of the free press had changed markedly to include nine free daily morning papers and nine free Sunday local/regional papers (www.newspapersociety.org.uk).

The decline in free newspapers' fortunes across the 1990s is as readily explained as their expansion a decade earlier. The sustained economic recession which began in 1989 reduced free newspapers' advertising revenues at a time when rising production costs, especially the substantial increases in the cost of newsprint, were reducing profitability and triggering closures (Oakley 1995: 24). Moreover, the increasing tendency of national papers to 'regionalise' editions and focus editorial on stories of regional significance attracted advertisers away from the local newspapers allowing nationals to 'cream off some of the substantial advertising revenues which are available' (McNair 1994: 173). But most significantly, the declining fortunes of the free press at this time reflected their changing patterns of ownership, as founding individual owners like Eddie Shah sold their local newspaper holdings to the large corporate newspaper groups. The transition was breathtakingly rapid with 80 per cent of the free newspaper market moving to conglomerate ownership between 1988 and 1989 (Nicholson 1995: 17). The new corporate owners, however, typically used their free newspapers to protect and promote their paid-for titles. Free newspapers became the foot soldiers of corporate strategy intended 'to defend territories and re-establish monopoly positions for paid-for titles' (Fletcher 1995: 14). Group strategy concerning advertising also tended to favour the paid-for newspaper titles, so that free newspapers were not allowed to compete for advertising in particularly profitable areas such as house and car sales (Fletcher 1995: 14).

After their extraordinary success during the 1980s, a decade later free newspapers were safely incorporated into the larger newspaper groups and functioning as little more than financial pit props supporting an ever-declining paid-for local newspaper industry. But by the turn of the millennium, the emergence of a new style of 'daily' free newspaper targeted at young, urban, commuter readers has enjoyed a striking initial success with some of the 'new breed's cheerleaders' arguing that these new *Metro* or *Lite* newspapers might not only reverse the declining fortune of free newspapers, but provide a model for 'the future of print journalism' (Berry 2005: 55).

McJournalism and the rise of free urban newspapers

The increasing standardisation of the editorial content of local newspapers, especially the similar page layout and design, has prompted concerns about the McDonaldisation of the local press (Franklin 2005: 137–51). The local daily Free Urban Newspapers (dubbed FUN papers by their owners and editors) seem to exemplify this trend. Perhaps unsurprisingly Pelle Tornberg, head of Metro International, the company which publishes 59 editions of the *Metro* in 83 cities each day for 15 million readers worldwide, acknowledges that he used to call his *Metro* papers the 'Big Mac of newspapers' until a colleague informed him of the opprobrium attached to the term in some countries. Tornberg now prefers the word 'Glocal' to reflect the fact that while the *Metro* follows 'a strict editorial formula' and a 'standardised editorial style and design' which delivers 'the same editorial line, layout and template around the world, every Metro is perceived as being a local newspaper' (Tornberg cited in Marriner 2005b). Fast-food metaphors abound in discussions of these new papers with the managing director of the *London Evening Standard* describing the free daily *Standard Lite*, launched in April 2004, as 'a snack version of the full fat paper' (cited in Gibson (2004: 11)).

In the UK setting, Associated's *Metro* series of daily papers was the first to be launched and remains the most successful.[1] The *Metro* was launched in London in March 1999 with a print run of 80,000 copies distributed for free via bus, railway and tube stations throughout the capital; by 2005, the London *Metro* was distributing 496,724 copies daily (Newspaper Society 2005). Building on this initial success, Associated quickly rolled out other regional editions for distribution across the Midlands, Scotland, the North West, Yorkshire and the South West. The aggregate circulation of the current eight *Metro* papers is 1,009,367 copies daily,[2] which prompts some enthusiasts to claim that it is 'the fourth largest circulation in the country', just behind the *Sun*, *Daily Mail* and *Mirror*

(Meeke 2005). At times the rhetoric becomes hyperbolic with the *Metro* editor announcing the paper as 'the biggest free in the world' (Morgan 2001: 14). The programme of expansion continues with the launch of the Dublin *Metro* in October 2005 and new editions for South Wales (Cardiff) and Liverpool since March 2006. According to its website, the *Metro* provides a '20 minute informative and entertaining read' for its target readership of 'young, affluent, urban commuters' and reaches 1.8 million readers daily of whom '67% are ABC1 and 74% are under 45 years old' (http://cws.huginonline.com/M/132142/PR/200510/1014769_5.html). *Metro* proudly boasts that it is 'the widest read paper among the 18 to 45 urbanite audience it is aimed at' (Meeke 2005). Journalistic plaudits have accompanied this expansive distribution success, with the London *Metro* being nominated for Newspaper of the Year in the 2005 British Press Awards. The new *Metro* papers are evidently 'a far cry from those ad-jammed freesheets that have been stuffed through our letterboxes for years' (Berry 2005: 55).

The success of the *Metro* has inevitably attracted other titles into the free market. The morning editions of the *Metro* are now complemented by the *Standard Lite* which, since December 2004, has been distributed free across London between 11.30 and 14.30, just ahead of its sister paper the London *Evening Standard* (Gibson 2004: 11). Two hours later in Manchester, the *MEN Lite* has been distributed free since March 2005 and again is targeted at 25–44-year-old urban commuters (Milmo 2005: 20). Even the most august titles are seeking the enhanced readership which the *Lite* editions are presumed to deliver. The *Financial Times*, for example, publishes an afternoon paper, the *FTpm*, for corporate subscribers. More *Metro/Lite* papers will undoubtedly arrive. In July 2005, the Office of Fair Trading (OFT) invited tenders for the rights to distribute a free afternoon paper in the London underground; previously, Associated possessed exclusive rights to distribution in the Tube. Expressions of interest were promptly received from Desmond's Northern & Shell, Murdoch's News International, the Guardian Media Group and Associated (Marriner 2005b: 23). Globally, the expansion of daily free newspapers moves ahead apace, with the 2005 edition of *World Press Trends* identifying 112 free daily newspapers around the world, with these free papers representing 40 per cent of the newspaper market in Spain, 29 per cent in Italy and 27 per cent in Denmark (cited in *The Guardian* 1 June 2005: 21).

At first glance, these new daily free papers seem markedly different from their weekly predecessors. They undoubtedly represent the most expansive sector within the local press at a time of relative stasis in the fortunes of the weekly free papers in terms of the number of published titles and the distributions they achieve. But in other – and perhaps key – respects, they are remarkably similar.

Four points about these papers are worth noting and perhaps signal a less optimistic perception of their journalistic worth.

First, the new *Metro* papers display a discernible schizophrenia. The standardised, editorial style and layout of all the *Metro* titles, combined with the tendency to carry national and international stories on the front page, creates the impression of a national tabloid title. This impression is reinforced by the fact that the *Metro* distributes more than a million copies daily, designates itself the fourth largest paper in the UK, competes with national daily titles for readers and advertisers and costs Murdoch's the *Sun* 40,000 sales daily (*The Guardian* 5 July 2005: 19). But paradoxically the Newspaper Society, the body that represents the interests of local and regional newspaper publishers, claims the *Metro* titles as its own and lists them as regional newspapers (Newspaper Society 2005). The *Metro* seems to have a genuine identity crisis: a series of regional papers occasionally masquerading as a national.

Second, the rationale for launching these daily free newspapers, like their weekly predecessors, has 'more to do with business than journalism' to reiterate Preston's (2003) assessment. Associated Newspapers was explicit in identifying the need to boost the flagging circulation of the London *Evening Standard* – down 50,000 between 2003 and 2004 – as the key driver in the decision to launch the *Standard Lite*. The hope that the *Lite* would serve as a spoiler intended to deter Richard Desmond's anticipated launch of a rival free newspaper, cited as a secondary impetus behind the new paper, offers a similar economic, rather than journalistic, rationale for the new paper (Gibson 2004: 11). In Manchester too, the publication of the *MEN Lite* owes more to the continuing circulation (mis)fortunes of the 'sponsoring' title, the *Manchester Evening News*, than any journalistic ambition for the new title. This foregrounding of business above journalistic ambition raises a connected issue and again highlights the similarities with the old style weekly free papers, namely the total reliance of both the new and the old style free papers on advertising income as a revenue source. This reliance makes them inherently more vulnerable to the influence of powerful advertisers and may trigger self-censorship rather than risking any loss of vital income.

Third, the economic and business model on which these papers are based and which provides the impetus for their launch, places a number of constraints on their editorial content. Each paper in Associated's *Metro* series, for example, like the Swedish-based International *Metro*, complies with strict templates to deliver a homogenised editorial format across the different regional titles. In May 2004 when the new East Midlands and South West *Metros* were launched, Associated confirmed that 'the new titles will carry almost identical news content to existing *Metro* editions elsewhere in the country' (Pondsford 2004: 6). The journalistic ambitions for enrichment of editorial content here are evidently modest compared to the corporate ambitions for increased advertising revenues via increased distribution of virtually the same newspaper.

The target readership for these newspapers, moreover, is defined much more narrowly than most free papers. The particular group identified is the 18–44-year-old, affluent, urban commuter typically characterised by the ill-defined label the 'iPod generation'. Predictably, editorial concerns attempt to engage and resonate with the presumed requirements of this readership group to the relative exclusion of others. But the cultural interests and journalistic demands of the iPod generation do not exhaust either editorial potential or readers' interests. Consequently, the editor's claims that 'what we provide is a very comprehensive news digest plus Metrolife, a very authoritative three pages of arts and five or six pages of listings a day which is very young, very cutting edge' are dismissed by less partisan observers who suggest that 'there is nothing too demanding here ... you can absorb just about everything in them on a short train or bus trip. You can, if you wish, keep your iPod plugged into your ear or play with your mobile phone as you flick through the pages' (Berry 2005: 55–6).

The *Standard Lite* and *MEN Lite* differ crucially from the *Metro* series, of course, because each is connected to a sister paper from which it can draw editorial inspiration and stories and tap into the relatively rich journalistic resources which only paid titles can provide. In these circumstances a higher-quality and broader range of editorial than the *Metro* titles can deliver within a substantially reduced resource context might be anticipated. But the paid titles then run the risk of 'cannibalisation'; namely, why should anyone buy the paid title if the free paper, distributed two hours earlier, is of an equivalent editorial standard? The danger of lost sales to the paid title is obvious. The *Standard* rejects such concerns arguing that the *Lite* is targeted at new readers and intended to persuade the '24 out of 25 Londoners who don't read the *Standard* to pick it up'. The new edition will complement the 'full fat' version rather than kill it (Gibson 2004: 11). A comparison of the contents of an early issue of the *Standard Lite* with the same day's late edition of the *London Evening Standard* illustrates the differences between the two papers; it might also be presumed to signal the editor's perceptions of what his readers value in the paid title (Table 14.1).

The striking differences are the absence of virtually any business coverage in the *Lite*, the substantially reduced sports coverage and the exclusion of any comment, while the news coverage is reduced less significantly from 16 to 12 pages. Columnists, it seems, are highly valued and at a journalistic premium: news but not views are available for free. As one observer commented, 'What you don't get for free is big name writers and columnists' (Berry 2005: 56).

This last observation connects to the fourth point concerning these papers; namely they are resourced on a journalistic shoestring. Associated, for example,

Table 14.1 Comparison of editorial contents in *Standard Lite* and *Evening Standard*

	Standard Lite	Evening Standard
Front page	'Tube strike at Christmas'	'Met: shock findings on race and sex'
News	12 pages	16 pages
Features/Lifestyle	5 pages	8 pages
Comment	None	3 pages
TV	3 pages	3 pages
Reviews	3 pages	3 pages
Business	1 page	8 pages
Sport	5 pages	9 pages

Source: Gibson (2004: 11)

believed that 35 journalists were sufficient to staff the first London *Metro* in 1999 while the paid-for *Evening Standard* employed 250 journalists (Berry 2005: 57); the editor has only six news journalists based at the London *Metro* and four in the Manchester office (Morgan 2001: 14). These very meagre numbers of journalists employed by the *Metro* have evident implications for both newsgathering practices as well as the eventual news content. The editor is quite explicit about the former; at the *Metro*, journalism is a desk-based job for a new generation of journalists. And fewer of them! Journalists 'work on the phone and on screen', he claims.

> Our news reporters are a product of the internet generation ... we don't have on-the-road reporters. Our reporters are internet literate and do a lot of casting around on websites ... the amount of information out there accessible from an office base is so huge that arguably what we are doing now, you could not have done a generation ago.
>
> (Jotischky in Morgan (2001: 14))

In sum, the *Metro* lacks both the resources and ambition to send its journalists beyond the office to investigate and seek out any but the most obvious stories which can be derived from the web or which come into the office unsolicited from news agencies. Investigative journalists have always been the curse of cost-cutting accountants and they have no place at the *Metro*. As Berry (2005: 57) observes, the *Metro* papers are 'great processors of available news; they are not in the business of digging out the difficult stuff'. The editor concurs. The *Metro* is 'basically a subs paper', he claims. 'Copy tasting is crucial as the digest of daily news is culled from PA agencies countrywide and international wires' (Morgan 2001: 14).

Berry raises two final concerns about these new style free papers; both connect to the potential impact of the free upon the paid newspaper sector. First, the business success of the *Metro* may prompt managers of paid titles to reduce journalistic staff to cut costs and achieve a competitive edge with evident consequences for editorial quality, namely more 'processors' and fewer 'diggers' of news. Second, the *Metro/Lite* papers may threaten or even 'kill off' a paid-for competitor or even the sister paper from which it derives its copy. Berry (2005: 58–9) 'fears' this could happen at the *Evening Standard*.

In the age of ambient news (Hargreaves 2003) when information is readily available and free from so many sources, the emergence of the *Metro* and *Lite* free daily newspapers may seem an obvious development. A *Metro* features editor poses the question directly. 'Our readers are used to getting news free from the TV, radio or the Internet, so why should they pay for a newspaper?' (Meeke 2005). The answer is clear. Free newspapers are based on an economic logic which prioritises business above journalistic ambitions and delivers highly standardised, stylised and McDonaldised papers, which are unable and unwilling to employ sufficient journalists to guarantee independent, high-quality news and a wide range of editorial. Instead these papers may be obliged to rely on agency copy, general interest and wacky stories lifted from the web, and information subsidies and press releases from local interest groups. The resulting editorial mix, as Berry (2005: 59) notes in a phrase which risks challenge for understatement, lacks 'the depth and detail of information on which a healthy democracy depends'. If that is the case and if, when selecting stories, the editor of the *Metro* is really looking for the '"F*** me Doris" factor so beloved of Kelvin McKenzie when he edited *The Sun*' (Morgan 2001: 14), then the cost of such free newspapers is too high.

Notes

1 As a matter of record, the first free daily newspaper, the *Daily News* was launched in Birmingham by entrepreneur Chris Bullivant in October 1984. The paper distributed 276,000 copies, claimed a readership of 427,000, and a 25 per cent share of the local newspaper advertising market. Reed Regional Newspapers bought a 51 per cent stake in the paper in 1987, merged it with other local titles, and confidently predicted a move to profit as well as the launch of similar titles in other metropolitan areas such as Manchester, Glasgow, Liverpool and London. But the free newspaper formula, which had been successful for weekly papers, struggled when applied to a daily. The *Daily News* was unable to resolve distribution problems and consequently failed to sustain adequate advertising revenue. Additionally, the paper confronted severe competition from the existing local paid titles. The *Daily News* changed its name to the *Metro News* and moved to weekly publication in May 1991. It closed shortly after (Nicholson 1995: 17).

2 This overall distribution is simply an addition of the following regional titles: *Metro* London 496,724; *Metro* Scotland 118,036; *Metro* North West 108,745; *Metro* Midlands

86,365; *Metro* Yorkshire 75,337; *Metro* North East 53,443; *Metro* East Midlands 42,716; and *Metro* South West 28,001 (Newspaper Society 2005).

References

Berry, D. (2005) 'News shouldn't be a free ride', *British Journalism Review*, 16 (2), pp. 55–9.

Bourke, D. (2003) 'The charge of the frees', *Press Gazette*, 28 February, pp. 16–17.

Fletcher, W. (1995) 'Born free, tamed by the old school', *Press Gazette,* 18 December, p. 14.

Franklin, B. (1998) 'No news isn't good news: the development of local free newspapers', in Franklin, B. and Murphy, D. (eds) *Making The Local News: Local Journalism in Context*, London: Routledge, pp. 125–40.

Franklin, B. (2004) *Packaging Politics: Political Communication in Britain's Media Democracy*, London: Arnold, 2nd edn.

Franklin, B. (2005) 'McJournalism? The McDonaldization thesis, local newspapers and local journalism in the UK', in Allan, S. (ed.) *Contemporary Journalism Studies: Critical Essays*, Milton Keynes: Open University Press.

Franklin, B.; Hamer, M.; Hanna, M.; Kinsey, M. and Richardson, J. (2005) *Key Concepts in Journalism Studies*, London: Sage.

Gibson, O. (2004) 'London's falling standard hopes for lite relief', *The Guardian*, 15 December, p. 11.

Hargreaves, I. (2003) *Journalism: Truth or Dare?* Oxford: Oxford University Press.

Hayes, A. (1996) *Family in Print. The Bailey Newspaper Group, A History*, Gloucestershire: Bailey Newspapers Group.

Marriner, C. (2005a) 'Pelle the conqueror', *The Guardian*, 28 November, p. 5.

Marriner, C. (2005b) 'The free sheet decider: does it come off on your hands?', *The Guardian*, 22 July, p. 23.

McNair, B. (1994) *News and Journalism in the UK – A Text Book,* London: Routledge.

Meeke, K. (2005) 'The shortlisting of the *Metro* as national Newspaper of the Year has been controversial', *Press Gazette*, 4 March, www.pressgazette.co.uk/article/030305.

Milmo, D. (2005) 'Manchester to get "Lite" evening paper', *The Guardian*, 15 March, p. 20.

Morgan, J. (2001) 'Welcome to Metroland', *Press Gazette*, 12 January, pp. 14–15.

Newspaper Society (2005) www.newspapersoc.org/uk/documents/factsandfigures/circulation/circ-jan-june–05

Nicholson, R. (1995) 'The last days of empire', *Press Gazette,* 18 September, p. 17.

Oakley, R. (1995) 'The root cause', *Press Gazette,* 27 November, p. 24.

Pondsford, D. (2004) 'Metro distribution set to top a million', *Press Gazette*, 28 May, p. 6.

Preston, P. (2003) 'The regeneration game', *The Observer*, 14 September, p. 8.

Chapter 15

Local news, global politics
Reporting the London bomb attacks

Stuart Allan

'I was on Victoria Line at about 9.10 this morning', wrote Matina Zoulia, recalling her experience on an underground train crowded with rush-hour commuters. 'And then the announcement came as we were stuck at King's Cross station that we should all come out'. She described how the passengers took their time, slowly making their way from the halted train. 'As I was going towards the exit there was this smell', she stated. 'Like burning hair. And then the people starting walking out, soot and blood on their faces. And then this woman's face. Half of it covered in blood'.[1]

The morning in question was that of 7 July 2005, when four 'suicide bombers' detonated their explosive devices on three London Underground trains and a bus in the centre of the city, killing themselves and 52 other people, and injuring more than 700 others. Responsibility for the attack was promptly claimed by a previously unknown group calling itself the Secret Organisation Group of Al-Qaeda of Jihad Organisation in Europe. A statement posted on an Islamist website declared that the attacks represented 'revenge against the British Zionist Crusader government in retaliation for the massacres Britain is committing in Iraq and Afghanistan', and that the country was now 'burning with fear, terror, and panic'. For Mayor of London Ken Livingstone, it was a 'cowardly attack' that would fail in its attempt to divide Londoners by turning them against one another. In his words:

> This was not a terrorist attack against the mighty and the powerful. It was not aimed at presidents or prime ministers. It was aimed at ordinary working-class Londoners, black and white, Muslim and Christian, Hindu and Jew, young and old. Indiscriminate slaughter irrespective of any consideration for age, class, religion, whatever. That isn't an ideology. It isn't even a perverted faith. It is just an indiscriminate attempt at mass murder.[2]

Londoners, he was convinced, would 'stand together in solidarity alongside those who have been injured and those who have been bereaved'. His reference to 'presidents and prime ministers' pertained to the fact that 7 July was also the first full day of the thirty-first G8 summit at Gleneagles, Scotland, where Prime Minister Tony Blair and other leaders of the member states were meeting to discuss issues such as global climate change and Africa's economic development (the latter having been the focus of the Live8 concert held five days before). Livingstone himself was in Singapore where he was supporting London's bid to host the 2012 Olympic Games.

For many Londoners, news of the explosions punctured the euphoria surrounding their city's Olympic success, the decision to award the Games having been announced the previous day. Splashed across the front pages of the morning's newspapers were triumphant stories, complete with photographs of jubilant crowds celebrating the day before in Trafalgar Square. In the immediate aftermath of the blasts, however, the day's initial news agenda was being quickly cast aside, rewritten on the fly by journalists scrambling to cover breaking developments.

This chapter, in taking as its focus the news reporting of the London bomb attacks, seeks to explore how the component elements of a local news story of instant global significance were drawn together. Singled out for particular attention will be the ways in which ordinary Londoners caught up in the explosions and their aftermath – such as Matina Zoulia, cited above, whose eyewitness account appeared in a weblog – contributed to the mainstream news coverage on the day. The social phenomenon of citizen reporting, especially where new technologies such as camera-equipped mobile telephones were pressed into service, demonstrated its potential to challenge more traditional forms of local journalism in new and unexpected ways.

Breaking news

'In 56 minutes', an Associated Press (AP) reporter observed on the day, 'a city fresh from a night of Olympic celebrations was enveloped in eerie, blood-soaked quiet'. Three of the four bombs involved had exploded within a minute of one another at approximately 8.50 a.m. on the London Underground system in the centre of the city. British Transport Police were immediately alerted that there had been an incident on the Metropolitan Line between Liverpool Street and Aldgate stations (some 25 minutes would pass, however, before they were notified of the explosion at the Edgware Road station).

By 9.15 a.m., the Press Association had broken the story with a report that emergency services had been called to Liverpool Street Station. By 9.19 a.m., a 'code amber alert' had been declared by Transport for London officials, who had begun to shut down the network of trains, thereby suspending all services. It appeared at the time that some sort of 'power surge' might be responsible. At 9.26 a.m., Reuters.co.uk's news flash stated:

> LONDON (Reuters) – London's Liverpool Street station was closed Thursday morning after a 'bang' was heard during the rush hour, transport police said.
>
> The noise could have been power-related, a spokesman said. Officers were attending the scene.

Speculation mounted about the source of disruptions, with a number of different possibilities conjectured. 'It wasn't crystal clear initially what was going on', John Ryley, executive editor of Sky News, later recalled. 'Given the Olympic decision, the G8 and the world we now live in, it was my hunch it was a terrorist attack' (cited in *New York Times* 11 July 2005). At 9.47 a.m., almost an hour after the first explosions, a fourth bomb detonated on the number 30 double-decker bus in Tavistock Square. The bus had been travelling between Marble Arch and Hackney Wick, diverted from its ordinary route because of road closures. Several of the passengers onboard had been evacuated from the Underground. At 11.10 a.m., Metropolitan Police Commissioner Sir Ian Blair formally announced to the public that it was a coordinated terror attack, a point reaffirmed by Prime Minister Tony Blair at 12.05. In a televised statement, a visibly shaken Blair condemned the attacks as 'barbaric', appealed for calm, and offered his 'profound condolences to the victims and their families'. It would be 3 p.m. before it was formally announced that deaths had taken place.

Radio is at its best with breaking news. Several of London's local radio stations pulled their regular schedules so as to provide rolling news coverage. Capital Radio went all-news from 10.00 a.m., simulcasting with Capital Gold, Choice FM and Xfm. EMAP's Magic and Kiss FM broadcast bulletins every ten minutes. Mark Storey, head of programming at EMAP, later suggested that radio played a role in 'galvanising' the capital following the attacks (*The Guardian* 5 August 2005), a point underscored by the number of listeners who contacted stations with eyewitness accounts. In the case of BBC Radio Five Live, presenter Matthew Bannister readily acknowledged the importance of their contributions.[3] 'The first eyewitness was on the air at 9:25 am', he recalled, 'with sirens wailing in the background'. The caller provided an account of the evacuation of the Liverpool Street station and the arrival of 'dozens of ambulances' as the area was cordoned off. Next up, the British Transport Police confirmed that there were 'walking wounded', and that two additional Underground stations had been closed, before another eyewitness relayed details about people with 'smoke-blackened faces' receiving medical attention outside Aldgate East Underground station.

'For Londoners', Bannister remarked, 'an incident on the tube with all its associations of claustrophobia and lack of escape routes is a nightmare vision'. Bearing this in mind, he was 'conscious of the need to keep calm and to balance reporting the news as quickly as possible with the need not to speculate ahead of the known facts'. All too aware that 'incautious speculation' can make a grim situation even worse, not least by causing panic amongst listeners, he observed the 'key rule' of ensuring that the precise source of each 'scrap of news' was made absolutely clear. 'At 10 o'clock', he stated, 'the first eyewitness who had actually been on one of the trains described an explosion, with many people injured and screaming in agony, and the top of the train blown apart'. All talk of the 'power surges theory' abruptly ended as a result; and by 10.10 a.m. the first report concerning a bomb in Russell Square – thought to have exploded in a litter bin – was broadcast. 'My task during the following couple of hours', Bannister stated, 'was to link different reporters, eyewitnesses and experts as the picture of a major terrorist attack on the capital became clearer'. A number of 'word pictures', as he characterised them, would stay with him for a long time afterwards.

The pressing need to secure pictures in a more literal sense was driving the imperatives of television news. Several news organisations were caught without their lead news crews, some of whom were in Singapore covering the International Olympic Committee's decision, while others were in Scotland reporting on the G8 meeting. Once the scale of the attack was clear, senior journalists and editors were pulled back, but in the meantime, newscasts were going to air even though hard information remained frustratingly elusive. ITV was the first television network to make the decision to interrupt its regular television programming. At 10.12 a.m., ITV1 cut away from *The Jeremy Kyle Show* to its rolling service, the ITV News Channel. Jonathan Munro, deputy editor of ITV news, stated:

> As people started coming out of Aldgate with blackened faces we realised something was seriously wrong. We already had three teams on the ground – a team at Stratford for the Olympics had crossed straight over to Liverpool Street. We had a reporter at Aldgate and a team from London Tonight ran up the road to King's Cross – it was easier for us than some as our headquarters are so close to where it was happening.
>
> (cited in Pike (2005))

Reporters and crews from ITV regional companies such as Meridian and Central – *London Tonight* is ITV's regional newscast for London – were stepping into the breach to help network journalists. Some of the first live pictures of the

Tavistock Square bombing area were secured, courtesy of traffic cameras being repositioned by Trafficlink, a company with which it had established an arrangement for regional news. '[Trafficlink] were able to move these cameras round to see what was happening', explained David Mannion, editor-in-chief of ITV News. 'We had an instant new source of pictures around London' (cited in *The Guardian* 8 July 2005). The live link-up was operating within 20 minutes of the story breaking, despite the difficulties ITV News was otherwise experiencing due to its people being unable to pass through the cordons surrounding the area where its base is situated in central London.

Evidently some 3.2 million people watched *BBC News* on BBC1 at midday, confirming that it is the Corporation's newscasts to which audiences are most likely to turn during times of crisis (6.9 million viewers reportedly watched the *Six O'Clock News*). Earlier in the morning, BBC1 had been slower than ITV to interrupt its regular programming by switching BBC1 over to BBC News 24, the rolling news station. It similarly exercised caution in its characterisation of the attacks, allowing a further hour to pass before stating the possibility that Al-Qaeda may have been behind the bombings at 11.32 a.m. Roger Mosey, then head of BBC television news, justified the decision to avoid early speculation by emphasising the need to adopt a measured tone in the coverage so as 'to give people a sense of scale' about what was happening. 'We get confirmed facts on air immediately but it's true we're cautious about some wire copy or internet-type rumours that we can't substantiate ourselves', he affirmed. 'At times on Thursday we were getting "eyewitness accounts" saying completely contradictory things that couldn't possibly all be true' (cited in *The Guardian* 11 July 2005; *New York Times* 11 July 2005).

Still, this more cautious approach attracted some criticism from rival news organisations. Nick Pollard, head of Sky News, contended that the Corporation was 'jumping through hoops of their own making' in this regard. He maintained: 'they clearly made a decision to be very, very conservative and stuck with one caption saying "police investigating incidents on the underground" for about an hour-and-a-half'. Sky News, in sharp contrast, adopted a bolder approach, characterising the attacks as acts of terrorism at 10.45 a.m. In Pollard's words:

> Our philosophy is that we will tell viewers what we believe is going on, we will attribute every source, claim and figure that we quote. We will also tell viewers what we don't know. I have a feeling that viewers, who are now quite attuned to 24-hour news, understand the rhythm and dynamics of an evolving story and would rather be told what we believe is the detail of an unfolding story, rather than waiting until the whole story is known.
>
> (cited in *The Independent* 1 August 2005)

Pollard remains convinced – in the face of countercriticism from the BBC, who had waited for the official police statement that Al-Qaeda was involved – that this approach does not lead to serious compromises being made with respect to the accuracy of reporting. An apparent case in point was the experience of Sky News producer Bob Mills, who had witnessed the number 30 bus explosion on his way to work that morning. He broke the news on Sky at 9.50 a.m., later recalling:

> I was walking alongside the number 30 bus, which was absolutely packed, as it went through Tavistock Square. As the roads were so congested it was crawling along at walking pace. I don't believe in mobile phones, which meant I dashed into a hotel to let my wife know that I was ok. I was in there for about 30 seconds, I rushed out, looked up and the bus blew up. There were bodies everywhere and it was silent. I thought everyone had perished. If I hadn't made that call I would have been next to the bus as the bomb went off.
>
> (cited in *Press Gazette* 14 July 2005)

Despite being certain that 'the bus had been blown up', he was asked by producer colleagues to say only that it was an unconfirmed explosion. Nevertheless, he was able to dispense with the 'power surge theory' once and for all (and with it related claims about derailments, collisions and sabotage). 'I was in journalist mode', he remembered. 'I knew that the story needed to be told as soon as possible. I was sure people needed to know, at that point I even thought the police and ambulance service needed to know – even though they weren't far away' (cited in *Press Gazette* 14 July 2005).

In the case of the local press, the London *Evening Standard* – the only paid-for citywide daily newspaper – had swiftly scrapped its plan to produce a special Olympic edition in order to focus resources on the blasts and their aftermath. A concerted effort was made to bring all editions forward by an hour. By 9.45 a.m., 'Bombs on tube kill commuters' was the front-page headline on its early edition. 'By our lunchtime edition we poured all our resources into it and included a dozen pages', managing editor Doug Wills stated. The next edition, off stone at 3 p.m., was headlined: 'Carnage'. The overall print run was increased by 100,000 copies, even though it was all too apparent that serious difficulties would be encountered when distributing copies in the city centre. 'Our distribution team used their integrity and knowledge of London to move the copies around', Wills maintained. 'It was all hands to the pump and everyone managed to get the information out across the city as soon as it was possible' (cited in Lagan (2005)). Readers in London, he believed, 'were able to get the full details from the *Standard* of what was happening an hour or so after the first blasts and in updated editions right through the day'. Expressing his obvious pride in colleagues' efforts, he added: 'We were publishing the fact that it was bombs, not a power surge, hours before TV' (Letters, *Press Gazette* 22 July 2005). This claim, while overstated, underscores a truly impressive achievement.

Citizen journalists

Particularly vexing for reporters during the crisis, especially those in television news, was the issue of access. Unable to gain entry to London Underground stations due to tight security, the aftermath of the explosions was out of sight beyond the reach of their cameras. On the other side of the emergency services' cordons, however, were ordinary Londoners on the scene, some of whom were in possession of mobile telephones equipped with digital cameras. As would quickly become apparent, a considerable number of the most newsworthy images of what was happening were not taken by professionals, but rather by these individuals who happened to be in the wrong place at the right time. The tiny lenses of their mobile telephone cameras captured the perspective of fellow commuters trapped underground, with many of the resultant images resonating with what was aptly described as an eerie, even claustrophobic quality. Video clips taken with cameras were judged by some to be all the more compelling because they were dim, grainy and shaky, but more importantly, because they were documenting an angle to an event as it was actually happening. 'Those pictures captured the horror of what it was like to be trapped underground', Sky News executive editor John Ryley suggested (cited in Pike (2005)). 'We very quickly received a video shot by a viewer on a train near King's Cross through a mobile', he further recalled. 'And we had some heart-rending, grim stories sent by mobile. It's a real example of how news has changed as technology has changed' (cited in *Independent on Sunday* 10 July 2005).

This remarkable source of reportage, where ordinary citizens were able to bear witness, was made possible by the Internet. A number of extraordinary 'phonecam snapshots' of passengers trapped underground were posted on Moblog.co.uk, a photo-sharing website for mobile telephone images. 'Alfie' posting to the site stated: 'This image taken by Adam Stacey. He was on the northern line just past Kings Cross. Train suddenly stopped and filled with smoke. People in carriage smashed tube windows to get out and then were evacuated along the train tunnel. He's suffering from smoke inhalation but fine otherwise' (cited in www.boingboing.net 7 July 2005). By early evening, the image had been viewed over 36,000 times on the Moblog.co.uk website (cited in *New York Times* 8 July 2005). Stacey himself was reportedly astonished by what had happened to the image. 'I sent it to a few people at work like, "Hey, look what happened on the way to work"', he explained. 'I never expected to see my picture all over the news' (cited in Forbes.com 8 July 2005). Elsewhere, Adam Tinworth, a London magazine editor and freelance writer, later recollected: 'I was grabbing photos to give people a feel of what it's like to be an ordinary person'. He posted a range of images on the web, including shots of blockaded streets, while he waited in a cafe for his wife to call. 'I started posting pictures simply as displacement activity while I waited to hear if she was OK', he said. 'Eventually I did, but there was so much interest in the photos and descriptions of what was happening that I kept on going, and took my lunch break from work to grab some more' (cited in *National Post* 8 July 2005).

Handling Tinworth's images online was Flickr.com, also a photo-sharing service that enables people to post directly from a mobile telephone free of charge. More than 300 bombing photos had been posted within eight hours of the attacks. With 'the ability for so many people to take so many photos', Flickr co-founder Caterina Fake stated, 'the real challenge will be to find the most remarkable, the most interesting, the most moving, the most striking' (cited in AP 7 July 2005). Individual photographs were 'tagged' into groups by words such as 'explosions', 'bombs' and 'London' so as to facilitate efforts to find relevant images. Many of these photographs, some breathtaking in their poignancy, were viewed thousands of times within hours of their posting. 'It's some sense that people feel a real connection with a regular person – a student, or a homemaker – who happens to be caught up in world events ... how it impacts the regular person in the street', Fake remarked (cited in *PC Magazine Online* 7 July 2005).

It was precisely this angle which journalists and editors at major news sites were also looking for when quickly sifting through the vast array of images emailed to them. 'Within minutes of the first blast', Helen Boaden, BBC director of news, affirmed, 'we had received images from the public and we had 50 images within an hour' (cited in *The Guardian* 8 July 2005). Pete Clifton, a BBC online interactivity editor, elaborated: 'An image of the bus with its roof torn away was sent to us by a reader inside an hour, and it was our main picture on the front page for a large part of the day'. Evidently several hundred such photographs, together with about 30 video clips, were sent to the BBC's dedicated email address (yourpics@bbc.co.uk) as the day unfolded. About 70 images and five clips were used on the BBC's website and in television newscasts. 'London explosions: Your photos' (http://news.bbc.co.uk/1/hi/in_pictures/4660563.stm) presented still images, while one example of a video clip was an 18-second sequence of a passenger evacuating an underground station, taken with a camera phone video. 'It certainly showed the power of what our users can do', Clifton added, 'when they are close to a terrible event like this' (cited in BBC News online 8 July 2005).

Over at the ITV News channel, editor Ben Rayner concurred. 'It's the way forward for instant newsgathering', he reasoned, 'especially when it involves an attack on the public'. ITN received more than a dozen video clips from mobile phones, according to Rayner. The newscast ran a crawl on the bottom of the screen asking viewers to send in their material. Every effort was made to get it on the air as soon as possible, but not before its veracity was established. This view was similarly reaffirmed by John Ryley, the executive editor of Sky News. 'We are very keen to be first', he maintained, 'but we still have to ensure they are authentic'. Nevertheless, according to Ryley, a video clip from the blast between King's Cross and Russell Square stations that was received at 12.40 had been broadcast by 1 p.m. 'News crews usually get there just after the event', he remarked, 'but these pictures show us the event as it happens' (cited in *The Guardian* 8 July 2005).

'This is the first time mobile phone images have been used in such large numbers to cover an event like this', *Evening Standard* production editor Richard Oliver declared. It shows 'how this technology can transform the news-gathering process. It provides access to eyewitness images at the touch of a button, speeding up our reaction time to major breaking stories'. Local news organisations, in his view, 'are bound to tap into this resource more and more in future' (cited in *National Geographic News* 11 July 2005). Such was certainly the case with national news organisations. One particularly shocking image of the number 30 bus at Tavistock Square, for example, which had been received at the website within 45 minutes of the explosion, was used on the front page of both *The Guardian* and the *Daily Mail* newspapers the next day. Some images were quickly put to one side, however. 'We didn't publish some of the graphic stuff from the bus explosion', stated Vicky Taylor, an online interactivity editor at the BBC: 'It was just too harrowing to put up.' Nevertheless, she said, the use of this type of imagery signalled a 'turning point' with respect to how major news organisations report breaking news, in her view (cited in *The Australian* 14 July 2005). 'What you're doing', Taylor observed, 'is gathering material you never could have possibly got unless your reporter happened by chance to be caught up in this' (cited in AP 7 July 2005). For Sky News associate editor, Simon Bucks, it represented 'a democratisation of news coverage, which in the past we would have only got to later' (cited in Agence France Presse 8 July 2005). Beyond question, in any case, was the fact that many of the 'amateur photos' taken were superior to those provided by various professional photographic agencies.

In the eyes of some critics, however, serious questions need to be posed regarding why citizen reporters are moved to share their experiences in the first place. John Naughton, writing in the *Observer* newspaper, expressed his deep misgivings: 'I find it astonishing – not to say macabre – that virtually the first thing a lay person would do after escaping injury in an explosion in which dozens of other human beings are killed or maimed is to film or photograph the scene and then relay it to a broadcasting organisation', he wrote. Naughton refused to accept the view that such imagery is justifiable on the grounds that it vividly captures the horrors of the event, contending that 'such arguments are merely a retrospective attempt to dignify the kind of ghoulish voyeurism that is enabled by modern communications technology'. Broadcasting organisations, he maintained, should refuse to use this type of 'amateur' material. In recognising that 'enthusiastic cameraphone ghouls on 7 July' were offered 'the chance of 15 minutes of fame' by picture-messaging to broadcasters, he questioned how many of them avoided attending to the pain of others as a result. '[I]f I had to decide between the girl who chose to stay and help the victims and the fiends who vied to take their pictures', he declared, 'then I have no doubt as to where true humanity lies' (*The Observer* 17 July 2005).

Looking ahead

This chapter's discussion has examined some of the ways in which ordinary people's eyewitness accounts, photographs and video clips improved the quality of the news coverage available during an extraordinary crisis, helping to engender a heightened sense of locality via the inclusion of alternative sources of information and first-person perspectives. Not surprisingly, there appears to be a rapidly forming consensus that the implications of citizen journalism for more traditional approaches to news reporting are deserving of close attention as a matter of urgency (see Chapters 3, 10 and 18).

Particularly salient in this regard is the acute challenge citizen journalism represents for local news organisations already struggling to cope with the Internet. London's *Evening Standard* may have been quick to respond to the attacks with its print editions, as managing editor Doug Wills maintained above, but such was hardly the case with its news site. Monitoring events online as they unfolded was Kieran McCarthy, who contends that at '11:30 am, two hours after the bombs went off and at the same time as the BBC website has gone down due to demand [a claim disputed by the BBC], the *Standard* is leading with stories on Big Brother and George Clooney'. According to McCarthy, there was '[n]ot a single mention of the bombs' by that time. Even when the *Standard* eventually reported its first story online, ' "Explosion" heard at station', the latest 'revelation' on actor Clooney was still the lead item on the webpage. 'The *Evening Standard* only excelled itself in one respect', he observes wryly: 'tardiness' (Letters, *Press Gazette* 28 July 2005).

What makes this example illustrative of broader concerns is that it occurred while a sharp retraction of the local daily's online news provision was underway. Three days earlier, Dominic Timms in *The Guardian* had reported: 'Associated

New Media has axed news staff on the London *Evening Standard* website to focus on entertainment amid fears that the online service is cannibalising sales of the newspaper' (*The Guardian* 4 July 2005). Local city coverage, it was announced, was to be dropped in order to refocus the news site around entertainment (film, theatre and restaurant reviews in the main, together with an online dating service).[4] Such a strategy carries the risk of making the *Standard* look increasingly irrelevant to those who care about what is happening in their community, especially in the case of young people more likely to go online for their news than to pick up a copy of a newspaper.

Local news organisations serious about connecting with their audiences, not least with those engaging in acts of reporting during a crisis, need to think through the possible consequences of their relative commitment to the Internet. The London attack was the first major incident in Britain where citizen journalism played a prominent – indeed vital – role in recasting familiar conventions of news reporting, but it most certainly will not be the last.

Notes

1 Entry in Guardian Unlimited news blog; http://blogs.guardian.co.uk/news/archives/2005/07/07/your_eyewitness_accounts.html
2 For a copy of the statement, see: www.london.gov.uk/mayor/mayor_statement_070705.jsp
3 See Bannister (2005); see also essays by Farrington (BBC Radio Five Live) and McLure (*Legal Times*), respectively, in the same issue.
4 According to the same *Guardian* item, the *Standard*'s site had been attracting 18 million page impressions, and close to 2.7 million unique users, in the days prior to the attacks.

References

Bannister, M. (2005) 'Suddenly my hands were shaking', *British Journalism Review*, 16 (3), pp. 7–11.
Lagan, S. (2005) 'Londoners turn to Standard as horror of attacks unfolds', *Press Gazette*, 14 July.
Pike, C. (2005) 'Blasts were watershed for rolling news, claims Sky', *Press Gazette*, 14 July.

Part 4

Constructing the local news agenda

Chapter 16

Local government public relations and the local press

Shirley Harrison

Setting the agenda

It has been argued that the public sees the world, not as it is, but through the filter of the media (McCombs 2005). While this may hold good for the public's view of events occurring on the other side of the world, of which the ordinary person will have little or no knowledge, it is not so straightforward a proposition when applied to the local media. Certainly journalists working in the local media select their material from a variety of sources and present it from their respective editorial standpoints. But their readers can, on the whole, be expected to have a more intimate knowledge and understanding of that world than any simple reliance on accounts in the local press. Hence, local newspapers have traditionally had to pay particular attention to the concerns and sensitivities of the community in which they circulate. Local journalists need to consider the sources from which they draw their material with equal care: they are writing for readers who may have greater local knowledge than the reporter.

The local news agenda is constructed from a number of sources with the journalist and newspaper editor acting as gatekeepers (Gandy Jnr 1982: 1–18). The proportion of material provided by local government press offices which appears in the local media varies widely. One study of a sample of newspapers in Northumberland gave the figure as more than 90 per cent (Franklin and Van Slyke Turk 1988: 29–41). These 'information subsidies' are provided by a number of sources, as other chapters in this section reveal and analyse. The discussion here examines the rise of the local government public relations officer (PRO) and the various ways in which local government officers interact with local journalists, explores the changes in the relationships between the two, and provides some insight into the way local authorities influence the reporting of local issues. We return to the issue of the information subsidy at the conclusion of the chapter.

The role of local government public relations

The doings of the council and councillors have long been the mainstay of local newspapers, as they are today. However, the way in which a local authority can shape the agenda of the local media has changed as local government has evolved.

The changing face of local government

Once, the city fathers were just that – aldermen (no women) and councillors who looked after their domain in a paternalistic fashion, cultivating (where they needed to) the minuscule electorate personally. As more people became eligible to vote, those who were seeking election found they needed to communicate with this expansive electorate. So councillors announced their policies and the local newspaper reported their speeches. In the first half of the twentieth century all cities, most small towns and rural communities were informed about the doings of their local parish, district or county council by their local paper which was probably locally owned.

Although there have always been policy differences between the political parties represented on local councils, a pragmatic consensus existed until relatively recently. Councillors tended to be senior, respected members of the community, typically above average age and tended to serve for lengthy periods in office. The 1964 general election, however, created something of a revolution among the traditional constituencies. The mood of the times, together with the Labour Party's seemingly unassailable position nationally, led to a resurgence of interest in politics and many young people joined the main political parties as active and energetic members. By the late 1960s some were standing as local councillors (Wigfield 1988: 9). This change opened the door to committed full-time councillors, many of whom progressed to become members of parliament, ministers of state and, in the case of former Lambeth councillor John Major, prime minister.

But elected councillors are simply the public face of local government. Town halls are staffed by local government officers, the employees who implement the policies of the council. The increasing complexity of local authority functions led in the 1960s to an expansion in employee numbers with large departments such as education, housing and social services each employing perhaps 1,000 or more staff. The chief officers of such departments wielded great power and controlled large budgets, leading sometimes to conflicts between them.

In 1971 a group of chief officers met under the chairmanship of Malcolm Bains, former county clerk of Kent, to consider the management of local authorities. The Bains report, published the following year, recommended that councils adopt corporate management, with a senior management team and a chief executive working jointly for the good of the whole authority, a model which was gradually adopted throughout local government (Smith 1986: 32; Franklin 1988: 1–59). Since then, councils have become still more corporate, adopting the Cabinet style of government and outsourcing much of their work. Bains also recommended the appointment of press and information officers. The number of local authority officers working in this field has grown and they, too, are working to a corporate agenda.

The 1970s also saw large-scale local government reorganisation with the creation of the large metropolitan shire counties in 1974 (abolished in 1986) and the creation of a two-tier county–district structure for everywhere except London and the major cities (again reorganised in the 1990s). A Scottish Parliament and a Welsh Assembly have been created, some towns and cities now have elected mayors, and plans for regional assemblies across England (essentially to fit in with European Union notions of regions) have met with varying degrees of enthusiasm. Nonetheless, the government remains intent on regionalising public services: Her Majesty's Courts Service in 2005 and the National Offender Management Service (an amalgamation of prisons and probation) in the pipeline at the time of writing.

Local councils have in the past few years become increasingly subject to inspection, performance monitoring and scrutiny. Within the council itself, there should be a Cabinet and one or more scrutiny committees, their purpose being to hold the Cabinet to account, to develop and review policy and to monitor and review service delivery. The Audit Commission is charged with grading councils under the Comprehensive Performance Assessment system. League tables of performance and 'best value' are produced. Local authorities have become more professional, more business-like and are under the public microscope to a greater extent than at any time before.

So, over the past 40 years there have been four major developments which have naturally led to the establishment of the public relations function in local councils. These are first, a greater politicisation of local government; second, a move towards more corporate and professional management in local councils; third, substantial changes in the names, identities and functions of local authorities in all parts of the country; and fourth, the need for councils to account publicly for their performance.

Before the local government reorganisation of 1974, there was a handful of press and public relations officers working for the counties and two London boroughs. By the mid-1990s all counties, London boroughs and metropolitan districts employed one or more public relations specialists. By 2005 all local councils had some kind of professional public relations function, either employed in-house or provided by another local council or private sector company.

The Chartered Institute of Public Relations Local Government Group (CIPR LGG) had increased its membership to more than 300 in January 2005 and expects to continue to recruit professionally qualified chartered practitioners at the rate of about 60 per year (CIPR LGG 2005: 3).

Local government public relations in practice

Just as local government has changed and evolved into a more professional activity, local authority PROs have adapted and progressed into quite a different species from the publicity officers of the 1970s and early 1980s. Their role was generally to promote the town or city, using advertising and PR 'stunts', sometimes with the intention of encouraging tourism or inward investment, sometimes simply for the sake of generating publicity for the council. During the 1990s PR departments became more concerned with internal communications and with communicating better with their local residents, using research techniques to identify the views and priorities of local people, including setting up citizens' panels.

Local councils are now much more concerned about public satisfaction, and their public relations staff are primarily concerned with excellence in communication. This is reflected in the new nomenclature: fewer PROs exist in local councils nowadays. Instead their job titles tend to include the words 'communications' (comms), 'marketing' or 'customer'. Their day-to-day work depends on the type of authority, the status of the public relations function within the authority, the size of the PR department or unit and the character of the authority itself. For example, Birmingham City Council, the largest unitary authority in the UK, has a 34-strong communications division which covers marketing, sponsorship and the council's web presence as well as the PR team of 15, with a ratio of one PRO to every 66,140 residents. Westminster City Council in London with 7 PROs (a ratio of 1:31,714) is moving 'from pure PR to an approach that integrates media, marketing and internal communications' (*PR Week* 2004: 24–5).

The importance of good communications was underlined by research undertaken in 2004 by MORI for the Local Government Association (LGA). This identified a strong link between council communications and overall performance in the Comprehensive Performance Assessment (CPA). The research showed that those councils which received a grading of 'excellent' or 'good' under the CPA spent more on the communications function than those given any of the three lower gradings (*PR Week* 2004: 22; LGA 2004: 28). Although most authorities produce their own newspaper or magazine for distribution to local residents and have a presence on the web, they are still very much involved with the local media. Media relations continues to be a prime function of local government communications staff.

The work of local government communications officers

The LGA (2004) report on a survey of communications in local authorities, attracting responses from 236 heads of communication, showed that almost 80 per cent of local authorities have communications as a corporate priority. Councils are becoming more strategic in their thinking about communicating with the media: two out of three have written media strategies. In terms of dealing with the local media, 90 per cent report good relations with their local press. The more local, the better: only five out of ten claim to have a good relationship with their regional press or their local radio, and they do not have very strong links with regional and national television. Councils want to deal professionally with the media: 69 per cent of respondents said they provide media training for councillors and officers.

The type of work undertaken by local council communications staff continues to focus on issuing news releases and answering media enquiries but there has been a 'noticeable increase' (since the survey conducted in 2002) in strategic thinking across the communications process and a 'greater readiness to examine the impact of communications work', together with a recognition of the importance of developing crisis media plans (LGA 2004).

In terms of the volume of work, half of the local authorities surveyed had produced fewer than 20 news releases in the previous month, with only one in ten producing more than 75. Forty per cent had dealt with less than 50 media enquiries the previous month, but unitary authorities, metropolitan boroughs and county councils had dealt with most media calls. One in six metropolitan boroughs had officers and members making more than 50 appearances in the local media, but for most councils there were fewer than ten in the month before.

While researching this chapter, I contacted members of the CIPR LGG in July–August 2005. It was evident that communications by local authorities were indeed becoming 'more strategic' and that this was wider than simply producing a strategy for media relations. Alex Aiken, head of Communications at Westminster City Council, made the point that,

> There is too much focus on media strategy, not enough on communications objectives. The media plan should support the business objectives of the organisation – to reduce fear of crime, recruit more foster carers or improve recycling. Too much emphasis on media relations on its own can detract from understanding the role that communications can play in supporting the business.

Kate Bond, Corporate Communications manager for the borough of Telford and Wrekin, also talks about communications objectives rather than simple media relations.

> Local authority communicators are increasingly recognising the importance of strategic communications ... With such an important role in local communities, councils must be seen to be providing value-for-money services, and actively seeking ways to promote their services so residents know and understand how their money is being spent.

Local councils' communications departments are likely to be in a better position to adopt and refine a communications strategy because their plans are more likely to be informed by research. They commonly use Market and Opinion Research International (MORI) surveys to determine residents' views about council services. Southampton City Council's public relations manager, David Bennett, values their 'increased' use of consumer research in media planning: 'for example we use MORI and one of the key questions for me has been each time "Which media tells you most about your local council?"'

Notwithstanding the augmentation, and sometimes replacement, of press officers by 'communications strategists', there is still, as the LGA report confirms, a concentration on dealing with the media, whether proactively or simply by reacting to calls. Kate Bond detects a move away from the reactive type of media relations towards active media management.

> In the past, local authority communications have been driven by the media, with councils reacting to the questions asked by the media. Perhaps this was seen as the easiest way to manage the media, but for those councils who have embraced communications, it is widely accepted that councils must manage the media by taking the good news to them.

Sally Rodé is Corporate Development Officer (Communications) for Forest Heath District Council in Suffolk, a rural area covering three market towns and 22 villages, where local newspapers are widely read: 'Our aim is to encourage our local newspapers, radio stations and television to carry as much positive information from us as possible and help us consult with our residents'.

In the same vein, Islington Council in London aims 'positively [to] manage the reputation of the council with local and national papers and broadcast media' with a focus on 'anticipating areas of the council's work which will come into the media spotlight – for both good and bad reasons'. The Council's press officer, Charles Dean, points up the connexion between good communications, good reputation and good performance:

The Audit Commission's annual report said "Islington is the fastest improving local authority in the country, rising from a poor rating in 2002 to a good rating in 2004" and good communications played its part in this achievement.

However, there is no guarantee that good news will appear in the local press. No matter how reliant the local newspaper may be on the information provided to it by the local council, the only way councils know they can promote a positive message is to pay for it by way of advertising.

Devolved communications

While the smaller local authorities typically have a unit of two or three officers providing communications services for the council, the counties and metropolitan boroughs tend to have large corporate communications departments including a centrally provided press office. The corporate press office would be the single point of contact for journalists wanting to contact the council on any subject, whether with a simple query, a request for an interview or photographs, or to discuss a possible feature. Journalists have often complained that this is unhelpful and inefficient, especially when they know to whom they want to speak, and thus the corporate press office has been seen as a hurdle to jump rather than a helpful way to the information.

Good practice now suggests that media guidelines should be produced by the press office and training be given to staff throughout the authority, so that all officers can play an active part in raising the council's profile. Guidelines and training courses are produced by Dorset, Lancaster and Worcestershire among others (IDeA 2005), and typically include information on the local media (contact, circulation, copy dates and so on); responsibility for dealing with difficult enquiries; how to handle straightforward media relations; what makes a good story and how to sell it to the local paper; general guidance on some of the legal issues relating to communications (such as during pre-election periods); how to write a press release; and organising press briefings and photo shoots.

Solihull's media protocol is available to all staff via their intranet. It provides information on the role of the central press office and sets out rules for working with the media. Buckinghamshire's protocol was produced to assist devolved communications:

> local journalists are encouraged to contact council officers direct for factual information, and Cabinet Members direct for policy statements. All thirteen of the local media who responded to an in-house survey on the changes said that the new media protocol had improved their relationship.
>
> (IDeA 2005)

Local news online

Another change in the organisation of media relations is the advent of the online press office. Recognising that news happens and journalists report it outside the normal nine-to-five working day of the local government officer, councils have typically had an on-call system, or no way at all of contacting the council out of hours. An online press office is one way of solving this problem, and a number of councils have adopted this in recent years. The benefits of an electronic system also include providing a better gateway into the organisation, offering customised e-briefings to journalists and providing webcasts of council meetings.

Andrewes (2005: 48) of Cardiff City Council conducted research into what makes an excellent online press office, as part of her CIPR Diploma. She found several examples of good practice.

- Wiltshire County Council, for instance, provides a Press Club to journalists who have registered as members. This offers a 'customisable media resource' which incorporates news and audio releases, briefings, a diary, photo library and contact details for communications staff.
- Wandsworth Council in London operates a briefing service called News Extra, which provides press kits containing press releases, backgrounders, internal links, details of spokespeople and how to contact them, links to relevant committee information and reports and direct links to related independent news stories.
- Lancashire has linked with Google to provide a targeted search facility which references news and information about the council from any source – its own material and what is being said about the council by anyone posting material on the Internet worldwide.
- Poole provides a News Direct service online, enabling journalists to receive updates on news and events as they happen. The briefings are provided in news release format and include links to other associated information, to background papers and to elected members with direct involvement. It also links directly to DiscussIt, the council's online discussion board, which has comment and opinion.

In embracing technology, however, councils have introduced more features than simply providing online press offices. West Sussex County Council has, since 2002, run a radio service providing prerecorded material which enables the council to control the message. Chris Ryder is broadcast media relations manager for the council and he describes the service thus:

We do our own interviews, so there is no interference into questioning and we provide a monthly interview with the CEO on his own radio page. As I am a former radio reporter myself, the interviews are hard-hitting so we have established ourselves quickly as a credible source for local broadcast media.

West Sussex is evidently very successful at controlling the message: there is 95 per cent take-up from local radio stations, many of whom now take interviews directly from the council site rather than rerecording their own (Andrewes 2005: 48).

Media relations

In keeping with the strategic approach, more councils are undertaking media relations audits. They know what happens to the material they release to the media, and some also know the effect it has on local residents' perceptions.

Thurrock Council, for example, has a media management system which tracks their news releases. In a typical week in August, a 'slow' news month, eight releases were sent out to up to ten local media outlets (newspapers, radio and television). All recipients used at least one of the stories and seven releases were used altogether: every story published had a positive slant. Ninety councils have bought the database system, Newsflash, to help them coordinate such basic statistics automatically (IDeA 2005).

Sometimes the media themselves are involved in auditing media relations. IDeA (2005) gives an example of best practice from Greater Manchester, where eight of the local authorities commissioned a journalists' survey.

In the LGA survey, nine out of ten communications managers described their relationships with the local media as good. This is echoed by Alex Aiken.

> Most authorities have 'good' relations with the local media, but this usually means a robust daily exchange, promoting positive stories, rebutting damaging and usually inaccurate accusations. This is certainly the case in Westminster.

It is also the case in Telford and Wrekin.

> Our relationship with the local media is extremely good. It is based on the principle that we expect fair and balanced coverage and they, in turn, expect us to meet their deadlines and be honest and straightforward in our dealings with them. The media is a vital link between the council and the community and they actively promote the good work that the council undertakes, but on the occasions we get it wrong, we say so.

In Southampton the relationship is 'better now than it ever has been'. Similarly, Islington Council has taken pains to foster a good relationship with the local media, which 'stems from the fact that we understand their needs'. This is a common theme in press officers' relationships with the local press: unsurprisingly, many of them are former journalists. (David Bennett of Southampton was news editor of the local BBC radio station, reported for South Today on television, and started his career on the local paper; Sally Rodé worked as a journalist for 28 years before being employed by Forest Heath Council).

The MORI survey and anecdotal evidence suggest that the relationship between local authority press offices and the local media has improved in recent years. This is to some extent attributed to the better understanding of the needs of local journalists, resulting in part from local journalists taking jobs as local authority press officers, and also to a greater professionalisation of the communications function. Council press officers understand the importance of deadlines and try harder to meet them; they no longer offer 'no comment' in response to enquiries; they meet regularly with local journalists and editors; they offer interviews with councillors and officers as the rule rather than the exception. As David Bennett explains,

> We understand deadlines, the need for accurate information, and cutting through the local government bullshit – and if that means representing the media's point of view against some tramline local government official who can't understand the need for urgency in a response, for example, we'll do that. It's the quid pro quo for managing the media when they get things wrong.

Council press officers also claim to be more open and transparent than was the case formerly. At Telford and Wrekin, Kate Bond says that

> The media are welcomed into the council for regular informal briefings with politicians and officers ... [we] build up strong relationships with the media and can talk to them many times each day. Press officers also make an effort to meet with journalists regularly and have honest and open discussions with them.

There is another driver towards openness and honesty, however. Sally Rodé points out that the biggest impact on councils has been the Freedom of Information Act. 'Saying "I can't answer that because it was an exempt report to councillors" is no longer an option because the journalist immediately lodges an FoI request!'

Notwithstanding the apparent improvement in relations, some councils believe that the local press is less important. For Alex Aiken of Westminster this is not only because the local press is less engaged with council business and has a 'poorer understanding' of the local council's role, but also because the local press itself is only one of a number of sources of local news and information:

> the growth of competing sources of news and information, and changing media habits amongst local people – the shift to broadcast media – means that local newspapers have less influence and tend to be read only by those with an interest in local government ... Regional television and local radio remain the prime communication channels for use. The Council's own magazine and A–Z comes second, followed by local newspapers and then the website.

Southampton Council discovered through its MORI survey that the local evening newspaper is no longer the main source of news about the local council, but 'it ties neck and neck with our own door-to-door magazine'.

Joint work with the local media

A number of local authorities are involved in joint work, including training, campaigning and emergency planning, with their local media. Worcestershire County Council, for example, developed a training pack for 'rookie' reporters as part of their project to try to improve the positive profile of youths in the 13–16-year-old age group (IDeA 2005), and Islington aims to promote good practice by sharing its press officers' experience with trainee journalists at the local university.

To be successful, media protocols need to be worked up jointly between the partners, as has happened in Buckinghamshire. Its media protocol was devised in conjunction with officers, elected members and local media representatives, 'with the aim of making the council more open and accountable to residents and partners via the media' (IDeA 2005).

In Southampton the council does joint emergency planning with the media and has also run a joint environment campaign on noisy neighbours with a local radio station. In Islington the council has worked with the local media on campaigns

> where their co-operation can boost public awareness or the take-up of our services – recent examples include an award winning environmental initiative – Eyes for Islington – and a successful road safety campaign which reduced both accidents and the pressure on the streets created by the school run.

Forest Heath council has been 'trying to encourage residents to help shape the future look of their district and our print media has been running a series of stories showing how individuals can make a difference'. Where the local council and the local paper have a common agenda, joint campaigns are a logical step: encouraging volunteering, campaigning for inward investment, promoting recycling and discouraging vandalism and graffiti are all possible subjects for collaboration.

Joint working is not always favoured, however. David Bennett in Southampton does not train officers and members with the help of local journalists because, he says, 'I have always felt it unfair that a Cabinet Member might for example be trained by someone who the following day is asking them hostile questions'.

Relevance of the local media

As we have already seen, some council communications chiefs think the local media are becoming less relevant as circulations dip and local people find other ways of getting information and news about the council. Consequently, local authorities have been quick to embrace technology and have developed extensive websites. These often include a news section, sometimes featuring recent and archived press releases. There may be FAQ sections, information on events, opening times, statistics, downloadable maps and photographs, research, reports, results of planning decisions and minutes of meetings – much of the information which journalists themselves can use without needing to contact the press office. But this information is also available to local residents, thus sidelining the local paper. However, as Sally Rodé notes, 'there are still a few souls out there who like reading newspapers and listening to local radio rather than sitting in front of a computer for hours'.

Westminster Council has conducted research in this area, as Alex Aiken explains, 'Research we have undertaken at Westminster and Richmond upon Thames shows that both the council website and community websites score poorly against local media and council publications'.

Local people know that, along with paid advertising in the newspapers, council publications and websites provide the 'official' view, whereas the local paper is seen as more objective and independent. David Bennett believes in 'the role of the Fourth Estate, examining our affairs in a credible way' and says about websites:

> [they] fulfil an objective, but they don't for example carry the imprimatur of independence the local media do (which means I feel that our messages are more trusted there), nor have they yet established habit – i.e. the local paper or local radio station is consumed by citizens every day as part of their routine in a way websites aren't.

Kate Bond agrees with this view, 'The third party endorsement of a local paper in reporting the news is important to give a story credibility. Local press is influential', and adds this comment about the use residents make of websites, 'The public use websites for factual information about service delivery, but local press talk about issues which affect people day in, day out'.

Councils have found that linking with external news providers can be useful in trying to promote credibility and trust. Jennifer Andrewes notes that,

> branded news agencies such as the BBC rank highest among reporters in terms of credibility ... Maidstone provides an excellent example of a site that provides a range of useful links to other national, regional and local news organisations, television and radio links, as well as directions to nearby councils and public information sites such as Up My Street, rail, health and education providers.

Information subsidies

This chapter has argued that local authorities are becoming more strategic, more focussed, more professional in the development of their relations with the local media. Local councils know what they want from their local paper – positive reporting – and are investing resources and effort to achieve it. Notwithstanding the view that the press is independent, objective and provides a dispassionate view of the local authority, it is clear that councils are providing the local media with a good deal of help to do their job.

Whether this is seen as a good or bad thing is a moot point reflecting, at least in part, the interests of the observer. Of course, it is commendable that local authority press officers are working hard to ensure that local journalists can get the information they need; that there are media protocols so that everyone knows what to expect and where they stand; that the stony-faced 'no comment' from a pompous councillor who has no sense of accountability is a thing of the past. It is certainly helpful to journalists that they can use the online material so generously made available to them and that their needs are better understood. It is probably an improvement that local councils' press offices are run by former journalists who know whereof they speak.

However, the issue of how great the information subsidy is or should be is a crucial one for the Fourth Estate. We have seen in this chapter that councils provide radio interviews (without any 'interference' from awkward questions) and that these interviews are broadcast wholesale. We have seen that press releases are used as a matter of course rather than being used as a starting point for a press enquiry. The information subsidy is great, and growing, but the credibility of the local media as an independent commentator on local council affairs does not appear to be diminishing.

In the previous edition of this book I concluded by saying that,

> One could argue that the town hall is becoming the last bastion of good municipal journalism. Without the carefully prepared material provided by professional local government PROs, local newspapers are unlikely to be able to perform their role as 'principal institutions of the public sphere'.
>
> (Curran 1991: 29)

Perhaps the last word should go to a working PRO and ex-journalist, Alex Aiken from Westminster:

> I fear that increasingly council media officers are used as an extension of local newsrooms. I estimate at Westminster we spend at least 30% of our time, equivalent to one and a half press officers costing £50,000 on servicing the local media, which reaches less than 10% of the population. Yet a story on regional TV can reach half the population, yet make far fewer demands. Many of the requests from local papers are for obvious facts and figures and pleas for letters and press releases to fill gaps in pages. In this sense media officers are simply filling gaps in the newsroom staff.

References

Andrewes, J. (2005) 'Developing an online press office: principles of excellence', *Profile*, March/April, p. 48.

CIPR LGG (2005) www.cipr.co.uk/lgg/news/IPRBusinessPlan2004–2006.pdf (accessed August 2005).

Curran, J. (1991) 'Re-thinking the media as a public sphere', in Dahlgren, P. and Sparks, C. (eds) *Communication and Citizenship: Journalism in the Public Sphere*, London: Routledge.

Franklin, B. (1988) *Public Relations Activities in Local Government*, London: Charles Knight.

Franklin, B. and Van Slyke Turk, J. (1988) 'Information subsidies: agenda setting traditions', *Public Relations Review*, Spring, pp. 29–41.

Gandy Jnr, O. (1982) *Beyond Agenda Setting: Information Subsidies and Public Policy*, Norwood, NJ: Ablex.

IDeA (2005) www.idea-knowledge.gov.uk (accessed 18 July 2005).

LGA (2004) *Communications in Local Government: A Survey of Local Authorities Conducted by MORI for the Local Government Association*, London: LGA Publications.

McCombs, M. (2005) 'A look at agenda setting: past, present and future', *Journalism Studies*, 6: 4.

PR Week (2004) 'Local Representation', *PR Week*, 12 November, pp. 24–5.

Smith, G. (1986) *Local Government for Journalists*, London: LGC Communications.

Wigfield, A. (1988) Quoted in an interview with the author in Lanstone, S. 'Improving service delivery in a local authority', MBA thesis, University of Sheffield, Sheffield.

Chapter 17

Hungry media need fast food
The role of the Central Office of Information

Brent Garner

> The citizen has the right to be told and the Government has a clear duty to
> tell him what it is doing in his name, and with his money, and why.
>
> (Sir Henry French 1949)

In theory what Sir Henry French asks for is straightforward: the people in a
democracy have a right to know, the government a duty to inform, and by implication the media a duty to deliver this information after proper scrutiny. In practice it is more complicated. Most writers on politics and the media in recent
years have concentrated on how politicians, especially those in government,
manipulate the media: few have written on how the media manipulate the politicians, virtually none on how a third party fits into this relationship, namely the
£6.2 billion public relations industry. I suggest that this burgeoning industry with
its range from reputation management to the growth of the celebrity, has rede-
signed the playing field with enormous consequences, not only for the national
media but also for the regional newsgatherers who might consider themselves
less susceptible.

Day-to-day government activity is routinely channelled to the public through
the parliamentary press corps, a media village at the heart of Westminster, in
which all regional newspaper and broadcasting groups have residents. These 'vil-
lagers' are also well placed to report the peculiarities of MPs from their region,
the local relevance of parliamentary activities, even spice it all up with gossip. In
this they find most MPs more than willing to cooperate since appearances in the
local media could translate into votes at an election. This relationship has existed
since the media were allowed into the House of Commons, and reports relied on
memory men until the likes of Dickens and Thackeray were allowed to take
notes and MPs would choose their moment when the best shorthand writers
were in the gallery so as to get the best coverage – not unlike the tendency of
MPs to bunch around speakers when TV cameras were admitted in the twentieth
century.

But even the combination of the press corps and cooperative MPs could not hope to cope with the level of activity generated at Westminster if policies were to be explained and citizens adequately informed. As both the media and the parliamentary machinery grew, the needs for intermediaries also expanded, and the number of communicators became the 3,000 or so there are today, grouped under the collective name of the Government Communication Network (GCN). The GCN's website explains: The GCN 'brings together all the communication professionals working in UK government departments and agencies. They include specialists in media relations, strategic marketing, electronic, internal and stakeholder communication, as well as writers, editors and designers'. This is a far cry from the first team of communicators which travelled the country in 1911 explaining the government's national insurance policies in community halls.

The Central Office of Information (COI), has been a main player in government communication since it succeeded the wartime Ministry of Information 60 years ago. Prime Minister Clement Attlee, announcing the new organisation, told parliament, 'It is essential to good administration under a democratic system that the public shall be adequately informed about the matters in which the Government action directly impinges on their daily lives' (HC December 1945).

Initially the public were informed about fairly innocent matters like how to cook dried eggs or save fuel, but from the start there were rumours of other kinds of 'cooking'. The *Daily Express* and the *Daily Mail* (Scammell 1995: 167) with typical British understatement called the COI 'propaganda agents for the Party in power' and a 'direct menace to one of our fundamental freedoms', while the 1948 publicity bill for Attlee's government, 'unprecedented in peacetime' and in real terms rivalling the Thatcher government's controversial spend in the 1980s (Scammell 1994: 166), was attacked by the Conservative Opposition. Sir Fife Clark, the third director general, had good reason to write in 1970 that the COI had been 'born in an atmosphere of suspicion on the part of the press and the Parliamentary opposition' (Clark 1970: 155).

It was the Thatcher years, however, that saw a quantum leap in this 'atmosphere of suspicion'. Since Lord Young's budget campaigns in the mid-1980s, first in the Manpower Services Commission and then at the Department of Employment, critics have claimed that the practice of government information has radically changed.

> The increased use of advertising was part of a broader but radical shift in government communication strategy during the 1980s, reflecting successive administrations' concerns to manage political communications by and about government and its activities.
>
> (Franklin 2004: 73)

Scammell was similarly suspicious. 'The peaks in employment advertising, the timing of the general election (and the involvement of Saatchi and Saatchi)' she suggested, 'seem more than mere coincidence, a fact not lost on critics of government publicity' (Scammell 1995: 208).

These criticisms peaked at the end of the 1980s when two quality broadsheets within a couple of months devoted entire pages to 'public concern' over official government information. *The Guardian* on 15 March 1989 questioned the quality of government statistics and *The Independent* on 10 May claimed that the government had 'become increasingly sophisticated in handling the news'.

The explanation is that on 9 February 1989, Bernard Ingham, Mrs Thatcher's chief press secretary, had also been appointed Head of Profession putting him, according to one critic, 'effectively in sole charge of the Government's propaganda machine' (Harris 1990). Previously the Head of Profession had been director general of the COI, which although accountable to a Cabinet Office Minister, was not attached to a departmental information division.

Being increasingly sophisticated in handling the news was a continuing criticism when New Labour achieved power in 1997. It is well documented that first Peter Mandelson, now UK European commissioner, and then Alastair Campbell, were tagged master spin doctors, the former for his influence in making the party electable and the latter for bringing his depth of knowledge of the media to the key media liaison role within government as Tony Blair's first press secretary. There was a significant difference between the two in that while Peter Mandelson was a politician, Alastair Campbell was not. But his role differed from Bernard Ingham's in that while Mrs Thatcher's press secretary was a career civil servant, Tony Blair's had been part of the Labour election campaign. The nature of the role Campbell inherited was changed by Order in Council so that, while occupying a civil service post he was also able to speak for the Party. The reason was simple, he told me. He wanted to be able to rebut inaccurate stories without having to hesitate over whether or not they were inaccurate in explaining government policy on the one hand or Labour Party values on the other. Waiting for a party spokesman to tackle the second point would simply mean missing deadlines, he said.

That the notion of spin became an issue is well documented elsewhere and came to a head when there was major disagreement between Martin Sixsmith, head of communications at the Department for Transport, and Jo Moore, special adviser in the department (i.e., party appointee) which resulted in them both departing from their posts in February 2002 after the latter suggested that the attack on New York's Twin Towers the previous September was a 'good day to bury bad news'. Bob Phillis, chief executive of *The Guardian* was asked to chair a review of Government Communication, an outcome of which was to once again split the two roles Campbell occupied.

The review restored the civil service role invested in the Prime Minister's official spokesman with a separate director of communication at No. 10 who could speak for the Party. The review also established a new post at Permanent Secretary level whose sole remit was government communication. Finally, the review abolished the Government Information and Communications Service (GICS), regarded as not fit for purpose, and replaced it with the GCN with the remit of consolidating standards and good practice and moving government communication into new areas.

As Howell James, the first incumbent of the role of Permanent Secretary Government Communication, explains:

> Effective Government communication exists in a challenging media environment. We live in a world of media plenty – hundreds of channels and outlets and constant noise levels, where complex arguments need to be made meaningful to different audiences. The skills of professional communicators are needed now more than ever to find new ways to connect government and citizens, to use new technologies to speed up the flow of information and give people more convenient access to the information they need. Government needs to hear from citizens and customers, from parents and carers, from members of different communities and religious groups, and understand their views, their concerns, their experience, their expectations.
>
> (GCN website)

Throughout these changes, criticism of alleged government propaganda did not generally extend to the regional COI for obvious reasons. An official pamphlet (COI 1984) said: 'Export publicity for industry is one of the regional officers' main functions. They supply to headquarters articles, photographs, radio tapes and other materials for overseas and are responsible for regional tours by official visitors from overseas and for the resultant publicity'. The most high profile of the other duties was making press arrangements for royal visits. Twenty years later and the regional teams are still championing the cause of exports, though now on behalf of the government agency, UK Trade & Investment, and not directly with embassies. The number of royal visits supported has diminished as the Royal Household has increased its level of involvement regionally. But issues such as the environment, transport, agriculture, trade, crime, regeneration, skills – all the mainstays of government activity – are still communicated out of each regional capital of the country, and now also out of Cardiff and Edinburgh. But the changing face of the communications world is seeing the nature of the work change. New services, such as monitoring and evaluation tools, have been developed and the COI offers a postgraduate degree programme for public sector communicators as part of the mix of development opportunities raised by GCN. It would take a truly dedicated conspiracy theorist to interpret this work as political manipulation.

The COI's regional network, the Government News Network (GNN), carries all government news, national or local on its website, which has therefore become one of the most used government sites. The branding came about as a result of an attempt to change the nature of the Network when, as part of the five-yearly review of the COI in 2003, it was transferred to the Cabinet Office. The aim was to shed its need to be commercial but the move coincided with a time when government was looking to the public sector to reduce spend, and finding new money to effect this change proved difficult. Three years later, one of Howell James's first decisions when appointed Permanent Secretary for Government Communication, was to return the GNN to the COI so that all communications disciplines could be offered from the same source and, therefore, in the round.

Way back at the beginning of the COI, Lord Radcliffe, director of its predecessor, the Ministry of Information, said governments 'always tend to want not a really free press but a managed or well conducted press. I do not blame them. It is part of their job' (Hennessey 1989: 364).

He pointed out that governments were 'not powerless or ill-equipped in this issue' since they 'have all the resources of modern public relations at their beck and call'. In fact they have two sets of resources, the Party machine and the GCN, and there are proprieties that divide the tasks between the two. The divide that most people are aware of is that overtly party political messages will not be handled by information staff who are civil servants. But this guardianship of propriety does not prevent the GCN serving the elected government of the day in the best way that it can. In fact like all other parts of the machinery of government, it is there to be used and used well.

The GCN guidelines state: 'Communicators and other public resources are provided to help ministers explain the government's policies in a positive light', but adds, 'Government communicators or other resources cannot be used for image-making which is the province of the party-political machine'. The basic conventions state: 'The activity should be relevant to government responsibilities; it should be objective and explanatory not biased or polemical; it should not be – or be liable to be – misrepresented as being party political and should be conducted in an economic and appropriate way' (GCN website).

When that archetypal spin doctor, Niccolo Machiavelli, advised his political masters to appear 'merciful, trustworthy, humane, upright and devout' he was addressing the same issues. But he spelled out clearly that it was appearing to have these qualities, not necessarily having them, that counted. 'Everyone can see what you appear to be, whereas few have direct experience of what you really are' (Machiavelli 1988: 623).

Media advisers still nod approvingly in this direction. Pat Cadell, President Carter's political adviser, lamenting his chief's defeat by President Reagan, said: 'Too many good people have been defeated because they have tried to substitute substance for style' (Scammell 1995: 20). Of course, that is the view of a political adviser in the USA. But even here in Britain, a secretary of state in a recent British administration told a gathering of regional press officers that when on regional tours he would prefer to be photographed early in the morning planting a tree, preferably accompanied by a member of the local community than have the media called to the station hotel at 14.00. He was not a rare political animal nor even an unprincipled politician; he simply knew what it took to persuade the local media to turn out to give him coverage.

Journalists and academics queue up to criticise this suspicious 'new' art of political marketing, laying the blame at the door of politicians, especially those in government and their co-conspirators. Just 21 years short of the five-hundredth anniversary of the first printing of The Prince, one of the most respected academics (Keane 1991: 101) wrote: 'The belief of politicians that half of politics is image making and the other half the art of making people believe the imagery whatever "the facts", is rampant'. He argued that 'lying in politics' was one of the five interlocking types of political censorship in the new era.

But just as Machiavelli's advice has been simplistically misinterpreted, giving him a not entirely deserved bad press, what Keane calls 'lying', at least insofar as it applies to information officers, is a disingenuous description of what modern communications are about. The remark Lord Tyrell, Permanent Under Secretary at the Foreign Office, made to a reporter is perhaps a richer description more worthy of consideration, 'You think we lie to you. But we don't lie, really we don't. However, when you discover that, you make an even greater error: You think we tell you the truth' (Sigal 1973: 131).

Of course since Lord Tyrell's time the world has changed, the media are more widespread and probing and the Freedom of Information Act means that little can be concealed even if concealment was the intention. But to talk of information being true or false is questionable at best. Without borrowing a phrase from Yes Minister's Sir Humphrey, information can be meaningfully categorised as accurate or inaccurate. The distinction between information and knowledge is at least as broad and useful as that between 'law' and 'justice'. Where law and justice coincide can be, and quite often is, coincidental as good lawyers and bad judges regularly prove. Or between news and truth. It was a reporter who first spelled out this distinction:

> news and truth are not the same thing, and must be clearly distinguished. The function of news is to signalise an event, the function of truth is to bring to light hidden facts, to set them in relation to each other, and make a picture of reality on which men can act.
>
> (Lippman 1965: 226)

The same is true of the distinction between information, which is the commodity the government information officer deals in, and knowledge, which is what the reporter should turn this information into through judicious reflection. There may have been occasions when 'official sources' have been 'economical with their information', but they are exceptions and can easily mislead a critic into thinking the exception is the rule and fail to see things that should be more obvious and are certainly more significant.

A former head of information responsible for unemployment statistics put it this way:

> In my book there is no such thing as a pure statistic. A statistic's in the eye of the beholder. A fall in unemployment of fourteen thousand eight hundred to one journalist will be good news, because it is a fall. To another it will be fiddling the books if at a time when the way they are counted has changed. To an economic journalist who will compare that fall with the previous month's fall of sixty thousand it will be an indication that the scene is beginning to change. Now there are three interpretations of one figure.
>
> (interview with the author)

Clearly the government information machine influences the contents of the news media but this is a finding that cannot be accepted in isolation. Structural changes in the media world offer a better explanation of why this is so than theories of political conspiracy or politicisation of the civil service – though this argument will tend to disappoint, lacking as it does the sexiness of conspiracy.

Even in the tranquil years of the 1970s an editor of the *Standard* said that news management was the most difficult of all pressures for an editor to withstand: 'In a sense, most government announcements and political activities involve an element of news management. This is related to presentation and timing if nothing else' (Wintour 1972: 44). And Tony Bevins, political editor of *The Independent* wrote in 1989, 'So much of news the public reads, sees, and hears is manipulated by someone somewhere; that manipulation has become common-place in modern journalism' (*The Independent* 10 May 1989).

These opinions are shared by regional journalists. A specialist correspondent on a Yorkshire evening newspaper said of GNN press officers:

> It would be impossible for them not to be political because they are in a political job and it offers them all kinds of ways of manipulating the news agenda. With the best will in the world it is pretty well inevitable. Take just one example: Ministers come out into the regions for a working breakfast and announce a project or a policy. This is good copy. I'm not sure whether anybody could be precise in drawing a clear dividing line between what is strictly a departmental matter and what gives party political advantage. Choosing the event and to some extent setting the agenda seems to be a perk for whoever is in the driving seat.

I would argue, neither originally nor particularly controversially, that public relations generally, of which the GCN is part, subsidises the media with 'free information' and that helps the news agenda.

There is a dimension to the 'information subsidy' which influences the nature of the local news agenda even more than the national one. As staff on local media is reduced – a 42-page free newspaper may be put together by a single journalist – the public relations officer by tailoring information to the media's requirements can make this subsidised information even more valuable. The 'packaging of politics' (Franklin 2004) is unquestionable (even if the effects of this packaging are questionable) but there is a persuasive argument that government information officers were following tabloid trends in the local media rather than setting them.

A study of the media as far back as the issue of the poll tax referred to the 'rise of the public relations state' and quoted the American critic Gandy's claim that at every level of government, there are information specialists who make sure that the government's message is reported the way it is meant to be reported. It was Gandy who claimed that these information specialists operate 'information subsidies':

> These are not bribes or material handouts, but measures to reduce the cost to information seekers of obtaining information they need to construct news. By making life easy for the news seekers, information managers can influence and even determine the flow and character of coverage about their activities in the news media. That is obviously, the basis on which all public relations and publicity work rests.
>
> (Deacon and Golding 1994: 415)

The old brigade of provincial editors would have snorted at this interpretation but there are few regional journalists today who do not recognise the reality. A local radio news editor said there was 'no doubt the GNN press releases put items on the agenda which, given enough time and resources, we would ignore'. And a study (Franklin and Turk 1988) of the take-up of local government press releases showed a remarkably high rate of 96 per cent. One of the authors of that study (Franklin 2004: 110) later explained the economic reason for the high 'strike rate' with which few journalists would quarrel. The local media have space that has to be filled quickly and cheaply. A press release written by former journalists (which many government information officers are) takes less editing than Mrs Pickle's local village notes or Mr Pickle's 2,000-word report on the village cricket team. And this study was borne out in 2004 when every story carried in the half-hour evening news programme of one television region was supplied by GNN. Admittedly this was a rare occurrence in a summer when news was slow but nevertheless occurred and makes the point.

The growth of what Franklin calls the fifth estate – 'if media constitute a fourth estate, the public relations professionals undoubtedly form a fifth' (Franklin 2004: 110) – has clearly accelerated over the last few decades. But it is not a new phenomenon. An eighteenth-century play had a Mr Puff, 'professor in the art of puffing', identifying different types which include 'as the circumstances require, the various forms of letter to the editor, occasional anecdote, impartial critique, observation from correspondent or advertisement from the party' (Sheridan 1779).

A century and a half later, the journalist and critic, Walter Lippman, argued that the development of the publicity man

> is a clear sign that the facts of modern life do not spontaneously take a shape in which they can be known. They must be given shape by somebody, and since in the daily routine reporters cannot give a shape to facts, and since there is little disinterested organisation of intelligence, the need for some formulation is being met by interested parties.
>
> (Lippman 1965: 218)

The obvious consequence of this persuaded every sizeable organisation – a New York press survey had found 1,200 press agents regularly active before the First World War – that it was 'safer to hire a press agent who stands between the group and the newspapers'. Today churches, charities, pressure groups as well as big businesses have a press office. In November 2005 a survey by the CIPR showed the UK PR industry employed 43,000 people in a business worth a total of £6.2 billion. Public and not-for-profit sectors are among the heaviest users of PR, accounting for 36 per cent of the turnover of all PR consultancies and employing 52 per cent of all in-house PR professionals, reported *PR Week* (11 November 2005).

But the fight for control of news agendas is not between journalist and 'press agents'. What the journalists largely do – especially in the regions but even in the national media to a large extent – is choose between what organisations offer them through public relations: a motor manufacturer launching a new model in Spain; a multinational tobacco company sponsoring research, an antismoking lobby dressing up as skeletons outside the building in which the research is being announced; a pop group releasing a new album; a rival group accusing them of stealing one of their tunes; Greenpeace interrupting a prime minister; the GNN organising the opening of a new road; a report from an antidrug group in an inner city; a procannabis group issuing their own report; briefing by a government department or a counter-briefing by the Opposition. This is virtually endless and easily demonstrated by reading, listening or watching the news any day with care.

And if any of these organisations wants to improve its chance of getting its message in the news, or even of getting itself off the agenda, it hires a professional. Lippman saw this in the USA 50 years ago:

> So if the publicity man wishes free publicity he, speaking quite accurately, has to start something. He arranges a stunt, obstructs the traffic, teases the police, somehow manages to entangle his client in an event that is already news.
>
> (Lippman 1965: 218)

In a world that is tabloid, politicians have learned they have to swallow the pill, however bitter, or disappear. One former government minister said when in opposition,

> To be in the media is to exist as a politician. Politicians now see themselves as another consumer product and anxiously ask: 'Are they still buying me?' In other words, there is a temptation for my whole political existence to be determined by media coverage, constantly living in a world of the immediate, superficial and easily consumable concepts.
>
> (Battle 1995)

The media, financially neutered, have to be fed an easily digested, if tasty, diet of fast food. This has tended to turn politicians, who cannot live without them, into showmen. We do not just live in a public relations state; we live in a public relations world. And that grindingly obvious fact explains better, if less sensationally than plots in corridors of power, the shape of the news agenda, including the political news agenda.

References

Battle, J. (1995) *The Catholic Post*, RC Diocese of Leeds newspaper, October.

Clark, Sir Fife (1970) *The Central Office of Information*, London: George Allen and Unwin.

COI (1984) *Government Communicates: The Work of the Central Office of Information*, London: HMSO.

Deacon, D. and Golding, P. (1994) *Taxation and Representation: The Media Political Communication and the Poll Tax*, Academia Research Monograph 11, London: John Libbey.

Franklin, B. (2004) *Packaging Politics; Political Communication in Britain's Media Democracy*, London: Edward Arnold (first published in 1994).

Franklin, B. and Turk, J. V. S. (1988), 'Information subsidies: agenda setting traditions', *Public Relations Review*, Spring, pp. 29–41.

French, Sir Henry (1949) *Report of the Committee on the Cost of the Home Information Services*, Cmnd 7836, London: HMSO.

GCN website: www.comms.gov.uk

GNN website: www.gnn.gov.uk

Harris, R. (1990) *Good and Faithful Servant*, London: Faber and Faber.

Hennessey, P. (1989) *Whitehall*, London: Secker and Warburg.

Keane, J. (1991) *The Media and Democracy*, Oxford: Polity Press.

Lippman, N. W. (1965) *Public Opinion*, New York: The Free Press.

Machiavelli, N. (1988) in Skinner, Quentin and Price, Russell (eds) *The Prince*, Cambridge: Cambridge University Press.

Scammell, M. (1995) *Designer Politics*, London: Macmillan.

Sigal, L. V. (1973) *Reporters and Officials: The Organisation and Politics of Newsmaking*, Lexington: D.C. Heath and Co.

Wintour, C. (1972) *Pressures on the Press: An Editor Looks at Fleet Street*, London: Deutsch.

Chapter 18

The role of the freelancer in local journalism

Ros Bew

Background and introduction

We are all journalists now.

(Hargreaves 1999)

To Ian Hargreaves' prescient words I would now add 'freelance'.

As I write, the UK has experienced terrorism from suicide bombers. A good number of the first dramatic pictures of the aftermath of explosions came from the mobile phones of those caught up in the horror. The most dramatic pictures and eyewitness accounts of what happened during the tsunami disaster in the Far East at the end of 2004 came direct and 'wholesale' from the people themselves as they struggled to survive. Repercussions from this kind of 'citizen's journalism' have yet to be seriously felt, properly assessed and played out but it has invigorated the debate about whether journalism is a profession (Bell 2005; Greenslade 2005; see Chapters 3, 10 and 15). My aim in this chapter is to give a journalist's overview of the changes taking place in free-lance journalism as well as some practical guidance for anyone considering a freelance career.

The research is not quantitative. It's a snapshot of what is going on in the fast-moving business of journalism and how that affects, shapes and challenges the freelance journalist working in the local context. It is a compilation of views from freelancers and their employers: their anecdotes and experiences, all of which vary tremendously. Everyone I spoke to agreed that change continues apace. No one is sure where the industry is heading although the latest buzzword is 'convergence' which seems to imply the appearance of the superjournalist rather like superman or superwoman equipped to work across all media. But during my 25 years in the broadcast industry, change has been a constant companion, so nothing new there. It's the nature of the business and not a whole lot different for print journalists.

Technical advances, a ferocious concern for bottom-line accounting coupled with management's desire to break down job barriers, mean journalists have almost become autonomous islands whether in the newsroom or working from their own office. Advances in information technology, most particularly the Internet, means it's much easier now to file from anywhere. Smaller, lighter and, very important, cheaper pieces of recording and camera kit put broadcast and, increasingly, still photography within the reach of many. So practical logic would suggest that it is much easier to be a freelancer, whether in print or broadcast, working for local or national outlets. The market is also much bigger and more varied. There are more than 250 commercial radio stations. If you take into account all commercial, analogue and digital services the total is more than 500 services, according to the Commercial Radio Company Association (CRCA) press office. The BBC has 40 local radio stations, six national radio services covering Wales, Scotland and Northern Ireland and 14 regional TV services which also includes services in Wales, Scotland and Northern Ireland (www.bbc.co.uk). Despite the overall decline in newspaper readership and the disappearance of local dailies, there are still some 1,283 regional and local papers (Newspaper Society 2005b), although many are simply subgroupings of a major regional title, rather like local radio stations with specialist opt-outs serving smaller communities (see Chapter 2).

Over the last ten years the National Union of Journalists (NUJ) has experienced a steady growth in the numbers of accredited freelance journalists. It has about 8,000 freelance members and that probably represents about half the real number at work (NUJ 2005). According to the NUJ, the explosion of specialist magazines and writers in niche areas and the ease with which one can set up one's own website or blog means there are a large number of people trying their hand at being freelance journalists. Worryingly, according to the NUJ, many who call the union seeking advice demonstrate a lack of some of the basic knowledge and necessary skills, for example, understanding the laws of slander and libel, or how public administration and the political system work. The NUJ has received so many requests for help that, according to their spokesperson, they ran the first ever journalism course aimed at freelancers in the autumn of 2005 entitled 'Essential Journalism'.

The NUJ has spotted a need, which universities up and down the country have also been exploiting, as any student looking for a place to study will know. There are now hundreds of different journalism courses on offer. They vary enormously from quick six-week turnarounds to year-long postgraduate courses, which include compulsory work placements. The demand has never been greater and appears to be growing. But is the work there to absorb all this talent and interest and how does a freelancer get a look-in?

Broadcast

There's little doubt that broadcast is where it's toughest for the would-be free-lance journalist. The BBC has just gone through another of its seismic cutbacks with about 3,800 jobs being axed. Even if this is in part a bit of window dressing to placate the government and move numbers off the payroll, it still means tough times for broadcast journalists but especially those working as freelancers, whether nationally or locally. But the fact is, locally and regionally, the cutting back has been going on steadily for years. In the 1970s, local radio had a generous team of staffers who were well supported by a range of freelance workers from reporters to presenters, many of whom had specialist knowledge, for example, in farming, business or sport. There were quirky personalities too who ran their own radio shows, and not for pocket money either. That kind of local input, a good chunk of which came from local print journalists, continues to disappear. In some places it has gone almost entirely. But there are more radio stations so broadcast journalists are working in tighter, more focussed areas. The BBC says it is committed to increasing the localness of its services over the next ten years. This includes improving technical resources in regional TV and the expansion of 'Where I Live' websites. 'Where I Live' offers updated local news and useful information. The viewer or reader simply types in their postcode. The News-paper Society sees this development as a threat to its traditional territory and remit to serve local communities. In its submission to the government review of the BBC's Royal Charter, the Society warned the BBC to 'stay off its patch' (Newspaper Society 2005a). If the BBC's strategy is followed through, then this suggests opportunities for local freelance journalists will start opening up again.

There's also been an explosion in the development of commercial radio stations but now mergers are commonplace in the commercial sector. With mergers, individuality can be lost. At one recently acquired station, which had valued its independence, they are already experiencing group branding and imaging. This particular station is waiting to see with some concern how programmes might be franchised across the group. One local freelance presenter – described as being too quirky – has been axed.

But it's not all gloom. The same station and others make regular use of free-lance journalists in the newsroom. They tend to come in two kinds: the 'old' hand who mixes shift work with other jobs, and the new student journalist gaining experience. The old hand is still in great demand. With a solid back-ground in the broadcast business they are relied upon to do the work and have sound judgement. In short, they are journalists with training in media law and an understanding of public administration. The stations I spoke to make regular use of such freelance journalists. But the key thing here is that they have put in some years already on the staff. Very often they are women who have decided to take time out to start a family or older journalists who have retired (Delano 2003). There's no doubt from everyone I have spoken to that they are, as always, the first to be offered the weekend shifts or holiday and pregnancy cover. They're seen as a 'safe pair of hands'. This is why many successful freelance journalists believe it's essential to establish yourself and build a track record and contacts, and then take your chances as a freelancer. This is particularly true of the broadcast media which demand more technical skills than print.

Increasingly, for the broadcast journalist their first experience of working will be as a freelancer. Local radio stations unashamedly make extensive use of freelance broadcast students, work that is often unpaid, or if it is paid, very poorly (Harcup 2003: 19). It is difficult not to speculate that the plethora of courses and large numbers of young would-be broadcasters have contributed to the loss of jobs, so great is radio and TV stations' reliance on trainees, interns and short-term contracts. The extent to which work at the BBC is under pressure is demonstrated by the change to its work placement scheme for trainee journalists. Demand is now so great that placements are no longer run on an *ad hoc* local basis but organised centrally with quotas being applied to stop some universities from hogging all the places. However, according to all the editors I spoke to, anyone who is any good will be snapped up. In fact, they said it is difficult to find good young broadcasters who are committed as well as talented. The advice is to work for as many local stations, and at the same time, as is possible. As one colleague put it 'experience is a tradable commodity'.

But there is a fundamental downside to working as a freelancer whether you are starting out or have years of experience. Freelance journalists are unlikely to get the top news story, unless, of course, they break it themselves. The headline stories will always go to staffers. Former editors and producers who now freelance know and expect this to be newsroom policy. The exceptions to this rule are specialists in business or sports reporting. This holds true for broadcast and print.

Print: 'We cover every spit and cough'

It's among our local daily and weekly papers that the most interesting and major change has been taking place which is shaking up everyone's idea of the role of the freelance journalist, and indeed what exactly is meant when people talk about 'journalists'. It started about 15 years ago and was outlined by Pilling (1998: 188). It is the pursuit of the 'super-local' news. The increasing pursuit and space dedicated to super-local news has given rise to what some editors call the 'village correspondent' or the freelance 'semi-journalist'. As one editor of a highly successful, as in popular, weekly put it: 'we cover every spit and cough'. He has a vast army of village pump correspondents who are paid retainers as freelancers to supply copy on everything from the local fete to the darts match. His paper regularly carries 25 pages of local news. He believes it's this focus on the minutiae of readers' lives which has kept the paper going, and has, in fact, raised its readership at a time when most are experiencing declining sales. 'The more eyes and ears I have out there the better. People today want "really really" local news. They want to see themselves in print'. At one major regional newspaper there were far more people writing for it today than there were 20 years ago. But there were also far fewer journalists in the traditional sense, whether freelance or staffers. By traditional the editor of that paper meant trained experienced journalists.

'The local pages are the most read, after the TV listings', says another editor who went on to add that 'our agenda is led by the readers and the last pages ever to go would be the local ones'. In his view in what some regard as the good old days of sound journalism (whenever that was), reporters wrote about what they thought was important and what they thought readers should be reading. That attitude has been turned on its head. Readers dictate what they want. Today there can hardly be any journalist or reporter left who is unaware of the importance of their newspaper's market and who they have in mind when they are writing. This is a key issue when offering articles, but more of that later. So what does all this mean for the regular journalist, if that is what one calls them, and the type of journalism on offer? The local pages submitted by semi-journalists can be a legal minefield, so increasingly the role of qualified journalists is as subeditors keeping a check on what is sent in. One editor I spoke to described it as 'gate keeping'. She welcomed new technology, which meant she had dramatic pictures and eyewitness accounts of local floods almost immediately after the event had happened. But she still needs her qualified journalists as she put it, to pull it all together, make sense of it and check out the details of the story. There will always be a need for gate keeping – someone who will check pictures and copy for authenticity and legality. She saw the role of the regional or local journalist as editing the flow of an ever-increasing and, at times, overwhelming supply of information. For her, the local and regional newspaper's key strength is how trustworthy it is regarded to be by its readers. However, the pay for these village pump correspondents on whom the local and regional papers now depend can be outrageous. I was told of £10 for a weekly football column in one case. But for the budding school-aged journalist, this can be a good way of getting early experience.

As a result of concentration on 'really really' local news, local and regional newspapers are less interested in national news tending to leave that to radio and TV but that does not mean there's more space for what has been in the past traditional local fare – court and council reporting. This is bad news for the freelance journalist. Covering court and council proceedings requires specific knowledge and qualifications. This is one area where freelancers have traditionally managed to get regular work either directly or through a local agency. It's also where many have managed to start out before moving on. But as one editor told me: 'we want more issue-led human-interest stories, which are better researched and more selective. We're not interested in verbatim reports from council meetings and court cases. Those agencies which understand this will continue to be used; those that don't won't'. The implications of this, in terms of the public knowing and understanding what is going on around them, are complex. But that particular editor's comments reflect commonly held views among many editors and offer some insight into how freelancers should approach their work and sell their stories.

With the growth in village correspondents and easier access through the Internet, we are moving ever closer to what they call in the US 'citizen's journalism'. Everyone it seems is a writer, reporter or photographer if they want to be. So where does this leave the freelance journalists trying to pursue their chosen profession? While some journalists and editors think the local opportunities for the professional freelance journalist, with accredited qualifications and experience, are disappearing, others argue that the sheer size of local papers coupled with the plethora of specialist supplements need the skills of more journalists than ever. Some newsrooms claim they have as many core journalists, both freelance and staff, as they had ten or twenty years ago. Where numbers had fallen, papers claim they are now on the increase. What seems to be likely is that the role for some of those journalists has changed, from originating articles to editing the input of the local or village correspondent. Editors point out that the local supplements offer more opportunities today for the freelancer especially for the ones with niche knowledge, as in sport, farming and business. 'Can't find enough with good knowledge and skills' was a complaint repeated by editors time and again.

What is the best way to start out whether in broadcast or print? Most editors and a good number of freelance journalists believe that experience as a staff reporter is essential. That seems to make good sense. However, there are those who are carving out a good career without having had a long track record slaving away in a newsroom subbing copy or writing cues for presenters. One person who is successfully bucking the trend is Janet Murray. She is a strong advocate of being a freelancer having become one almost immediately after training. She believes so passionately that it is possible to be successful and make a reasonable living being a freelancer that she set up the first ever website dedicated to the needs and interests of the freelance journalist. The website allows journalists to network, swap information and seek advice and help. Courses on taxation, negotiating skills, marketing and business planning are all in the offing. From setting up The Journalists Forum in November 2004, and having grown from three to 1,200 members in a little over a year, Jan launched Journobiz in March 2006 – expanding the forum into a wider community site for media professionals. Crucially, Janet Murray believes that talent and good journalism skills alone won't guarantee a successful career as a freelancer, whether you are working in the local sphere or aiming at the national press. So what does it take and what is the best way to carve out a career and, more importantly, make a living in what is clearly a tight and increasingly difficult market place?

How to get started and the practical stuff: 'Invest to accumulate'

Thankfully much of the old suspicions and prejudices about freelance journalists not being up to the job or they would be on the staff, or that they are past it or unreliable, have just about disappeared. So many people from different professions are on short-term contracts or working as consultants (another word for freelancing) that this kind of view is just plain ignorant. The challenges for today's freelance journalist, local or national, are more complex than ever, so where to start?

There are still a few old hacks who regard experience alone as being the only way to a successful career. This nostalgic experience, by the way, is usually gained in the rough macho-driven environment of a stuffy newsroom – a rite of passage involving fetching coffee and listening with suitable awe to the stories of some old buffers reminiscing about great scoops in the face of fantastic odds. This is of little use to anyone and thankfully that has just about disappeared with more structured experience on offer. So, experience as a staff journalist can stand you in good stead. You will come to understand the ebb and flow, ups and downs of the local radio station or newspaper. You'll find out which months are quietest and how to be creative in order to fill pages or airtime. In short, you get the real inside track and get to know the local heartbeat which will be incredibly helpful when you start trying to sell your ideas from outside. This is a time to build up a network with other journalists and to get to know local organisations and contacts within the communities you hope to report on. You'll get to know your patch and identify the buttons which get the local community going. Above all, don't underestimate the constant inspiration and challenge you get from your colleagues' work. As a freelancer, the one thing I found I missed was the injection of ideas and thought from time shared over the coffee machine, hammering out ideas or current issues. Camaraderie and teamwork is enjoyable. If you can't bear to lose this, then perhaps being a freelancer is not for you.

Although as the NUJ has discovered, there are a good number of successful freelance journalists who have no training, it is nonetheless essential, more so today than it has ever been – whether it is a short course which is all that you can afford or the much more expensive but thorough postgraduate diploma. But once trained up, your skills shouldn't be allowed to languish. Updating, renewing and widening them at regular intervals is essential. The NUJ offers many short courses offering specialist skills. It also runs specific courses aimed at the freelance journalist, which build on the trade skills learnt at university. These courses can be found on its recently created training website (www.nujtraining.org.uk). 'Invest to accumulate' is Janet Murray's motto and over the coming years this is going to be more true than ever before. Journalism of the twenty-first century will demand that we be multidexterous – able to broadcast and write for websites, write for print but also offer spin-off stories for TV and radio programmes. Some journalists, particularly the freelance ones, are already working comfortably across media.

Aside from the practical journalism skills, there are a whole raft of other skills and knowledge, which you are also going to need. It is often these which let down even the most talented freelancer. As a freelancer you are joining a vast army of the self-employed. You will be running a business. This is not something we are very good at teaching in the UK. We still see business as something separate from everything else. Art colleges grasped this some time ago. The bottom line is that you will be running your own business.

Over the last decade, tax and employment legislation have been changed deliberately to make it easier and more financially rewarding for people to be self-employed. There are tax benefits to encourage and help self-employed people set up their own office, invest in equipment and run their business. Freelance staff working newsroom shifts have greater employment rights than they used to. But the administration involved in running a business can come as a shock. The self-employed freelance has to pay for everything from pens to paperclips – a shock if you have been used to staff support. Right from the start you should find a good accountant. Most will be happy to have a chat to get you going and explain what you should be doing from the off. You can do most of the record keeping yourself but then the final sums and working out of tax can be done by the professional who will reduce their costs so long as you have filed away receipts and kept details of money in and money out. Banks too are well set up to give advice and often have special no-charge deals for those starting out. It's important to establish regular office systems: filing of notes, keeping receipts and logging how much is coming in and going out. This is a bore but it becomes much easier and prevents the build-up of inscrutable and mysterious bits of paper when the income tax return is due.

Now to the bottom line – money! Be clear about what you are being paid and how. Generally print is better than broadcast in that there are clear rates paid for lines, headlines and so on. But you need to check them out. Bear in mind that the lineage and fee for the final broadcast item may not represent the amount of research you put in.

Discuss these issues before you get started. You will need good negotiating skills. Radio seems to have no fixed proper rate. It is almost at the whim of the editor or producer. Shift working, though, does normally come under some agreement but check it out including such mundane things as whether you get transport home late at night.

Once a commission is agreed confirm the details by email. Make sure all parties are happy with the intended outcome. Courses on how to negotiate – and you will need these skills when talking about fees or working conditions – are available through various organisations including the NUJ.

'The Medium is the Massage': Marshall McLuhan

Financial advice is not the only thing missing from many journalism training courses. We could do with some practical lectures or workshops on how to market yourself beyond setting up websites or blogs. Marketing starts with knowing the output of the newspapers or radio stations you hope to work for. Obvious? Yes, but this was the top of the list of advice from all the editors I contacted. Too often they find reporters are clearly ill-informed and haven't bothered to read, look at or listen to the product. Most editors will happily spend some time with a newcomer going through their portfolio and discussing the kind of thing they would be interested in. So, put one together even if it's primarily of work done during a course. It is important to be professional about yourself and your talents. This may sound harsh and at odds with the ideals of good journalism but regard yourself and your work as a product to be marketed. Take a cool look at what you have to offer, where your strengths and weaknesses lie and how you think you might stand out from the rest of the crowd. Too often freelance journalists only want to report on the classic fun subjects – films, theatre, food and gardening. If you can develop a niche knowledge as in sport or business, so much the better. One journalist who has been in the business for many years took some advice early on and passes it on for good measure – 'develop a specialism and you have a job for life'. So is it worth all the hassle? All the freelance journalists I spoke to say, however much they may moan, they prefer the independent work pattern and the fact they can often offer a different approach in their work and wouldn't go back to the increasingly centralised office. As one former staff journalist turned freelancer put it – 'It's about me now!'

Notes

Interviews with 18 journalists from broadcast and print provide the research data for this chapter. Except where stated, it was agreed that they would speak frankly on condition that that their views were quoted anonymously. Interviewees came from a wide spectrum: some were experienced editors of regional papers covering weekly and evening editions; some were editors and producers in local radio; others were freelance journalists contributing to both print and broadcast. I would like to thank them for being generous with their time and for their helpful suggestions in pursuing additional routes of enquiry.

References

Bell, E. (2005) 'London's citizen reporters prove their worth with their coverage of bombing', *The Guardian*, 11 July.

CRCA – Commercial Radio Company Association (2005) interview, July.

Delano, A. (2003) 'Women journalists what's the difference?', *Journalism Studies,* 4 (2).

Greenslade, R. (2005) 'Seen it, shot it, sold it', *The Guardian*, 8 August.

Harcup, T. (2003) 'Priced out of a job', *Press Gazette*, 27 June, p. 19.

Hargreaves, I. (1999) *Reporters and Reported,* Unpublished lecture series, January–March, Cardiff University: JOMEC, Cardiff.

Newspaper Society (2005a) *Review of the BBC's Royal Charter: Newspaper Society's Submission,* London: Newspaper Society, 18 July.

Newspaper Society (2005b) www.newspapersoc.org.uk (accessed October 2005).

NUJ (2005) interview, July.

Pilling, R. (1998) 'The changing role of the journalist: from faithful chronicler of the parish pump to multiskilled compiler of an electronic database', in Franklin, B. and Murphy, D. (eds) *Making the Local News: Local Journalism in Context,* London: Routledge, pp. 183–96.

Chapter 19

Trading on trust: news agencies, local journalism and local media

Martin Hamer

Introduction

Press – or news – agencies are major sources of news and information to both media and nonmedia organisations on a global, national and/or local scale. Many local, regional and national newspapers rely heavily on agency copy which, since it is typically supplied to so many and varied types of media, usually needs to be impartial. Agencies like Reuters, an international company, have

> historically, been one of the most formative influences in the development of the very concept 'news' in the western world, aiming to satisfy the news appetite of many daily retail media, regardless of political persuasion, so they put forward the concept of 'impartiality' as a valued journalistic objective.
> (Boyd-Barrett 1980: 19)

Thus, news agencies have played an 'agenda-setting' role (Boyd-Barrett 1980: 19). The Press Association (PA), the national news agency for the UK and Ireland, itself claims it has an agenda-setting function by influencing what happens in the media (The Press Association Group 2005b). The local media serve a specific geographical area and are expected to meet the needs of the local audience in terms of news, comment and a channel for the expression of local culture (McQuail 1992: 151). In this way, the local agencies may also be said to set the local news agenda although it could be argued that the agenda is already set for them through the needs of their customers. Whichever way round, it also follows that relations between the agencies and the local press need to be cordial at worst and very close at best, with trust forming a major part of this partnership. Sanders, for example, claims: 'Trust is the whole basis upon which the reporting edifice is founded.' News agencies trade on trust and need a reputation for accuracy, speed and reliability (Sanders 2003: 109). Using an albeit limited number of examples from the UK, this chapter examines relationships between news agencies, both local and national, and the local and regional press, in terms of how much agency copy is supplied and used, who sets the news agenda as a result and what are the implications of this reliance on agency material for broader issues of democracy.

Press agencies

Press agencies are organisations which gather and distribute news to a range of media on a local, regional, national or international scale. Some are government-owned or state-backed. The laying of the Atlantic cable in the mid-1860s meant the telegraph – a means of transmitting information – became intercontinental and led to a proliferation in the number of national and international news agencies, or wire services, which distributed news to a variety of clients. Hackett and Zhao say it suited the political economy of the news agencies to provide purely fact-based copy. To serve this range of subscribers with varying partisan orientation, the wire services needed to provide 'middle-of-the-road, factual reportage, to which individual newspapers could add their own "spin"' (Hackett and Zhao 1998: 72).

The PA's arrival in 1868 came at a time when news was becoming a much sought-after commodity. The abolition of the 'taxes on knowledge' paved the way for the establishment of both an independent, 'free' and cheap press. It meant that more newspapers could afford technological innovations, like the new printing presses. It had been argued that an affordable press was an important part of an educated democracy (Lee 1978: 117–18). The main stumbling block for newspapers was that the telegraph wires were controlled by a few private firms, operating under the Magnetic and Electric Companies banner. For events outside their own circulation areas, provincial newspapers were particularly at the mercy of the telegraph news wires as these companies 'held a monopoly control of the supply of news by telegraph and they exploited that power ruthlessly … it was no wonder, therefore, that provincial news bosses had long cherished the vision of a news agency of their own'. The telegraphed reports were highly expensive and often full of errors (Moncrieff 2001: 10–11). The 1868 Telegraph Act nationalised the UK's telegraph companies, providing the catalyst for the emergence of a news agency like PA (Moncrieff 2001: 10).

The big agencies provide what are known as wire services (Boyd-Barrett 1998: 19). In the United States, the arrival of the wire services in the nineteenth century meant that news was sold as a commodity to newspapers irrespective of their political leanings (Jaehnig 1998: 98). Print and online publications rely on the news agencies for much of their daily news (Franklin *et al.* 2005: 166), though agency content tends to be considered as wholesale resource material which needs to be reconfigured for a specific audience (Boyd-Barrett and Rantanen, 1998: 6). Rolston and McLaughlin (2004) show how the press, while relying heavily on news agency copy, can still present local angles on wider stories, though the outcome can sometimes be 'strained' and 'bizarre' (Rolston and McLaughlin 2004: 191–201). Franklin discusses how shortages of staff journalists, including at the BBC, means that reliance on the ready supply of news provided by the news agencies like the PA and Reuters is considerable, particularly in understaffed local radio newsrooms where journalists are under considerable pressure to produce regular bulletins across the day (Franklin 1997: 143). Many press agencies employ freelance journalists (Van den Bergh 1998: 196–7), but most will also have permanent staff.

One of the chief dogmas of journalistic practice in the western world is the notion of objectivity, the view that news reporting should seek to be impartial and balanced, an ideal sought by the PA (and the BBC). This is in an attempt to make sure that full and fair accounts of reported events are given, though British newspapers are not bound by this convention in the same way as the broadcast industry (Sanders 2003: 42).

As with many other media organisations, new technology – including the arrival and seemingly unending growth of the internet as both a source of news and a new customer base – has helped press agencies expand in recent years. In addition, the introduction of equipment like high-powered laptop computers and portable phones means that reports and images can be filed electronically within seconds, enhancing the speed, accuracy and efficiency of the editorial operation (Franklin 1997: 102). This is clearly of great benefit to press agencies which face constant deadlines as they cater for such a great variety of customers. Journalists can also keep abreast of world events and copy being produced by news agencies via the internet on their mobile computers (Franklin 1997: 102), which can be seen as increasing the value of the agency material. It also indicates an agenda-setting function on the part of the press agencies.

Surviving and serving

The PA, now under the Press Association Group umbrella, describes itself as 'one of the leading providers of media services in the UK and home to the country's national news agency … supplying fast, fair and accurate news and information' (The Press Association Group 2005a). Editor Jonathan Grun (2005), who has overall responsibility for the agency's editorial output, gives an idea of the scale of PA's output, 'Every regional evening, morning and Sunday newspaper and radio and TV station takes PA services – ranging from the main news, sport and picture wires, to page ready news, racing, TV and ready-packaged video bulletins'.

Based in Fleet Street until the 1990s, PA has a network of offices and regional bureaux around the UK and Ireland. Its main locations are London, Howden in East Yorkshire, Glasgow and Belfast. It employs almost 1,400 people from reporters, subeditors, photographers, page production specialists and weather forecasters to IT, commercial and other support staff. It is a private company with 27 shareholders, most of whom are national and regional newspaper publishers (The Press Association Group 2005b).

Newspapers, particularly the provincial ones, were clearly PA's main customers when it was founded. Former political editor, Moncrieff (2001: 11), author of *Living on a Deadline* which details the agency's history, says it was registered as a limited company in 1868, with the 'aim of giving the kind of reports newspapers – and other subscribers – wanted, when they wanted them and at the length they wanted them'. In the agency's centenary history book, Scott (1968: 26) says its *raison d'être* was the result of a desire by the provincial newspapers to organise and control their own collection and supply of news. It would be open to any provincial newspaper proprietor who wanted telegraphic news (Scott 1968: 28). PA made its intentions clear from the outset. Edmund Robbins, one of PA's very first subeditors, recalled: 'There were three cardinal principles to be remembered always. First, accuracy, the second, promptitude, the third, absolute impartiality' (Scott 1968: 47).

The PA very nearly went out of business in the 1990s, its existence threatened by a section of the regional press it was formed to serve. A company called UK News had previously served only regional evening papers from its Leicester base, but it was then decided it would also feed the two conglomerates, Mirror Group and Express Newspapers (publishers of ten national titles between them), with a national service. It was announced in August 1995 that both groups would end their contracts with PA at the end of that year. UK News was also strengthened by support from two big regional newspaper chains, Westminster Press and Northcliffe, the latter being part of *Daily Mail* owners, Associated Newspapers. Stung by this massive threat to its monopoly, PA reduced the price of its daily news service to other newspaper groups. Fortunately for PA, just as UK News was recruiting staff in preparation to start its big news operation in a few months' time, Westminster Press pulled out as a cost-cutting exercise and an ensuing row between the other three major shareholders over how to reallocate the shares led to the Mirror Group renegotiating a five-year deal with PA on the reduced rates. The Express Group followed suit and agreed to a three-year deal (Greenslade 1995). It had also been stated that journalists at both The Independent and the Express group had voiced concern over taking an untried service from UK News while losing the PA one (Morgan 1995), which indicates a fairly substantial reliance on tried and trusted agency copy by at least some of the national newspapers. It also fuelled the debate over which was the more important concern, the cost of an editorial service or the quality.

Grun recalls that the UK News saga changed the way PA operated, saying that prior to the threat, 'we had the wrong attitude to our customers. In some ways, you could argue that we sent the signal to some of our regional customers that we didn't want them as customers any more ... it was wrong'. He reflected that it took the setting-up of UK News to make PA sit up and take notice of how it must adapt to meet the changing needs of its customers (Grun in Hamer (2000: 18)). PA's provision for the regional press included a special evening newspaper service, known as PACE, delivering a daily average of 30,000 words between 06.00 and 15.00, while national and international news is sent camera-ready (ready for printing) to many daily regional newspapers (Hamer 2000: 19). Grun says: 'PA's original historic mission was to be the national level eyes and ears of the regional media'. To some extent, this still seems to be the case. He adds:

> As a result, they are able to carry cost effective national news. At a local level, they are able to take our national stories and localise them to suit their region. And we also provide vital coverage for their region from outside their area – for example, our Westminster and City desk staff file some stories which may not be of great interest at a national level but is very significant in a particular region. In addition we now produce a number of regional newswires.
>
> (Grun 2005)

Regional endorsement of PA's service came from a newspaper customer in its centenary year; the *Yorkshire Post* paid tribute to the agency, saying

> The trustiness of the PA is one of the supreme merits of British journalism ... the fact is that most of our newspapers contain so much news wired from the PA that it would look monotonous if every message from its giant building in Fleet Street had a Press Association by-line or label.
>
> (Andrews 1968)

Some official bodies clearly see PA as a convenient and objective way of getting news out to the rest of the media. David Tuck, assistant press secretary to the Queen at Buckingham Palace, sees PA as a 'tried and tested means of ensuring that an official statement is swiftly and accurately made available to the broadest range of print and broadcast media' (Hamer 2000: 45). Several regional newspapers also appear to let PA set a part of their news agenda with the page-ready operation in which it supplies camera-ready pages, containing both text and statistical information, for newspapers (Hamer 2000: 26). Assuming news agenda-setting has some importance in the daily life of the nation and plays a part in the democratic process, then bearing in mind the range and extent of PA's editorial services and the powerful and wide-reaching custom base that it serves, it would appear to have a significant role in leading the news agenda for at least some of the media in the UK and Ireland. I help to produce material for several regional news indexes for the BBC, which is traditionally among the biggest customers of the PA. A substantial amount of the agency's copy is used either as a primary news source or to supplement stories, though the BBC has a two-agency rule which usually requires confirmation from more than one source before a news story is published. It is also noticeable that PA does not cover every regional story; indeed for a national news agency, this could be deemed impossible. However, this does raise the possibility that local agencies best serve the interests of the local media.

Grun says the PA has strived to ensure its services are of the highest quality and represent good value to customers. More importantly, he says the services have been developed 'in partnership with customers to ensure they are relevant to their businesses' (Grun 2005). While working at the agency between 1989 and 2001, I can confirm that PA staff members are encouraged to be as accommodating and as helpful as possible with all customers, whether national or local, without them being allowed to dictate things. Historically, PA has also used a fair number of minor agencies around the UK and Ireland, providing it with match reports and stories, though quite possibly not as many as previously used to be the case. Grun is clearly content with PA's relationship with journalism at the regional level: 'We enjoy cordial relations with many agencies and local media generally' (Grun 2005). This has clearly not always been the case, most particularly at the time of the threat posed by UK News when PA, by its own admission, had neglected to some extent the needs and views of its local customers. Does this suggest that a local agency is better suited to meeting these demands than a major press agency like PA?

Covering the local patch

Barnes News Service, which is based in Wigan, Greater Manchester, could be termed a local press agency. It was started in the 1960s (at the same time that the ailing *Evening Chronicle* merged with the *Manchester Evening News*) as a one-man operation by Jeff Barnes. The current editor, David Calderbank, says the agency has grown over the years, although staff numbers – four reporters – are now lower than previously. Barnes serves all different types of media, including radio, television and websites with words only although the agency does work in tandem with two freelance photographers at different ends of the 'patch', which is the area that the agency covers. This stretches from the Wigan area through central Lancashire and west Lancashire to Preston. The majority of the material supplied by Barnes is sports-related, though the local agency also produces news, including court reports. Calderbank (2005) says it is very much a team effort.

Calderbank says the service supplies all the evening papers on that particular patch. They include the *Manchester Evening News*, *Bolton Evening News*, *The Gazette* (Blackpool), *Lancashire Evening Post*, *Liverpool Echo* and *Daily Post*. All the weeklies in the coverage area also tend to rely on Barnes. The same applies to all the local radio stations stretching from Carlisle to Manchester and Merseyside, while most of the national daily newspapers tend to look to Barnes News Service for cover, at least initially. 'For them it's not cost effective to tie staff up, particularly on crown court cases', he says. The local newspapers, he explains, still want local news, while the demand of the daily newspapers has changed considerably during the past decade or so, though this is more down to the changing tastes of news desks rather than the introduction of new technology. In relation to the PA, which uses Barnes copy, he says that the growth of the national news agency, particularly during the past ten years, has had an impact but not a significant one: 'They tend to cover the stories staffed by the dailies, so the market for us isn't big any way, apart from ordered cover'. The BBC also uses copy, particularly for court stories, from local agencies such as Barnes, mainly for the financial reason given earlier by Calderbank. When asked whether Barnes News Service has contributed to the reporting of significant events in the local communities which it covers, he feels that the agency has helped to get the message across, but is not sure that it has played a 'vital role'. On the subject of how Barnes relates to the rest of the media, he says, 'We have a reasonable relationship with most rival agencies but not a lot of contact. Our relationship with local papers is strong' (Calderbank 2005).

My experiences, as someone who has used copy supplied by Barnes News Service – while working at both the PA and the BBC – and also commissioned the agency to cover stories, are that a local agency like this depends on a strong, flourishing partnership with its customers, whatever type they might be. It is particularly with material like the type supplied on court stories that the local press agencies like Barnes prove invaluable as no section of the media wants to get things wrong, particularly pertaining to legal matters, so there can be nothing better than receiving material from somebody who was actually present. As Calderbank says, media organisations do not want one journalist tied up at a court case (unless it is a particularly big one) and so local agencies prove very useful. It would appear that the local media, and national to some extent, would appear to depend very much on local press agencies like Barnes – though more in certain areas of reporting than others. It is also clear that a well-established local agency like Barnes knows its patch as well as, if not better than, any other media organisation and therefore can be said to be best-placed to supply local media with local stories. The local media would also seem to be a local agency's biggest customers in terms of copy required and, therefore, this is where it concentrates its efforts. In fulfilling this local need, they may also be said to be serving the democratic process at the regional level.

Conclusion

At first glance, press agencies like the PA and Barnes News Service are very different organisations, certainly in terms of size of staff and their respective output (PA clearly does far more than simply provide text, which is basically the full extent of Barnes' remit). The PA also has a customer base which stretches the length and breadth of the UK and Ireland – and beyond in some cases – while Barnes provides a parochial service as it covers a regional patch. However, with regard to the media they both serve, the range of customers to which they each supply information is not dissimilar; each provides copy to print, broadcast and online services and both organisations clearly need to be seen as reliable and trustworthy to their customers. In some cases, for example with the page-ready service, the PA basically provides some whole pages for a regional newspaper (it could almost be said to be a publisher in this respect), which suggests that it sets the news agenda to some extent. One of the main services provided by Barnes is court copy which, for legal reasons alone, has to be accurate. PA is also a major supplier of stories from the courts, suggesting that in this respect at least both national and local agencies serve the democratic process. Where there may be a substantial difference is at the local level of news supply. As a national news agency, PA's horizons are broader and bigger, and it needs to be all things to all types of media. It might appear that it is left to the local agencies to satisfy the appetite of local media which sometimes require parochial stories, not of any great interest on the wider scale, but still important locally and to the overall democratic process. Big or small, for both the sake of journalism and democracy, it is surely important that press agencies need to be trusted by their customers due to the fact that they are relied upon for a sometimes varied and often considerable number of stories. It might be said it is probably for logistical and financial reasons, more than anything, that the media trust the agencies to provide an important part of their editorial output. But nevertheless, on the whole, trust them they appear to do.

References

Andrews, Sir L. (1968) 'The daily thirst for news – the P.A. has met it for 100 years', *Yorkshire Post*, 13 March.

Boyd-Barrett, O. (1980) *The International News Agencies*, CA: Sage.

Boyd-Barrett, O. (1998) '"Global" news agencies', in Boyd-Barrett, O. and Rantanen, T. (eds) *The Globalization of News*, London: Sage.

Boyd-Barrett, O. and Rantanen, T. (eds) (1998) 'The globalization of news', in *The Globalization of News*, London: Sage.

Calderbank, D. (2005) Interview by email, 19 July, 19.04.

Franklin, B. (1997) *Newszak and News Media*, London: Arnold.

Franklin, B.; Hamer, M.; Hanna, M.; Kinsey, M. and Richardson, J. E. (2005) *Key Concepts in Journalism Studies*, London: Sage.

Greenslade, R. (1995) 'Casualties of Monty's war', *The Times*, 20 December.

Grun, J. (2005) Interview by email, 1 September, 14.20.

Hackett, R. and Zhao, Y. (1998) *Sustaining Democracy? Journalism and the Politics of Objectivity*, Toronto: Garamond Press.

Hamer, M. (2000) *The Press Association at Work,* Unpublished.

Jaehnig, W. (1998) 'Kith and sin: press accountability in the USA', in Stephenson, H. and Bromley, M. (eds) *Sex, Lies and Democracy: The Press and the Public*, New York: Longman.

Lee, A. (1978) 'The structure, ownership and control of the press, 1855–1914', in Boyce, George; Curran, James and Wingate, Pauline (eds) *Newspaper History from the 17th Century to the Present Day*, London: Constable.

McQuail, D. (1992) *Media Performance*, London: Sage.

Moncrieff, C. (2001) *Living on a Deadline,* London: Virgin Books Ltd.

Morgan, J. (1995) 'Eleventh-hour hitch for UK News national deal?', *UK Press Gazette*, 11 December.

Rolston, B. and McLaughlin, G. (2004) 'All news is local: covering the war in Iraq in Northern Ireland's daily newspapers', *Journalism Studies*, 5 (2), pp. 191–201.

Sanders, K. (2003) *Ethics & Journalism,* London: Sage.

Scott, G. (1968) *Reporter Anonymous*, London: Hutchinson & Co Ltd.

The Press Association Group (2005a) www.thepagroup.com/ (accessed 12 September 2005).

The Press Association Group (2005b) www.thepagroup.com/about/shareholders.php, www.thepagroup.com/ourpeople/index.php, www.thepagroup.com/about/locations.php and www.thepagroup.com/about/editorial.php (accessed 18 September 2005).

Van den Bergh, P. (1998) 'The business of freelance journalism: some advice from an old friend', in Franklin, B. and Murphy, D. (eds) *Making the Local News*, London: Routledge.

Part 5

Read all about it! Editorial content in the local press

Chapter 20

Letters to the editor in local and regional newspapers

Giving voice to the readers

Karin Wahl-Jorgensen

The letters to the editor section has a unique place in local journalism, because it is the only place in the newspaper where readers have their say, in their own words, on the small and large issues that preoccupy communities everywhere. In this chapter, I take a closer look at letters to the editor in Britain's local and regional press. On the basis of interviews with 15 local and regional newspaper editors[1] I examine what role the section plays in the paper, how letters are selected for publication, which letters and contributors the editors prefer, and which topics and debates are most widespread. Finally, I look at how new technologies have changed the letters section.

Introducing letters to the editor

Journalists view the letters section as a crucial part of the newspaper, describing it as a 'platform for debate' that gives voice to the readers. As one editor suggested, 'the letters page is for local people who are often afraid of getting in touch with officialdom. By writing a letter, they can have a say' (Robert Williams *Monmouthshire Beacon*, personal communication, 1 September 2005).

Readership surveys and staff assessments indicate that the letters section is one of the most widely read items of the newspaper, after the front page (Gregory and Hutchins 2004; Tunstall 1996). Hynds (1991: 134), who conducted a large-scale survey of newspaper editors in the United States, found that letters sections are seen as central to newspapers in 'identifying public concerns and issues, contributing to a forum for the discussion of these issues, making readers feel represented, and lending variety to the editorial page'. Along those lines, letters sections serve a series of practical purposes for local papers. First, they strengthen ties between newspapers and their communities, and are frequently viewed as a tool to maintain or boost circulation and sales revenue (Wahl-Jorgensen 2002; Tunstall 1977). In interviews, editors described the letters page as 'good PR for the newspaper' (Malcolm Pharo *Somerset Guardian*, personal communication, 12 August 2005). Ian Mean, editor of the *Gloucester Citizen,* suggested that 'a paper with a poor letters page has poor contact with its community' (personal communication, 16 August 2005). Second, the section provides the newspapers with much-needed feedback on their coverage. This is especially useful for the free and paid-for weeklies – the vast majority of local newspapers (cf. Franklin (2005)) – which cannot afford to conduct audience surveys. One editor said that the letters section is a 'measure of the paper's health, of whether you're striking a chord. If you run something and you suddenly get a lot of letters, you know you've got it right. It gives you the feeling that you're in touch with your grassroots' (Sara Hadwin, personal communication, 29 July 2005).

Finally, letters sections are often a source of ideas for feature stories. Ian Mean said that 30 per cent of neighbourhood news stories in the *Gloucester Citizen* come from letters. Gerry Keighley of the *South Wales Argus* (personal communication, 10 August 2005) recalled receiving a letter alerting the newspaper that the council was ceasing its funding for Meals on Wheels. The *Argus* picked it up as a story, raising a public outcry about the decision, which was eventually reversed. Shira Valek of the *Barry & District News* and the *Penarth Times* said that she turns letters into stories whenever they contain something 'new, of human interest, or something good that's happening in the community' (personal communication, 11 August 2005). Another editor suggested that drawing on letters as the basis for stories 'is a way of empowering people to take part, to feel that we care about them' (Don John *Glamorgan Gem,* personal communication, 29 July 2005). More pragmatically, such story ideas are indispensable for resource-starved local newspapers, which are otherwise heavily reliant on press releases from local authorities and groups (Harrison 1998: 167).

Selection of letters for publication: criteria and preferences of editors

Though editors around the world proclaim that their letters section is a 'wide open' forum for public debate (Wahl-Jorgensen 2002a), they cannot deny their work as the 'gatekeepers' of public debate. Through their selection and editing, as well as through phone conversations and other interactions with letter writers, they play an active role in shaping the discussions of local communities.

Having said that, the gatekeeping role of editors at the local level is more limited than that of editors at national papers. Editors at the newspapers I studied publish the vast majority (60–90 per cent) of the letters they receive.[2] Most are reluctant to turn down contributions, even if they are personally offended by the content. As one editor put it, 'I don't have to agree with the letter, but I do have a duty to defend free speech' (Keighley, personal communication; cf. also Wahl-Jorgensen 2004).

Most papers will not print contributions that are anonymous or lack contact information. Also, editors usually reject contributions from outside the paper's circulation area, ones that have been submitted to several papers, or ones with potentially libellous content. Editors prefer shorter letters, and rarely publish ones that are longer than 200 words. However, they endeavour to edit down longer contributions that add to the debate, even as they lament that getting them into a publishable shape can be one of the toughest jobs in the newsroom. It is difficult because letter writers often express themselves in what editors describe, variously, as 'convoluted', 'confused' and 'rambling' language – the language of the impassioned amateur writer, rather than the polished professional journalist. Editors struggle to preserve the personal voice and the substance of the letter, seeing it as their role to 'manage the debate, rather than censor it' (Don John, personal communication).

Libel is of particular concern because editors are legally responsible for the content of letters even if they haven't written it. As Don John of the *Glamorgan Gem* put it, the letters section is 'one of the most dangerous pages in the newspaper, because people can slip in the most diabolical things' (personal communication). Letters that set off alarm bells include ones that use abusive language, attack particular individuals or make unsubstantiated allegations against local groups or institutions.

Other letters that are automatically excluded are ones that incite racial hatred. Along those lines, all the editors I interviewed had a policy of never publishing letters from the British National Party or its members, or anyone else who 'preaches hatred'. For example, after the London bombings of 7 July 2005, some editors reported a rise in racist letters. As Gerry Keighley of the *South Wales Argus* put it, 'we received a lot of letters that expressed institutionalised racism, where people refer to immigrant bombers, suggesting that the whole immigrant population are terrorists. They are expressing their fear about a small number of extremists, by saying that the entire community is a threat' (personal communication).

Most editors are reluctant to publish letters from national charities. As one described it, 'very worthy organisations like the Glaucoma Association will regularly send letters out to all local newspapers to tell people how important it is to get your eyes checked regularly. It's a press release but they've made it to look like a letter to the editor' (Hadwin, personal communication). Editors appreciate having such letters in stock to use as fillers for days and weeks where letters from local contributors are thinner on the ground.

Editors generally prefer letters that relate directly to the local news agenda and will generate further debate. This means that they're not particularly keen on thank you notes, which are nevertheless very common contributions, recording appreciation for community participation in festivals, fund-raising events and memorials. However, because thank you notes are often brief, they are useful as fillers. Editors also believe that thank you letters boost community spirit.

Editors' practices of letter selection and rejection vary according to the ebb and flow of letters. The newspapers I studied – daily and weekly – had anything between 5 and 40 letters for each issue, and devoted between one and three pages of newsprint to readers' letters. However, letter writers tend to be less active in the summer months and around Christmas. Also, the quantity of letters depends on events in the community. Around election time, editors are overwhelmed by party-political letters – their least favourite (cf. Franklin and Richardson (2004) for a more detailed discussion). In general, when large debates erupt, letters follow.

Debates

The letters bag of local newspapers reflects ongoing debates on issues central to the well-being of the community – on topics as varied as the viability of wind farms, the availability of parking for disabled drivers, the development of sports facilities, the antisocial behaviour of teenagers and the loss of local post offices. These are debates that follow on from news stories, but are also fostered by community events, council meetings and chat between neighbours. Such profoundly localised debates are remarkably similar across newspapers and regions. They are the 'issues that matter everywhere' (Gerry Keighley, *South Wales Argus*, personal communication).

Most editors will prefer letters that discuss local issues covered by the paper, but occasionally national stories get an airing – including the debate over ID cards, the war in Iraq and the bombings of 7 July 2005. While local issues take up the majority of the letters pages, these issues often tie into larger national debates and concerns. In the letters sections of the local newspapers I studied, there were debates on the same topics that dominate the pages of national broadsheet newspapers, including antisocial behaviour, the quality of public health and transportation services, and the rising price of petrol, to mention just a few examples. Recalling letters written by local farmers during the foot and mouth disease crisis, Sara Hadwin suggested that 'if you've got some large national crisis like the foot and mouth disease, it is illuminating to have someone say, "This is how this affects me"' (personal communication).

The debates unfolding on the letters pages illustrate how these sections function as vibrant public sphere institutions, or sites where 'private people come together as a public' to discuss matters of common concern (Habermas 1989: 27). As such, the letters page is relentlessly political and reflects a variety of views, often confrontational and controversial. While the drift of news content in local papers is generally away from controversy and openly political content, letters sections thus stand out as a last bastion of rigorous discussion (cf. Wahl-Jorgensen (2005), Franklin (2005), and Murphy (1976)). Nevertheless, heated political debates are not particularly popular with editors. Though they celebrate the section as the place for the airing of views and opinions by 'regular people', they also profess a clear preference for the personal stories and anecdotes of readers, rather than the expression of views on local issues.

Local editors are keenly aware of their niche in the market. They know that their papers are the main source of information about the local community, and view it as both their responsibility and strength to provide such information. As one editor explained his policy:

> We are looking for letters written by local people about local issues. Someone writing in who isn't local, writing about something that isn't local, is lower priority. We get an awful lot of circular letters. Charities seeking money get lesser-known celebrities to write hundreds of letters to publications all over the country. People who write letters about their pet issues – Iraq, vivisection or something Tony Blair's done – will get everyone's e-mail address and send around their letters.
>
> (Phillip Welch, personal communication, 1 September 2005)

As such, letters from individuals are seen as more unique and authentic contributions. Consistent with editors' view of the letters section as a platform for the opinions of individual readers, they also prefer to limit contributions from activist groups, charities and other organisations, whose views are typically represented in the remainder of the newspaper.

However, not all readers' letters are created equal. Editors generally prefer letters that tell stories based on an individual's experience, rather than ones that 'rant and rave' about local politics. For example, Robert Williams of the *Monmouthshire Beacon* said that the best letter he had received on the day I visited his newsroom was about an elderly man who was pleading for help in finding his lost walking stick, 'because it's so important to this one person' (personal communication). Editors celebrate 'gut reaction letters' into which people pour their feelings. As Ian Mean, editor of the *Gloucester Citizen* put it, his favourite letters are the ones that tell 'emotive and human' stories (personal communication). Citing the example of a compelling letter of apology from a driver who was involved in a crash which killed the passengers in the other car, he argued that 'people in times of sadness or great grief can write very emotive letters'.

Editors are adamant that the top priority for the letters section is to allow regular readers a say, and therefore limit contributions from local political figures. They suspect politicians of having an 'axe to grind' or riding their 'hobby horse', and believe that they are using the page for 'self-promotion' (cf. also Wahl-Jorgensen (2001)). As Christopher Hansford of the *Bath Chronicle* (personal communication, 1 September 2005) said, 'sometimes politicians get wind of just how good a platform the letters section is, and use it that way.' Viv Hargreaves of *The Forester* lamented that

> certain politicians will always beat a drum about a subject, and I'm selling a newspaper, so I don't want to bore the readers. A politician's letter is not going to motivate them to read the paper ... Political letters are desperately boring. They are a big turn-off for the reader, just knocking the other party, really not selling the paper.
>
> (personal communication, 11 August 2005)

She also pointed out that the publication of a letter from a local councillor usually elicits a reply from their opposition, leading to a 'personal ding-dong between councillors' which has little relevance to public debate. Such contributions move the section away from the idea that it is for 'ordinary people'.

Finally, editors are less keen to include the letters of their 'regulars', or those letter writers who are frequent contributors (cf. also Wahl-Jorgensen (2006a: chapter 8)).

These 'usual suspects' (Mean, personal communication), who see themselves as 'frustrated newspaper columnists' (Jonathan Isaacs, personal communication, 1 August 2005) often have what editors describe as 'bees in their bonnets' (Williams, personal communication) and 'pet issues' (Carol Deacon, personal communication, 8 August 2005). These pet issues often include significant topics, such as the future of the Welsh language (Keighley, personal communication) or the renovation of historical landmarks (Pharo, personal communication). For some editors, however, these contributions create a 'stale debate' which is boring to readers. A debate is 'stale' when no new ideas or information are added. As Don John of the *Glamorgan Gem* put it, 'one of the warning signs is when your regulars begin to repeat themselves' (personal communication). Also, editors seek to limit contributions from regulars because they seek out a diversity of voices. As Sara Hadwin explained it, if the same few individuals dominate the letters debate:

> the other readers are going to think, it's not fair ... The point of letters is to give different people a platform. You don't want your regular contributors to hog it. So I used to ration them, and a good letter from somebody else would take precedence.
>
> (personal communication)

Editors, therefore, prefer letters from 'new writers', also because they see letter writing as a means of enhancing bonds between the paper and its readers. Most editors are particularly keen to hear from young writers, who are underrepresented in the letters pages, and whose interest in their local paper is vital to its future financial success. When young readers do write in, their letters are often given top billing on the page.

Overall, then, the preference of editors is for letters that are written by private individuals about very personal experiences. This makes for what they perceive as a more engaging public debate, but also one which is less political, focused as it is on private story-telling, rather than matters of common concern (cf. Wahl-Jorgensen (2001)). However, because papers publish almost every letter they receive, their preferences rarely translate into practices of selection. As a result, the letters pages of British local papers continue to be an idiosyncratic mix of personal anecdotes, calls for charity funding, thank you notes, and a vibrant public debate on political issues. Nevertheless, the overall tone of the letters debate tends to be against change of any sort. Having said that, many editors are keen to include a 'balance of letters', and therefore express a yearning for letters that go against the majority public opinion, for instance, letters that support wind power or new housing developments.

Letter writers: a profile

Though editors often insist that letters are a 'barometer of local feeling' and represent the opinion of the community, they also recognise that their contributors are not necessarily representative of the readership of the paper and the community more generally (cf. also Sigelman and Walkosz (1992: 944)). Letter writers are 'local people who feel motivated and involved in a given issue' (Don John, personal communication). People who make the effort to pen a letter 'feel anger, passion, or the urge to set the record straight. They want to uncover something that they feel others should know about' (Deacon, personal communication).

Such observations are consistent with the findings of scholarly work on letters. On the basis of a nation-wide survey, Hart (2001: 420) concluded that typical letter writers are elderly white men who own their home. They are well-educated and civic-minded, and vote in all elections. Similarly, work by Reader *et al.* (2004) confirmed that letter writers are older, wealthier and better educated than average.

Viv Hargreaves of *The Forester* in rural Gloucestershire described her letter writers as 'conservative with a small c'. She suggested they are 'notoriously stubborn, and can't see that things would be better with a slightly different approach'. One editor described letter writers as people who 'have civic pride, have seen things change in their communities, and don't like it' (Gerry Keighley, personal communication). Most of the editors I interviewed would agree with this description of contributors, consistently describing them as 'resistant to change' and prone to nimbyism. This feature of the letter-writing public makes the section a site for the airing of views that are more extreme, strongly held, and unchangeable than those of the population as a whole, as suggested in studies of letters debating issues as varied as religion and immigration (Mutz 2004: 33; Kerr and Moy 2002: 63). Indeed, the consensus among journalism scholars is that letters are, at best, 'hazy reflections of public opinion' (Grey and Brown 1970: 450). As McNair (2000: 108) suggested, 'the reader's letter was and remains an important medium for accessing the views of those members of the public who are motivated and literate enough to compose and submit a few paragraphs in the required style'.

New technologies, new voices?
The future of letters to the editor

The Internet has created new opportunities and challenges in all aspects of local news production, including the letters pages. Most local newspapers now receive the majority of letters on e-mail. Editors approve of this development because it has increased the volume of letters – some suggest that e-mail has doubled or tripled the number of contributions (Christopher Hansford, personal communication, 1 September 2005). It also reduces the workload of journalists: e-mailed letters are not only easier to read than handwritten ones, but they arrive already typed up and computerised, and thus easier to 'enter into the system'. This also means that there is a quicker turnaround from the receipt of a letter to its publication which is particularly important for daily papers.

Some editors also believe that the ease of sending letters on e-mail might mean that new and different letter writers have come to the fore. Anita Syvret, the editor of the *Gloucestershire Echo,* suggested that

> a lot more readers can dash off a three-paragraph e-mail when a story in the *Echo* has irritated them ... The range of contributors also widened. It probably also went slightly upmarket, to include those with computers at home.
>
> (personal communication, 9 August 2005)

Other editors suggest that the e-mail option is more likely to mobilise the favoured younger letter writers.

However, the new technologies are not without their drawbacks. One problem is that they make possible the proliferation of 'astroturf' or 'synthetic grassroots opinion' (Berman 2003: 4) in the form of letter-writing campaigns organized by political interest groups. Along those lines, using e-mail for letter-writing campaigns has even become part of the electoral campaign strategy of political parties. As Franklin and Richardson (2004: 459) found, 'during the 2001 United Kingdom General Election campaign, the letters pages of local newspapers were colonized by political parties as part of their broader media based campaign strategies'. Several of the editors I interviewed reported being overwhelmed by 'spam' lobbying e-mails and were targeted by political parties' orchestrated campaigns at election times.

Another challenge to the letters page is the opening-up of competing forums for discussion on their newspapers' websites. Thus, the majority of the papers I visited now have discussion forums on which readers may post opinions about local issues. One of the newspapers – the *Gloucester Citizen* – is experimenting with a new special section, 'Views from the Net', which publishes excerpts from forum discussions on the editorial pages (Mean, personal communication). The *Citizen*'s approach represents a trend towards using technologies to further engage readers and improve feedback opportunities and participation. On balance, most editors view the new technologies as useful tools for engaging readers and facilitating the publication of letters.

Conclusion

Readers' letters remain a vital part of local newspapers, despite changes and challenges to the form. Editors view the letters section as a key democratic responsibility, but also a useful tool for maintaining good relations with the community. Letters are not necessarily reliable indicators of local public opinion, because the keenest contributors are also the people who have the strongest, most polarised and unchangeable opinions. Nevertheless, the letters section is one of the few places that provide a sense of the hotly debated topics in each local community, and they are invaluable in forging and maintaining ties between newspapers and their readers.

Notes

1 I interviewed editors in the South of England and South Wales. Of these interviews, 12 were conducted in person, and three over the phone. I spoke to four editors in Wales and 11 in England. Seven of the interviews were with editors, letters editors, and opinion editors of regional dailies, and eight were with weekly editors. All interviews took place in July, August, and September, 2005. These interviews, while not representative of the diversity of local journalism cultures in Britain, give a sense of how local and regional newspapers deal with letters.

2   See Wahl-Jorgensen (2002b) for a more general discussion of the criteria and preferences
for selection of letters at local and national papers in the United States. These include the
requirement that letters be relevant to the news agenda of the paper, that they be brief,
entertaining, and written by individuals who are authorities on the subject, either by
virtue of their professional background or their personal experience.

References

Berman, A. (2003) '"Turf" war: copy desk vs. copycats', *Editor & Publisher*, 136 (6), pp. 4–5.
Franklin, B. (2005) '"McJournalism": the local press and the McDonaldization thesis', in
Allan, S. (ed.) *Journalism: Critical Issues*, Maidenhead: Open University Press, pp. 137–50.
Franklin, B. and Richardson, J. (2004) 'Letters of intent: election campaigning and orches-
trated public debate in local newspapers' letters to the editor', *Political Communication,* 21
(4), pp. 459–78.
Gregory, L. and Hutchins, B. (2004) 'Everyday editorial practices and the public sphere:
analysing the letters to the editor page of a regional newspaper', *Media International
Australia*, 112, pp. 186–200.
Grey, D. L. and Brown, T. R. (1970) 'Letters to the editor: hazy reflections of public opin-
ion', *Journalism Quarterly*, 47, pp. 450–6.
Harrison, S. (1998) 'The local government agenda: news from the town hall', in Franklin, B.
and Murphy, D. (eds) *Making the Local News,* London: Routledge, pp. 157–70.
Hart, R. (2001) 'Citizen discourse and political participation: a survey', in Bennett, W. L.
and Entman, R. M. (eds) *Mediated Politics: Communication in the Future of Democracy*,
Cambridge and New York: Cambridge University Press, pp. 407–32.
Hynds, E. C. (1991) 'Editorial page editors discuss use of letters', *Newspaper Research Journal*,
13, pp. 124–36.
Kerr, P. A. and Moy, P. (2002) 'Newspaper coverage of fundamentalist Christians, 1980–
2000', *Journalism and Mass Communication Quarterly,* 79, pp. 54–72.
McNair, B. (2000) *Journalism and Democracy: An Evaluation of the Political Public Sphere,* London:
Routledge.
Murphy, D. (1976) *The Silent Watchdog: The Press in Local Politics*, London: Constable.
Reader, B.; Stempel, G. and Daniel, D. K. (2004) 'Age, wealth and education predict letters
to the editor', *Newspaper Research Journal*, 25 (4), pp. 55–66.
Sigelman, K. and Walkosz, B. J. (1992) 'Letters to the editor as a public opinion thermometer:
the Martin Luther King holiday vote in Arizona', *Social Science Quarterly*, 73, pp. 938–46.
Tunstall, J. (1977) 'Letters to the editor', in Boyd Barrett, O.; Seymor-Ure, C. and Tunstall,
J. (eds) *Studies on the Press*, London: Her Majesty's Stationery Office, pp. 203–48.
Tunstall, J. (1996) *Newspaper Power: The New National Press in Britain*, Oxford: Clarendon
Press.
Wahl-Jorgensen, K. (2001) 'Letters to the editor as a forum for public deliberation: modes of
publicity and democratic debate', *Critical Studies in Media Communication,* 18, pp. 303–20.
Wahl-Jorgensen, K. (2002) 'The normative-economic justification for public discourse:
letters to the editor as a "wide open" forum', *Journalism and Mass Communication Quarterly*,
79 (1), pp. 121–33.

Wahl-Jorgensen, K. (2004) 'A "legitimate beef" or "raw meat"? Civility, multiculturalism and letters to the editor', *Communication Review*, 7 (2), pp. 89–105.

Wahl-Jorgensen, K. (2005) 'The market vs. the right to communicate: the anti-political local press in Britain and the journalism of consensus', *Javnost/The Public*, 12 (3), pp. 79–94.

Wahl-Jorgensen, K. (2006) *Journalists and the Public: Letters to the Editor, Citizen Participation and Democracy*, Creskill, NJ: Hampton Press.

Chapter 21

Open source?

Hearing voices in the local press

Karen Ross

Introduction

Every so often, in defending the local press against the competing lure of the
internet, the Newspaper Society (2003), the body representing the UK regional
and local newspaper industry, states boldly that 'the public' trust their local press
more than other media because these newspapers are both more accountable to
readers but also closer to their interests. For example, the incoming president of
the Newspaper Society in 2005, Sir Nicholas Hewitt, insisted that

> no other media has the resources to collect and distribute local news in the
> depth that we have. I am sure the figures show that the more local the news
> is, the stronger the title. But it is not just about local news, it is about what
> local news we carry and how we present it.
>
> (Hewitt cited in *Press Gazette* (28 July 2005))[1]

However, are Sir Nicholas and the local press industry correct in their insis-
tence that the local press really does serve its local community and not only
represents their interests but also represents that community back to itself? In
other words, are local media concerned both with accountability and democracy, at least in terms of community participation? This chapter constitutes a
very modest attempt to posit a few responses to this question, and draws from
a small-scale empirical study of sources in the local press to do so. Using a case-
study approach, three local newspapers were monitored every week for ten
weeks, generating 539 articles and 925 sources for analysis. I argue that the
privileging of elite white male voices which has been revealed in studies of the
national press is also evident in the local sector, despite the fact that the local
press has much more freedom to promote more diverse views because it is not
tied to a national agenda. In addition, many more women journalists work in
the sector and some work (see p. 242) suggests that women journalists are
more likely to use women sources in their stories than men (Zoch and

VanSlyke Turk 1998; Armstrong 2004). The chapter concludes that the common-sense values of newsworthiness and the propensity to seek out the usual suspects to speak in the news combine to produce a circuit of meaning which is dominated by elite male (white) perspectives which prevent a more diverse range of experiences being heard. This circle of meaning seems more powerful than any individual journalist's desire to do something different, more powerful than any gender-based proclivities to tell different stories.

How to make source

Many studies of the press have looked at aspects of content or professional practice or bias but few have seriously considered the use of sources in news. In the few studies of news sources which have been undertaken, findings usually show that the principal contributors are elite white men, with the 'ordinary' citizen, women, and members of ethnic minorities being far less frequently identified, since journalists are much more likely to seek out elite sources whom they believe will give their reports the requisite degree of gravitas and authority (Dolan 2005). Even during election campaigns, which are the times when the public's voice is most frequently sought by journalists, the people who actually populate news stories in the British press are party leaders (who currently also happen to be men) and the stories in which they speak focus on topics which interest the two major players in the game of politics – journalists and politicians – rather than the public (Stephenson 1998). Similarly, in almost every study which specifically looks at gender salience in source selection, men are always more frequently used than women (Grabe *et al.* 1999; WACC 2000).

Looking for evidence that the press is genuinely interested in and will air the views of the general public is mostly a thankless task. In most sections of the local press, a banana-eating dog or a cat which walks on a lead is more likely to provoke the interest of a local reporter than an antiwar demonstration in the town centre. Although the news media are often conceptualized (at least by their own members) as the contemporary manifestation of the public sphere as idealized by Habermas, few media scholars would argue that 'the public' has much of a role in this so-called 'public' sphere. In work focused on the representation of public opinion and citizens, 'the public' are most often described as apathetic and framed as passive rather than active citizens (Lewis *et al.* 2004; Thomas *et al.* 2004). This rather classic example of framing results in a public constructed as uninterested (see also Miller (2004)) and accorded scant credit as narrators of their own stories but creating this particular rendition of 'the public' gives a pretty obvious lie to those other publics who are anything but passive observers such as antiwar and antipoverty demonstrators[2] and voting refuseniks.

A case study

Rationale and methods

This chapter draws on a small-scale empirical study which explores who is invited to speak in the local press using a case-study approach featuring three local newspapers published in the Midlands: the *Birmingham Post*, the *Coventry Evening Telegraph* and the *Leicester Mercury*. If we accept even the most benign form of agenda-setting on the part of the local press, then who is allowed to speak in the news is just as important as which stories are selected for inclusion. Who speaks matters because access to the media is access to influence. Even in so-called nonpolitical stories, the people chosen to comment on a new building development or the closure of a hospital or the incidence of distraction burglaries help to shape how issues are (perhaps 'should' be) considered and viewed and contribute to an 'understanding' of whose views are important. For this reason, I concentrate on two specific aspects of sourcing: the relative use of the elite and 'ordinary' voices, and the differential use of women and men as sources.

Given that the literature relating to the national press suggests that public voices are more likely to be sought out during election campaigns, the monitoring period for the case study was chosen to include the run-up to the 2005 British general election, the election campaign period itself, and the period immediately after the election in order to identify whether this was also the case for the local press. I used the strategy of a constructed fortnight as the sample frame, with monitoring beginning on Monday 13 March and continuing until Friday 16 May, taking Monday 13 March as the first day, Tuesday 21 March as the second day and so on, until I had monitored ten (week) days over ten weeks. The three newspapers were chosen mostly as a convenience sample as I had ready access to all three, but also because they share a broad regional geographic boundary, serve broadly similar communities and have similar circulations in relation to population size.

At this point it is perhaps worth saying a few words about the vital statistics of each of the selected newspapers. The *Birmingham Post* was first launched (as the *Birmingham Daily Post*) in 1857 and is now part of the Trinity Mirror Group and has a circulation of around 13,000. It is a daily paper published Monday–Saturday and at the time of writing, has a woman editor, Fiona Alexander. It styles itself as a more 'thoughtful' paper – it is the only regional broadsheet in Birmingham – than its sister paper, the *Birmingham Mail*, and its own publicity says that it has the 'business readership' at the heart of the paper.[3] The *Coventry Evening Telegraph* was founded in 1891 as Coventry's first daily newspaper and is also now a member of the Trinity Mirror Group. It has a circulation of around 58,000. It is an evening paper, published Monday–Saturday. It has an all-male editorial team (editor: Alan Kirby) and has a readership profile which is split one-third, two-thirds, ABC1 and C2DE. The *Leicester Mercury* was first published in 1874 and is now a member of the Northcliffe Group. It has a circulation of around 84,400 and is an evening paper published Monday–Saturday. Its senior editorial team of 11 staff (editor: Nick Carter) includes two women (deputy editor and features) and its readership profile is very similar to that of the *Coventry Evening Telegraph*.

As this study is interested in the generality of news stories and their sources, rather than particular types of story or particular categories of source, the first 20 stories in each newspaper were coded in terms of story type, gender of source/s, status of source/s and other variables such as sex of the reporter. Occasionally, fewer than 20 stories were coded for an individual newspaper because news items ran out early on and were replaced by features, lifestyle or sports sections. For the purposes of this study, I only coded those items which were 'straight' news including 'soft' news stories, but excluded news summaries, editorials, opinion pieces and letters to the editor. I also filtered out all stories which did not include at least one quoted source and ignored those stories which were 'national' rather than 'local' in flavour. A total of 30 issues of the three newspapers were thus monitored (3 newspapers × 10 monitoring days) and a total of 538 articles were analysed and 925 individual sources coded.

Open source? Findings and analysis

Table 21.1 demonstrates the huge variety of story themes across the three sampled newspapers.

As might be anticipated, the news agenda for the local press is very different to that of the nationals, with 'human interest' stories being by far the most frequent story category. Such stories have indicative headlines such as: 'Charity gives Iraq baby care lifeline' (*Birmingham Post* 14 March); 'Retirement will be perfect fit for shoe salesman' (*Leicester Mercury* 14 March); 'Flying the flag for VE celebration' (*Coventry Evening Telegraph* 15 April). There is a clear clustering of story types between the three newspapers, suggesting that there is a broadly accepted 'sense' amongst local journalists concerning what a local newspaper should contain. What is perhaps surprising about the breakdown of story categories here is the relatively low number of stories which are either about politics in general (nine stories) or the general election in particular (five stories), given that the monitoring occurred before, during and after the 2005 general election (see Chapter 23). Whilst we would not expect the local press to be covering national political or election stories to any great extent, it would be reasonable to expect to see stories about local campaigns and candidates, but only the *Birmingham Post* had a sufficient volume of stories about the general election to make this category one of its top five. The *Birmingham Post* certainly has the feel and style of a broadsheet newspaper, unlike the *Coventry Evening Telegraph* and the *Leicester Mercury* which

Table 21.1 Story category by newspaper title

Story category	Newspaper title			Total
	Birmingham Post	Coventry Evening Telegraph	Leicester Mercury	
Human interest	10%	31%	23%	122 (23%)
Employment/economy	17%	10%	6%	59 (11%)
General crime	7%	8%	9%	43 (8%)
Environment	8%	7%	10%	43 (8%)
Health/well-being	10%	4%	8%	37 (7%)
Education/training	6%	6%	5%	5%
Transport/traffic	4%	2%	5%	4%
Arts/culture	3%	4%	6%	4%
Burglary/theft	1%	3%	3%	3%
General election	9%	<1%	1%	3%
Charity event	1%	6%	3%	3%
Death	4%	1%	3%	3%
Musical event	3%	5%	—	3%
Sports-related	—	3%	3%	2%
Politics	2%	1%	2%	2%
Enterprise	4%	2%	1%	2%
Pets/animals	1%	<1%	2%	2%
Faith-based	1%	1%	1%	1%
Community consultation	—	—	2%	1%
Violent crime	5%	<1%	<1%	1%
Local celebrity	—	<1%	1%	<1%
Industrial action/ complaints	1%	1%	—	<1%
Sex-related (discrimination)	2%	—	—	<1%
Nuisance crime	—	1%	1%	<1%
Council negligence	—	1%	1%	<1%
Sex-related crime	1%	—	2%	<1%
Local defence/crime prevention	—	—	1%	<1%
Local disaster	1%	<1%	—	<1%
Race-related	1%	—	—	<1%
Grand Total	157 (100%)	209 (100%)	172 (100%)	538 (100%)

are very clearly marked out as local red-tops, including their use of relatively short articles, a high number of unattributed items and a large number of photographs and advertisements. The *Birmingham Post*, on the other hand, tends to longer articles and often includes 'national' stories.

We would also expect that members of the public would be more heavily represented in local news stories during a general election campaign because of the presence of opinion polls and surveys which are a staple of the national press during this time and Figure 21.1 shows that this was also the case with the local, showing a steady rise in the use of 'ordinary' people up to the week of the election itself, and then a decline.

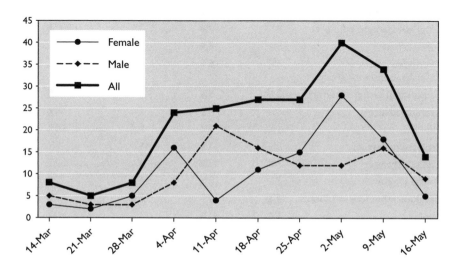

Figure 21.1 Frequency of members of the public used as sources by date

As far as the news sources themselves are concerned, of the 925 attributed sources analysed, the *Coventry Evening Telegraph* used slightly more sources across their articles than the other two, and the *Birmingham Post* slightly less, in proportion to their total number in the sample. However, the *Birmingham Post* uses a rather more diverse range of sources than either of the other two local papers.

Whilst Table 21.2 shows that members of the public are better represented as sources in this sample of news stories than is demonstrated elsewhere (Haney and Greene 2004), they still only comprise less than a quarter of 'all' sources, with far more preference given to 'elite' voices such as those from the business world (usually managers of businesses), traditional professional occupations such as GPs, lawyers, and teachers, together with councillors and local

Table 21.2 Status of source and newspaper title

Status of source	Newspaper title			Total
	Birmingham Post	Coventry Evening Telegraph	Leicester Mercury	
Business person	8%	13%	13%	112 (12%)
Joe Public [a]	5%	12%	17%	111 (12%)
Joanne Public [a]	5%	13%	16%	112 (12%)
Professional [b]	13%	9%	7%	88 (9%)
Local councillor	5%	8%	9%	68 (7%)
Local government employee	4%	9%	7%	65 (7%)
Police officer	5%	8%	5%	60 (6%)
Charity/voluntary sector/ campaign/consumer group	6%	6%	4%	5%
Education (teacher/lecturer)	8%	5%	4%	5%
Criminal justice	6%	4%	4%	4%
MP/PPC	11%	2%	1%	4%
Professional assoc.	8%	<1%	<1%	3%
Events organizer	1%	3%	2%	2%
Trades Union	3%	2%	<1%	2%
Religious group/organization	<1%	1%	2%	<2%
Tie-in to story	1%	<1%	2%	<2%
Emergency services	<1%	<1%	2%	1%
Mother	<1%	2%	2%	1%
Civil servant Gvnt. agency/quango	<1%	<1%	2%	1%
Father	2%	<1%	<1%	<1%
Alleged criminal	<1%	—	—	<1%
Celebrity	<1%	—	—	<1%
Minor political party	<1%	—	—	<1%
Victim	<1%	—	—	<1%
Political party worker	<1%	—	—	<1%
Student	—	<1%	—	<1%
Total	236 (100%)	374 (100%)	316 (100%)	925 (100%)

a Joe and Joanne Public were coded where the source was not described by a specific
   occupational descriptor
b the kinds of professional occupations coded here included GPs, hospital consultants and
   managers, teachers and lecturers; where other occupations were frequently mentioned, they
   were given their own code, for example, police officers, local government workers, MPs.

government workers. As before, the *Coventry Evening Telegraph* and the *Leicester Mercury* have more or less the same categories of source topping their lists, whereas the *Birmingham Post* is more likely than the other two, to use MPs or political candidates and representatives of professional associations such as Chambers of Commerce. This further emphasizes the *Birmingham Post*'s rather different sense of itself, as somewhere between a local and a national newspaper.

What Table 21.3 makes clear is that human interest stories attract the largest volume of sources and, unsurprisingly, are also the story type in which members of the public are most likely to be asked their opinion or to be quoted. There is very little difference between the volume of women and men sources in this category of story, although there are clear differences when the next most frequent category is considered. For women, their second most frequent appearance is in stories relating to employment and the economy which, on the face of it, is a little surprising. However, a number of these stories related to the closure of the MG Rover plant at Longbridge in Birmingham, where the wives of men made redundant were interviewed about the impact the closure will have on their families. For male members of the public, the second most frequent story topic in which they were asked to comment was 'general crime', as it was for police officers and councillors.

If we begin to drill down the data a little more, we quickly find that there are clear gender skews both in the status of female and male sources, and also in terms of the kinds of stories in which women and men appear.

What we see from Table 21.4 is that women are three times more likely to be asked to speak as members of the public than men and that they are overrepresented as education workers and spokespeople for the charitable and voluntary sector, areas of work which are typically undertaken by women. By contrast, men are twice as likely as women to be asked to speak as business people, three times more likely to speak as local councillors and nearly three times as likely to speak as police officers. But these gender-biased proclivities on the part of journalists are not a consequence of women's absence from these occupations. Of 68 local councillors used as sources, 60 were men, despite the fact that in 2004, 29 per cent of all councillors were women,[4] an average which was more or less constant across the three regions in which the sample newspapers are published. Similarly, of 58 police officers used as sources, nine were women, even though in the West Midlands Constabulary, an area which covers two of the three sample newspapers, 24 per cent of police officers are women.[5] So, additional factors must be determining the selection of particular sources by journalists, such as persistently going for the usual suspects.

Table 21.3 Story category (top 10) by status of source used (top 5 plus Joanne and Joe Public)

Story type	Status of source						
	Police officer	'Professional'	Councillor	Local govt. spokesperson	Business	Joanne Public	Joe Public
Charity event	1	4	4	1	1	3	8
Environment	2	4	5	7	9	3	1
Musical event	1	1	1	2	9	4	3
Sports-related	1	2	1	4	10	4	3
Arts/culture	2	8	1	3	1	5	8
Human interest	13	19	14	10	23	33	35
Employment/economy	2	8	8	3	20	14	7
Education/training	2	4	2	2	13	6	6
Health/well being	5	16	3	4	2	7	4
General crime [a]	13	3	7	2	4	7	12
Grand Total (460)	42 (9%)	69 (15%)	46 (10%)	38 (8%)	92 (20%)	86 (19%)	87 (19%)

a excluding burglary/theft

Table 21.4 Status and sex of sources

Status of source	Sex of source	
	Female (%)	Male (%)
Business person	8	16
Joanne Public	36	—
Professional	7	12
Joe Public	—	14
Local councillor	3	10
Police officer	3	8
Education (teacher/lecturer)	9	4
Local government employee	5	6
Charity/voluntary sector Campaign/consumer group	11	3
MP/PPC	3	4
Criminal justice	2	5
Mother	5	—
Trades Union	1	2
Professional assoc.	<1	3
Tie-in to story	2	1
Events organizer	2	2
Emergency services	<1	2
Religious group/organization	<1	2
Civil servant, govt. agency/quango	1	1
Father	—	2
Alleged criminal	—	<1
Celebrity	—	<1
Minor political party	—	<1
Victim	1	<1
Govnt. Minister	—	<1
Political party worker	—	<1
Total	302 (33%)	623 (67%)

As well as gender skews in terms of source selection more generally, there are also some (albeit small) differences in the kinds of stories in which women and men feature, as Table 21.5 below shows, although these are less marked than gender differences in status. This is quite a positive finding as it suggests that journalists are moving away from the habit of only asking women to talk about health and only asking men to talk about the economy.

Table 21.5 Sex of source by story category

Story category	Sex of source	
	Female	Male
Human interest	74 (25%)	143 (23%)
Employment/economy	32 (11%)	68 (11%)
General crime	20 (7%)	56 (9%)
Environment	24 (8%)	50 (8%)
Health/well-being	17 (6%)	37 (6%)
Arts/culture	15 (5%)	24 (4%)
Music event	12 (4%)	23 (4%)
Education/training	20 (7%)	24 (4%)
Transport	12 (4%)	25 (4%)
Sports-related	12 (4%)	19 (3%)
Burglary/theft	6 (2%)	18 (3%)
Charity event	12 (4%)	18 (3%)
Enterprise	6 (2%)	19 (3%)
Various other	40 (13%)	59 (8%)
Total	302 (100%)	623 (100%)

On the other hand, the absolute number of women and men sources still favours men, so that even in the category of 'human interest' which appears to favour women, the actual numbers of women and men quoted in these 122 stories are 75 and 138 respectively. In only two categories (local celebrity and sex-discrimination) do absolute numbers of women sources (4, 3) exceed men (3, 1). In only one category (pets/animals) do women and men achieve parity (4 sources each), but in all the others, women are outnumbered on a ratio of at least 1:2, and often more than this. It is only as members of the public where the absolute numbers of women and men sourced across all story types are almost identical (112 and 111 respectively). It is extremely disappointing to find the same gender skew in an analysis of local press reporting as found in studies of national newspapers, that is, 1:2 (women to men) whereas it would be expected that, relieved of the need to report the major national stories, journalists might look a little more imaginatively at their local community

Importantly, a preponderance of male journalists in regional newsrooms cannot be 'blamed' for this persistent disavowal of women's views since, where the sex of the journalist could be identified, 44 per cent of articles were written by women and 55 per cent by men (two stories had a female–male team). Although some research suggests that women journalists are more likely to use women sources in their stories than their male colleagues (Zoch and VanSlyke Turk 1998; Armstrong 2004), the findings of this study challenge that suggestion, since the proportion of women sources used by women journalists (34 per cent) is only slightly higher than the number used by their male colleagues (33 per cent). What this suggests is that research findings derived from analyses of the national press or national media more generally should not be casually assumed as indicative of trends in the local press.

Conclusion

Through the exercise of its alleged commitment to providing news of interest to its local community, the local press has an ideal opportunity to subvert the national agenda and mainstream proclivities towards the use of elite male sources and a bias which privileges the maintenance of the status quo. But what the findings from this, admittedly modest, study show is that who speaks in the local press is alarmingly similar to the national picture, despite the higher proportion of women journalists working in local newsrooms.

Without a better understanding of the dynamics of local press newsrooms, it is impossible to securely interpret why local journalists, women and men, continue to privilege elite male voices. One possible explanation is that notions of newsworthiness and source credibility, which have traditionally privileged these particular perspectives, exert a stronger influence than a desire to more accurately reflect the views or seek the opinions of their local constituency in all their vast diversity. It is of significant concern that in a region like the West Midlands which has an ethnic minority population of around 600,000 (approximately 18 per cent),[6] that less than 4 per cent of all quoted sources were members of identifiable ethnic minority communities and of these, 26 per cent were women. It is of significant concern that only one-third of 'all' sources were women and that only a quarter of sources were asked to speak or be featured as 'ordinary' people. This bias in source selection makes clear the news media's considerable gatekeeping function in determining both content and perspective of news stories and indicates the importance of familiarity, easy access and shared ideas about relevance and credibility, as key features of the source selection process. If the local press is to continue to call itself 'local' in any meaningful way, it probably needs to work a bit harder to more genuinely reflect the views and interests of local communities back to themselves.

Notes

1 'NS chairman: local press has positive future', *Press Gazette*, 28 July 2005, www .pressgazette.co.uk (accessed 28 July 2005).

2   A political environment which has witnessed a catastrophic decline in voting over the past 20 years, but saw 200,000 people support Live8 in Hyde Park in July 2005, less than two months after the worst turnout for a British general election for 80 years (*The Observer*, 8 May 2005), is not one of public apathy but of outrage.

3   www.trinitymirror.com/

4   *The National Census of Local Authority Councillors in England 2004.* London: Employers' Organisations for Local Government.

5   West Midlands Police website: www.west-midlands.police.uk/our-people/women.asp

6   Extrapolated from the Office for National Statistics, 2001 Census.

References

Armstrong, C. L. (2004) 'The influence of reporter gender on source selection in newspaper stories', *Journalism and Mass Communication Quarterly*, 81 (1), pp. 139–54.

Dolan, K. (2005) 'Blinded by "objectivity": how news conventions caused journalists to miss the real story in the "Our Lady" controversy in Santa Fe', *Journalism,* 6 (3), pp. 379–96.

Grabe, M.; Zhou, S. and Barnett, B. (1999) 'Sourcing and reporting in news magazine programs: 60 minutes versus hard copy', *Journalism and Mass Communication Quarterly*, 76 (2), pp. 293–312.

Haney, C. and Greene, S. (2004) 'Capital constructions: newspaper reporting in death penalty cases', *Analyses of Social Issues and Public Policy*, 4 (1), pp. 129–50.

Lewis, J.; Wahl-Jorgensen, K. and Inthorn, S. (2004) 'Images of citizenship on television news: constructing a passive public', *Journalism Studies*, 5 (2), pp. 153–72.

Miller, D. (2004) 'System failure: it's not just the media – the whole political system has failed', *Journal of Public Affairs*, 4 (4), pp. 374–82.

Newspaper Society (2003) 'Response to Government Communications Review Group (May)', www.newspapersoc.org.uk (accessed 28 July 2005).

Stephenson, M. (1998) *The Glass Trapdoor: Women, Politics and the Media During the 1997 General Election*, London: Fawcett.

Thomas, J.; Cushion, S. and Jewell, J. (2004) 'Stirring up apathy? Political disengagement and the media in the 2003 Welsh assembly elections', *Journal of Public Affairs*, 4 (4), pp. 355–63.

WACC (2000) *Who Makes the News?,* London: World Association for Christian Communication.

Zoch, L. M. and VanSlyke Turk, J. (1998) 'Women making news: gender as a variable in source selection and use', *Journalism and Mass Communication Quarterly*, 75 (4), pp. 762–75.

Chapter 22

Out damned plot

The *Evening Standard* and the introduction of the London congestion charge

Ivor Gaber

This chapter offers a case study of how one particular newspaper – the London *Evening Standard* – reported what its own motoring correspondent described as 'the biggest road experiment the world has seen' (23 February 2003). It is based on a review of more than 500 articles that appeared in the paper between January 2002 and May 2003.[1] At the core of this analysis is what appeared to be an attempt by the *Evening Standard* to 'prove' that London's Mayor, Ken Livingstone – a politician that the paper had been crossing swords with for the best part of two decades[2] – was secretly 'rigging' London's traffic lights. This was, allegedly, being done so as to create congestion in the run-up to the introduction of the congestion charge so that, when the charge was introduced and the lights returned to normal, people would attribute the easing of the congestion to the new scheme.

The allegation was first made in an article dated 19 March 2002 headlined, 'Ken's "secret red light plan" to keep out cars'. In it the paper reports that 'Mayor Ken Livingstone is working on "secret" plans to prevent motorists driving into London – by rigging the traffic lights, it is claimed today' (19 March 2002). The phrase 'it is claimed today' is often used by journalists to disguise the fact that this 'new' piece of news is either not so 'new' or is of dubious provenance. The source of this 'secret plan' is nowhere to be found within the 718 words of the article. There is also an absence of any details of the 'plan', no quotations from it, no indications of its origin or even suggestions (in the most general terms) about the reliability of the 'source'. The greater part of the article is devoted to the 'furious reactions' of the motoring organisations and of Conservative boroughs inside and outside the proposed congestion charge zone. The paper states, without any attribution, that 'His [the Mayor's] engineers are modifying them [the traffic lights] so traffic flow into the city can be dramatically reduced via a central computer and drivers will face a "sea" of red lights that will hamper their progress in outer and inner London.' The newspaper then asserts that 'Only by cutting off the flow at the outskirts, critics claim, can congestion charging be proven to "work"' (19 March 2002), but again neither the original statement nor the 'critics' are identified.

It is not in dispute that protecting the identity of sources is a fundamental principle of free and independent journalism. However, when using unnamed sources, it is important to indicate something of the status of the source in order to enable the reader to make an evaluation of the credibility of the information being provided. 'Secret plans' might or might not have existed, the article merely asserted they did without making any attempt to provide any corroboration in the face of a blanket denial from Transport for London (TfL) – the Mayor's executive agency for transport – which the paper only carried at the very end of the article: 'TfL denies that it has "secret plans" to stifle traffic flow to ensure the success of congestion charging. A spokesman insisted that although traffic lights were being linked to a central computer, this was to eradicate congestion' (19 March 2002).

On the following day the *Standard* ran an editorial condemning this 'secret plan'. It began: 'Mayor Livingstone is reported to be working on a secret plan to "rig" traffic lights to discourage motorists from entering central London' (20 March 2002), without any reference to the categorical denial that TfL had given the paper the previous day.

The following month the paper's coverage moved from 'critical' to virtually 'oppositional'. In the first 150 words of an extraordinary 'profile' of the Mayor (running to more than 2,000 words in length) the paper described the Mayor thus:

> Ken Livingstone metamorphosed into a snapping, snarling brute ... the Mayor's voracious demands for money ... he damned them ... they avoided his wild eye ... It was frightening and it was ugly. Ken at bay, raging against his own impotence, gripped by paranoia.
>
> (29 April 2002)

On 31 May the *Evening Standard* returned to the central allegation with an article headlined: 'Traffic lights rigged so car charge looks good'. The report began: 'Ken Livingstone is refusing to come clean on "secret" plans to rig London's traffic lights, it was claimed today' (31 May 2002). This was a curious inversion of the 'innocent until proven guilty' concept. An allegation had been made, it had been robustly denied, but instead of accepting, or at least quoting, the denial, the Mayor was charged with 'refusing to come clean'. In other words, Livingstone either admits the charge and is seen as a cheat, or denies it and is seen as both a cheat and a liar – the possibility that the allegation might be wrong does not, apparently, enter the equation.

The repetition of the allegation that the Mayor had deliberately 'rigged' central London's traffic lights was repeated in June. Indeed, by this stage the *Evening Standard* was seeking to give the impression that its 'revelation' was an established 'fact'. In an article on 19 June headlined 'Traffic light chaos will spread to the suburbs' the paper claimed that: 'The traffic light chaos inflicted on central London by Ken Livingstone's transport officials is to be extended'. The paper stated 'Since the *Evening Standard* first revealed how the traffic signals had been secretly re-phased, TfL has faced a flurry of accusations about its motives' (19 June 2002), without any mention of the fact that this 'revelation' had been consistently denied by TfL and that most of the accusations had been generated by the newspaper itself. But in an apparent retreat from the original allegation the paper reported that 'Tories on the London Assembly say the idea is to "soften up" Londoners for the congestion charge by causing jams now which would be eased once the charge is introduced next year. Most experts regard that as "too cynical"' (19 June 2002). This was the first recognition by the paper that there might be a political motivation behind the traffic-rigging allegations and that 'experts' were doubting the veracity of the claim.

Nonetheless, on 4 July the *Evening Standard* launched a new front, a 'Gridlock London' campaign. It opened under the headline 'Here's why we're all driven crazy; a new *Standard* campaign exposes the traffic schemes designed to make congestion charging look good' (4 July 2002). Thus, the allegation of 'rigging' congestion had by then become such an established fact that it could be used in the headline, without any qualification, and formed the basis of the paper's new campaign. The next day the paper produced virtually a 'special edition' devoted to their 'Gridlock' campaign, containing no fewer than five articles running to more than 4,000 words. The main news story began thus:

> The full extent of the traffic light chaos bringing the capital's roads to a standstill can be revealed today. Documents obtained by the *Evening Standard* show just how widespread the campaign to re-phase London's signals in favour of the pedestrian has become. They detail 111 changes in central London, at some of the busiest junctions, which have already caused delays and gridlock for thousands of motorists since they were implemented.
>
> (5 July 2002)

This introduction implied that:

- the *Standard* had, through investigative journalistic techniques, obtained a secret document which it was revealing to its readers that day;
- that the changes in traffic-light sequencing were a deliberate 'campaign' (with all that this implied); and

- that no fewer than 111 changes hade taken place to favour pedestrians over other road-users.

All three statements were misleading. First, the 'documents obtained by the *Evening Standard* had been sent to the newspaper by the TfL press office in response to the *Standard*'s 'Gridlock' campaign.[3] Second, the use of the word 'campaign' by the paper implied something that had been planned with some ultimate goal, which had been robustly denied by the Authority on numerous occasions and which the *Standard* itself, just the previous month, had quoted 'experts' as dismissing as 'too cynical'. And, finally, the paper apparently misunderstood the information it had received; the document they were sent indicated that the total number of lights being changed to favour pedestrians was not 111 but 63 – the remaining 48 changes being the result of either construction work in Trafalgar Square or were related to bus priority schemes.[4]

The article repeated the central charge of a 'secret plan', although making sure that it was attributed elsewhere (in this case to a somewhat amorphous 'many') but, for the first time, blamed not just the Mayor but also Derek Turner, the TfL official in charge of the scheme. Having profiled the Mayor, in less than flattering terms, the paper turned its attention to Turner. The profile was headlined 'Red Derek' – on the face of it the term 'Red' presumably referred to red traffic lights, but was also redolent of the attacks made by right-wing newspapers in the 1970s and 1980s against the 'hate figures' of the so-called 'loony left' such as 'Red Robbo'. The article began: 'Derek Turner, Transport for London's single-minded – some would say ruthless – Managing Director, said he wants to be remembered for two key achievements'. The use of the word 'ruthless' which is not attributed, set the tone for the article which was full of words suggestive of rage and unreasonableness including 'unprecedented anger', 'viciously attacked' and 'exasperated' (5 July 2002).

On 24 July a computer controlling 800 traffic lights in central London developed a fault and massive traffic congestion followed. Despite the fact that this had nothing whatsoever to do with congestion charging, casual readers of the *Evening Standard* might have been forgiven for thinking that the two were somehow linked. The *Standard*'s report contained two sentences relating to the scheme (shown in added italics) which stood in splendid isolation from that which came before and after:

'These are the worst conditions we have seen for a long time with motorists completely blocked in', said Rebecca Rees of the AA Motoring Trust. *Thousands of traffic lights are being re-phased as part of Mayor Ken Livingstone's Transport for London (TfL) plan to give pedestrians longer to cross roads, to redirect traffic away from sensitive sites and to speed bus trips. Critics claim that the re-phasing will be reversed when congestion charging starts, to give the impression that the £5 a day scheme is improving traffic flow.* The computer failed at 6.15am. TfL said engineers were immediately scrambled to fix the software problem.

(24 July 2002)

On the same day the paper published another article about London's traffic problems, this time concentrating on Trafalgar Square. The piece was largely devoted to an attack by Kevin Delaney of the RAC Foundation on the redevelopment of the Square. The article, just over 700 words in length, contained no fewer than 450 words of direct or indirect quotations from Delaney. It was 'balanced' with the following: 'Transport for London, headed by Mayor Ken Livingstone, is attempting to make the area more welcoming for pedestrians' (24 July 2002) – a full 18 words of refutation. This item was subsequently followed up by a letter for publication from the Mayor which was not printed. A similar fate befell letters on this subject from the Mayor or TfL on 18 July, 19 July, 1 August, 9 August and 12 August.[5] Over the same period the *Standard* did publish two letters from Derek Turner and one from the Mayor (although this was accompanied by three letters directly attacking him).

August also saw the start of a new theme in the paper's coverage – the elaboration of a series of 'horror' stories that would follow the introduction of the charge. These included:

- 'Crooks scamming Britain's car registration bureaucracy may sabotage congestion charging, and law-abiding motorists could foot the bill' (9 August 2002);
- 'Ambulance chiefs today warn that lives will be put at risk by Ken Livingstone's congestion charging scheme' (14 August 2002); and
- 'Mayor Ken Livingstone's congestion charge will trigger gridlock on vital London routes as commuters struggle to avoid the £5 a-day payment, a new survey shows' (15 August 2002).

In September the 'conspiracy' cropped up again with the following intriguing opening to an article by former *Evening Standard* editor Simon Jenkins:

Wherever two or three Londoners are gathered together, they whisper of 'the plot'. Why has traffic on key routes in central London slowed ... a mass of metropolitan rage congeals around one conviction, that someone, somewhere is strangling the traffic. Whodunit? ... The number one suspect must be the Mayor. He has both motive and weapon. Next February he is introducing the one policy he can call truly his own, the one on which he says he will stand or fall ... Next year he wants to show that traffic speeds have risen. What better prelude than to create chaos now and boast a better future tomorrow? He must have done it.

(28 November 2002)

Just two days before Christmas 2002, the *Evening Standard*, returned to the conspiracy:

Ken Livingstone's transport chiefs have arranged for almost a third of the roadworks causing gridlock in London to disappear dramatically prior to the congestion charge. In what critics have branded a 'con', officials have admitted that they will suspend the Mayor's roadworks programme for two weeks before and six weeks after the introduction of the scheme. Projects already under way should be completed and no new maintenance work will be commissioned. The revelations have been seized upon by the Mayor's opponents as evidence that he orchestrated the gridlock to make his congestion charge seem more effective.

(23 December 2002)

In the New Year the paper reported how the changes to London's traffic lights, about which they had been so exercised a few months previously, were now coming into effect not as a result of some 'plot' to cripple London's traffic flow but as part of the congestion charging scheme. The report, neutral in tone, appeared to accept that the explanation for the changes in London's traffic lights was to ease, not create, congestion:

London experienced its first taste of congestion charging today as key parts of the capital's new system went live. Scores of traffic lights at strategic junctions were switched to new timings to see if major routes into the city centre can take the strain when road pricing under Mayor Ken Livingstone's ambitious scheme begins. The aim is to prevent gridlock on the zone borders as drivers divert to avoid the £5 a-day charge. The new timings will hold back vehicles heading into London on major highways until roads on the sensitive boundary are clear.

(7 January 2003)

As if to confirm this new mood of understanding, peace appeared to break out on the following day. The overtures began with the *Standard* reporting that Ken

Livingstone had conceded that he had been to blame for much of the traffic congestion of the past few months, not because of any conspiracy to make the congestion charge scheme appear to be working, but because he (and TfL) had been overambitious in terms of the number of road improvements they had sought to undertake at the same time. And, as if mirroring the Mayor's magnanimity, an editorial in the paper accepted the Mayor's concession and made no embarrassing references to conspiracies or secret plans: 'We have had our disagreements with Ken Livingstone in the past', they wrote.

> However, we must give credit where it is due and congratulate him on his candid admission that he is to blame for much of the misery suffered by motorists in central London over the last year, highlighted by our Gridlock London series. He confesses today that he is guilty of trying to carry out too much repair work on roads at the same time … 'It is quite clear in retrospect they strained the capacity of London', he admits. This is frank and honest and we wish that other politicians were as willing to own up and say 'sorry' when they get things wrong.
>
> (8 January 2003)

The following day the *Standard*'s motoring editor wrote his own 'clear the air piece'. He began by welcoming the Mayor's apology and went on to give his own explanation about why traffic in London, throughout 2002, was in such a mess. 'It's easy to see why it all went horribly wrong' he wrote.

> To ensure that nothing would interfere with the smooth running of congestion charging that starts next month, and on which the Mayor's re-election may depend, his transport department forced far too many major schemes – such as those at Vauxhall Cross, Trafalgar Square and Shoreditch – into too short a timescale. It caused meltdown.
>
> (9 January 2003)

The significant point about this explanation is that it recognised that at the heart of the issue was, in all probability, traditional British cock-up rather than conspiracy. In TfL's enthusiasm to 'ensure … the smooth running of congestion charging' they had hurried through too many schemes in too short a time.

However, having 'cleared the air' about the 'secret plan', the paper's overall hostility to congestion charging remained, as evidenced by a spate of scare stories about the scheme that were run through January and February. These included:

- 'Thousands of drivers will be forced to pay up to £1,200 a year just to park their cars when congestion charging begins, it emerged today' (21 January 2003).

- 'Householders will have to pay more for home repairs and improvements in central London as tradesmen struggle to offset the cost of the congestion charge, it has emerged' (22 January 2003).
- 'Congestion charging will cost the Government £500 million when businesses hit by loss of trade demand huge rates rebates, a new study warns' (28 January 2003).
- 'Crime will almost certainly rise outside the congestion charging zone as offenders attempt to escape being caught on new CCTV cameras, police have warned' (3 February 2003).
- 'Parking fees near the congestion charging boundary are to rocket by up to 60 per cent in a bid to stop drivers leaving their cars just outside the zone' (10 February 2003).
- 'Householders who live just outside the congestion charging zone were today warned to brace themselves for a slump in the value of their homes' (12 February 2003).
- 'The recruitment of teachers to inner-city schools will be "devastated" by congestion charging, the head of a London grammar warned today' (14 February 2003).

In the days immediately following the introduction of the charge, the pages of the *Evening Standard* were replete with horror stories about the effects the charge was having, or at least was about to have. On the first day of the charge the *Standard* sent out its reporters to find the traffic chaos that the scheme was bound to have caused – instead they found near-empty roads. (Perhaps the *Evening Standard* was partially responsible for this having spent the past year building up a sense of fear and dread about the introduction of the charge – had they themselves unwittingly contributed to the dramatic drop in traffic that coincided with its introduction?)

Headlines, as any journalist is keen to tell a disappointed source, are not written by the reporter but by subeditors back in the office and hence on occasion do not always reflect the story that follows. But they are emblematic, they are the mood music people hear as they read the paper and they, to a large extent, reflect the values of the paper. Hence, reviewing the headlines in the *Evening Standard* in the days following the introduction of the charge provides a useful insight into how London's evening newspaper was reporting what was undoubtedly one of the capital's biggest news stories in recent times.

On the first day the paper's congestion charge lead was 'Half-term cuts traffic gives Mayor breathing space on historic first day' (17 February 2003), which seemed to imply that introducing the charge at half-term had been a coincidence or had been, in some way, 'unfair'. The story below the headline reflected the paper's negativity towards the scheme: 'London today took a big leap in the dark. After years of planning the historic day arrived when Londoners were charged for the privilege of driving into the capital'. Motoring organisations quoted in the story reported that traffic was flowing smoothly; in the absence of the predicted traffic chaos *Standard* reporters had to look elsewhere for their daily dose of negativity. An interesting juxtaposition was to be found in one of the paper's stories from the first day. Under a headline '6,000 passengers stranded as rail power lines collapse' the paper reports that the collapse of power lines had led, according to the *Standard*, to 'rail chaos'. And, although this had nothing to do with the introduction of the congestion charge, the second paragraph of the story read: 'Adding to the chaos expected to accompany the introduction of the congestion charge' (17 February 2003).

Throughout the remainder of the first week the traffic refused to gridlock and the predicted 'chaos' failed to materialise, but the paper remained undaunted, as this selection of headlines from the second day indicates:

- 'Why congestion fee is a tax on education in London';
- 'Jammed lines stop motorists paying fee';
- 'Thousands of drivers fail to pay £5 charge'; and
- '10 tube trains went past before I could get on'.

(18 February 2003)

On the third day of the charge the paper reported a survey by Trafficmaster which found that there had been dramatic improvements in road journey times since the introduction of the charge. Under the headline 'Journey times down half inside zone on 8 routes into London', the *Standard* reported: 'The extent to which car journey times in London have been slashed since the start of the congestion charge was revealed today' (19 February 2003), which, to anyone who had relied on the newspaper for objective reporting about the impact of the charge on London's traffic, would have come as an almost complete surprise. But, undeterred, the *Standard* still ensured that the majority of the day's stories remained steadfastly negative in tone.

On the Friday of the first week, a change of mood was detectable. An article by the *Standard*'s motoring editor indicated a more measured approach. The article began with a recognition of the enormity of the change and an indication that it might just succeed: 'We're in the middle of the biggest road experiment the world has seen' and it went on to give one of their first upbeat assessments of the scheme: 'With a few exceptions, the level of planning by the Mayor's office has been impressive' (20 February 2003).

The second week saw the first positive congestion charge headline – 'C-Charge: a triumph so I plan to freeze the fee for 10 years says the Mayor' (25 February 2003), followed two days later by a somewhat bizarre piece by the *Evening Standard* columnist Simon Jenkins who wrote: 'Mr Livingstone and Mr Kiley have earned the benefit of everyone's doubt. They thought the unthinkable and did the undoable. They delivered a transport policy on time, on budget and without flinching from hysterical media and political attack' (27 February 2003), failing to mention that the prime source of the 'hysterical media and political attack' was the very newspaper for which he was writing.

With the initial phase out of the way, and the paper's worst fears about traffic or technological meltdown not having been realised, there was a distinct change in the tone of the *Evening Standard*'s coverage, as it began to analyse the impact of the scheme more objectively and to note both its good and bad effects. Towards the end of the month Derek Turner, the man whom the paper had described as the architect of congestion charging, announced that he was leaving his TfL post. The paper reported that it was well known 'that Mr Turner has long had a difficult relationship with the Mayor and his personal transport advisers at City Hall' (25 March 2003). That might or might not have been the case, but what must have taken *Standard* readers by surprise was the assertion that followed:

> Tension between the two camps heightened last year when Mr Turner authorised the alteration of traffic light changes without making the Mayor fully aware of what the impact would be. As a result the Mayor was accused of fiddling with the lights to deter motorists and saw his popularity dented.

Up until this point readers could have been forgiven for having the clear impression that, if anyone was responsible for 'rigging the traffic lights', it was the Mayor but now here he was being painted as the victim of Derek Turner's machinations!

Analysis of the *Evening Standard*'s coverage of this issue, and in particular of the 'traffic lights conspiracy', reveals an almost textbook case of the creation and development of a media myth. It is possible to observe its 'birth', to analyse its metamorphosis from hypothesis through to accepted fact, and then to monitor its virtual disappearance. The idea that London's traffic congestion in 2002 had been deliberately created as a means of making the congestion charging scheme appear a success the following year, was made as little more than a stark assertion, based on an unspecified 'source', with no evidence proffered in its support. From this point it became an accepted fact in the pages of the *Standard*, with the paper then invoking its own coverage to justify the story and to explain virtually all of London's traffic problems.

In retrospect it appears that this central allegation probably originated with the Conservative Group on the Greater London Assembly. This is a perfectly legitimate activity for an opposition party to pursue. What is more questionable is the role of the *Evening Standard*, for the newspaper picked up the Conservatives' campaign, developed and exploited it. But did so without:

- making clear where the allegation originated;
- offering any evidence to substantiate the claim; or
- providing coverage of the build-up to congestion charging that could be reasonably described as fair and accurate.

The *Evening Standard* is the monopoly supplier in the London evening newspaper market and thus has a responsibility to provide Londoners with an accurate and reasonably balanced coverage of affairs in the capital. In the case of congestion charging, it appears that through much of the build-up to the introduction of the charge, they failed to do this. Their performance since then, with the exception of the period immediately following the introduction of the charge, has been significantly better, providing Londoners with fair coverage of something which, one way or another, is likely to affect more of the capital's population than any other measure that London's government has the power to implement.

Notes

1   This chapter is based on a research project funded by the Greater London Authority which investigated the media coverage of the London congestion charge. A complete version can be found in Gaber (2004). I am grateful to Emily Seymour for her assistance.
2   For a detailed analysis of the context in which the *Evening Standard* and the national media reported Ken Livingstone and the London congestion charge see Curran *et al.* (2005).
3   Information given to author by TfL Press Office.
4   Document sent to the *Evening Standard,* shown by TfL Press Office, to the author.
5   Information supplied by the Mayor's press office.

References

Curran, J.; Gaber, I. and Petley, J. (2005) *Culture Wars: The Media and the Left in Britain*, Edinburgh: Edinburgh University Press.
Gaber, I. (2004) *Driven to Distraction: An Analysis of the Media's Coverage of the Introduction of the London Congestion Charge*, London: Unit for Journalism Research, Goldsmiths College, University of London.

Chapter 23

Downgrading the 'local' in local newspapers' reporting of the 2005 UK general election

Bob Franklin, Geoff Court and Stephen Cushion

When Alan Milburn was appointed election coordinator for the Labour Party in November 2004, he announced that the 2005 general election would be fought 'as much locally as nationally' (*The Guardian* 11 November 2004). His remark seemed to suggest that Labour, along with the Conservatives and Liberal Democrats, would target local journalists and local newspapers in the coming election as vehicles for conveying Party messages to local readers and voters (Franklin and Parry 1998; Franklin and Richardson 2002; Lilleker and Negrine 2003). Six months later and two weeks into the campaign, some national journalists mistook the word for the deed and began to complain about politicians' courting of local journalists to the exclusion of national reporters. *Independent* journalist Stephen Glover, for example, claimed the *Daily Mail*'s Quentin Letts had been denied entry to a Conservative event in Gloucestershire that was 'limited to local journalists' (*Independent* 18 April), while the editor of the *Yorkshire Post* outlined the courtship rituals deployed by Labour spin doctors to seduce local journalists, which included 'choreographed regional Party "launches", local versions of the theme for the day and a succession of morale-lifting visits, single acts in a well-rehearsed theatrical performance'. When the 'Blair/Brown road show' visited the northwest, the editor of the *Liverpool Echo* claimed, 'only local and regional journalists were granted interviews despite the nationals' hopeful attendance' (*The Guardian* 25 April 2005, p. 5). But such blandishments evidently proved ineffectual. As election coverage unravelled, it became clear that local journalists' reporting of the 2005 general election was unprecedentedly national in focus, preferring to foreground reports of visiting cabinet ministers and other 'celebrities' above the reporting of local issues.[1]

Local journalists and election coverage

Local newspapers' election coverage has changed markedly across the last 20 years (Franklin 1989; Negrine 2005). In 2005, four broad trends were evident. First, a sharp decline in local weekly and daily newspapers' election coverage accompanied by a similarly marked increase in regional newspaper reporting. Second, the collapse of election coverage focused on local rather than the national concerns mentioned above. Third, a growing emphasis on trivial and entertaining coverage rather than sustained discussion of policy concerns, and fourth, a more adversarial editorial stance towards policy and politicians in both the major parties. Each trend is analysed in turn but we begin by considering journalists' assumption, expressed in interview and manifest in coverage, that the election is not a story which interests their readers.

Apathy rules, OK?

For some local journalists, a general election is still a significant occasion that delivers national politicians and exciting story opportunities to their patch. But the default assumption of the majority of journalists interviewed for this study was that readers are bored by election coverage. An editorial in the *Morley Observer* exemplified the world-weary attitude of many journalists.'I'm finding that as I get older', the journalist claimed, 'tolerance levels and boredom thresholds are on the decline. With this in mind, it is somewhat of a relief that we are nearing the end of the election campaign. I must admit that whenever I switch on the television or radio, avoiding a political debate/discussion has become a priority' (*Morley Observer* 29 April, p. 10). The *Halifax Courier* offered prophylactic relief recommending a local hotel which offered 'Escape the Election Breaks' for readers who were 'really fed up with the election campaigning' (20 April 2005). The Leeds *Metro* identified the Lake District as another 'election-free zone' for people who wanted to vote but 'shouldn't have to put up with it every minute of the day' (12 April 2005), while the *Spenborough Guardian* reported the failure of a 'Question Time-style event' when only three questions were submitted by voters. 'Apathy defeated the event', the paper claimed, 'The public seems to be turned off by politicians and their trade' (15 April 2005).

A distrust of politicians (especially Tony Blair) was identified as the culprit. 'Lack of trust of politicians is behind voter apathy' the *Spenborough Guardian* headlined, suggesting that 'the major reason for low turn out at national and local level is the poor esteem in which politicians are held' (15 April 2005). Ironically, journalists were highly critical of the perceived electoral apathy which they imputed to their readers and editorialised to motivate them to engage with the electoral process. The *Mirfield Reporter* issued a clarion call to those readers who 'so lack interest in the democratic process' that they 'need to be surgically removed from their settee if a certain soap opera is on. But as always we would urge people to get out and vote … whoever they support … The right to vote is something to be treasured. Prove yourself worthy of it next Thursday' (*Mirfield Reporter* 29 April, p. 8).

Journalists offered a number of explanations for readers' disaffection with the election: the 'phoney election war' figured prominently in most accounts. 'The election date was the worst kept secret in Britain', a journalist claimed:

> We knew it four years ago and everything for the past year was geared up to May 5th. But when Blair called the election … you had two major events coinciding in the same week – the death of the Pope, his funeral and the royal wedding. Easter was in the mix as well, so it had a very disjointed start. To be honest I think the ordinary person in the street didn't notice when the election campaign started and they were thinking 'They're only saying what they've been saying for the past four years, is there anything new here? No, there's not'! As a journalist, I just didn't notice a change between the phoney war and the campaign. It was as if you were waiting for something to spark the election into life – a Prescott punch – but it never came.
>
> (Interview 27 May 2005)

One journalist suggested another reason might be readers' confusion resulting from the clash between Party and national media agendas – 'there was almost a battle of wills going on. *Today*, *Breakfast News* and others were saying "we're going to do our package on Iraq" but it bore no relation to what the parties were doing'. A Labour regional press officer endorsed this view suggesting that 'Iraq did not play as a story in the local press. It was only an issue for the *Guardianista* – the *lentilista*. People who want to create a wonderfully intellectual society but a place where I don't think any bins would get emptied' (16 May 2005).

The ups and downs of election coverage: contrasting trends

Local newspapers provided considerable coverage of the 2005 general election. The 27 newspapers analysed published 1,466 election items including 986 (67.3 per cent) articles, 75 (5.1 per cent) editorials and 405 (27.6 per cent) readers' letters across the four weeks of the campaign. Newspapers devoted 49,935 square inches of their columns to election news, which was a substantial increase on the 2001 election (Table 23.1).

Table 23.1 Local newspapers' election coverage in 1987, 1992, 1997, 2001 and 2005

Election Year	Article	Editorial	Letter	Total
1987	921 (77.1%)	35 (2.9%)	238 (19.9%)	1,194 (100%)
1992	1544 (74.9%)	42 (2.0%)	475 (23.0%)	2,061 (100%)
1997	858 (68.8%)	86 (6.9%)	304 (24.4%)	1,248 (100%)
2001	934 (74.7%)	64 (5.1%)	252 (20.2%)	1,250 (100%)
2005	986 (67.3%)	75 (5.1%)	405 (27.6%)	1,466 (100%)

In 2005, the number of editorials increased by 17 per cent and letters by 61 per cent, but these aggregate figures obscure significant reductions in coverage across the majority of newspapers (Table 23.2).

The modest coverage provided by free newspapers in 2001 (23 items), for example, plummeted in 2005 with nine free papers publishing a meagre four articles and two letters across the campaign. Coverage in weekly paid papers was also reduced. Only three of the 15 weeklies (the *Dewsbury Reporter*, the *Mirfield Reporter* and the *Todmorden News*) sustained their 2001 output of election articles, while other weekly papers – including the *Brighouse Echo* (down from 45 in 2001 to 25 in 2005), the *Heckmondwike Herald* (52 to 28), the *Morley Observer* (27 to 6) and the *Wakefield Express* (22 to 11) – reduced their coverage significantly. A further four newspapers halved the number of election reports they published. By contrast, editorials increased slightly from 21 to 23 in 2005 while readers' letters expanded from 119 to 159. The daily *Halifax Courier* reduced its election coverage across all editorial formats. The 337 items of coverage published in 2001 reduced to 201 in 2005: the number of editorials and readers' letters halved.

Regional newspapers, however, upped their game considerably and account for the overall increase in coverage. The *Yorkshire Post* increased the number of published articles (37 per cent) and editorials (63 per cent) and tripled the newspaper's mailbag by publishing 153 readers' letters. The new Leeds *Metro* reported the election with enthusiasm, publishing 223 election related items but curiously chose to eschew editorials.[2] Table 23.3 places this decline in journalists' attention to elections in longitudinal context.

Journalists offered two explanations for the decline in coverage. The first rests on the market considerations which drive the newsgathering and reporting processes locally. A journalist recalled a meeting

> to discuss how we were going to cover the election. We had lots of ideas but the central question was 'will it actually assist in maintaining sales?' … Unfortunately in these heavily commercialised days if you put material in the paper and the circulation goes down sharply, then you're not doing yourself any favours. You've got to balance your public service obligations and tailor that to what best suits your readership.

A related concern was the dwindling size of newsrooms with an experienced political journalist claiming,

> we could have done more. In the past we allocated a reporter to each candidate which meant six or seven journalists, but this time there was just two of

Table 23.2 Items of election coverage by newspaper title in 2005 and 2001 (in brackets)

Paper Title	Paper Type	Circulation	Article	Editorial	Letter	Row Total
Aire Valley Target	Free	30,426	2 (2)	—	0 (2)	2 (4)
Bradford Target	Free	47,971	0 (2)	—	1	1 (2)
Calderdale News	Free	30,052	—	—	—	—
Huddersfield Weekly News	Free	65,848	1 (1)	—	—	1 (1)
North Leeds Weekly	Free	31,918	1	—	—	1
East Leeds Weekly	Free	36,362	1	—	1	2
West Leeds Weekly	Free	36,455	—	—	—	—
Weekly Advertiser (Dewsbury)	Free	42,173	0 (1)	—	—	1 (1)
Wharfe Valley Times	Free	43,981	1 (13)	—	—	1 (13)
Batley News	Weekly	9,624	19 (28)	2 (3)	16 (13)	37 (44)
Brighouse Echo	Weekly	6,596	25 (45)	0 (2)	1 (3)	26 (50)
Colne Valley Chronicle	Weekly	5,662	8 (17)	1	13 (8)	22 (25)
Dewsbury Reporter	Weekly	7,030	42 (35)	4 (4)	32 (24)	78 (63)
Hebden Bridge Times	Weekly	3,486	16 (15)	—	4 (5)	20 (20)
Heckmondwike Herald	Weekly	4,284	28 (52)	4 (3)	10 (12)	42 (67)
Holme Valley Express	Weekly		8 (17)	1 (0)	13 (8)	22 (25)
Huddersfield District Chronicle	Weekly		8 (14)	1 (0)	13 (8)	22 (22)
Mirfield Reporter	Weekly	7,030	38 (33)	4 (3)	29 (15)	71 (51)
Morley Advertiser	Weekly	3,937	8 (11)	0	1 (6)	9 (17)
Morley Observer	Weekly	3,049	6 (27)	2 (2)	11 (2)	19 (31)
Pudsey Times	Weekly	23,760	1 (6)	—	—	1 (6)
Spenborough Guardian	Weekly	4,284	29 (52)	4 (4)	9 (10)	42 (66)
Todmorden News	Weekly	4,402	15 (14)	—	2 (2)	17 (16)
Wakefield Express	Weekly	34,301	11 (22)	—	5 (3)	16 (25)
Halifax Courier	Daily Evening	23,583	153 (244)	8 (16)	40 (77)	201 (337)
Yorkshire Post	Daily Regional	57,976	391 (281)	44 (27)	153 (54)	588 (362)
The Metro	Daily Regional	75,781	174	—	49	223
Total			986 (934)	75 (64)	405 (252)	1,466 (1,250)

Table 23.3 Number of election items by newspaper type across five general elections

Newspaper type	Editorial format	Year				
		1987	1992	1997	2001	2005
Free	Article	50 (73.5%)	103 (83.7%)	54 (71.6%)	21 (91%)	6 (60%)
	Editorial	0 (—)	3 (2.4%)	3 (4.1%)	0 (—)	0 (—)
	Letter	18 (26.5%)	17 (13.8%)	16 (23%)	2 (9%)	4 (40%)
	Total	68 (100%)	123 (100%)	73 (100%)	23 (100%)	10 (100%)
Weekly	Article	251 (71.1%)	595 (67.5%)	329 (73.8%)	388 (73.9%)	262 (59%)
	Editorial	11 (3.1%)	12 (1.4%)	32 (7.4%)	21 (4%)	23 (5.2%)
	Letter	86 (25.8%)	274 (31.1%)	83 (18.8%)	119 (22.1%)	159 (35.8%)
	Total	348 (100%)	881 (100%)	444 (100%)	528 (100%)	444 (100%)
Daily	Article	231 (73.8%)	359 (68.6%)	167 (47.2%)	244 (72.4%)	153 (76.1%)
	Editorial	4 (1.3%)	12 (2.3%)	25 (6.8%)	16 (4.7%)	8 (4%)
	Letter	78 (24.9%)	152 (29.1%)	162 (46%)	77 (22.8%)	40 (19.9%)
	Total	313 (100%)	523 (100%)	356 (100%)	337 (100%)	201 (100%)
Regional	Article	389 (83.7%)	476 (91%)	308 (82.4%)	281 (77.1%)	565 (69.7%)
	Editorial	20 (4.3%)	15 (2.9%)	26 (7.0%)	27 (7.5%)	44 (5.4%)
	Letter	56 (12%)	32 (6.1%)	41 (10.6%)	54 (15.5%)	202 (24.9%)
	Total	465 (100%)	523 (100%)	375 (100%)	362 (100%)	811 (100%)

us covering the whole thing with other people brought in as necessary to cover days off and when events clashed.

A second explanation reflects parties' strategic emphasis on contesting key marginals, which is transforming the traditional idea of a 'general' election by generating markedly different levels of political activity in different constituencies. Where politicians go, journalists follow. Where there is only modest electoral activity, coverage will be sparse; to rephrase Lloyd's argument, this is 'what politics has done to our media' (Lloyd 2004). In 2005, newspapers which had no key marginal in their circulation area were left effectively without an election contest to report. A senior journalist explains:

> The problem is the key marginals. In Yorkshire we had fifty-five seats, but there was only an election being fought in eight or nine. In the rest there was no election at all. I live in a safe Labour seat and you get a single piece of literature from the Tories or Lib Dems, just a leaflet. But on election day, I came into work through Leeds North West where suddenly there was an election. You actually saw people on the streets, banging on doors, cars going around with election stickers, candidates with loudspeakers. There was an election going on there but in the rest of Leeds there was no election at all.

Down with the local?

In interviews, journalists routinely expressed their belief that 'a good election story is a local story'. 'We're always chasing that local angle', a reporter claimed. 'Whenever the big wigs came, perhaps to talk about asylum we would get local figures and challenge them. We're always trying to localise the story'. When a political celebrity can be associated with a local issue, the editorial cocktail becomes irresistible. Consequently, the *Halifax Courier* produced a front-page splash about bullying in local schools, highlighted by the case of 'Brave James' who received a letter of support from Chancellor Gordon Brown, following an incident of bullying at James' school (4 April 2005).

But the editorial mix of local and national concerns is complex (Tables 23.4 and 23.5).

Table 23.4 reveals newspapers' highly variable commitments to a local or national focus in election coverage. Free papers' (100 per cent) and weekly papers' (70.7 per cent) attention to local news is evident while the local daily (32.8 per cent local) and regional newspapers' (11.2 per cent local) preference for national news is similarly clear. But what is significant in 2005 is the shrinking provision of local election stories in the weekly and daily papers which in 2001 devoted 79.6 per cent and 60.5 per cent respectively to coverage with a local flavour. For their part, the larger regional papers have become more nationally focused. In 2001, 24.6 per cent of election reports in the *Yorkshire Post* were locally focused; in 2005 the equivalent figure was 12.8 per cent.

Table 23.4 Local and national emphases in different types of newspaper in 2005

| | Type of issue reported in item | | | | Total | |
| | Local | | National | | Count | Row (%) |
	Count	Row (%)	Count	Row (%)		
Free weekly	10	100	0	—	10	100.0
Weekly paid	314	70.7	130	29.3	444	100.0
Daily	66	32.8	135	67.2	201	100.0
Regional	91	11.2	720	88.8	811	100.0
Total	480	32.7	986	67.3	1466	100.0

This complex reporting of local and national concerns is further nuanced when distinctive editorial formats are considered (Table 23.5). In 2005 almost two-thirds of articles (61.9 per cent) focused on national concerns compared with 30.8 per cent in 2001.

Table 23.5 Local and national emphases in election coverage by editorial format in 2005

| Format | Type of issue reported | | Total |
	Local	National	
Article	376 (38.1%)	610 (61.9%)	986 (100%)
Editorial	11 (14.7%)	64 (85.3%)	75 (100%)
Letter	93 (23%)	312 (77%)	405 (100%)
Total	480 (32.7%)	986 (67.3%)	1466 (100%)

The local element in election reports has halved. Similarly, editorials (85.3 per cent) have become more nationally focused than in 2001 (65.6 per cent) while readers' letters have shown a more modest move to an increasingly national orientation (74.2–77 per cent) in 2005. This paradox of marginalising local news in local newspapers is striking and requires explanation.

The increase in editorials and readers' letters in 2005, with their traditionally greater emphasis on national concerns, offers part of the explanation (Table 23.1 and Franklin 2004). But journalists' suggestion that Party press offices were issuing fewer news releases focused on local stories, preferring to win editorial space by offering photo opportunities of visiting celebrities and politicians is undoubtedly nearer the mark. 'It is very sad', a senior news editor recalled, 'but you could probably count on the fingers of one hand press releases which took up a local issue ... This time it was more "Oh we're flying someone in for a visit. It's a photo opportunity of a minister, come and do it"'. The reporter's comment also reveals the degree to which journalists are reliant on Party press officers for election stories and the extent to which the fourth estate allows the fifth estate to set the election agenda. A regional press officer confirmed this emphasis on celebrities and senior politicians:

> A minister coming to town is a story pretty much anywhere. It did get rather silly in key seats where people kept pouring in to support their friends or certain individuals they get along with; it's the 'him off the telly syndrome'.

Analysis on newspaper election stories revealed that 49 per cent of all published items featured celebrity politicians, while the inclusion of celebrities in election stories was greater for the *Yorkshire Post* (62 per cent), the *Metro* (62 per cent) and the *Halifax Courier* (54 per cent).

Dumbing down? Lampposts, garden gnomes and 'scandal busters'

Journalists respond to readers' apathy in two ways both of which result in some degree of trivialising or 'dumbing down' of election reports. First, journalists try to lighten election coverage by publishing personalised profiles of candidates which provide human interest detail rather than outlines of candidates' policies. The *Dewsbury Reporter*, for example, described female, Muslim Conservative candidate Sayeeda Warsi who has a seven-year-old daughter Aamna as

> a Dewsbury girl born and bred ... A local lass. Once a high flying lawyer with her own practice, Mrs Warsi is used to life in the fast lane and certainly believes she could make it as an MP ... She believes her experience as a charity worker – she founded a charity for Asian widows and orphans – will help her every step of the way.

> (8 April)

A journalist acknowledged 'it's important to try to humanise the election ... so we had a feature on what it's like to be an MP's wife'.

A related editorial strategy for engaging readers involves publishing quirky, amusing stories but with an electoral content. 'We had some good election stories', an editor recalls.

One that sticks in the mind was the Tory candidate who, while she was out delivering leaflets, came across two new lampposts erected within three feet of each other. It made a great picture; a nice little story and we sent it up a bit. How many politicians would it take to change a light bulb? That sort of thing.

In this tradition, the *Yorkshire Post* published a story about 'a man who once pushed a monkey nut for seven miles with his nose' who chose to show his support for Blair by kissing the politician's photograph for eight hours; the head-line declared 'Self-publicist plants 100,000 big Xs on Blair photograph' (6 May).

The most striking story in this tradition of trivialising was published in the *Metro*. Under the headline 'The Scandal Busters' the *Metro* claimed, 'every general election needs a juicy scandal. But as there hasn't been one this time we've decided to invent some and ask 3 top PRs to devise strategies to dig the three party leaders out of the imaginary holes we've made for them' (3 May, p. 7). Michael Howard's dilemma is that his maid turns out to be an illegal immi-grant, while Tony Blair discovers a property he owns is being rented 'by a woman whose professional name is Lady Spankalot. She invites photographers into her home and they have field day in her dungeon, pictures of which are splashed across every newspaper's front page'. The rationale for such stories is that they enliven the election debate, but some journalists are embarrassed by their growing presence in election coverage; others are 'depressed by the constant trivialisation'. Apart from increasing the national rather than local focus of election news, it is difficult to understand what such stories bring to electoral debate. Harder still to imagine that they encourage civic engagement.

Journalists as adversaries

Finally, local newspaper reporting of the 2005 election was characterised by a more adversarial stance against the politicians and policies of both the Labour and Conservative parties, than in previous elections.

Since 1987, coverage has been characterised by a 'balance of partisanship' in which any political commitments articulated by one paper were 'neutralised' by the opposite political leanings of another, generating a remarkably even-handed coverage across the 27 newspapers published across West Yorkshire; this changed in 2005 (Table 23.6).

In 2001, reporting of the Conservatives was fairly even-handed with 46 per cent of comments being positive and 54 per cent negative: in 2005 supportive comments reduced to 31 per cent while critical commentary jumped to 69 per cent. Journalists' already critical approach to Labour (37 per cent positive but 63 per cent negative in 2001) became more severe in 2005 when the Party enjoyed only 26 per cent positive but 74 per cent negative appraisals. In sum,

Conservatives received one positive for every two critical appraisals in 2005: Labour one for every three. Table 23.6 reveals the partisanship of particular newspapers. The *Batley News*, for example, was twice as critical of Labour as of Conservatives while the *Brighouse Echo* offered Labour twice as many positive as negative comments. For their part, the *Holme Valley Express* and the *Huddersfield District Chronicle* were unrelentingly negative about the Conservatives. The most noticeable shift was the *Halifax Courier* where the relatively balanced reporting of the Conservative Party (68 favourable and 86 negative comments) became highly critical in 2005 (30 positive but 70 negative). Labour fared less well. In 2001, three out of every four appraisals of the Party were supportive but in 2005 that ratio had fallen to just one in every two comments. A similar pattern of increasingly adversarial and critical coverage of both parties is evident at the *Yorkshire Post* (Table 23.6).

Table 23.6 Positive and negative appraisals of parties in local newspapers in 2005

Paper title	Type	Conservative		Labour		Liberal Democrat	
		Positive	Negative	Positive	Negative	Positive	Negative
Aire Valley Target	Free	0	0	0	0	0	0
Bradford Target	Free	0	0	0	3	0	0
Calderdale News	Free	0	0	0	0	0	0
East Leeds Weekly	Free	0	0	0	0	0	0
Hudd. Weekly News	Free	0	0	0	0	0	0
North Leeds Weekly	Free	0	0	0	0	0	0
Weekly Advertiser (Dewsbury)	Free	0	0	0	0	0	0
Weekend Times	Free	0	0	0	0	0	0
West Leeds Weekly	Free	0	0	0	0	0	0
Wharfe Valley Times	Free	0	0	0	0	0	0
Batley News	Weekly	5	24	5	48	6	3
Brighouse Echo	Weekly	6	9	11	5	6	0
Colne Valley Chronicle	Weekly	2	15	4	8	5	2
Dewsbury Reporter	Weekly	8	36	20	36	20	1
Hebden Bridge Times	Weekly	7	11	7	20	10	0
Heckmondwike Herald	Weekly	12	17	9	16	7	3
Holme Valley Express	Weekly	2	15	4	8	6	2
Huddersfield District Chronicle	Weekly	3	13	4	7	4	1
Mirfield Reporter	Weekly	8	35	15	35	16	1
Morley Advertiser	Weekly	1	3	3	4	1	0
Morley Observer	Weekly	2	2	4	18	0	0
Pudsey Times	Weekly	0	0	0	0	0	0
Spenborough Guardian	Weekly	13	15	10	15	13	2
Todmorden News	Weekly	7	7	5	11	10	0
Wakefield Express	Weekly	9	5	18	9	7	0
Halifax Courier	Evening	30	70	54	104	33	6
Metro	Region	39	69	60	159	38	7
Yorkshire Post	Region	115	252	155	623	87	59
Total		268 (30.9%)	598 (69.1%)	388 (25.6%)	1129 (74.4%)	269 (76.6%)	87 (24.4%)

Interestingly, there were striking differences within the various editorial sections of the newspapers. Journalists' articles tended to be written with a critical edge with both Labour and Conservatives receiving twice as many critical as supportive comments, while editorials and readers' letters typically hammered both parties (Table 23.7).

Table 23.7 Local newspapers' appraisals of parties by editorial format in 2005

Item type	Conservative		Labour		Liberal Democrat	
	Positive	Negative	Positive	Negative	Positive	Negative
Article	237 (37.3%)	398 (62.7%)	347 (32.7%)	715 (67.3%)	235 (79.4%)	61 (20.6%)
Editorial	7 (21.9%)	25 (78.1%)	4 (4.9%)	78 (95.1%)	1 (25%)	3 (75%)
Letter	24 (12.1%)	175 (87.9%)	37 (9.9%)	336 (90.1%)	33 (58.9%)	23 (41.1%)
Total	268 (30.9%)	598 (69.1%)	388 (25.6%)	1129 (74.4%)	269 (75.6%)	87 (24.4%)

For their part, columnists were allowed to let rip to generate an expansive mailbag. Writing in the *Yorkshire Post*, Bernard Dineen denounced 'Labour's so-called immigration controls' and declared Gordon Brown's 'pledge not to raise income tax' to be 'Labour's biggest lie'. But on occasion the hyperbole is so intense that it prompts reflection about the value of Simon Kellner's vision to create what he terms a 'viewspaper'. Consider the following rant.

> Of all Labour's failures violent crime is the worst. There are 500 victims of violence every hour. Lawlessness affects every part of national life ... Police are hamstrung by political correctness and red tape ... Everything that has gone wrong in society stems from Blair's side of politics.
>
> (*Yorkshire Post* 5 May 2006, p. 12)

This sort of partisan bile may offer catharsis to a frustrated journalist but seems to add little to election discussion or electoral understanding.

Conclusions

Local newspapers' reporting of the 2005 general election generated a number of significant paradoxes. First, a general election is an important event for any local community (and for the journalists who report it) and yet most local newspapers offered their readers substantially reduced election coverage. In contrast, the regional *Yorkshire Post* published an unprecedented volume of election reports (especially readers' letters). Second, this reduced coverage in the 'local' press was less locally focused preferring to report national concerns, but especially national celebrity politicians. Third, despite journalists' expressed commitments to even-handedness in election reports, there is evidence in 2005 of an increasingly adversarial editorial posture to politicians in the two main parties but also evidence of a greater partisanship in coverage in particular newspaper titles. The balance of partisanship, which prevailed in previous elections, has been lost.

The declining coverage reflects the shift to corporate ownership of the local press with management requirements for editorial content which will deliver more readers, more advertisers and more profits: and all this with less journalists! The resulting coverage tries to 'humanise' or trivialise the election story. Journalists offer a complementary explanation. They suggest the reduced coverage is a consequence of the emergence of the 'non-general election' campaign in which parties target key marginals for frenzied campaigning while relegating the remaining and safer seats to an electoral second division in which voters and readers are ignored. This targeting of particular seats left some local newspapers with simply no evident electoral contest to report and provided a further example of 'what politics is doing to our media'.

Notes

1   Studies funded by the Nuffield Foundation and conducted between 1987 and 2005 have analysed election coverage in a comprehensive sample of free weekly, paid weekly and daily evening and regional morning newspapers, circulating in the ten selected West Yorkshire constituencies of Batley and Spen; Bradford North; Bradford South; Colne Valley; Halifax; Leeds East; Leeds North; Leeds West; Pudsey and Wakefield. A total of 7,219 items of election coverage across the five election campaigns have been coded for 38 variables and analysed using SPSSx. Additionally, interviews have been conducted with journalists and editors of local newspapers (38) and politicians and Party press officers (37). The authors are grateful to the Nuffield Foundation for its financial support.

2   Published by Associated Press and listed as a regional newspaper by the Newspaper Society, the *Metro* newspapers – published in major urban centres, such as London, Glasgow, Leeds and Birmingham – are designated FUN (free urban newspapers) papers targeted at commuters and young readers (22–44 years – the iPod generation). They are distributed free at rail and bus stations and attract considerable local and regional advertising (see Chapter 14).

References

Franklin, B. (1989) 'Local parties, local media and the constituency campaign', in Crewe, I. and Harrop, M. (eds) *Political Communication: The General Election 1987*, Cambridge: Cambridge University Press, pp. 211–21.

Franklin, B. (2004) 'Talking past each other? Journalists, readers and local newspapers' reporting of the general election campaign in the UK', *Journal of Public Affairs*, 4 (4), pp. 330–46.

Franklin, B. and Parry, J. (1998) 'Old habits die hard: journalism's changing professional commitments and local newspapers' reporting of the 1997 general election', in Franklin, B. and Murphy, D. (eds) *Making The Local News: Local Journalism in Context*, London: Routledge, pp. 209–28.

Franklin, B. and Richardson, J. (2002) '"A journalist's duty"? Continuity and change in local newspapers' coverage of recent UK general elections', *Journalism Studies*, 3 (1), February, pp. 35–52.

Lilleker, D. and Negrine, R. (2003) 'The rise of a proactive media strategy in British political communications: clear continuities and evolutionary change 1966–2001', *Journalism Studies*, 4 (2), pp. 199–212.

Lloyd, J. (2004) *What The Media Are Doing to Our Politics*, London: Constable.

Negrine, R. (2005) 'The role of the UK local press in the local constituency campaign', *Journalism Studies*, 6 (1), pp. 103–16.

Chapter 24

Ethics for local journalism

Chris Frost

Can journalism ethics be local?

Local and national journalism have very different jobs to do, but are the ethics of local journalists different than those who work on the nationals? Of course, the same standards are expected from both national and regional journalism. The same producer guidelines apply wherever you work in the British Broadcasting Corporation (BBC) while all independent broadcasters are bound by the same Ofcom content code. Local newspapers work to the same code of practice as nationals and editors of both serve on the Press Complaints Commission (PCC), the national self-regulatory body that hears complaints against the press.

The PCC's code of practice, the National Union of Journalists' code of conduct, the BBC's producer guidelines and Ofcom's content code, all cover the ethical areas that most people believe should be considered by journalists: truth-telling and accuracy, privacy, discrimination, children, vulnerable people, intrusion, corruption, damaging reputations unfairly and harassment (Frost 2000; Keeble 2001; Sanders 2003).

Complaints about the local press

A consideration of the complaints made to the PCC reveals that as many complaints are received about regional newspapers in England and Wales as there are about national newspapers. The PCC's 2003 annual report, for example, shows 41.4 per cent of complaints against nationals and 40.8 per cent against regionals (www.pcc.org.uk/2003/statistics.html). Looking at complaints accepted by the PCC and then adjudicated, the picture shifts. In its first 13 years of operation, 60 per cent of the 500 or so complaints adjudicated by the PCC were against national newspapers (Sundays and dailies) with only 40 per cent levelled against local dailies, evenings and weeklies.

When the different types of complaints adjudicated and upheld by the PCC since its inception in 1991 are considered, national newspapers have received more complaints overall, while all types of newspapers are subject to a similar percentage of complaints about accuracy. National and regional newspapers receive more complaints about privacy invasions than weeklies, but national newspapers are far more likely to receive complaints from well-known people than regional papers. National newspapers are also much more likely to trigger complaints about harassment, misrepresentation (including hospitals) and discrimination. Regional papers, on the other hand, are more likely to commit an intrusion or worry innocent relatives. While all newspapers face complaints about interfering with the privacy of children, it is regional papers, weeklies in particular, which are most likely to commit such breaches of privacy. Table 24.1 reveals that there are quite significant differences concerning the complaints made and upheld against the different newspaper types reflecting the quality, scope and ethical probity of their distinctive journalistic practices.

Table 24.1 Complaints upheld by the PCC listed by different newspaper types[a]

	Weekly	Regional Evening	National Daily	National Sunday
Confidential sources	0	0	0	0
Financial journalism	0	0	1	0
Discrimination	0	0	6	0
Children	20	14	11	13
Innocent relatives	7.3	24	1.2	0
Intrusion	9.76	4.76	2.41	1.25
Payments	0	0	1.2	2.5
Harassment	5	0	13	13
Misrepresentation	0	0	8.4	15
Hospitals	0	0	0	6
Listening devices	0	0	0	1
Accuracy	49	48	51	53
Opp to reply	4.9	0	1.2	2.5
Comment	0	4.8	0	1.3
Privacy	7.3	33	31	35
Well-known	0	0	28	38

a 1991–2004. Figures represent percentage of each type of complaint, not actual numbers of complaints. No regional dailies as complaints upheld are too few to be statistically significant.

Accuracy is regularly cited as a key journalistic virtue, a view supported by most books about journalism ethics and journalists who argue that the search for truth and its accurate representation is a key journalistic role (Frost 2000; Keeble 2001; Bell 1998; Sanders 2003; Randall 1999).

There is not enough space here for a lengthy discussion on the nature of truth, what separates it from accuracy and the need for both in their place. What is clear is that readers don't like it if a journalist spells their names incorrectly or confuses details of a story in which they are involved (Frost 2001: 82). For this reason, local newspapers probably tend to get more complaints than national newspapers about relatively trivial errors. The local newspaper is well used to readers ringing up and pointing out minor errors and the sensible editor, of course, prints corrections, issues admonishments to reporters and, where necessary, publishes an apology. These remedies usually ensure the paper's standards are kept high and prevent complaints from going further. This probably explains why the number of complaints made to the PCC is equal between nationals and regional papers, but the number of complaints upheld by it is very much tilted towards the national press.

Leaving aside truth, accuracy and privacy, Table 24.1 shows that national newspapers are much more likely to have a complaint upheld about discrimination or working in hospitals than local newspapers, while the latter are far more likely to have complaints upheld about children, innocent relatives, intrusion or not giving an opportunity to reply.

The statistic about the opportunity to reply is an apparent surprise. Weekly papers, with their letters pages and relatively open-access news pages should find offering a reply very easy. In fact, the numbers of complaints here are very small and only two local newspapers refused to offer a right of reply. It is magazines (not identified on the chart) which are the worst offenders concerning the right of reply.

A key element in the continuing popularity of local papers is their ability to record and celebrate the minutiae of community life. Births, marriages and deaths have always been a staple of the local paper. The main ethical concerns for local newspapers inevitably wrap around these age-old preoccupations. Concerns about privacy and intrusion are obvious when dealing with people's relationships. Accuracy and concerns about the reporting of children are bound to crop up in discussions of marriage and birth. Death and its reporting have enormous ethical concerns such as intrusion and invasion of privacy.

Births and reporting children

Local newspapers are keen to report births, and similarly eager to cover schools and the rearing of children. Many of us have children, or hope to have children and all of us have been children, so we are all concerned to read and learn about issues connected with bringing up children, their education and their welfare.

But journalists confront increasing problems in reporting school life, for example. Many schools refuse to allow the publication of photographs or reports of school sports days, plays and other events, often quoting the Data Protection

Act. This limitation on reporting events which local editors consider to be of public interest can lead to conflict. Where there is conflict about whether pictures or stories should be obtained, there are usually ethical dilemmas.

There are some legitimate concerns about publishing pictures of children. Newspapers have long been aware that extreme care needs to be taken with the publication of pictures of children for fear they will be targeted by abusers. Full names, and certainly addresses, are often withheld in order to reduce the risk of children and their families receiving harassing phone calls or visits. Usually this can be achieved by withholding the home address and using only the school or area address.

Names of children should be used with care in any story about their direct welfare. Naming a child involved in a story about bullying or about a contagious illness, for instance, may lead to harmful effects for that child. Most codes of conduct suggest that children in such positions should not normally be named; only the strongest public interest defence will be accepted by the PCC in such a case. Since the PCC started taking complaints in 1991, it has strengthened its stance on the coverage of children and the invasion of their privacy (Frost 2004).

Concerns for the welfare of children have prompted a much more negative approach to the coverage of young people. The difficulties in covering the everyday good-news stories of children have led many editors to give up the struggle and there is now less coverage of award ceremonies or sporting achievements. But when a young person behaves anti-socially, the government has made it clear it wants newspapers to publicise this with pictures of the offender and details of their offences and the Anti-Social Behaviour Order made against them (www.guardian.co.uk/uk_news/story/0,1428113,00.html). This raises broader ethical concerns about local journalism and the way it records society.

Stories about children and babies often focus on health issues, whether this relates to an epidemic of measles or meningitis in school, or the birth of the first New Year baby. Local journalists do not figure in the PCC's complaint list about hospitals. Pictures of New Year babies are published with the permission of the proud parents and the local hospital. Local journalists rarely need to invade hospitals to talk to victims of some tragedy, although they do need to contact hospitals to seek condition reports about accident victims and other people at the centre of stories. This is no longer the easy task of earlier years. The Data Protection Act has given considerable protection to people concerning any data collected about their health and hospitals will no longer routinely issue condition reports without the patient's permission. Any good local reporter probably has a contact somewhere in a hospital who can find out basic information of this kind. However, handing out this kind of information is potentially a serious disciplinary (or even criminal) offence for the source. Ethically, a journalist needs to be aware that a contact in this position should be used sparingly and should be protected: journalists have a moral duty to protect confidential sources of information. This means the source should not be identified without their agreement. Since such a source could face dismissal and possibly prosecution, the journalist who uses such a contact will have to consider putting themselves at risk of jail. For instance, a *Daily Mirror* journalist who refused to name a contact who provided inside information about the medical history of Moors Killer Ian Brady narrowly missed a jail sentence (www.legalpractitioner.co.uk/artmedia1.htm).

This protection of sources goes beyond hospitals and a source who provides inside information becomes a confidential source. The development of a confidential source of information is normally achieved on the basis of consent. A reporter is approached by someone with a story and the reporter then decides whether to agree to promise confidentiality to that source. No reporter is obliged to do this, although without such a promise, the source may decide not to deliver the story. But the kind of long-term relationships that good reporters build with people on the inside of organisations may mean an automatic assumption of protection as might the provision of information in circumstances that clearly put the source at risk.

Marriages and other family events

Between birth and death is a whole range of community events to record and celebrate. Many of these events are one-off celebrations, such as marriages or anniversary parties. When recording these family events, care needs to be taken about addresses. Reporting that a certain house, that might be replete with wedding presents or just the normal household possessions, will be empty for a specified time while the family celebrate a wedding or attend a funeral, is information that many burglars would relish. The PCC takes this advice further, instructing papers not to publish the addresses of a whole range of people from police and prison officers to judges and cabinet ministers who might be put at risk as a result. It would certainly be unethical to needlessly place people at risk of physical harm. Sometimes the press wish to attend an event or find out information about a person. When invited, of course, this is not a problem. It is also important to know when access is a right even if an invitation is not offered (weddings are public events from which one cannot be refused entry, for instance). Other events (such as wedding receptions) might need subterfuge in order to gain entry. This requires the reporter and editor to consider whether there is sufficient public interest in the story to warrant such a subterfuge, which by itself would probably be unethical. This means looking beyond whether the story is one that will interest the public to consider whether it is something they need to know; that is, in the public interest.

Although local papers do not cover celebrity in the same degree and kind as national papers, intrusion is nonetheless a more substantive problem, according to figures from the PCC. More complaints are made and upheld about intrusion in local papers than the nationals. Invasions of privacy, however, while rarer in the local weekly, are at about the same frequency as a percentage in local evening papers as they are in the nationals.

This underlines one of the main considerations journalists should make about privacy: journalists may need to invade privacy in order to serve the public interest.

The range of story types that encompass the public interest is wide but it is generally defined in the UK as:

- exposing criminal or anti-social behaviour;
- preventing people from being misled;
- exposing dangers to public health and safety; and
- exposing significant incompetence in public office.

All of these are important to a local newspaper. Stories exposing health and safety problems, anti-social behaviour or public authority incompetence are now the bread and butter of many local newspapers' coverage. But rather than being stories about celebrities, these reports will focus on a local vicar, a head teacher, or perhaps a police officer or traffic warden. People who rarely appear in the paper may suddenly be exposed for alleged bullying, or corruption or just plain incompetence. Ethically those who hold high social status or positions of power on trust from the public, either because they are paid by the public or because their position and status in society depends on it, must answer for their conduct to that society. The doctor who refuses to turn out to help a patient, the teacher who harasses a child are both potential stories for the local newspaper. Yet, their surprise at being exposed may well lead them to complain to the PCC more readily than the celebrity who is regularly featured in the national press.

It is worth pointing out that while celebrity coverage is not an issue for local papers according to PCC figures, this may be because a local newspaper's definition of celebrity, or at least being well-known in a community and hence of news interest, is different. Any national celebrity living within their circulation area is usually not reported frequently or that person would be in every issue of the paper. But people with local status such as mayors, councillors, head teachers, police chiefs, charity leaders and heads of community groups are written about regularly in the local paper and so their rights of privacy could be said to be reduced compared with the ordinary citizen. Research has shown that the public feels that there should be different levels of privacy for different groups in society

(Kieran *et al.* 2000). Children should have the strongest right to privacy, whilst criminals should have practically no right to privacy at all. Authority figures appear somewhere in the middle of this taxonomy. They have considerable rights to a private life, but fewer rights than those who do not hold public office and are in the public eye. For instance, a police chief should be more answerable for his or her public and private behaviour than a factory worker and consequently a local radio station or newspaper is arguably more justified in invading the privacy of such a person. A reporter might also be justified in using covert means of investigation such as hidden cameras or false identity in order to find out information that should normally remain private.

These kinds of decisions, of course, might also affect a national reporter, but just as the scale of privacy varies according to the subject of the story, the threshold might also change depending on the market. A local newspaper might have a more important reason to breach the privacy of a person than a national paper. For instance, if the local paper found that a head teacher of a local primary school had unusual, but not illegal, religious convictions or sexual practices, then it might be appropriate to breach that person's privacy in order to inform local parents who could then make up their own minds about sending their children to that school on the basis of an informed choice. Making the story a matter of prurient interest for all in the country by publishing in one of the Sunday papers might not be in the public interest (although it would certainly interest them) as that public is different.

Deaths and the darker side of life

Death is an event that is often newsworthy. A celebrity death is news for the nationals, but a regional paper knows that almost anyone dying in their locality will probably be known to some readers and is therefore likely to be a story. Writing about the death of someone in the local community is not in itself intrusive, although details of the circumstances might well be; it is here that a determination of the public interest is important. The death of a local politician or a well-known local figure such as a priest or teacher is bound to be of interest to readers and in the public interest. How that person died might also interest the public: if he or she had died whilst in the bed of a lover, for instance, most people would be interested to read that additional detail. But does that give the newspaper the right to publish such private details causing possible embarrassment and upset to the deceased's family? In order to justify invading privacy in this way, journalists have to consider whether it is in the public interest to know these details. Does the public need to know that the deceased had a lover and that this is where he or she died? Or is it enough to know about the death? We certainly don't need to know on the basis that it would affect our judgement of the person next time we come to vote. However, it could be argued that it would allow us to make a better assessment of our decision-making processes, depending on whether that person's character had been successfully judged or not. It can also be argued that what interests the public may well also be in the public interest.

The so-called death knock is an area of considerable ethical concern for journalists working on local papers. Visiting bereaved relatives is one of the standard jobs for local journalists and one that brings mixed responses from journalists and members of the local community. There are anecdotal stories of journalists being threatened by neighbours of the bereaved when looking for a story. There are two main ethical issues here. The first is whether it is an invasion of privacy to publish a story about someone who has died and the second is whether it is right to approach the relatives of someone recently deceased to ask them about their loss.

Whether the death is newsworthy because of its circumstances or because of who died, many stories of deaths are carried in local newspapers because they are newsworthy and because one of the duties of newspapers is to be places of record.

As to the second point about approaching the family of the victim: if someone's death is worth recording, then surely their life is worth recording, and it is in the public interest to learn a little about the person whose death the paper is notifying. Who better than their family to inform the paper about the person who has died? Many families welcome reporters into their home to talk about their loss and record their memories of their loved one in the local paper. Sanders quotes several examples of families welcoming death-knock reporters as well as examples of bad practice. (Sanders 2003: 100). It is for this reason that the death knock cannot itself be unethical, provided it is done with thought and sensitivity.

The key to the death knock is sensitivity and compassion. The family must be given the opportunity to refuse to be interviewed or to be interviewed later. Reporters need to allow the family to tell the story in their own way. They should not be rushed nor have words put into their mouths. They also need to see 'their' words accurately reported. This last can be problematic. Every child who dies is portrayed by their family as a little angel whose talent and boundless potential meant their removal from this world was a tragedy. Never mind that to others he or she was a bully, or a feckless young criminal or both. Accuracy and truth can have some serious tussles when dealing with reports about the dead. If the parents or other family members refuse to be interviewed or will not give permission for use of a picture, then pursuing the matter would almost certainly constitute harassment.

Local journalism, of course, involves dealing with people who become day-to-day contacts. But often, when a major story breaks, less sympathetic treatment at the hands of the national media may often make them nervous of speaking again and it can take a local journalist some time to rebuild the relationship. This may be the reason why the local press faces more upheld complaints about intrusion. The nationals are accused of harassment, but less often with intrusion. It will be the local paper that often first breaks a story that is then seen as intrusive, particularly when the story is followed up by a national. It is impossible to tell whether the complaints come because the local newspaper will tend to be seen as intruding on even quite trivial stories, or whether the intrusion complaints only really start to arise after the intervention of the national press. Certainly a local reporter needs to think carefully about ethics and practicalities before providing sources to out-of-town reporters.

Another aspect of local journalism that is of lesser concern for the nationals is the relationship between the powers in the locality and the reporter. Much has been written about Alastair Campbell when he was director of communications at Downing Street and his relationship with the press. But the relationship between local government and reporter can be equally delicate. The relationship between local business and the reporter is also often much closer than the same relationship on a national newspaper. This is not to say that a local paper would or should refuse to carry a story that attacks the local mayor or a local business, but that the effects, for the paper itself, could be more direct. Revealing that a new housing estate of 5,000 homes was built on a toxic waste tip, for instance, would be meat and drink for a national paper; for a local paper too, but the fall-out in terms of home owners, local builders, estate agents, tourism chiefs and business development agencies would be much greater. Many local papers have slogans or policies that suggest they are working for or supporting the local community. Carrying stories that damage that community, even when true, carry far more risk for a local paper. Again, the national can come in, write the story, and then go on to the next, largely unworried by the rage and anguish they leave behind. The closer community relationship means it is local reporters who may be threatened in their offices, or have hate mail or worse delivered to their homes for covering stories whether they expose the hate antics of the far-right extremists or the dubious business practices of the local gangsters.

The key factor that differentiates local journalism ethics from national journalism is the proximity of the local journalist to the community. The reporter's loyalty, or duty to the local community and reader, places a different emphasis on first the approach to the source and the story, and then the way the story is used when published. There is often a more thoughtful approach with a lesser attempt to sensationalise and more attempts to provide balance and allow all sides to put their case.

References

Bell, M. (1998) 'The journalism of attachment', in Kieran, M. (ed.) *Media Ethics*, London: Routledge, pp. 15–27.

Frost, C. (2000) *Media Ethics and Self Regulation*, London: Routledge.

Frost, C. (2001) *Reporting for Journalists*, London: Routledge.

Frost, C. (2004) 'The press complaints commission: a study of ten years of adjudications on press complaints', *Journalism Studies*, 5 (1) pp. 101–14.

Keeble, R. (2001) *Ethics for Journalists*, London: Routledge.

Kieran, M.; Morrison, D. and Svenig, M. (2000) 'Privacy, the public and journalism: towards an analytical framework', *Journalism: Theory, Practice and Criticism*, 1 (2), pp. 145–69.

Randall, D. (1999) *The Universal Journalist*, London: Pluto Press, 2nd edn.

Sanders, K. (2003) *Ethics and Journalism*, London: Sage.

Shannon, R. (2001) *A Press Free and Responsible*, London: John Murray.

www.pcc.org.uk/2003/statistics.html (accessed 30 August 2005).

www.guardian.co.uk/uk_news/story/0,1428113,00.html (accessed 30 August 2005).

www.legalpractitioner.co.uk/artmedia1.htm (accessed 30 August 2005).

Chapter 25

Football fanzines and local news

Chris Atton

Introduction

In an overview of professional practices in sports journalism, Rowe (2005: 133) argues that sports reporters are caught between two impulses: first, to present their work according to the 'rationality associated with journalism and modernity'; second, to succumb to the 'subjectivist sporting tribalism of fan discourse'. Rowe finds that sports journalists tend to minimise investigative or muckraking journalism in order to preserve their relationships with their sources. These sources, particularly at a local level, may be so specific to particular clubs that to jeopardise them might well prevent further reporting. The investigative work that does take place in sport tends to begin with general reporters who have better resources and are better trained in that field or, increasingly, becomes the province of the business correspondent. The sports journalist's dependence on a small set of primary definers results, Rowe (2005: 127) argues, in a 'rather sycophantic cultivation of key sports sources'. There is also the requirement to cultivate readerships without alienating them by unfavourable reports of their team, turning the journalist into a fan where 'critical, reflective commentary [becomes] difficult' (Rowe 2005: 133). That most sports journalists enter the profession because of their love of a particular sport might only exaggerate this tendency.

Rowe's (2005: 134) dichotomies, whilst they might reliably indicate realistic pressures in professional sports journalism, place amateur sports fans in a marginal position: 'populist sports fandom ... undermines their [sports journalists'] claim to reputable journalism'. Since the focus of this chapter is the football fanzine, it is appropriate to ask to what extent we might consider the work of the fanzine writer (an amateur sports fan) as 'reputable journalism'. If, as Rowe seems to claim, fandom enables only uncritical, unreflective commentary, can the fanzine ever be a source for local sports news? To answer this question we need to explore a number of issues. Chiefly, we need to consider the content of the football fanzine and the social and cultural processes by which it is generated. We shall do the latter by arguing that the football fanzine is a continuation and an embodiment of the values of the radical community press of earlier decades, rather than simply a continuation of the punk fanzines of the 1970s, with which it is most commonly associated (Hebdige 1979; Triggs 1995). We shall then examine the claims for the fanzine's content as news, in particular asking whether its news values and sourcing routines suggest continuities with mainstream local sports journalism. Finally, we shall look at the relationships between the professional sports media and the football fanzine. In short, this chapter will ask: to what degree does the football fanzine function as local sports journalism?

Radical local news media

We turn first to a brief overview of the nature and values of nonprofessional local news production which, it will be argued, provide a foundation for understanding the role of the football fanzine as a specialist form of local news. The radical community press that flourished throughout the UK in the 1970s and 1980s (Dickinson (1997), Harcup (1994, 1998), Minority Press Group (1980) and Whitaker (1981)) has largely disappeared. Whilst there remain small-scale community newsletters, the dominant community media projects during the 1990s and into the 2000s are narrowcast television and radio stations. The technical infrastructure and specialist skills required mean that such projects need to rely on organisational and business models that have more in common with mainstream media enterprises than their radical print predecessors. Thus, the independence (financial and organisational) and the participatory, grassroots arrangements for the production of an 'alternative journalism' tend to be diluted. The licensing regulations for such stations (the system of Restricted Service Licences) place further limits, constraining both content and reach.

By comparison, the radical community press of the 1970s and 1980s sought to be free from commercial considerations and to provide 'ordinary people' with news and information that was directly useful to them in their daily lives. The publicity material for the *Liverpool Free Press*, for example, identified three prime elements that it shared with many alternative media ventures: commercial independence (anticommerciality, even) and the journalistic freedom that it was felt to bring; editorial independence from political parties and other organisations; and the empowerment of specific communities of interest, which in the case of the *Liverpool Free Press* and similar papers was also a local community (Whitaker 1981: 103).

> Whereas the mainstream local media privileged news constructed from the perspective of those in positions of authority, the radical local press constructed its news from the perspective of those of low status, producing what

have been termed 'parish magazines of the dispossessed' (Harcup 1994: 3). And in answer to Tony Harcup's question: 'Whose news is it anyway?' (Harcup 1998: 105) we might answer: 'their news'. Local people would not only become primary sources and major interviewees in stories, they could also become news-gatherers. Reporters would build up networks of local people: not only political activists, but local residents' groups, parents, workers, the unemployed, the homeless, and encourage them to supply leads for stories.

(Atton 2002: 116)

These features are still evident in issue-focused, international media of social movements (for example, Indymedia – Atton (2004, chapter 2)). In terms of local, radical community media we can consider the football fanzine as continuing a tradition, an alternative way of doing journalism that has largely been lost at a local level. To what extent, though, might the fanzine be considered as journalism?

Fanzines as journalism

Amongst the expanding research into fanzines, consideration of whether fanzines constitute journalism is absent. Typically, the fanzine is considered from within cultural studies or cultural sociology, where it is characterised as a 'site for cultural contestation' (Jary et al. 1991), where identities may be formed and communities developed. Jenkins (1992: 213) has argued that fandom constitutes 'an alternative social community' where cultural production is employed 'as a means of building and maintaining solidarity within the fan community'. Fanzines are major sites of cultural production and represent or stand in for, activate or establish, a community. The dominant sociological understanding of the fanzine is that the power of 'amateur' work lies in its subcultural location (Hebdige 1979). In her survey of British fanzines, Triggs (1995: 74) argues that '[f]anzines are vehicles of subcultural communication'. Similarly, the roots of the British football fanzine have been seen to lie in the punk fanzine. Jary et al. (1991: 584) see in them 'the same orientation to contradiction, the oppositional stance', mentioned by Hebdige (1979: 584). Here the primary function of the fanzine is to stand in for a social relationship. Studies of football fanzines emphasise the sociocultural value of the fanzine for its producers and readers (Haynes 1995). This approach considers the fanzine primarily as a communication medium and a cultural location for the development of individual and group identity; it has tended to ignore any content that is not directly useful to an understanding of identity. Moorhouse's (1994) examination of Celtic and Rangers fanzines, for example, concentrates on comment and opinion dealing with sectarianism and supporters' attitudes to the rival team. It is acknowledged, of course, that the football fanzine also acts as a focus for 'the lack of supporter involvement in decision-making processes' of their favoured club (University of Leicester, Centre for the Sociology of Sport 2002), but even here there is little attention paid to how news content informs this aspect of the fanzine.

Fanzines 'focus on the accumulation and display of detailed information about a topic ... fans come to perform their own detailed critiques of their chosen subjects. Such displays of specialised knowledge are common across the range of fanzines' (Atton 2004: 139–40). Such accumulation and display of expert knowledge has the capacity to challenge professionalized notions of authority and expertise. To be considered an expert by readers means that the fanzine writer accrues a high degree of cultural capital. This expertise is typically displayed directly and not through the mediation of other sources (such as primary definers of other experts). It is from this direct display of expert knowledge that the writer achieves credibility. This suggests that the fanzine is a site for a type of journalism quite different from that of the professional sports journalist.

Online fanzines

We must also note the movement of many, if not almost all, football fanzines to the Internet. This offers a number of advantages both for a publication wishing to deal with news and for any alternative publication. Printing costs and the limits of voluntary labour (time and numbers involved) have chronically affected the frequency and, more generally, the longevity of the printed alternative publication. Football fanzines are rarely produced more than ten times each season; many restrict themselves to quarterly publication. One of the few exceptions is the Middlesbrough fanzine, *Fly Me to the Moon*, which has been published for every home match since it began 15 years ago (more than 350 issues, currently with a print run of 1,500 copies). Jary *et al.* (1991) found that 52 per cent of fanzines were produced by between three and five writers. The reliance on the efforts of a small group of dedicated fans, together with financial limits, must make the move to web-based publication tempting. Printing costs, the labour of layout and the effort involved in distribution are, if not entirely absent (printing, of course, is absent), significantly reduced. The independent and personal nature of the fanzine has led, as it has in other areas of fanzine production (such as music, film and television fanzines), to more than one fanzine being produced for a single subject. Football clubs boast as many as half a dozen publications; with this variety comes competition and the need for self-promotion to achieve and maintain reputation and visibility. The fanzine can use its web presence as advertising for its printed form and many use the platform to encourage subscriptions. (Although the movement of fanzines to the Internet has not replaced the print fanzine, the latter often remains alongside its online version, sold outside the ground, on the terraces, in pubs and clubs and by mail order.)

The commercial potential of the football fanzine has not gone unnoticed by marketeers. Content aggregators and web hosts have recognised this since the 1990s and organisations such as Rivals.net, Footymad.net and Fansfc.com provide space for football fanzines that is supported by advertising, typically for sports-related goods and services such as club souvenirs, sporting equipment, club strips, and gaming and betting services. Such aggregators bring together online football fanzines arranged by leagues and divisions, an entry for each club providing details of all fanzines using the service. There exist differences between providers, however. Whilst Rivals.net and Footymad.net host fanzines in the conventional sense, Fansfc.com offers a more centralised information service. Its news is organised first by league and then alphabetically by each club. Under each club the news is provided anonymously, each item timed and dated, as we might find in professional online media news providers. A generic email address is provided to enable readers to 'mail the FCEditor' and a similarly generic address offers 'email the journo'. Despite the anonymity and the apparent centralisation of editorial content, readers may also 'work for FansFC!' by emailing the editor. It is not clear how fans contribute or what expertise or credentials are required; the layout of the site suggests that fans will have their contributions anonymised, with little scope for individuality (unfortunately, my request to the editor for clarification went unanswered). There are limited links to other sites under each club, including each club's official site and selected fan sites (often single sites). Each club entry also offers a free subscription to the FansFC weekly newsletter for that club. The range of fan sites linked to here is far more limited than those provided through Rivals.net and many of the links are broken, suggesting an operation that is not regularly maintained.

The news provided by Fansfc.com falls into three categories. First, items that essentially summarise (with sources acknowledged) news taken from commercial news media. These are largely national sources, such as the *News of the World* and the Scottish *Daily Record*. Second, items which use direct quotes from players, trainers and managers; and third, briefer items which summarise with no quotation. These last two appear to be original content. However, the commercialisation of fanzine activity need not be seen as a dilution of the 'purity' of the fanzine. On a site like Rivals.net each publication remains editorially independent of its host. This arrangement enables the online fanzine to present news in a far more timely fashion than its print counterpart. The printed fanzine has been, and continues to be, dominated by comment and opinion. Editorial comment and personal columns are common, as are satire, jokes and cartoons. These remain a feature of the online fanzine, but those using commercial providers to (in the jargon of the day) 'power' their publications are developing news strands as standard. This represents a significant shift in the content of football fanzines; whilst long interviews with players, managers and other 'primary definers' from the club have been long-standing features of fanzines before their appearance on the Internet, news has tended to be ignored, since the periodicity of the printed fanzine has meant that any news gathered would be out of date by its publication. In this respect at least, the fanzine has played second fiddle to the local daily or weekly news media in timeliness, if not in access to sources.

Nor is this emphasis on news solely down to the fanzine editors taking advantage of the online medium. The web hosts Rivals.net and Footymad.net themselves have determined this in large part by their adoption of a standard format for the presentation of each fanzine, where the web space for each fanzine is organised by common features. Whereas side bars on each fanzine's home page link to archived stories, columns, discussion forums, information about the printed fanzine and links to other fanzines for the club, the central feature of the home page is a news column densely surrounded by advertising. It is to the nature and content of this central news content that we now turn, using examples drawn from a range of fanzines hosted by the providers already mentioned, who represent the major hosts for British online football fanzines. We shall look particularly at the sources for this news, its authors and its relationship with commercial news providers, especially those local to the club.

The nature of fanzine news

Rivals.net divides its content into two broad areas: 'Football365' and 'Rivals Football'. Football365 provides general football news, which conforms to professional standards and tends to be generated from commercial news providers. Rivals Football is the site's home for online fanzines. The number of fanzines that are linked to each club varies. Whilst a single fanzine links to the club's name, the fanzine itself may link to many more (Rochdale links to six other sites). The number of contributors tends to be small, conforming to the Jary *et al.* (1991) finding. The Aston Villa fanzine *Heroes and Villains* is typical: its news is bylined by two contributors, Mark Fletcher and 'Legion'. This fanzine also provides us with examples of the three standard news styles used by the fanzines: stories reproduced verbatim from professional news media; stories summarised from the professional media; and original journalism. Stories from commercial news providers dominate. *Heroes and Villains* uses a range of sources:

- the official club site and its press releases;
- national media such as the British Broadcasting Corporation's (BBC) online sports service;

- international media, such as Skysports.com;
- specialist media (*Sporting Life*); and
- local media (*Express and Star*).

In all cases the contributors use the online editions of these media. They provide a credit and a link to the original story as well as reproducing the story in its entirety, with no further editorial comment. The news stories in the Manchester United fanzine *Red Issue* (on the Footymad site) are all credited to a single, anonymous editor and almost all derive from national mainstream sources. In some cases the story is summarised with a credit; in others the story is reproduced in its entirety with a credit or web link to the original. Sources include *The Observer, The Times, The Sun,* the *Daily Mirror* and the *Sunday People.* The editor is acting here as a cuttings service, providing a news digest across a broad range of tabloid and broadsheet papers, just as the editors of *Heroes and Villains* do across a range that includes broadcast media. Whilst this does not constitute original journalism, it is an important service to fans. Moreover, the Internet enables frequent updating; *Red Issue* might post up to a dozen stories a day (though half that number is more typical). During the research period (June 2005) these were dominated by Malcolm Glaser's takeover of the club, as well as articles on new players and players seeking transfers. Other fanzines, such as *Talk of the Tyne* (a Newcastle United fanzine on Rivals.net) and *Ready to Go* (Sunderland) rely more on the local press for their news. This is not always limited to the local press of the immediate area; *Talk of the Tyne* quotes from the *Birmingham Evening Mail* in a story about the Birmingham club Aston Villa (though this might well be due to the use of an intermediate, unacknowledged source).

Inevitably, news content will be determined by the activity of the club, itself a result of the size, significance and economic position of the club. Some fanzines will have very little to report if their clubs are hardly ever in the transfer stakes or not lucrative enough to tempt takeover bids. Whilst *Red Issue* was posting multiple news items daily during the sample period for this research, the most recent post on Stirling Albion's *Rave On* site (on Footymad) was 7 May 2005. This simply contained details of the team line-up for a forthcoming match.

Arsenal World on the Footymad site is typical in a further use of the mass media: as a source for critique. It features a narrower range of news sources, emphasising national media sources such as Sky and the *News of the World.* Indeed, one story ('Colegate – a modern love story', 5 June 2005) is an opinion piece sourced and inspired by an interview given by player Ashley Cole to the *News of the World* and subsequently reported on Sky Sports. In another opinion piece, Jack Harrison, a regular contributor, asks fans: why do you enjoy 'the inflated claims, mad murmurings and downright lies of the tabloid press ... ? ... because you like media speculation, in particular, you like transfer talk' ('Transfer traumas', 14 June 2005). There is not a fanzine that does not engage with the media coverage of its team or of the sport in general. This critique is generally negative, yet the reliance of the fanzine on those same media as news sources shows that, whilst editors and writers might well be dismissive and sceptical of the comment and opinion in the professional media, they trust its reporting expertise enough to use it as primary source material for their own news.

There is evidence of original reporting, however. Match reports are common, though hardly unique to fanzines. There is little evidence of any investigative journalism, though many fanzines publish (often lengthy) interviews. It appears that, however critical a fanzine might be of its club's financial or management dealings, this does not seem to affect its access to significant individuals in the club. *United We Stand* (a Manchester United fanzine on Rivals.net) has published interviews with the club's deputy chief executive, key players and Alan Green, a sports commentator who has been accused of bias against the club. The news pages of Middlesbrough fanzine *Fly Me to the Moon* (Rivals.net) also contain significant amounts of original journalism based on lengthy interviews with key figures in the club. During the research period, the latest in a long-standing line of such features was with the club's commercial manager, Graham Fordy. Whilst ostensibly providing news about the club's latest fund-raising project, the piece was more an occasion to provide discursive and detailed analysis of the club's finances and its future prospects. Here we see the coming together of the fanzine writer's own expertise and knowledge with the access to sources and journalistic skills we would normally associate with the professional, local sports journalist. Generally, these pieces are written by the editor, though not all use news so explicitly. Robert Nichols's piece 'Many Viduka returns?' (15 June 2005) demonstrates well the typical fanzine editor's specialist expertise; it is based on his knowledge of the club and its players, its history and performance. However, despite its appearance in the news section of the fanzine, in its seven paragraphs of highly informed comment there is only marginal and vague reference to news sources ('it has been reported ... '). Unusually, *Fly Me to the Moon* has also used a local sports journalist as a regular interviewee to generate a regular column. During the 2002–3 season, Paul Kerr, a BBC Radio Cleveland sports commentator and 'Boro' fan, offered comment and opinion in a series of interviews with the fanzine's editor, Robert Nichols. As with *Arsenal World*, summaries and critiques of mainstream media are common. *Fly Me to the Moon* has formalised both in a weekly feature by fan David Bates ('Boro in the Media Spotlight'). His combined news digest and commentary draws on national broadcast media, 'the Sunday papers' and the *Gazette* (Middlesbrough's evening paper).

Fly Me to the Moon was the 2005 winner of EMAP's sports fanzine award and overall winner of their award for best British fanzine. Interestingly, the judges did not base their decision on the fanzine's news coverage. Whilst acknowledging its 'acute knowledge' of the club, their summary emphasised its 'cartoons, a spoof Radio Times round-up ... it stood out as one of the funniest fanzines around' (www.emapfanzineawards.co.uk/winners_2005.html). That fanzines choose to enter themselves for such awards demonstrates that many, despite their scepticism towards the coverage that the mass media might provide, wish to be recognised and taken seriously by those very same media. *Hob Nob Anyone?*, the Reading FC internet fanzine (www.royals.org/about.html), lists all its appearances in the media: national and local press, national specialist football press, television and radio, and other Reading fanzines. Notably it cites two weekly columns its writers contributed to local papers: The 'Jim and Mick Answer Column' in the *Reading Chronicle* (during the 1996–7 season) and 'The *Hob Nob Anyone?* Column' in the *Reading Evening Post*, which ran during the 1998–9 season. It also mentions a weekly teletext column that appeared on regional Meridian TV during the 1998–9 and 1999–2000 seasons. Here we see an inversion of the fanzine's reliance on professional news sources; in this case the fanzine supplied expert commentators to local media.

Conclusion

This brief survey has shown varied approaches to the use of news by online football fanzines. The dominant model seems to be the editing and republishing of mass media sources, though we have seen how some fanzines generate their own news as well as using professionalised news output to generate expert comment and opinion. There is little evidence here of the fanzine's contribution to agenda-setting and decision-making. In this respect fanzine writers are similar to Rowe's assessment of the professional sports journalists as reporters with little claim to 'reputable journalism'. However, we should not ignore the evidence of original news production in fanzines, though it might not be overwhelming. Arguing for a model of communicative democracy, Hartley (2000) has proposed redaction as an emerging practice of public communication, where there is a focus on the processes of reduction, revision, preparation, editing and publishing, and where journalism as original writing is less prominent. This practice is evident in the fanzines examined here, where we find a hybrid form of news production. This hybridity is further nuanced by the embedding of editorially independent fanzine sites in content aggregators such as Rivals and Footymad. 'News is no longer the preserve of journalistic organisations', argues Chalaby (2000: 34) in an exploration of the diversification of news providers through the Internet. Whilst the fanzines examined here do not enable such a grand claim to be argued conclusively, they do at least suggest that they are able to function as effective news digests and as originators of news, as well as sites for expert, amateur commentary.

References

Atton, C. (2002) *Alternative Media*, London: Sage.

Atton, C. (2004) *An Alternative Internet: Radical Media, Politics and Creativity*, Edinburgh: Edinburgh University Press.

Chalaby, J. K. (2000) 'Journalism studies in an era of transition in public communications', *Journalism: Theory, Practice and Criticism*, 1 (1), April, 33–9.

Dickinson, R. (1997) *Imprinting the Sticks: The Alternative Press Outside London*, Aldershot: Arena.

Harcup, T. (1994) *A Northern Star: Leeds Other Paper and the Alternative Press, 1974–1994*, London and Pontefract: Campaign for Press and Broadcasting Freedom.

Harcup, T. (1998) 'There is no alternative: the demise of the alternative local newspaper', in Franklin, B. and Murphy, D. (eds) *Making the Local News: Local Journalism in Context*, London: Routledge, pp. 105–16.

Hartley, J. (2000) 'Communicative democracy in a redactional society: the future of journalism studies', *Journalism: Theory, Practice and Criticism*, 1 (1), April, 39–48.

Haynes, R. (1995) *The Football Imagination: The Rise of Football Fanzine Culture*, Aldershot: Arena.

Hebdige, D. (1979) *Subculture: The Meaning of Style*, London: Routledge.

Jary, D.; Horne, J. and Bucke, T. (1991) 'Football "Fanzines" and football culture: a case of successful "cultural contestation"', *Sociological Review*, 39 (3), 581–97.

Jenkins, H. (1992) '"Strangers no more, we sing": filking and the social construction of the science fiction fan community', in Lisa A. Lewis (ed.) *The Adoring Audience: Fan Culture and Popular Media*, London: Routledge, pp. 208–36.

Minority Press Group (1980) *Here is the Other News: Challenges to the Local Commercial Press*, London: Minority Press Group.

Moorhouse, H. F. (1994) 'From Zines like these? Fanzines, tradition and identity in Scottish football', in Grant Jarvie and Graham Walker (eds) *Scottish Sport in the Making of the Nation: Ninety Minute Patriots?* Leicester: Leicester University Press, pp. 173–94.

Rowe, D. (2005) 'Fourth estate or fan club? Sports journalism engages the popular', in Stuart Allan (ed.) *Journalism: Critical Issues*, Maidenhead: Open University Press, pp. 125–36.

Triggs, T. (1995) 'Alphabet soup: reading British fanzines', *Visible Language*, 29 (1), pp. 72–87.

University of Leicester, Centre for the Sociology of Sport (2002) *Fact Sheet 7: Fan 'Power' and Democracy in Football*, www.le.ac.uk/so/css/resources/factsheets/fs7.html (accessed June 2005).

Whitaker, B. (1981) *News Limited: Why You Can't Read All About It*, London: Minority Press Group.

Chapter 26

Freedom of information and local journalism

Heather Brooke

On 1 January 2005, two new laws came into force that finally give local journalists and members of the public a means of shining light into the dark spaces of local government. The Freedom of Information Act (FOIA) 2000 and the Environmental Information Regulations (EIR) 2004 offer the public a new legal right to official information. Little scholarly attention has been paid to these new laws to date (Brooke 2007) though some academics are instigating new research, notably Steve Wood at Liverpool John Moores University, the University College London's Constitution Unit and Patrick Lavelle at the University of Sunderland's Journalism Department.

Journalists, campaigners and activists have been the main users of the new laws. Freedom of information isn't just for the front pages of the big national newspapers or broadcast investigative documentaries. Newspapers such as the *Kent Messenger* group, the *Eastern Daily Press* in Norwich, *The Scotsman*, Glasgow's *Sunday Herald* and Trinity Newspaper Group papers such as the *Western Mail* in Wales and *Newcastle Chronicle* are all using the act vigorously. Newspapers and journalists are missing a trick if they fail to use the FOI, according to Kevin Booth, editor of the *Evening Press* in York. 'FOI should become a fundamental part of the way all of us conduct our news gathering operations', he told the *Press Gazette* (Francis 2005). 'It has enabled us to put into the public domain stories that would never have come to us before.'

'All the journalists I've spoken to say the main advantage of FOI is that it sets the agenda', says Paul Francis, political editor of the *Kent Messenger* group (interview August 2005). 'We can make judgements about what is going to interest our readers rather than having to rely on council press releases.' What he finds particularly striking is that, of the many stories emerging through FOI, very few, if any, would have emerged from official information channels such as cabinet meetings, agendas or reports. Few councils, it seems, are adopting the openness agenda.

This is not altogether surprising as the UK is one of the last industrialised countries in the world to adopt freedom of information laws. Unfortunately, this delay has not produced a thoroughly modern law, but one more at home in a third-world dictatorship. It contains a large number of exemptions, opportunities for delay and a ministerial veto that allows politicians to overrule the FOI regulator. Nevertheless, the law presents a crack in the stony edifice of official secrecy and journalists would do well to know the law so they can chisel away to a more open and accountable government. This is the real strength of FOI – it allows journalists to use their expertise in uncovering information about issues the public finds interesting. Local officials often have little idea about what the public want to know and even less interest in opening themselves to public scrutiny. FOI allows the public, and by default the press, the ability to set the priorities of government, which is as it should be in a democracy.

At the *Eastern Daily Press* in Norwich, editors and reporters are advised to view FOI as an important tool in their journalistic toolbox. By August 2005, the paper had put in 51 requests, of which only nine had been refused and three of those were under review by the information commissioner. Resulting stories ranged from finding out about food hygiene in local restaurants and schools to full details of a £229 million Private Finance Initiative (PFI) deal to build a new hospital for Norwich.

Trinity Mirror regional papers were training staff on the FOIA from early 2005 and all titles have 'FOI champions' and regular reviews of how it can be applied, according to Darren Thwaites, editorial development manager for Trinity Mirror Regional (Francis 2005). 'Staff are now asking, "what is it that we – and our readers – want to know?" and making requests they think will generate the information', Thwaites says. 'Asking the right questions is crucial but, if you do get it right, the successes can be spectacular. Newsrooms are thinking much further ahead.'

Local journalists also have an advantage over their national counterparts when it comes to freedom of information requests. First, exemptions in the FOIA favour Whitehall in what is very much an example of 'one law for us and another for them'. For example, Section 36 provides an exemption for information prejudicial to the 'effective conduct of public affairs'. Usually information can only be withheld under this exemption if it meets a public interest test; however, when the House of Commons holds the information, there is no public interest test!

Second, power in the UK resides in the central government and because of this, the most powerful politicians will expend their energy protecting this citadel from public scrutiny. A local council will simply not have the same resources to suppress information as say, the cabinet office (though they may give it their best effort). Finally, when it comes to appeals, I have a strong hunch that any robust rulings made by the information commissioner will be made against local councils rather than central government. Already in late 2005, the majority of FOI stories were coming from local rather than national newspapers.

The basics: Freedom of Information Act 2000 and Freedom of Information Act 2002 (Scotland)

The FOI Acts of both countries are almost identical, but where there are differences, the Scottish law is generally slightly better. The FOIA affects more than 100,000 public bodies including the police, local and central government, most quangos, schools and universities, and the National Health Service (NHS). There are several bodies not covered that ought to be: the courts and tribunals, the royal family, Network Rail and, oddly enough, the Press Complaints Commission. A better law would simply have defined any organisation receiving the majority of its funding from the taxpayer as a public authority (this is how most American state FOI laws are drafted). As it is, each public body must be named in Schedule 1 of the law for it to be covered. You can check the list online at the Department for Constitutional Affairs website: www.foi.gov.uk/ coverage-guide.htm

Making a request is easy. It must simply be in writing – either by letter, fax or email – for the law to apply. Include a name and correspondence address so the authority can contact you, though legally it does not have to be your name. The agency cannot ask why you want the information – that's none of their business – but they may ask you to clarify your request if they are unclear about what you need. It is important to make your request as specific as possible but not so specific that you self-censor your request. If you don't know how to narrow your request, then the public body is under an obligation to help you under Section 16 of the Act – the duty to advise and assist. This means that file structures or other record-keeping data must be given to you in order to help you formulate your request.

You can give the request to anyone in the public authority, but it is best to send it to the FOI Officer, Press Officer or the person who holds the information. The authority must answer your request promptly and in no more than 20 working days. Some time extensions are allowed, for example, if the agency needs to consider the public interest or if schools are in recess, but the authority must tell you about any delay.

The law's main right of access is this:

> Any person making a request for information to a public authority is entitled
> – (a) to be informed in writing by the public authority whether it holds information of the description specified in the request, and
> – (b) if that is the case, to have that information communicated to him.

Jack Straw said when he introduced the bill, it would 'transform the default setting from "this should be kept quiet unless" to "this should be published unless"' (HC 2R, 7 Dec 1999, Col 714). The law creates a 'duty to confirm or deny', that is, the authority must inform the applicant in writing whether or not it holds the information. There is also a duty to disclose that information to the applicant.

This means that officials must expend a lot of time and money to keep something secret. They can no longer simply ignore the inquiring member of the public or press. A public servant's quickest and cheapest response to a FOIA request is simply to answer it. Realistically, though, this is unlikely, but the law now gives you the right to challenge such secrecy.

Information can only be refused if it meets an exemption outlined in law. Admittedly, there are many exemptions to choose from: 23, plus requests can be refused if they are vexatious or exceed the fee limit of £600 for central government and £450 for other public bodies.[1] It is important to remember that exemptions are discretionary: they don't have to be used. If they are applied, the majority have a public interest test, which means information must be disclosed if it is in the public interest and the default position is for disclosure.[2] The only appeal against absolute exemptions is to argue on a point of law.

Most of the exemptions are qualified by a public interest test. This means that if you want a report on a fatal train disaster, which may be covered by both exemptions under Section 30 (about investigations and proceedings) and Section 31 (prejudicial to law enforcement functions), the public authority will have to prove why the public interest is best served by secrecy if it wants to withhold it. And the public interest can change over time, so while there may be a legitimate need to suppress the report while the investigation is ongoing, once it is complete, the public interest will move toward disclosure.

Fees

You will most likely not be charged for your request though legally the public body can charge you a reasonable fee for photocopying and postage. However, the cost of searching and collating material counts toward the overall cost of your request and if that goes above £600 for central government and £450 for all others, the agency is no longer obliged to answer. This works out at two-and-a-half days' search time for an employee paid at £25 an hour. So you must ensure that your request can be answered within this time. You have three months to pay the fee, after which the authority will give you the information. If you wait longer than three months, the authority does not have to answer your request. If you think the fee is unreasonable you can ask for a detailed receipt of how they calculated the total and appeal to the information commissioner for a review.

If you are unsatisfied with the agency's response, then you can ask for an internal review. If your request is still refused, you can then take your complaint to the information commissioner. He is the independent regulator of the FOIA and has the power to overrule a public authority's decision to withhold information. If he rules against you, the final appeal is to the Information Tribunal (though not in Scotland). Controversially, a cabinet minister can overrule the commissioners of both the UK and Scotland. The commissioner's ultimate sanction against a negligent public body is to charge them with contempt of court.

Publication schemes

The FOI law requires that all public authorities have a publication scheme, which is simply a listing of all the types of information the authority has committed to make public such as committee minutes, budgets, staff handbooks. This is a legal document, so if the council says it publishes all procurement contracts and then refuses to give you one, you can complain to the information commissioner. Most schemes are now online and found by searching the authority's website for either 'publication scheme' or 'freedom of information'. An increasing number of public authorities are also adding 'disclosure logs' to their websites that provide a listing of the FOIA requests received and material released in response to those requests. See, for example, the British Broadcasting Corporation's (BBC) disclosure log: www.bbc.co.uk/foi/docs/freedom_of_information.shtml #requests

Environmental Information Regulations 2004

You might wonder why there are two FOI regimes: one for environmental information and another for all other types of material. The answer is simply that the FOIA allowed for too much government secrecy! It was too weak and did not meet European obligations on access to environmental information. Rather than beef up the FOIA, politicians voted instead to create another law entirely.

You should have a familiarity with this law only because if you can phrase your request in such a way that it becomes 'environmental', it is much more likely to be answered. You can find out more about the EIRs in the environment chapter of *Your Right to Know* (Brooke 2007) or from the Department for Environment, Food and Rural Affairs (DEFRA) website: www.defra.gov.uk/corporate/opengov/eir/guidance/index.htm.

Why the EIRs are better than the FOIA:

1   requests cannot be denied on the basis of cost as with FOIA;
2   there are no absolute, or 'blanket', exemptions;

3 there are fewer, more narrowly drawn exemptions and they all must meet a public interest test;
4 requests can be made verbally, not just in writing; and
5 the exemption for commercial confidentiality must meet a stronger harm test.

Openness versus privacy

Even if you don't specifically want personal information, it is likely that as a journalist you will find officials claiming that something you want is exempt due to the Data Protection Act 1998. For example, central government claimed for years that it could not release the names and sponsoring companies of employees seconded to work in their departments. Eventually, they had to relent but there are plenty of similar cases ongoing. The confusion stems not just from government truculence but also the Data Protection law, which is possibly one of the worst laws on the statute books. It is thick with ambiguity, needless jargon and confusion, making it very difficult for public authorities to know what they can and cannot release.

The key factor in deciding what to release and what to withhold is based on what is reasonably considered private. The concept of privacy is itself hard to define – an 'I know it when I see it' kind of thing. Should the names of council staff be made public? I think so, as I am the one paying their salaries, but many council workers think differently. Not only do they think the public has no right to their direct telephone number at work but they don't think we even have a right to know who they are! Some of the first cases taken to the information commissioner were about precisely this type of information. The public has an interest in knowing the names and job descriptions of public officials who are carrying out work on behalf of the people. And they also have an interest in knowing how their public services work and how well those public employees are doing their jobs.

The information commissioner's guidance states that:

> It is often believed that the Data Protection Act prevents the disclosure of any personal data without the consent of the person concerned. This is not true. The purpose of the Data Protection Act is to protect the private lives of individuals. Where information requested is about people acting in a work or official capacity then it will normally be right to disclose.

Ask yourself: does the information sought relate to a person's public or private life? If it is about someone acting in an official or work capacity, then it should normally be provided on request unless there is some risk to the individual concerned.

Local government FOI laws

More than 80 per cent of regional daily newspaper editors and 60 per cent of weekly newspaper editors surveyed ranked secrecy among public bodies of high or very high significance, according to results from a press freedom survey released 17 February 2005 by The Newspaper Society (2005). The astounding level of paranoid secrecy and obstruction operating in UK local councils constantly surprises me. Councils have had decades to get used to openness and yet it seems to have made no difference to their attitude toward the public. A radical shift is needed if councils and indeed politicians are to regain public trust.

There are several local government acts that deal specifically with the public's right to attend council meetings and access relevant information. Some of these laws give the public greater rights than the FOIA, such as the right to background information about major decisions, but others are more restrictive. The main laws are:

- Public Bodies (Admission to Meetings) Act 1960 – the first 'freedom of information' law for local authorities gave the public a right to attend council meetings of local authorities, including parish and community councils, unless 'confidential' information was discussed and then they were automatically kicked out.
- Local Government Act 1972 – this law gave the public an additional right to attend council committee meetings, but the previous exclusion of the public and press applied if 'confidential' information was discussed. Schedule 12A of the law sets out 15 categories and exemptions where local authorities can withhold information from the public. There is no public interest test.
- Local Government (Access to Information) Act 1985 – this Act added subcommittees to the list of council meetings open to the public and press, and gave a right of access to reports held by the authority where the report and related documents are to be discussed in a meeting, unless the information is exempt or confidential. It also replaced the blanket 'confidential' information with exempt information, and the exclusion of the press and public was no longer automatic but had to be formally proposed, seconded and voted upon.
- Local Government Act 2000 – handed local councils secrecy on a plate under the guise of 'reform'. Instead of becoming more open, the law brought in new cabinet-style councils. Decision-making power was taken away from committees and given mostly to single-party cabinets.

Local newspapers have found it increasingly difficult to report on councils since implementation of the 2000 law, which is another reason the FOIA law was so welcomed by the regional press. 'Cabinets are usually a single-party group of politicians, which means they can manipulate and massage the information and make decisions on their own terms', said Paul Francis, political editor at the *Kent Messenger*. 'Older councillors are amazed at how sources of information have dried up. Even backbenchers of the same party are sidelined from the decision-making process' (Francis 2005). The FOIA won't help you get into a closed council meeting, but it can get you the paperwork and data used and discussed at the meeting and much other material that shows the inner workings of the council.

In 2006, the exemptions in 12A were made compatible with the FOIA by adding a public interest test. Remember, though, the FOIA deals with access to information, not access to meetings. So it is still possible that you could be excluded from a meeting based on a 'confidential' document that would subsequently have to be released under the Act.

You needn't have an encyclopaedic knowledge of all these pieces of legislation. All you need to do is ask in writing for the information. You do not have to explain how the laws give you the legal right to make a request: the FOIA is automatically invoked for all written information requests and takes precedence over the older laws.

How to use the FOIA and EIRs

Looking at the time limits of FOIA and EIR, it quickly becomes apparent these laws will be of little use for breaking stories. Instead, they are best used in two main ways:

- getting whole classes of information in the public domain so they can be used as an ongoing resource for daily stories; and/or
- for agenda-setting investigative stories that reveal major problems or issues in an organisation.

For the first type of request, think about the catalogues of information collected by your council. Most British people have little knowledge of the skeleton of records and databases that underpin government because historically such information has always been kept hidden from public view. This is very unlike the United States where I worked as a reporter. We were able to view most of the 'machinery of government', from line-item budgets and politicians' travel receipts to police reports, jail booking forms and food safety inspections. As a result, American reporters have a deeper understanding of the structure of government bureaucracy and know the manner and quality of information collected.

The good thing about FOI requests for whole classes of data is that you only have one battle to fight. Once you have won, the information should be readily available at all times. This is the goal. For example, in the United States there is actually very little reason for a local reporter to file an FOIA request now because so many have been asked and fought over that most of the information sought is already in the public realm.

If you are making this type of request, then it is important to ask it in a way that keeps the request within cost limits. So either ask for something environmental (where there is no cost barrier), such as food hygiene or fire safety inspection reports, or narrow your time-frame or geographic location. Ask for things that are so obviously in the public interest – food hygiene reports of hospital kitchens – that there is no way the council can refuse without looking foolish. They may still do so (councils are not known for their customer service acumen) but such behaviour will lead to more stories and possibly even a campaign. When Norwich City Council refused an FOI request from the *Eastern Daily Press* (*EDP*) for food hygiene inspections, the paper ran an article slamming the council. 'They were mortified and bent over backwards to give us information on over 100 cafes, restaurants, pubs and takeaways, which made fascinating reading and gave us a splash and a spread', says *EDP* assistant editor Paul Durrant (interview 25 August 2005).

Durrant advises reporters to research their request well and hone down the specific information required, rather than go on fishing expeditions and asking for everything. 'We've worked hard to cultivate FOI officers in the various councils and trusts so that we can speak to them informally before the formal request and maybe negotiate the best way forward within the cost restrictions', he said. 'We've also reminded them of their "duty to assist" and almost without exception this has paid off.'

Some examples of possible FOI/EIR requests to make to your council (*Your Right to Know*: 'Local Government' chapter):

Gifts, salaries, allowances and expenses The *Daily Mail* ran a story on 29 July 2005 based on an FOI request: 'The gates of wrath: Anger at councillor's £17,000 home improvement on taxpayers'. Former Scottish MSP David McLetchie had to resign when his misuse of taxi expenses was revealed in the *Sunday Herald*.

Amounts spent by the council on consultants The *Eastern Daily Press* made an FOI request for the salaries paid to two corporate officers brought in by Waveney District Council and discovered they were paid £21,000 of taxpayers' money for just eight days' work!

Trading standards Markets: have there been illegal or unsafe goods sold at the market? How often are inspections made? Inspection reports: for trades such as plumbers, businesses, shops, factories and farms. How often are they made? What are the results? How many are prosecuted and how many convicted?

Complaints   Get a listing of the most complained-about businesses or trades.

Regeneration   A huge amount of public money is spent on regeneration projects and wherever there is 'free' money, there are people eager to put it in their pocket. Keep a close eye on how this money is spent. In Tower Hamlets, councillor Kumar Murshid was censured for failing to declare his relationship with the chief executive of a training company that had received £2 million of public funds (Findings of Tower Hamlets Standards Committee October 7 2003).[3] You could also request minutes from regeneration committee meetings and operational budgets to uncover who is benefiting the most from these big, publicly funded projects.

Transport   The *Evening Press* in York used FOI and found the City of York council was making £20,000 a day from parking charges. The information was used as part of the paper's 'Stop the highway robbery' campaign. Ask for parking enforcement contracts, bus contracts, the number of bus accidents, even future transport plans drawn up by outside consultants.

Education   Education accounts for the largest proportion of local authority spending (41 per cent). A council's education department is responsible for schools, education, student awards, special education, and youth services. Requests can be made for food hygiene reports of school kitchens, the amount spent per school meal, qualifications of teachers, the number of teachers facing disciplinary action, number of expulsions per school. If schools are built or run by a private contractor, ask for the contract.

Environmental services   This includes such things as pest control, environmental nuisance (dog fouling, dumping, noise), rubbish collection, waste management, food safety, health and safety, recycling, skip hire, energy efficiency, air and water quality, contaminated land, biodiversity, drainage, abandoned vehicles and street cleaning.

Run-down parks and libraries   Ask for budgets and maintenance schedules for parks and other local amenities. Are staff numbers being cut? Ask for a list of all the open spaces and leisure facilities sold off in the last ten years. Ask for minutes from closed meetings where these sell-offs occurred.

There are many hundreds of requests you can make, limited only by your imagination and cunning. It may be a hard slog but the rewards are definitely worth it. Even if your requests are refused, that too can lead to a story. If all else fails – publicity is an excellent way to shame councils into better behaviour. *The Scotsman* launched a scathing attack on that country's refusal to publish the names of those receiving European farm subsidies when the names were released in England and Wales. When 70 local residents in Sheffield were kicked out of a council meeting in May 2004 after waiting for two hours to discuss a controversial construction of a Buddha statue, the local media publicised the ban. Soon after, Sheffield council admitted it had been wrong to ban the press and public from the debate.

Politicians will undoubtedly find it difficult to accept the new standards of public accountability and openness, but it is the role of the reporter acting on behalf of the citizen to make the costs of not doing so even greater.

Notes

1   Fees regulations were under review as this book went to press so check the Department for Constitutional Affairs website for the latest guidelines.
2   For a more detailed look at exemptions see *Your Right to Know* ('Laws of Access' chapter), or see the guidance issued by the Information Commissioner's Office or Department for Constitutional Affairs: www.dca .gov.uk/foi/guidance/exguide/index.htm
3   www.towerhamlets.gov.uk/templates/news/detail.cfm?newsid=2095

References

Brooke, H. (2007) *Your Right to Know*, London: Pluto Press (new edition).

Francis, P. (2005) 'Reporters unlock the secrets of FOI', *Press Gazette*, 21 July 2005, www.pressgazette.co.uk/article/210705/reporters_unlock_the.

Information Commissioner 'Freedom of Information Awareness Guidance No. 1: Personal Information', www.ico.gov.uk (follow links 'freedom of information' – 'exemptions guidance'.

Newspaper Society (2005) *The Challenge for Freedom of Information, Press Freedom Survey*, 17 February 2005, www.newspapersoc.org.uk/Documents/Publications/pr2005/press-freedom-survey.pdf.

Wadham, J. and Griffiths, J. (eds) (2005) *Blackstone's Guide to the Freedom of Information Act 2000*, Oxford: Oxford University Press.

Wood, S. (2005) *Complying with Freedom of Information Legislation: A Guide for Practitioners*, April 2005, www.freepint.com/shop/report/foi2005/.

Wood, S. (ed.) *Open Government: A Journal on Freedom of Information*, www.opengovjournal.org.

Index

Related titles from Routledge

Power without Responsibility
Sixth Edition

James Curran and Jean Seaton

This is a useful and timely book
Richard Hoggart, *Times Educational Supplement*

In a fast-changing media scene this book is nothing less than indispensable
Julian Petley, *Brunel University*

Power without Responsibility, the best guide to the British media
Nick Cohen, *The New Statesman*

Power without Responsibility is a classic, authoritative and engaged introduction to the history, sociology, theory and politics of media and communication studies. Written in a lively and accessible style, it is regarded as the standard book on the British media. This new edition has been substantially revised to bring it up to date with new developments in the media industry. Its three new chapters describe the battle for the soul of the Internet, the impact of the Internet on society and the rise of new media in Britain. In addition, it examines the recuperation of the BBC, how international and European regulation is changing the British media and why Britain has the least trusted press in Europe.

ISBN 10: 0-415-24389-0 (hbk)
ISBN 10: 0-415-24390-4 (pbk)

ISBN 13: 978-0-415-24389-6 (hbk)
ISBN 13: 978-0-415-24390-2 (pbk)

Available at all good bookshops
For ordering and further information please visit:
www.routledge.com

Related titles from Routledge

Media and Power

James Curran

Media and Power addresses three key questions about the relationship between media and society.

- How much power do the media have?
- Who really controls the media?
- What is the relationship between media and power in society?

In this major new book, James Curran reviews the different answers which have been given, before advancing original interpretations in a series of ground-breaking essays.

Media and Power also provides a guided tour of the major debates in media studies. What part did the media play in the making of modern society? How did 'new media' change society in the past? Will radical media research recover from its mid-life crisis? What are the limitations of the US-based model of 'communications' research? Is globalization disempowering national electorates or bringing into being a new, progressive global politics? Is public service television the dying product of the nation in an age of globalization? What can be learned from the 'third way' tradition of European media policy?

Curran's response to these questions provides both a clear introduction to media research and an innovative analysis of media power, written by one of the field's leading scholars.

ISBN 10: 0-415-07739-7 (hbk)
ISBN 10: 0-415-07740-0 (pbk)

ISBN 13: 978-0-415-07739-2 (hbk)
ISBN 13: 978-0-415-07740-8 (pbk)

Available at all good bookshops
For ordering and further information please visit:
www.routledge.com